THE BREACH

By

Randy Pool

This book is a work of fiction. Places, events, and situations in this story are purely fictional. Any resemblance to actual persons, living or dead, is coincidental.

ISBN: 1-4033-4662-3 (e-book)
ISBN: 1-4033-4663-1 (Paperback)

This book is printed on acid free paper.

1st Books - rev. 08/15/02

Chapter One:

"The Closet"

(Wednesday night/ Thursday morning)

Startled! Her head quickly jerked to the left towards the small oaken nightstand. There was no apparent sound or disturbance, only the glow of the large red numbers that brightly announced the early hour. At 2:34 am, nothing much stirred in Carrolton Virginia. Gertie slowly turned to her right to find Adam deeply enthralled in championship horseshoes or crabbing in the Chesapeake Bay, or some other pleasant dream. Convinced he had not nudged her, she found herself fully awakened for no apparent reason. She gently lay her head back upon her pillow, and carefully rearranged her netted rollers back into place. Closing her eyes, she tried to think of meadows and warm sunshine - but she was still unable to cross the threshold into sleep. Instead, her mind fixed on an old familiar hymn,

"Ere you left your room this morning - Did you think to pray?
In the name of Christ, our Savior,
Did you sue for loving favors, As a shield to-day?
O how praying rests the weary! Prayer will change the night to day;
So when life seems dark and dreary,
Don't forget to pray."

As her mind repeated the chorus for the third time, she decided that the Lord was calling her - again.

Slowly sliding her legs from under the heavy covers, she reached beside the nightstand for the aluminum walker. She gripped the plastic coated handles firmly before rising and placing any of her weight on her feet. Her fur-lined house-shoes lay in their space beside the bed and she gingerly slid each foot into place before taking her first step. They felt especially warm for this early autumn frost. The rubber tips squeaked once across the cold hardwood floor, and she quickly lifted the walker, so as not to awaken Adam. She made her steps deliberate and careful, and soon was through the landing and down the hall towards the den. Not wishing to flood the hallway with light, she focused what little night vision she still had on the moonlight coming through the windows. As she pushed the door slightly to the side she felt along the wall for the end table where her mother's porcelain lamp sat. She turned the brass key-shaped switch twice and a soft glow illuminated nearly a third of the room.

Gertie knew this feeling well. She was not prone to insomnia, heartburn, or restless anxiety. She was sensitive to prompting. As a young girl, she had found the greatest need of her life was to know intimately her Lord and Savior, and in simple prayer, she established that relationship. Through the years, she took seriously the calling to come apart from the affairs of this life and enter "her closet" alone to be with the One Who loved her and cared for her. In exchange, she found that there were distinct times when her Heavenly Father called her to "the closet" for a time of special prayer. As Job offered sacrifice for the possible sins committed by his children in their hearts, she had interceded for hers. As Abraham "bartered" with a just and holy God for the doomed city of Sodom, she had pleaded on behalf of lost loved ones. As Moses offered himself in place of a wayward Israel, she had felt the responsibility of praying fervently for her church, her community and her country. She was an Esther, who had just been summoned into the presence of her King.

———

10:43 PM didn't seem too late to Karen, but it was forty-three minutes past her curfew on a school night. Chula Vista, a suburb of San Diego, was a nice community for many Navy retirees who enjoyed the warm southern California climate. Karen, a senior at National City High School, knew as much Spanish as she did English. It was not uncommon for her to date Hispanics, but it was understood that the same time rules applied. The fact that she chose Wednesday night to arrive home late only multiplied the infraction - she had chosen the mall and a movie over prayer meeting . . .again.

Dr. Howard R. Pennington, Th.D, waited poised in the living room where no one ever sat. The three-piece living room set had been purchased over six years ago, and had never needed to be cleaned once. Only two years had passed since the plastic cover had finally been removed from the sofa. The den always seemed more comfortable for entertaining guests, so like most middle class homes, the living room was not a room for the living. But it was the room closest to the front door.

He first heard their voices whispering and chuckling incoherently, followed by an ominous and punctuated silence. As the young man's steps were heard hastening from the porch to his car, Karen fumbled with her keys. Howard did not rise to open the door for her. He wanted her to find him waiting. He quickly glanced at his watch again in order to be accurate with his indictments. As the door opened, their eyes met in a tense confrontation. Her cheerful smile quickly inverted as she braced herself for the sermon. Her eyes reflected no sense of guilt or remorse, but rather, an obstinate defiance that challenged the very authority of the man who stood before her. It was not hate, as much as it was simple teen-age rebellion. Karen was to be eighteen this next summer. When was this preacher going to realize that? He was still trying to run her life, just like he tried to run the lives of those in his congregation. When was he going to understand that she did not want to sing specials with the choir. She did not want to teach the pre-school. She didn't like "doing puppets". She wasn't the example he wanted her to be for the youth, and most of all, she did not want to be a "preacher's kid".

"I suppose you know what time it is?" he began curtly.

"Ten-ish, I suppose. The movie got out around 9:30 and we ran by Mickey-D's" she responded unapologetically closing and locking the door behind her.

"Try 10:45!" he rounded up for emphasis sake.

"O.K.! Forty-five minutes late. What's the big deal?"

"The big deal, young lady, is that we have rules in this house," he said, and suddenly found himself reverting to the same clichés he had heard through his own adolescence from both the TV and family.

"You have rules!" Karen shot back cutting him off, "I have choices!"

Though first taken aback by the outburst, he quickly detected that it was part of a rehearsed speech she had been waiting to deliver on just such an occasion.

"Furthermore," she continued, "I have been exercising those choices for some time now. *I choose who I will go out with.* I choose where I will go with him, and what we mutually decide we will do together." (He refrained from correcting her use of redundant expressions.) "And if you must know, I am also choosing to not start college next year, like you and Mom have already decided for me to do."

Fathers undergo no basic training to prepare them for raising children. Unfortunately, it is easier to become a father than to be one. They are denied the internal bonding that accompanies childbirth, and are usually too proud to allow some book to tell them how to do it. And yet, the relationship between a father and his daughter is magical. She is the only one who can still climb up into his lap long past the time when her size and weight should permit her. She is the only one who can convince him that shoes are a necessity of life. Is it any wonder that correcting daughters can be the most difficult task any father can be called upon to do? Most times, fathers must rely on the sternness of their voice to project their authority, but when that fails, the choices are limited. Corporal discipline had not been an option to Howard since Karen was twelve years old. Though abundantly educated in pastoral care and counseling, family life never seemed to fall within textbook examples. He was at a loss for what to do or say next.

"Karen . . ." he began slowly, but then felt the futility of his own words. "I think it best if we . . ." his voice trailed off as he felt himself being restrained from completing his own thought. "What I mean is . . . "

"Don't say it!" he heard almost audibly within his mind. *"Tell her you love her and you are glad she is all right. Tell her good-night!"* He shook his head as though to clear away the strange form of communication coming from within. He had not waited nearly an hour by the door on that hard sofa just to let her off the hook. He would not allow her to bark at him about choices and then declare her independence from them in such a defiant fashion. He deserved more respect than that, and now was the time to draw the line and re-establish some of the order that had been lost over the past two years.

"YOU ARE GROUNDED YOUNG LADY! Two weeks - no dates, no malls, no movies, no more - do you understand me?" He felt each word explode from his face with the anger it was meant to convey. But when he had finished, he felt no victory or resolution. He didn't even feel the satisfaction of having said it. It felt . . . reactionary . . .painful . . . it felt wrong.

"FINE! I can't wait till I'm out of this house . . . and away from . . ." she stopped herself just short of crossing the line, but her heart was already packed. She turned dramatically and marched up the stairs to her bedroom without trying to cushion her steps for the noise. Mother could hear for all she cared. After all, where was she anyway? Why wasn't Mom downstairs waiting with Dad? Did she not care what he was going to say to her? Was she not going to defend her? Why was she hiding in the bedroom pretending they were all such a happy family?

She threw open the door, and with the same pendulum swing of her arm, slammed it closed behind her. She threw her sweater in the corner and walked to the door of her walk-in closet. Opening the door, her eyes went instinctively to the plastic clothesbasket of stuffed animals half-buried in the back under some windbreakers. She remembered the closet seeming so much bigger when they had first come to live there. She remembered how safe she felt surrounded by all her "true friends", now collected together in the basket. She sat on the floor of the closet and began to cry. As she gazed upward, she saw the large suitcase they had stored in *her* closet. Just another reminder that not even her space was all her own. Well, things were going to change. The large suitcase was going! . . . *And her with it*!

———

The rains had begun early that day. Most Central American countries enjoy two seasons: wet and dry. When it was dry, it was hot. When it was wet, it was wet! In some regions, the rains were almost punctual. Beginning middle to late August, they arrived every afternoon. The south of Honduras had two faces to correspond with its two seasons. During the wet season, the undergrowth flourished, filling hillsides and roadsides to give the impression of jungle. What the south lacked was true foliage, partly because of the traditional farming practices. So when it was dry, it was dusty dry and hot. The landscape transformed to the desert scenery of southwest Texas. For the Departments of Choluteca and Valle, the rains came normally during the summer months (though referred to as winter), bypassing August usually, and continuing through till November. The best semblance of a schedule occurred when the rains appeared almost daily - sometime around three o'clock in the afternoon. But the rains had begun early that day, and had been pouring constantly throughout the afternoon and into the evening. The rivers would be filling sooner, and travel would become more difficult as the night progressed.

Ramón Aguila Reinaldo was known to his friends (what few he had) as "Moncho", and known to the rest as "El Rey", meaning "The King". Aguila was Spanish for "eagle" but that name was hardly ever used. For that matter, none of his names were used often, for he was not a man to associate with. He had come to the South from the department of Lempira in the northwest of a country not much larger than the state of Tennessee. He had come without family and had taken a wife, as well as several "*mujeres*" (women), from among the villagers of *Santa Tierra*. He was feared by most and for good reason: he had killed no less than nine men since he had arrived to their pueblo fifteen years earlier. Though most had been shot by the .33 revolver he carried conspicuously in his belt over his right front pants pocket, he still boasted of having killed two with a machete (both during the same fight), and one with a Rambo style hunting knife. Three of the deaths had resulted from an unsuccessful attempt at blood vengeance on the part of family members. The only scar he bore was a twelve inch line that ran just below his elbow to his wrist on his right forearm - the one and only contact made by one of the other men during the machete fight.

"*Mas cerveza, AHORA!*" Moncho yelled out - for more beer - his speech already slurred from passing the night in the small cantina. He went back to explaining to his two companions his impression of the degree of current corruption in the government. Using his hands, rather mostly his fingers, to help him form the words, he repeated the same old "*dichos*" (trite expressions) over and over to his uninterested drinking buddies, who only cared about how many more beers he could buy them. The owner of the cantina, Roberto, walked courageously to the table of "*El Rey*", and asked to see some more money. Insulted, Moncho stood to his feet, slurring obscenities, and running his hands through his pockets. The owner stiffened nervously when his hand passed over the handle of the pistol in his belt, but Moncho had no intention of shooting his only supplier of tomorrow's beer. When he realized he had lost most of his money that afternoon playing "*nipe*", a Latin version of poker, he glared at the owner of the cantina, but knew better than to demand drinks on credit. For tonight, the party was over - unless he could find more money. He tapped the steel chamber half-protruding from his belt, and smiled.

"We'll be back very soon", he sneered in Spanish, and he led his two drunken companions out the door.

———

Gertrude Anne Miller Baxter, the one and only daughter of the Thomas Millers preferred the name "Gertie", because Adam Baxter preferred the name "Gertie". Her family name of Miller had once been Mueller, but that was unimportant. She was a fourth generation American, and had broken all ties with her German heritage. She had faithfully prayed her Adam through World War II from the summer of 1941, when he was sent to Iceland, until the summer of 1944, when he landed on the beach of southern France with the U.S. Seventh army as part of *Operation Anvil*. Though a young man of twenty-five, he had suffered a minor leg injury that sent him home to his war bride of twenty-three. Together, they prayed through the remaining year of battles and then rejoiced, when the war finally came to a close. He always called her "Gertie", and she always loved to hear the way he said it.

Gertie had settled into the rocking chair beside the couch so she could reach both her Bible and her stationery. She had found that many times the Lord would show her someone to write and encourage while she was praying for him or her. She always included the time of day when the letter was written in the top right corner so they would know when she was thinking of them. It was not uncommon for friends to receive letters dated and timed in the early hours of the morning. Gertie found she listened better when there were no distractions. Opening her Bible, she found her large print devotional booklet. Though there were many organizations that mailed them out, she preferred the one sent quarterly to her church from her own denomination. She picked hers up faithfully every three months when it was laid out on the large wooden table in the vestibule of the church. She read the single page devotions and looked up the scripture texts for additional insights. Most of all, she enjoyed scanning the list of missionary birthdays for that day, in hopes of seeing a familiar name. Not that it mattered greatly, for she would pray for each one, by name, equally.

Opening the booklet, she found the devotion for that day, which was now only three hours old. The writer spoke of intercession, which came as no surprise to Gertie, and the text read from Ezekiel 22:30 - *"And I sought for a man among them, that should make up the hedge, and stand in the gap before me for the land, that I should not destroy it: but I found none."* Gertie closed her eyes and let the words sink deep into her spirit. *"I sought for a man . . . but I found none."*

"Oh Lord," she prayed, "what man are you seeking? For what are you seeking him to do? How do I pray?" She sat in the quiet for a moment, and then opened her eyes.

She turned the booklet to the section of missionary's birthdays. She adjusted her trifocals to see the smaller print of the birthday list. She spoke each name quietly and tried to pronounce each of the countries in which they served. Since the restructuring of the former Soviet Union, there were many unfamiliar names of countries now spanning Eastern Europe, but she made a gallant effort to sound them out. After all, she thought, at nearly 3:00 am, who would correct her?

Her eyes stopped on a familiar name, and she paused in her listing. How many years had it been since he visited their church with his wife and . . . was it three children? She remembered one was quite a young lady of fifteen, and in fact, their church learned of the great emphasis placed on the fifteenth birthday of a young girl in their country when the church hosted her own stateside *"quincienera"*. It resembled a miniature wedding, only without the groom! There had been attendants, gowns, and a beautiful pink cake. She must be at least eighteen now, Gertie thought smiling over the memory. Today was her father's birthday, Carey Eldridge, missionary to Honduras.

She remembered his name because it reminded her of William Carey, the Father of Modern Missions. From her own childhood she had studied missions through age level groups in her little Baptist church. She had served many years as president of the local Women's Missionary Union, working on both association and state levels. Though not currently holding a position, she still tried to frequent what meetings the weather and her health allowed her to attend. But for the past five years, her greatest contribution had been from her "prayer closet". Perhaps, she thought, it always had been.

She remembered Carey and his family, because they seemed so comfortable in their work. They enjoyed doing their presentations in the churches, and the whole family participated. Carey was light-hearted and injected humor into the slides at appropriate times, to help carry the congregation along. But she remembered there was a serious side to him that led you to know that he did not take lightly his calling or his mission in God's service. Gertie had been placed on their mailing list shortly after that furlough, and had kept up with their work and ministry for the past two to three years. She knew if she rummaged through the stationary drawer of the end table, she would find their last newsletter.

This must be the one I am to pray for specifically, she thought. She took the time to open the drawer and find the newsletter. Rereading the highlights, she found a section she had previously marked with a star, signifying a priority that had been expressed through the newsletter concerning their work in Honduras. The section spoke of Carey's prayer to open a new work in a small village in the mountains above their base city of operation. He requested prayer for wisdom in discerning the Lord's timing and, as the letter read, *"for the open door to soon be found in this small and poor community of. . . Santa Tierra"*.

———

Santa Tierra, like many villages in a country historically Catholic, had chosen for itself a religious name meaning, "Holy Land". Most village names honored patron saints that became the objects of annual festivals, whether celebrated religiously or not. Other villages bore similar sacred significance, such at *"El Corpus"*, ("The Body") with reference to the same "body" as Corpus Christi in Texas. *"Santa Cruz"* meant "Holy Cross", and *"Santo Domingo"* translated "Holy Sunday". Sixteenth Century Spaniards had grafted their religion along with their culture and language into this primitive Indian nation. What remained were the names, and a nominal following of syncretistic Catholicism. The village names sounded like old western towns whose pronunciation had been butchered for nearly two centuries by English visitors.

Carey Eldridge had learned in his second year on the field that a good local accent could cover a multitude of grammatical errors. After a year of language school in Costa Rica, and thirteen years on the field, he no longer translated in his mind, but simply spoke fluently, thinking in Spanish as naturally as he did in English. Carey was truly bilingual, but only because he didn't count his Greek as a verbal language. Though bilingual, Carey still carried Armando with him to his night services in the event of an emergency, or car trouble, so as not to be alone on the road. He was particularly glad to have Armando Ochoa with him that night.

The rains had started earlier than usual, and had filled the mountain streams that wound their way through the pass. *Santa Tierra* was situated about forty-five minutes from the paved hi-way, with only a rain-gutted dirt road leading into town. The five speed, double cab, Toyota Hilux with high wheel clearance and four wheel drive was a necessity for maneuvering the rock laden roads, steep grades and (on nights like this) the mud and swollen stream beds. Spanning most ravines was a small concrete ramp, called a *"quebrada"*, to allow the water to flow over the passage without eroding completely away the ground of the road. As the rains continued, the water flow from the mountain streams over a *quebrada* could become very swift and deep. Carey had learned the hard way not to underestimate the power of such a current. If the water could reach the top of his wheels, it could push him over the concrete ramp and into the stream. Some ramps where built with two to three foot drops that could overturn a pick-up like his. The wisest course of action was to wait on one side of the road until the rains slowed and the flow diminished. Some nights, he had waited as much as three hours. He was about to break his record.

Armando, known to all as "Mando" was twenty-seven years old, and a fairly new Christian. He was an iron welder, who made decorative gates and bars used on the windows of homes for protection. The ironwork called *balcones*, included a style of eight-foot high bar fencing that spanned the Eldridge's front yard facing the road. Mando had personally overseen the work on the Eldridge home with an eye to both security and beauty. He took pride in his skill and shared in the appreciation of the finished product.

It was while working on the Eldridge fence and gate that Carey had first talked to Mando about the "gated entrance" to heaven. Mando acknowledged the familiar idea of St. Peter and even related some equally familiar jokes. One day, Carey, using his EE (Evangelism Explosion) training, had asked him, "If you were to stand before that gate, and God Himself asked you why He should let you in, what would you say to him?"

As Mando stammered and tried to think of a good religious answer, one of his workmen, showing up for the first time, came to the solid metal port and tapped on it lightly. Carey, seizing the moment, turned towards the gate and called out, "Who is it?" After the worker gave his full name, Carey turned to Mando and winked, and in his sternest voice called to the person on the other side, "And why should I let you through my gate?"

After a pause, the voice on the other side replied, "Because I'm with Mando." Smiling, Carey quickly lifted the latch to let him join the other workers. He turned to Mando and explained, "You see, Mando, Jesus is the only way into heaven, He told us so, and the only way we can enter is to be able to say, 'I'm with Him'".

Mando smiled in understanding, and setting down his hammer, he said with all sincerity, *"I want to know this Jesus."*

———

"What hymns have we not sung yet?" Carey asked Mando, after a few moments of silence. The worship service had concluded just above *Santa Tierra*, and they had reached the swollen *quebrada* at the north entrance of town around 9:05 PM. For the next three and a half hours or so, they had sung every hymn and chorus either one of them could think of, some more than three times, and were beginning to run out of steam.

"I know one," smiled Mando, using his pocket flashlight to look at his watch. And in his most "professional" singing voice, he began to croon loudly, *"feliz, feliz cumpliaños, deseamos para ti,. . ."* which was the "Happy Birthday Song" found near the back of their Spanish hymnal. He sang from memory the familiar birthday blessing used in the church with a renewed gusto and enthusiasm. Carey smiled softly to himself, realizing it must now be past 12:00 am - tomorrow! and it was his birthday. The fact was, it was closer to 12:30, but the thought had just occurred to Mando, so he took the opportunity to be the first to congratulate the missionary on his special day. Finishing the song, he said slowly and proudly, "Appy Bert-day, 'ermano Cah-ry, Got ...Bles .... Ju!"

"Gracias, Hermano (brother)," Carey replied humbly. "I guess I didn't plan on being stuck here all night. I would rather we both be in our beds right now. But the rains have lightened up quite a bit this last half-hour. Perhaps, we can try very soon to cross."

Moncho led his *compañeros* staggering through the town to the plaza in front of the Catholic Church. Luís pulled on Moncho's shirt to stop him. "Where are we going to find more money for beer tonight?"

Moncho leaned towards his face, as though someone might be trying to listen to their conversation. "Did you see whose truck was outside the cantina?" he slurred.

"No," They both responded in unison.

"Felípe, . . .the supplier. He came to bring the rum and beer and to sell it to Roberto. He stayed late tonight, but he has to return to Choluteca before morning. He will have much money with him when he drives out of town."

"So . . ." They both joined in together, "We are going to rob Felípe?"

"Si, hombre," he replied straightening up, and turning toward the road out of town. "Follow me, I will show you where we will wait for him".

———

Gertie glanced at her ladies Timex. It was their smallest model with their largest numbers. She had wanted something dainty but practical on her last birthday, and Adam always knew how to please her. It was now 2:55 am, and she had just finished addressing the letter to "Brother Carey and Family"; she promptly wrote the time above the date so she wouldn't forget. "I doubt you remember me. . ." she began after her usual salutation and blessing. She proceeded to describe the church and dates when his family had visited. She double-checked her copies of their newsletters, and then asked about each of the children by name. She wished Carey specifically a very happy birthday, and that the Lord would bless him in a special way on that day. She then began to write from the heart, revealing how the Lord had awakened her that evening to pray for him. She felt burdened that there was a specific need or trial he was facing in which he could use some prayer support and encouragement. "I have no special revelation or vision concerning you or your work, I just feel impressed that you are either about to or are now facing some real difficulties." She hoped that the letter would not sound too "mystical". "Just know," she concluded, "that people are praying for you, especially on this day! May God bless you as you serve Him!" And then she signed it simply, "Yours In Christ, Gertie Baxter."

The hall clock chimed three times, and Gertie held the letter in her hand. She closed her eyes and prayed softly to herself. "Lord, You know I don't understand what I am doing, but You do. I thank you for calling me this evening to 'the closet'. I pray right now for whatever young Carey is facing on the field, that You would overcome it and turn it around for Your Honor and Glory. Protect him and his family from the attacks of Satan, and accomplish Your will in all that is done. May this letter find its way to him soon. In Christ's Holy name I pray, Amen."

Retrieving one of the newsletters again from the drawer, she addressed the envelope using the foreign names of the city, department and its code, and then wrote HONDURAS in all capital letters. One of her letters, addressed to Central America, routed itself through California first, because she had abbreviated Central America with C.A. She did not want this letter to be lost or delayed. In view of what Carey Eldridge was about to face, it was certain that God did not want this letter misdirected, either.

Chapter Two:

"The Accident"

12:55 am was considered late, even for Carey, to be returning home from an evening service. It could only mean car trouble or a road problem. Sometimes, the buses would break down climbing the mountain roads, and no other cars or trucks could pass around them. This had happened once, and Carey had slept in the cab and Mando had slept in the camper of the truck. The next morning, oxen were used to pull the bus back down into a wider place in the road for the owner to then work on it. It was "not knowing" that kept waking Susan up every twenty minutes to see if he had arrived. She slipped on her dressing gown and went to the kitchen for a drink of water. The three-gallon Coleman thermos on the kitchen counter held their drinking water, but this late at night, the ice had all melted and the water was near room temperature. Susan didn't care, it was wet, and that was good enough for her. Holding the glass between her hands, she realized it was already morning. . . and Carey's birthday. She closed her eyes, and whispered a prayer that was prayed by her and the children countless nights at bedtime when Daddy was out visiting a church or mission. "Dear Lord, please keep Carey safe on the road. Watch over his going out and his coming in and please bring him home soon." She had no way of knowing the significance of that prayer and most especially its timing.

———

"I think the water is lower now," Mando offered peering out through the sprinkled windshield with his flashlight. "Let me go and check it." Immediately, he began pulling off his shoes and opening the car door to roll up his pants legs.

"You be careful, if the current is strong, don't try it" Carey urged.

"*No problema!*" he called out wading into the stream crossing. Halfway across, the water was no higher than the top of his shins. Though it was wetting the bottom rolls of his pants legs, it was not pushing him over. The water had gone down enough for them to cross. He emerged on the other side victoriously and shined his flashlight from left to right signaling the "all-clear" for him to bring the Toyota across. Carey pulled the key back towards him to warm the glow plugs, and then started up the motor. Aside from wetting the brakes somewhat, the stream posed no real threat to the high wheel clearance of the truck. Carey reached across and swung open the passenger door for Mando, who was still lowering his pants legs, and called

12

out, *"Let's head-em up and move-em out, and maybe we'll make it home before 2:00"*. Mando hated it when he used English expressions he didn't understand.

———

"This one will do. Quick, help me," Moncho demanded, grabbing the fat end of a fallen tree limb. He instructed the other two to lift in the middle and help him pull it across the road. The branch was about seven inches thick and bowed so that it rose up well over a foot from the ground in the middle. Its length was more than enough to cover the width of the road. It lay there unnaturally though, because the nearest tree was still several meters away down the hill. Moncho chose this spot because of the bushes alongside the shoulder that could be used for cover until the unsuspecting motorist stopped to move the fallen limb.

The truck rumbled through the village of *Santa Tierra*, passing the cantina and the plaza. Everything seemed so quiet and serene at night, even after a storm. The services had been held in the home of a believer who lived above the village, and above the main *quebrada* that had delayed them for nearly four hours. The small group was composed of some seven adults and almost thirty children. Counting the curious, who often times stood outside the windows and front door of the home to watch the "evangelicals" sing and pray. Usually, fifty or more gathered for evening services. There had been considerably less this evening because of the rain. Carey had preached on the importance of praying daily to help the young Christian to grow. He had emphasized the scriptures of Philippians 4:6 and 1 Peter 5:7 and how they must give their cares in prayer to God. His greatest care for this village was to find a place where they could meet and an open door for the gospel. For the most part, the believers of the mission all came from two extended families. Carey glanced at Mando, who was trying not to fall asleep as the truck lunged and bumped over the rough terrain.

"Mando, what do you think it would take for us to reach the people of *Santa Tierra*?" Carey asked sincerely.

"I'm not sure, *Hermano*," he confessed, "Nothing short of a miracle, I suppose. The people are hard. They think little of religion, and less of *gringos*. The farther you travel away from the cities, the less contact these people have had with persons other than their own village." Mando thought carefully for a moment, and then chose to continue delicately, in hopes he would not hurt the feelings of his friend. "You have been coming to *Santa Tierra* for over eight months now, and many of the people only know your truck. They are not impressed by the sacrifice you make to come to their village, for they travel this road daily on foot or by horse. You must show them something different, something more."

"I understand," Carey acknowledged, "Thanks for being honest. I just pray the Lord will show me soon how I can reach out in a meaningful way that they would understand and accept."

BUMP! The truck bounced hard over a rock that jarred them both erect in their seats. Carey decided he best keep his eyes on the road for now. They still had over thirty minutes of this kind of ground left to cover till they reached the highway and its blacktop.

Moncho heard the sound of the motor first. He motioned to Luís to look over the embankment to see if it was the familiar red pick-up of Felípe. Luís crawled up over the edge and peered into the direction of the coming sound. The soft glow of the moon on the low clouds illumined the backdrop behind the road. As the vehicle came over the hill to make its descent toward them, Luís could make out the familiar shape of the cab of a truck. But as it veered right for the first curve, he could see the camper attached to the truck bed, and realized that this was not Felípe, but rather the *gringo* missionary who must have been above the village that night. He scurried back to Moncho to tell him that it was not the beer salesman. Moncho just smiled all the more.

"A *gringo*," he thought aloud, "they carry more money anyway . . . all the better!"

"No, Moncho! My cousin goes to his meetings. I can't do this!" Luís did not wait for the reprisal, he slid on down the embankment and hurried to the footpath leading back into the village.

"And you?" he snapped at the other. "Do you fear one *gringo*?"

"No, Moncho," he responded obediently, "What do I do?"

"Go across the road near the limb. Stay low behind the bush so that his headlights do not see you, and wait till he stops. When he steps out of his truck, grab him and hold him and I will come from the other side in case there is one with him in the truck," he said and pulled out his pistol to remind them both, they had the power on their side. "If he tries to fight you, I will be there."

The four wheel drive slowed the traveling to about 10 kilometers an hour (just over 6 mph), especially climbing or descending the steep grades where the larger rocks and mud called for more navigation than usual. Carey saw it first in the high beam of the headlights, it was an oversized branch lying in the road. It took an extra moment for it to register because of their tiredness, but soon they both felt a rush of adrenaline as he turned quickly towards Mando, "Is that what I think it is?"

Mando sat erect and grabbed the handhold above his door. "Yes, *Hermano*, what ever you do, don't stop!" The anxiety in his voice was obvious. They both understood the potential danger of such a sight.

Carey looked around quickly trying to assess the situation. There was no way to go around the branch, and it would be too difficult to shift into reverse and attempt to back up the hill given the rocks, curves and slippery mud. Forward appeared to be their only direction. The Toyota had a high wheel clearance, but not that high, he thought. The branch bowed upward near the middle to almost two feet he estimated.

"Don't think about it, *Hermano*, just go!" Mando said almost frantically.

"But what about the muffler?"

"If you break it, I'll reweld it! Just go!" he almost shouted. Carey shifted down into first and held tightly to the wheel.

Instead of slowing, as expected, the truck roared and lunged forward with the climbing power of its four-wheel drive. As its heavy front tires rolled over the limb, it raised up into the air like a bear. The man on Carey's side, fell backwards behind the bush as the limb shook under the weight of the truck. Clearing the front wheels, the middle of the branch could be heard rubbing the drive shaft and then rolling hard along the muffler until the back wheels met the wood. Then the back end rose up clearing the rear axle. Fortunately, there had not been any jagged branch cuttings to puncture the tires as they climbed the obstacle. Moncho watched in mute amazement, not realizing that the *gringo's* truck was so strong and so high off the ground. Felípe's truck could never have cleared that branch. But they had not escaped yet.

"Did you see anybody?" Carey asked quickly, shifting it back into second to try and put some distance between them and the branch.

"No! but to be honest, I had my eyes closed praying," Mando said smiling.

Neither man noticed the form rising from the right rear corner of the truck trying to find his footing to run along the road beside them. By the time Carey checked the passenger side mirror, Moncho had almost reached the back seat window. Carey saw the silhouette moving, but could not make out the features. "Mando, there is someone beside the car!"

Mando turned instinctively with his flashlight and shined it out the open window beside him. The sight was then reflected in the side mirror for Carey to see. It was a man, large and menacing, and in his right hand, he held a pistol. Carey prayed audibly, "Help us Lord Jesus!"

The combination of events that followed was more than coincidental. As Gertie and Susan prayed, Mando shined the light in the eyes of their attacker. Moncho, losing his night vision, hung his foot in a root from the tree where he had taken the branch. The large truck then began to slide towards the right from the rear in the mud and Carey compensated automatically by turning into the direction of the slide. At that moment, Moncho found himself falling face first onto the ground, the gun flying from his hand as he tried to break his fall. He landed on his right cheek in the mud, his body half on and half off the road. Unfortunately, the portion on the road was his upper torso, and Carey's maneuver to keep the truck straight slid the vehicle over his body. Moncho opened his eyes after hitting the ground in time to see the right rear wheel of the Toyota Hilux coming towards him, but there was not even time to scream.

"Was that another branch?" Mando asked having drawn himself back in from the window of the truck.

"I don't think so!" Carey responded, with a sickening feeling in his stomach. "Do you still see him out there?" He said, starting to slow down the truck. Mando shined his flashlight once again behind him out the window, looking carefully in the mirror, but the man was gone. He then stuck his head out the window, and shined along the roadside until the beam stopped on the fallen form alongside the road. "*Hermano*, there he is, but he is down!"

Carey stopped the truck. "Does it look like another trap?" He asked cautiously.

"I don't think so. I can see his right hand from here and the gun is gone. I think something has happened. Should we not go back to see?"

The question was a difficult one, for they both still felt the tingle of fear and the apprehension of exposing themselves to danger. But if the man were hurt, he would not be found till the morning and could possibly die. *"It is all right. The danger is over. Go now to him."* With the thought came a peace that Carey recognized. He shifted the truck into reverse and inched his way back to the place just past the slide.

The rains had now stopped and many of the clouds were beginning to clear. The full moon began to poke its way through the clouds. The silent partner that had fallen behind the bush lay quietly on the ground watching, but not moving. He did not wish to be noticed or remembered, so he lay very still and watched. Carey called from his door to the man with his head still turned in the mud away from them, but there was no response. Together, they walked carefully towards him, and were standing just over the body when they could see the muddy tire track beginning at his left shoulder, traveling diagonally across his shoulder blades, and across his right arm just above the elbow. Carey bent down trembling and searched the neck for a pulse. He looked up into the waiting eyes of Mando and shook his head no. They both stood motionless for an eternal minute, and then Carey slowly walked back to the truck and unlocked the door above the tailgate. Swinging it up and lowering the tailgate, he walked back to Mando and the body.

"What are you doing, *Hermano*?" Mando asked sincerely.

"We can't leave him here," he explained while glancing at his watch, "and it is now past 1:00 am; there is no one we can carry him to in *Santa Tierra*. I suggest we place him in the back of the truck and carry him to the F.U.S.E.P. (*Fuerza de Seguridad Publica*, or "Public Safety Force"), station on the highway just outside of Choluteca. They will need to be notified anyway, and they can help with the identification."

"You know that they will arrest you?" Mando said cautiously.

"I realize that," Carey replied, "but we can't just leave him here. Besides, the authorities will notify his family."

It was the latter that concerned Carey the most, because machete law was still common in the rural areas where he served. You did not bring home a dead relative in the middle of the night, especially if you were responsible for their death. A vengeful brother could strike you down without all the facts, and the authorities would seldom pursue it. It would be better to allow the local police to notify the family in the daytime. Mando agreed and together they lifted the heavy body into the back of the truck. There were no hymns sung for the remainder of their trip to the pavement.

The two "bounced" in silence along the dirt road, Carey traveling slower than usual, yet still occasionally hearing the muffled thud of the "cargo" against the back wall of the bed of the truck. It was a sickening sound that accentuated the tragedy and deepened the heaviness in their hearts. Carey's hands had begun to tremble as the realization of the night's events became clearer. He never saw anything more than the form in the mirror. Carey had not tried to hit the man, he had not tried to do anything except maintain control of the truck, and yet, now a man lay dead, and he had been the one to run over him. How could he not be responsible? He did not feel guilt of malice or of neglect. To some extent he felt trapped, like a victim himself of the circumstances. He replayed the tape in his mind of the branch, the urgency in Mando's voice, the form in the mirror, the slide and finally the "second bump". It had all happened too fast. He could not have done it differently without stopping at the branch and allowing himself to be robbed and possibly shot as well. . . *shot as well*! Where was the gun? They had not picked up the gun. He couldn't remember even looking for it. Their only concern had been to load the body and continue on down the mountain as quickly and safely as possible.

"Mando, we forgot the gun," Carey said, breaking the silence.

"Do you want to go back after it?" he asked half-serious.

"I suppose not, do you think they will believe us without it?"

"As much as they would have believed you with it. You do not have the license proving it was his. For that matter, I doubt he had a license proving it was his." Mando replied looking earnestly at Carey.

17

Mando had a point. The authorities would have to weigh the truth of their story solely on their testimony. Now Carey had another matter to worry about. Most authorities believed whatever gained them the bigger bribe - or so he had been told.

———

Capitán Juan Carlos Mendoza was not accustomed to the graveyard shift. One of his men had sent word that his wife had been taken to the hospital with severe *dengue*, a tropical cousin to malaria, and he needed a replacement for his shift. The Capitán had received the notice late that afternoon while preparing to go home, and decided to snatch five hours of sleep and return himself for the shift change at ten. With still four hours left to go till 6:00 am, he was beginning to fight the fatigue of two shifts during the same twenty-four hour period.

Though it was not unusual for vehicles to pass through the *posta* all hours of the night, he was most suspicious of those entering the city between 2:00 and 4:00 in the morning. He had just about decided to let this one past, so he would not have to rise from his chair propped up squarely against the wall of the guard post, when he saw that the truck was slowing and veering in towards him. He brought his chair to "all fours" and reached for his flashlight.

The red Toyota Hilux with the white camper was a familiar one to Mendoza. On many occasions, he had hailed a ride returning from another village, where he had been serving, and the "American missionary" had stopped and carried him in the cab, instead of making him ride in the back, as did most who stopped. He did not remember his name, but recognized his lighter complexion and his fading red wavy hair. As the truck pulled to his side, Mendoza smiled away his tiredness, his crooked teeth showing.

"*Buenas noches, Jéfe*" he called to the truck. "*Jéfe*", *or* "chief" was a typical expression of respect for strangers who appeared to be men of authority. "What keeps you out so late at night?"

"*Buenas noches, Capitán*," Carey did not remember his face, but he recognized the insignia on his uniform. "We have a problem, sir. Could you step around to the back of the truck?" he asked matter-of-factly while opening his own door to step down. Mando was also moving to the rear of the pick-up in order to open the tailgate door. The Capitán followed without question, then stood motionless with them at the rear of the Toyota for several moments.

"*Muerto?*" he inquired, asking if the man was dead.

"*Sí,*" was the quiet response from Carey, who knew the question required more information and explanation than that, but hoped he could sit down to give it. Mendoza lifted the gate in order to close it for them, and invited the two men into the guardhouse where they could calmly and comfortably give all the necessary details for his report. It was obvious they were troubled and equally obvious that they wanted to do what was right. This was not a time to make accusations. A younger officer might have seized the opportunity to exploit and extort them, but Mendoza was more interested in the truth than he was in a bribe. He suddenly felt very much awake.

The lone figure staggering back into the village used the road rather than the foot trail, primarily because he did not trust his own equilibrium enough to carry him along the path that followed the small section of canyon. It didn't matter, because there was no one to witness his return - the hour was too late at night (or too early in the morning) for him to be noticed. He came to his small adobe house and beat repeatedly on the wooden door, calling out for his wife to open it before it started raining again, though the threat of rain had long since passed. As he heard the wooden brace being lifted from its holders, he tapped the handle of the .33 pistol now pushed down into his own pants pocket. This pistol had given Moncho power. That power would now be his.

———

After twenty minutes of reliving the events of the evening, Carey dropped his head into his hands resting his elbows on his knees. Mando confirmed each detail with his own testimony, speaking as humbly as he could. It had occurred to both men, that the only other witness lay in the back of Carey's truck, and his version would not be heard. The question was whether this officer would believe their testimony or not. In the case of vehicular manslaughter, the law stated that the one responsible for the death must be held in custody until it could be determined that the death was an accident. In this case, the only eyewitness accounts were those of the accused.

"And there was no one else who saw what happened?" asked the Capitán.

"No sir, we were outside the village on a narrow incline where no one lives."

Mendoza paused in thought looking out the window of the small checkpoint. The one common factor they all shared was their need for sleep, but there was a dead man in the rear of their truck and he had to determine whether these two were telling the truth. He rose from his small-unpainted wooden desk and headed toward the open door. "Let's remove the body from the truck for now, and I will see what needs to be done."

It took all three of them to carefully slide the lifeless form from the bed of the pick-up and to transfer it to the floor of the guardhouse. There, the light revealed the face of the victim for the first time to Carey. His appearance had not been greatly marred by the accident. In fact, apart from the slight deformity of the left shoulder, which had been crushed under the wheel, the body showed no evidence of a violent death. His chest cavity had been crushed pushing the air out of his lungs at the point of impact. He had stopped breathing before his lungs filled with blood, so there was no bleeding from either the mouth or the nose. For all appearances, he simply looked asleep.

As Mendoza folded Moncho's arms across his chest in a restful repose, he noticed a long scar on the right forearm of the deceased. He turned the face slightly to the light and stared intently into its features. The face of death does not show the personality of the individual, nor does it allow one to see into the eyes of their soul as is possible in life. But there was something familiar about this man. After some thought, the Capitán's eyes sparkled with recognition. He knew this man, and what's more, he knew the kind of man he was. Mendoza had been called to *Santa Tierra* with two of his officers to interrogate a man involved in a machete fight resulting in two deaths. He recalled the injured arm, as well as the defiant face of the *"machismo"* who boasted his innocence by claiming self-defense. The only "testifying witnesses" had collaborated his story, almost verbatim. Though he was convinced of the man's guilt, he was powerless without proof to take action. Though two years had passed since the fight, Mendoza had not forgotten the face or the scar of the man who had defied him and the law. He looked up at Carey and said soberly, "I know this man. I know what kind of man he was. I believe your story and I see no reason for either of you to be held accountable for his accidental death. I have your directions (address) and phone number, and I will contact you if there are any more inquires, but as far as I'm concerned, you are both free to go. I will see that the body is carried back to the family in *Santa Tierra*, and I will explain what has happened. I would suggest you wait some time before you return there."

Carey and Mando exchanged glances and decided to quickly obey the Capitán's suggestion before he reconsidered. As they mounted the truck, Carey glanced at his watch. It was now 2:45 am and he knew, that if Susan was awake, she was near frantic. He pulled the truck back out into the road and headed over the large bridge into town. Mando lived just within the city limits. Carey would drop him off at his home and travel five more minutes to his own. The quiet streets made his entrance seem so ominous, as if the whole town already knew what he had done that evening.

He left the truck running as he opened the padlock through the hole in the metal sheeting of his gate. Susan always locked the gate at night from the inside, but Mando had cut a hole large enough for Carey to reach in and unlock the gate from the outside. He pulled the truck into the secure carport and closed the gate and the world behind him. Oso, their Doberman, came around from the back of the house to greet him, his stub of a tail whipping wildly. Carey had never felt as safe as he did at that moment standing on the inside of his own front entrance. He wondered how long it would take him to be willing to leave that safety, and face again the world that he had come to know that evening - the world of life and death.

As he gently unlocked and opened the front door, he stepped quietly through the living/ dining room and into the den, where he found Susan asleep on the couch. The lamp beside her still shined, and the newest edition of her favorite Christian novelist lay open across her chest. He switched off the light and decided to let her rest where she lay. After all, he had taken many an afternoon *siesta* on the same couch, and it was really quite comfortable. The truth was, he could not face the questions that would come if he woke her now. He would let her pass the night at rest, and tomorrow they would face the storm together. As he gently lifted her book, returning it to the coffee table, the thought came upon him suddenly, *"If there had to be a widow this evening, would you rather it had been her?"* For the first time, it occurred to him that the accident not only took a life, it most probably saved two.

Chapter Three:

"The Storm"

(Thursday morning)

The morning light filtered through the white shears of the bedroom window. The heavy curtains draped over only a portion of the upper third allowing the East Coast sun to greet Gertie and Adam each morning. She had wanted to start her days as soon as possible, so she seldom used the pull-down shades Adam had installed above the windows. But this morning Adam had risen first. He had started the coffee, retrieved the *Newport News Herald* from the front porch, and was catching up on the ball scores he had missed the night before.

Adam Baxter was a small man of quiet strength. He had celebrated three quarters of a century of life the year before, but still carried the stamina for morning walks in the mall. He liked basketball, professional bowling and horseshoes. Though he had never played basketball, he followed the NBA with a vicarious enthusiasm for anyone who could jump higher than he stood. His bowling trophies lined the homemade shelf above his desk in the den. He still tossed horseshoes.

With over ten years since retirement, he filled his days with home projects, exercise walks, and hours of study for his Sunday school class. Adam never waited till Saturday night to begin preparing. He had taught the Senior Men's Class at the First Baptist Carrolton for seventeen years, and still found himself learning something new each week. He often said, "The moment you stop learning is the time you stop teaching". His desk was a museum of reference works and Bible translations. He used articles from the teachers' aids, illustrations from current magazines, and he scribbled endless notes on legal pads that would later be compiled into a neat legible outline. He poured himself into his class, and it showed. For Adam, the labor of his latter years was to be spent enriching the hearts and minds of those entering that stage when most men began to feel useless. Each Sunday morning he gave the men of his class that much more to live for.

This Thursday morning, he chose to let his Gertie sleep in. He carried his cup of coffee to the den and searched for the last yellow legal pad he had been using the night before. His lesson for the next Sunday came from the book of Exodus, chapters 32 and 33. Adam was so glad his class had switched from the curriculum of themes to that which studied the books of the Bible. Following the program of study, he would be teaching the entire Bible in only nine years. According to the outline of the lesson, Moses had interceded for Israel at least three times in these two brief chapters. Adam was focusing on the first incident found in verses 1 through 14 of chapter 32.

The background of the story, to Adam, centered in Moses' absence from the camp at a time when they felt they needed him. He had gone to the mountain of God for the sake of the people, but they did not see it that way. They only knew that he wasn't there for them. Adam scribbled another note, "In the absence of authority, there is absence of discipline which leads to compromise and eventually to open rebellion". The sin of Israel could be seen in the heart of adolescence. How many young people had he known, whose fathers had left them out of their lives while "trying to provide for them", or even worse "trying to serve the Lord". Unknown to Adam that morning, another young girl, feeling the neglect of her pastor/father was about to follow Israel in her folly. Fortunately for her, she was not unknown to God.

———

Karen awoke to the din of the trash collectors tossing the heavy plastic containers back to the curb. The monotone beeping of the vehicle backing up in order to make the tight turn down the next block drove her head under her pillow, as she tried to block out the noise. It was 5:48 am and her clock wouldn't go off for another twelve minutes, but she decided the sooner she was washed and dressed, the sooner she could get out of the house. As she grabbed her gown, it occurred to her that the extra ten minutes would also give her a jump on her little brother in the use of the bathroom. He normally awoke around 7:00 and pounded on the door just as she was finishing her hair. The seven years difference in their ages had always made it difficult to relate to him. She felt more like his baby-sitter than his sister. Only in the past two years had they even offered to pay her for watching him. He was still too young to understand why a teenage girl needed more time in the bathroom than a ten-year-old runt.

Howard emerged from the walk-in closet with two ties as Donna finished making the bed.

"Which do you think?" he asked holding them up for her to decide. She never looked up.

"Which ever you think best," she sighed.

"I suppose the paisley is too much for today," he decided, returning into the closet to place the green paisley tie back on its appointed rack. He knew she was upset, but he didn't wish to talk about it before breakfast, especially with Karen still in the house. So they followed their morning routines in silence, showing courtesy but distance.

The Pennington family seldom shared meals together, and breakfast was no exception. Terry would not even come downstairs until Karen had left the house around 7:30. He walked three blocks to school and his classes did not start till 8:05. Karen rode a bus for twenty-five minutes, and had to rush to homeroom. Howard had attempted family devotions in the morning on three separate occasions when the children were younger, but it just never seemed to work. Now he read his Bible and prayed privately in his study, and was lucky if Karen came by the door before leaving the house to say good-bye.

The only link between family members was Donna Pennington. Everyone related to Mom. She had met Howard as a young "preacher-boy" in Fort Worth while he was attending seminary. She was a Texan, and he a Tennessean. She played piano, and he drove eighty miles one way to preach each Sunday at their little church in Parsons. Her family had served him lunch most of the two years he was with the church, and he came to know Donna for the beautiful and humble person that she was. He had "courted" her properly and with the blessings of her family. He had asked her hand in marriage two months before graduation. It was understood that they would most likely leave Parsons and possibly even Texas, although Howard had no plans to return to Tennessee. He felt the "Bible belt" was saturated with southern preachers, radio and TV evangelists, and every form of "ministry" you could tack a fish upon.

Howard decided to continue his theological training in California and pursue his doctorate at Mill Valley. By the age of twenty-seven, he had moved the family one more time to southern California to serve as pastor of a mid-size Baptist church that averaged roughly one-fifty in Sunday School. Donna had been pregnant with Terry at the time, and the move had been equally difficult for seven year old Karen. But Howard was a "mover and a shaker", and he soon adapted to the fast pace of California living. At one time, he even took Spanish classes in order to reach out to the Hispanic community near his home, but the church never embraced a Latino ministry, so he set his sights on building a larger urban congregation. He was now involved in the planning stage of a new facility for the church.

Donna had not adjusted quite as easily. For Donna, the role of pastor's wife became a passive one. In southern churches, they were considered important to their husband's ministry, supportive and visible. Her piano playing, once central to the work in Parsons, had been lost to a young man with a YAMAHA DX-240 upon their arrival to San Diego. Traditional ladies groups were not organized, nor did there appear to be a need for them. Ministry was different here, and Donna felt lost. At times, she felt the only thing she did have a handle on was her family, but even that was beginning to lose its grip.

Karen darted about the kitchen as though on a scavenger hunt, piecing together her lunch and drinking down the large glass of diet breakfast drink her mother had prepared for her. She never acknowledged her mother, who sat quietly at the table watching the storm whirl itself about the room. Donna glanced at the kitchen clock above the counter and noticed that it was only 7:15.

"You've got plenty of time, Karen, why not sit down and drink your breakfast? I have some toast comin' up in just a minute," she offered as pleasantly as she could.

"No thanks," she said coldly, finishing the last gulp of chocolate nutrition and tossing the plastic cup into the sink water. "I gotta meet some friends at the bus stop."

Without another word, she blew out the side door, letting the screen door slam behind her for punctuation. Donna bit her bottom lip knowing that Terry would traipse down the stairs in just a few minutes. There would be time for tears later. Besides, she had to be strong for her talk with Howard. Things had to change. He had to listen this time.

———

By 9:30, Susan had already fed the boys, Joshua and Caleb, and was beginning to wonder just how long Carey was going to stay in the bed. She knew he had come in late, but did not know how late. The last time she had looked at her watch had been at 1:45 am as she read on the couch. Her relief in finding him safe in the bedroom when she awoke that morning at 6:30 was enough. She let him sleep and decided to get the story later.

Susan was a practical woman who complemented Carey well. He took life as it came. She tried to see it coming. She had the family head for organization and he had the energy to carry out the plans. They worked well as a team and saw themselves as such. Susan liked working close to the home where she could give the time that Josh and Caleb needed. Josh was born during their first term shortly after language school, and Caleb shortly after their first furlough. Susan had been thirty-six when Caleb was born, and it had been a difficult pregnancy on the field. He was now twelve, and as tall as she was. Josh was fifteen and adventuresome. He enjoyed going out with his father to the remote villages. He showed much interest in the work, though he never indicated that he planned to serve on the mission field when he grew up. For Carey and Susan, it was enough that all three of their children had come to know the Lord early in life. The boys had adjusted well, and were as much "Honduran" as they were American in their interests.

Their oldest, Anna, was two years old when they left their home near Portsmouth, Virginia. She grew to young womanhood while in Central America. She, too, was extremely close to her father. Whenever he had errands to run, whether to the market, the post office, or to visit a church site in the afternoon to speak with a local pastor, Anna wanted to go. She just enjoyed his company. Sometimes they talked. Sometimes, they listened to the Panasonic cassette player between them on the front seat, as Daddy played 60's hits between his gospel tapes. She was especially partial to the *Beach Boys* and the *Herman's Hermits*.

The decision to send her to the states to finish high school had not been an easy one. Her educational needs were greater than other M.K.'s (Missionary Kids) in the mission. She had battled "slow learning" through the six years of correspondence classes that her mother taught her on the field. Before homeschooling was vogue, it was a necessity for missionaries who lived away from English schools. Her three separate academic years during their furloughs had helped her to "catch-up" some. But when the decision was made for her to attend the Embassy School in the capital, she began to fall behind in important subjects. After consultation with the mission and the area director, the family decided to look for educational opportunities in the U.S. Carey's younger brother, Billy, jumped at the chance to host his favorite niece in their home for her senior year of high school. With the agreement of his wife, they prepared their home for their new guest. Anna had mixed emotions about leaving. On the one hand, she looked forward to living in the states where she knew her living conditions would improve by at least four decades of technology, while on the other hand, she did not wish to be so far from her parents, especially her father. The one consolation was that Uncle Billy looked a little like Dad, and seemed to care for her just as much, though she knew it was not the same. She had always been and always would be a "Daddy's girl".

Susan gave a list of groceries to Josh and Caleb, primarily to get them out of the house, though she did need a few things. The large woven plastic baskets were normally carried by the women (usually on their head), but the boys didn't mind helping out and toting one each. They were to go to the meat market for four pounds of fresh ground beef, one frozen chicken (Susan still did not relish the idea of killing, plucking and cooking a live one like her neighbor), a pound of soft cheese called *"quesillo"*, and two bags of eggs. They then were to walk to the vegetable market nearby and buy five pounds of potatoes, some lettuce (if available), a large bunch of fresh carrots, a pineapple or two, bananas (naturally), and about two pounds of red beans. Their next stop was to a small grocery store where they would find five pounds of sugar, some tomato paste, and if there were *Lempiras* left over, some candy for them both. The near thirty pound load would be divided between them (with the eggs on top of one and the bananas on top of the other), and a pocket full of hard candy each. That should keep them occupied for at least an hour or more.

Susan then walked back to the den where she had left her book on the coffee table. She would read until Carey stirred. After only three pages, she could hear the shower water running from the master bathroom. She knew she would have at least fifteen minutes more until he would emerge from the bedroom, so she returned to her historical novel of the Jews return to Israel in 1948. The series of books were both informative and inspiring and that was what appealed to Susan. She finished the chapter and dog-eared the page just as Carey entered the den.

"Well, get enough sleep?" she asked pleasantly. She knew whatever had kept him out late the night before should be met with encouragement and not criticism or sarcasm.

"Six and a half hours is about normal for me," he responded, leaving room for questions.

"You didn't get in till 3:00 am? What happened?" she asked sincerely clearing a place on the sofa beside her, so that he could make himself comfortable.

"I don't know where to begin," Carey said slowly, choosing the wooden rocker across from her so that they could look at each other while they talked. "First, Mando and I got caught on the wrong side of a *quebrada* after the service, and had to wait almost four hours before we ever reached *Santa Tierra*."

Susan had traveled with him to the mission site on several occasions and knew the road well. She pictured the spot he was referring to in her mind and nodded quietly.

"Well, we finally got across, and then drove through *Santa Tierra* about 12:45 or so." Carey paused to frame his words for the next series of events. "Well, you know that steep hill just outside of the town?" he asked looking into her eyes. As he continued recounting the details of the accident, tears began to well up into his own, and as she heard his pain, they both began to cry.

Susan rose from the couch to kneel beside his rocker taking his hand into hers.

"I don't know what to think. . . I took a life last night," he cried.

She squeezed his hand and laid her head on his knee. Closeness was the only consolation she knew to offer. In her mind, she tried to imagine how it happened, how it might have been avoided. But the only alternative would have most likely have resulted in tragedy for Mando, Carey, or both. The truth was, a man had laid a snare into which he himself had fallen. Carey was not to blame for that.

"It was not your fault," she offered, "you could have been killed yourself, or Mando."

"I realize that," Carey said wiping his eyes. "When I saw you sleeping here last night, it was as though the Lord said, 'If there had to be a widow, would you rather it be her', meaning you!"

He paused for a moment to compose himself, then said clearly, "There is no doubt in my mind, that God spared our lives last night, I just don't understand why another man had to die. Would it not have been enough for the man just to slip down the embankment and wake up this morning with a headache?"

"I can't answer that, but I can tell you this, Carey Eldridge," she said, reaching up and taking his face in her hands, "I'm glad *you* woke up this morning in *your* own bed. And if that's selfish on my part, then I'm sorry."

Carey lifted her up and pulled her close to him as she slid onto his lap in the rocker. Together, they rocked in their oneness, and there was peace in the storm.

"*Oh, Dios mio!*" came the cry of despair from within the small two room home of Anita Peréz de Reinaldo, the wife of Moncho. Capitán Mendoza stood at the door with two other officers. The body of her husband lay covered with a blue plastic tarpaulin in the back of the gray Nissan pick-up. Though the floor of her home was dirt, they did not wish to enter with their heavy muddy boots. She pushed past them to the side of the truck as neighbors began to gather along both sides of the road to see. The face of death was neither uncommon nor disturbing in the rural areas. Drunken brawls, family feuds, and disease oftentimes left its stain in their wake. These were common facets to their lives, as was the death that accompanied them.

It was the curiosity of death's face that fascinated even the youngest of gawkers. How did they die? Was it violent or not? Even the local newspapers left little for the imagination, but displayed graphically in full color the unnatural twisted repose of death. Perhaps, the psychology of seeing it lessened the grip of fear that it held. Or perhaps, there was a sense of relief in seeing another's demise, as though the Reaper could only claim one soul at a time, like the lottery in reverse. Whatever the interest, it was suddenly stifled the moment the plastic was lifted from the body. They all stood in silent dismay.

"There is no blood," one whispered to his neighbor.

Anita held her breath. He was wearing the same clothes he had left the house in the day before, and though they were muddy, they were not torn.

28

He still had his shoes, which meant the authorities must have found him shortly after his death, but how? They live so far from the police. He never went down into the city at night, and the police never patrolled this far up the road. She looked at the Capitán with questioning eyes.

"He was found just outside of town last night. He had been run over by a truck in the road. We think he was drunk and passed out, and whoever hit him did not see him," Mendoza lied in order to protect the missionary. The figure at the left rear of the truck heard the lie, but knew better than to speak up for the moment. "He was carried to our station in town. So we are bringing him back to you this morning. We are sorry for your loss," he concluded half sincerely.

With that, the Capitán motioned to the two officers to carry the body into the house. He tried not to reveal the satisfaction he felt seeing this man brought to his own form of justice. He tried to sympathize with the widow and her loss, but it was not easy. She followed the men inside and cleared the pictures and dishes off of the only table in the house. They gently laid the body over the table and then exited dutifully.

As the truck backed out to the main road of the village, all but one turned their attention toward the house and to the widow who had begun to wail again. He watched the officers slide out of view thinking about the "secret" he now held - the truth of Moncho's death. He wondered if there was a way to make money with his secret. He would have to think much about that, but for now, it must be kept a secret. He turned towards Moncho's house that was now brimming over with by-standers. Above the roof, he could see the darkened clouds forming just beyond the mountaintop. It was going to storm again tonight, he thought to himself.

———

Howard closed the devotional commentary he had been reading and mechanically replaced it back into its slot on the bookshelf. He could barely remember what he had just read. He picked up his coffee cup and walked to the kitchen.

"Where's Karen?" he asked glancing around the room. Donna sat quietly at the small kitchen table cradling her cup between her hands.

"She stormed out of here about five minutes ago."

"But its not even 7:30 yet," Howard countered noting the time, again. His voice revealed his renewed annoyance with both his daughter and the situation she was creating in his home. It was obvious that Donna had been disturbed the night before by the conflict, and her demeanor had not brightened with the morning.

"Did you wish to say something more to her this morning that you failed to say last night?" she asked sarcastically. She looked up from her cup and caught his eyes. "I really don't think she was in a mood to see you."

Her voice cut deeper than her words. Howard knew that relations with his daughter had been strained for some time, but until now, he did not realize that he had been drifting from Donna, as well. He searched for the words to disarm the tension, but was distracted by the sudden entrance of Terry.

"Morning," he called cheerfully, "Sis already split?"

Terry's "hip" vocabulary was being influenced greatly by Brady Bunch reruns on cable. Although he knew better than to repeat such archaisms as "groovy" and "out-of-sight", some expressions still seemed appropriate, even if he was the only one who used them.

"It appears so," responded his father in a matter-of-fact tone. Donna just glared back into her coffee.

"Cool!" he said gleefully, "more breakfast for me!" He buttered both slices of toast that still sat warm in the small oven on the counter, and poured a large bowl of cocoa-something cereal. It was a new brand Mom was trying out, because it was cheaper.

As Terry slowly ate his cereal and slurped his milk, Howard found a lone grapefruit half in the crisper of the refrigerator. He sectioned it in silence, and then sprinkled two packs of artificial sweetener over it. Donna sat in mute contemplation, as three fourths of her family "endured" their breakfast together around the table. By the time he had finished his toast, Terry had sensed the awkwardness of the situation, and made an effort to dismiss himself as quickly and as politely as possible.

Several unspoken moments passed between them, then Donna looked up again with less intensity in her eyes. She knew they had to talk, but she had learned through her eighteen years of marriage, that every "discussion" became a debate in which he would eventually divert the issues enough to redirect the problem back to her. But this was not her problem - it was his. He was losing his daughter, and he still thought it was a simple power struggle.

"Do you want to talk about last night?" she began, hoping he would take the hint, pull off his jacket, and spend the morning with her there at the kitchen table.

Yes I do, I need help, I know there's a problem, but I don't know where to begin to straighten it out. Will you please help me? It was the same voice he had heard in his mind the night before. But it was foolishness. It was weakness speaking out of lack of sleep and concentration. Again, he shook it off. . . and again he later regretted doing it. Dr. Pennington, ThD, had a busy morning ahead of him, with appointments beginning at 9:00. He still had some sermon preparation to work on before that, and he had to finish his article for the church newsletter going out that day. There was no time for him to stop and discuss a "little family rift". Karen would be all right, he told himself, and so would Donna after she had a good night's sleep.

"I wish I could," he lied to himself, "but I have a building committee meeting this morning with the contractor, then, tomorrow night with some of the men of the church. We're getting some flack from Arnie again, and the men want some solid answers to the proposal and the budget concerns."

He pushed his chair back into its place and reached for his briefcase. Donna's head dropped back down toward her cup in defeat.

"I promise we'll talk about it tonight," he said softly in an apologetic tone. Donna acknowledged his answer and offered her cheek for his farewell kiss as he made his way to the door. But as she heard the car pull away from the driveway, she closed her eyes in surrender, and gave way to the tears she had tried so hard to hold back. The storm raged in her heart and the rain poured from her soul.

———

Gertie pushed the door to the den open with her walker feeling refreshed from her morning bath. She had slept till nearly 9:30, but Adam had barely noticed. He had been so enthralled in his Bible study, he had forgotten completely about breakfast.

"Will you look at this?" he called out excitedly. "It was God who told Moses about the wickedness of the people. He didn't just find them sinning when he returned, he was sent back because of their sin."

Gertie leaned over his shoulder and read from his large print Bible, *Exodus 32:7-10*:

> *"And the LORD said unto Moses, Go, get thee down; for thy people, which thou broughtest out of the land of Egypt, have corrupted themselves: They have turned aside quickly out of the way which I commanded them: they have made them a molten calf, and have worshipped it, and have sacrificed thereunto, and said, These be thy gods, O Israel, which have brought thee up out of the land of Egypt. And the LORD said unto Moses, I have seen this people, and, behold, it is a stiffnecked people: Now therefore let me alone, that my wrath may wax hot against them, and that I may consume them: and I will make of thee a great nation."*

"See, God was ready to destroy them before Moses ever knew there was a problem," he exclaimed pointing to the verses.

"So what's your point, pumpkin?" Gertie asked.

"The point is," he turned to look at her as he spoke, "God knows the situation before we do, and sometimes has to make us aware of it so we can get involved. We may not have any idea what is going on somewhere else, but God does, and He can draw us into it. Moses had no idea what was going on down the mountain. I always thought he found them carousing around and responded to what he saw. But this passage goes on to tell us how Moses interceded for Israel, based solely on what God saw."

Gertie smiled to herself. "I think I know exactly what you are saying, and you are so right, honey." She rotated her walker toward the couch where she had left the letter from the night before.

"To change the subject, are you planning a trip into town today?", she asked, easing herself back onto the sofa.

"I can, if you need something," he replied turning back to his desk.

"I just need a letter mailed. It needs to be weighed and it's going to Central America," she explained, making sure the seal was good.

"I would be happy to. I need to take a break from this for a spell anyway. Do you need anything else while I'm out?" he offered, closing up his Bible and commentaries.

"Just for you to come back before lunch," she warned, "I know how you like to stop for coffee at the diner and talk for hours."

"You don't have to worry there, sweetheart," he said with a kiss on her forehead, "I am anxious to get back to this study. I'll be gone no more than a half-hour. By the way, were you up early this morning?"

"Yes, dear. I was troubled, so I got up for prayer and to write that letter," she replied, picking up the crochet afghan she had started in the summer.

"Anyone we know?" he inquired.

"Yes and no. I know the Lord had me pray for the Eldridge family in Honduras, but I feel there is another about to go through a real trial. . . but I don't know who it is, or even where they live, . . , or what connection they may have with the Eldridges," she explained glancing over her trifocals.

Adam smiled that gentle smile she so loved, "Well, rest assured, God knows them, and whatever storm they are about to weather, He can see them through it. You just pray for them as the Lord leads."

"I always do," she replied smiling back.

Chapter Four:

"The Slough"

Rusty Patterson had a fresh dynamic about him that matched his handsome appearance. From his well-groomed hair to his stylish Pearl Vision frames, he exemplified the finest of generation X. Though only twenty-four, he had completed his Bachelor's through UCLA and his M.RE. (Masters of Religious Education) farther north in Mill Valley, where he had first come to meet Dr. Howard Pennington in a special chapel service. Dr. Pennington had been invited to address the seminary during their annual lecture series. Rusty had been greatly impressed with the organization and deliberation of this pastor and alumnus. He struck him as a man of experience who knew what he was doing, where he was going, and just what it would take to get him there. Rusty thought he could learn much from his maturity and therefore introduced himself to Dr. Pennington during the reception. From that conversation, and further correspondence through Rusty's final year at the seminary, the Cornado Baptist Church in San Diego extended a position of Associate Pastor/ Minister of Education.

His bright youthful appearance was a draw for the young couples whom Howard had trouble attracting. "Gated communities" had migrated from LA into the southern bay area like the swallows that returned to the mission of Capistrano each year. Young childless couples chose to live in amassed apartments with electronic gates. They left their "gated" homes each morning to drive into "gated" businesses using their parking cards for entrance. At lunchtime, they frequented no less than three "drive-thrus" for banking, paying bills, and eating, and then returned to their "gated" parking lots. After work, they returned to their "security gates" and the rent-a-guard granted them entrance into the safe haven of "home". It was as though personal contact must be kept to a minimum at all costs. This made the outreach techniques Howard had learned from Nashville, and later in Texas completely ineffective. He needed Rusty's perspective. The past two years had proved that to be true.

Rusty jaunted into Howard's office, smiling broadly (as usual) for Diane, Howard's secretary and receptionist.

"Is he busy?" Rusty asked cheerfully.

"Not at the moment, he is waiting for some contractor, but I think he is just reading right now, you want to go on in?" she offered politely, looking up from her computer. Diane had been pasting the "Nursery News" from the previous week's edition into the current set-up, and was just about to change the names for this week's administration of diaper duty. She was too young to remember the days when such articles were actually pasted with real "paste".

"Sure do," he said, continuing his stride past her and down the hall to the Pastor's office. He paused long enough to knock.

"Yes, come in," Howard replied softly from the other side of the closed door.

"Do you have a minute?" Rusty smiled.

"Sure, Rusty, come on in," Howard said closing the commentary he had not been reading.

"I have something I want to bounce off your wall," Rusty said enthusiastically. Howard enjoyed the freshness Rusty offered to the church staff. He knew he could never be like him, but the difference complemented him well, and Howard was mature enough to recognize that.

"I am preparing a study for the men's group. This Sunday morning is their monthly breakfast, and they have asked me to bring a devotional between their sausage links and hash browns." Rusty sat in the large burgundy chair to the right of Howard's desk.

"You have my undivided attention," Howard said swinging his swivel executive chair around to face him.

"OK, here goes. . . how many people were in Lot's family?" Rusty's hazel eyes glistened as he spoke.

Howard leaned back in thought. "I can only assume your answer is not four: Lot, his wife, and his two daughters. So why don't I just let you educate me this morning."

"OK, follow me now," he said eagerly. "We know Lot had two virgin daughters, that he offered to the men of the city."

Howard nodded.

"Can we assume that the angels who went to Sodom, though not omniscient like God, were at least briefed on their mission and what they should find?"

"I suppose," Howard conceded.

"Then look at what they said to Lot." He swung open his NIV study bible to Genesis 19, and began reading from the twelfth verse:

> *"The two men said to Lot, "Do you have anyone else here — sons-in-law, sons or daughters, or anyone else in the city who belongs to you? Get them out of here, because we are going to destroy this place."*

"They mention sons-in-laws, sons or daughters that are not in the house with them. Now, we know there were sons-in-laws, because they made fun of Lot in verse 14. Now my translation says they were pledged, but King

James says they were married, and the commentaries are split. So let's just call them what they are: "sons-in-law". The angels mention daughters that are not in the house, so they could be the married daughters, and the two in the house, the unmarried daughters. No problem, right?"

"I'm still with you, go on" Howard encouraged.

"OK, so we have unmarried daughters, and married daughters, and sons-in-law. What about sons? The angels mentioned Lot's sons not living at home. Is it safe to assume Lot may have had some sons as well?" he asked sincerely.

"I don't have a problem so far," Howard agreed.

"OK, here's the tally then. If Lot had *at least* two sons, not living at home. . . and *at least* two married daughters, also not living at home. . . and *at least* two sons-in-law that we know did not live at home, plus the four under his roof. . . then how many people were there in Lot's family and under his direction?"

Howard made the quick calculation and replied firmly, "ten."

"Right!" Rusty exclaimed, and then leaned forward for the kill.

"And how many people did God tell Abraham that He would spare the city of Sodom for, *if* he found them righteous?" he asked confidently.

Howard dropped his chair forward. He had not only realized the answer to Rusty's question, his mind had processed the implication as well. The look on his face was not what Rusty had expected, but it was evident that Howard had gotten the point.

"That's right," Rusty continued for him, "God said, if there were ten righteous people in Sodom, he would spare the city. Abraham knew there were at least ten people in Lot's family alone when he interceded for them, but what he didn't know was that Lot had lost control of his family. Trying to be a judge for the city, as it says in verse nine, he tried to be a positive influence over the people. We know from 2 Peter 2:7 that he was a righteous man, himself. The tragedy is that Lot tried to save the city and lost his family. Hence, he lost the city as well."

Howard closed his eyes momentarily as the words burned into his heart. Rusty thought he was trying to "fit it all together", and paused for him to respond. After an awkward moment of quiet, Rusty spoke up.

"When you compare the family life of Lot to the family life of Noah, you have two totally different pictures. My idea is to share with the men how important their ministry to their family is. You can become so enthralled in "church work" that you can lose your own family in the process. Perhaps even to the point of offering your own daughters to the world to abuse. Oh not directly or conscientiously, but by not being there for them when they need you - it's the same as turning them out on their own."

35

Rusty went on for a few moments longer with his application, but his words sounded distant, as though carried down a long hallway. He couldn't know he was pouring salt into an open wound. And as painful as that was, salt is intended to heal.

"So what do you think?" Rusty concluded.

Howard blinked back to reality and tried to disguise the fact that the bright enthusiastic young man in his office had just dropped a cedar of Lebanon on his head.

"Well, Rusty, it sounds plausible, and very interesting. I think your point is well taken, and it should communicate greatly with the men's group." Howard's voice was level and unrevealing. He slowly turned his chair back towards the desk giving the impression that he needed to return to some urgent work before him.

Rusty took the hint, and conveniently remembered the article he needed to finish for the newsletter. His step was less animated as he walked past Diane's desk.

"Is there something troubling Bro. Howard?" he decided to ask.

"I'm not sure, but he has been very quiet this morning. I bet he is just anxious over this building program. He meets with the contractor this morning and with the committee tomorrow night," she explained.

"Is Arnie still on that committee?" Rusty asked.

"I don't think so," Diane sighed. "But he has been vocal in his opposition. Maybe that's what is bothering Bro. Howard."

In his office, Howard had picked up the gold-framed family portrait he kept on his desk. The portrait was four years old, and in need of updating, but he liked it because Karen was still smiling. He looked into her eyes and wondered, "Would I ever see her smile at me again?"

———

Luís walked around the adobe house until most of the neighbors had returned to their homes. He entered quietly and gazed about the room. Anita sat rocking back and forth whimpering softly with her head buried in the shoulder of her father. The children had scattered back outside, the three smallest being too young to understand the death of their father. They played with sticks and chased the chickens in front of the house. Luís stepped across the room to the dining table where Moncho was laid. The rumors were true. There was no sign of a fight. To the astonishment of the people, Moncho appeared to be at rest. It was thought that he would have been shot or stabbed or worse, but the officer said he had been crushed under a car while lying in the road. Luís knew more than most, but he still did not understand how it could have happened. He expected to have heard of the death of the missionary, perhaps both shot and robbed, with only suspicion as to who had been responsible, but not this. The questions filled his mind, but one thing was for certain, Moncho had not been alone on that road after he left, and Luís knew who was with him. He wondered how long it would take for them to talk about what happened. Perhaps he would see him that night again at the cantina. Luís respectfully crossed himself and then passed by the widow extending his hand in condolences. She looked up at him and stared blankly. These were the eyes that grieved for duty, not for love. Her period of mourning would be relatively short, Luís thought to himself.

He stepped out into the afternoon sun and looked in the direction of the plaza. The tall edifice of the cathedral could be seen from any point in the town. It had been years since he had attended mass. Suddenly, the sharp reminder of his own mortality gouged at his heart. He had been with Moncho less than fifteen hours before, and now he laid dead in his own home. Maybe a man should be more prepared to meet his Creator, Luís thought. "I will go this Sunday with my sister," he said to himself, as he turned and followed the muddy path back to the main road leading down to the cantina. "And I will say a prayer for Moncho." The eyes that followed him from a distance were not fixed on prayer.

––––––

Karen floated through her morning classes, and ate her lunch alone. The seething had subsided, and given way to depression. She felt trapped in a family that did not recognize her individuality and personhood. She did not hate her father, but she hated the way she felt around him. He was so precise and organized, it seemed any disruption of his schedule threatened the security of the home. He planned their weekends, he planned their vacations, he had even planned her "sweet sixteen" birthday. That was when things really began to go sour, when he declared there would be no dancing at her party. He was so concerned about his image as a pastor, he had lost sight of her image as a teenager. What she needed was a sense of independence, at least one area of her life where she was in control. She needed a job - - money meant independence.

"Hey Karen, whats ya doin' sittin' all alone?" a voice called from behind her.

Karen turned to see Tasha Hardin with her lunch tray in hand. Though she still didn't feel sociable, she quickly donned a smile and invited her to sit. Maybe it would be better to talk and clear her mind. After all, Tasha worked, and she may just know where Karen could find an afternoon job.

"Tasha, I was just thinking about trying to find some work - you know, for after school. You wouldn't by chance know anyone whose hiring right now?" Karen began suddenly.

"Sure do," she said with half a mouth full of spaghetti. She swallowed hard, and took a long swig of her juice. "A girl I know just quit at *Sugar 'n Spice*."

"The clothing store?" Karen's eyes brightened.

"Yes!" Tasha squealed. "It would be perfect - girl, you even get a discount on what you buy there."

"But how old do I have to be?" Karen suddenly realized.

"They say eighteen, but they don't care, the girl who left was only seventeen. And besides, girl, you look eighteen! Just be sure to wear somethin' fine when you go in, like one of your Sunday outfits." Tasha twirled another mouthful onto her fork.

"Would you go down with me to apply? I've never done this before," Karen asked.

"Sure, girl. I work in the video store on the second level, and I have to be there by 5:00. We can go in about 3:30 if you want," Tasha offered wiping the sauce from the corners of her mouth.

"Wait a minute," Karen threw on the brakes, "I forgot, I'm grounded."

"Says who?" Tasha asked.

"Says my Dad, as of 10:45 last night. I came in late from the movies with Fernando. My Dad went ballistic! Anyway, I'm grounded for the next two weeks - *no dates, no malls, no movies, nothing!*" she exclaimed impersonating his voice.

"No problem!" smiled Tasha, spooning down some tan colored pudding. "Call your Mom before he gets home, and ask if you can go for the interview. She'll say yes, and then they'll have to fight it out. Eventually, he'll give in because it's a job, and parents like that sort of responsibility stuff."

"You think so?" Karen asked excitedly. It felt good to smile again.

"Think so? Honey, I KNOW SO! I've been working my folks for the past four years. Just pit them against each other, and you are in the clear," Tasha said confidently, picking up the tray to toss the empty cartons in the containers by the dish washers window.

"So I see you at 3:30 in front of the library, right?" Tasha called back from the window.

"I'll be there!" Karen said triumphantly.

As Tasha hurried through the doors, Karen sat quietly for the next few minutes, still alone, but not feeling quite as lonely. Her mind raced ahead to the prospects of her own finances, her own decisions, and eventually her own life. This had to be the right thing to do.

———

Carey was not resting because he was tired, he was depressed and feeling the weight of condemnation on his heart. The Accuser stood between him and the throne of God and pointed his odious finger between Carey's eyes and shouted, "murderer!" Carey had begun to wonder how he was going to inform the mission chairman about the "accident". His mind wandered, as he considered whether the police officer would come back later wanting "hush money" for letting them go. He pondered anxiously about what would await him on his next journey into *Santa Tierra*. Would there be an avenging relative waiting for him? Was his hope of opening a work there now destroyed? Should he go to the widow, and if he did, what would he say? "I'm deeply sorry for running over your husband, but it was him or me?" The more Carey thought, the deeper into the Slough of Despond he sank. He turned over and faced the back of the sofa and tried to close out the world, again.

———

"Twenty-eight minutes exactly!" called out Adam as he hurried through the front door. "I told you I would be back in less than thirty."

"Yes, you did," Gertie called back from the den, still crocheting. "Did you mail my letter?"

"As you wished" he said entering the room, kissing her once again on the forehead. "Did you miss me?"

"All twenty eight minutes of your trip away from me," she smiled.

"I told you I wanted to get back to my study," he said reopening the three translations on his desk. "Now where was I?"

"Somewhere on Mount Horeb, while the people were partying at the foot of the mountain. You were saying that God saw it happening while Moses was still up on the mountain," She recounted for him.

"Right, now Moses is going to intercede for Israel," Adam said eagerly. He reached above his head to the small cassette deck next to his largest bowling trophy, and restarted the easy instrumental tape of hymns. As the panpipes began to softly play *Blessed Assurance*, Gertie sang the familiar words to herself.

Adam began to read aloud from his NASB Study Bible,

> *"Then Moses entreated the LORD his God, and said,*
> *'O LORD, why doth Thine anger burn against Thy people*

> *whom Thou hast brought out from the land of Egypt with*
> *great power and with a mighty hand?'"* (Exodus 32:11)

"It sounds like Moses is acknowledging God's ownership of His people," he quickly scribbled down on his legal pad. "He is also reaffirming God's plan of their deliverance".

"Do you think it was necessary for Moses to remind God of what He had done?" asked Gertie breaking away from the repeated chorus.

"I don't think Moses is reminding God, as much as he is rehearsing the mighty deeds of God before Him as a form of praise. We must always enter into His courts with praise, and Moses is doing that first," Adam explained simply. "I think the meat of his intercession is to be found in the next verse, listen". Adam continued to read verse 12.

> *"Why should the Egyptians speak, saying, 'With evil*
> *intent He brought them out to kill them in the mountains*
> *and to destroy them from the face of the earth'? Turn from*
> *Thy burning anger and change Thy mind about doing harm*
> *to Thy people."*

"Here we find Moses reinforcing God's reputation. It is His reputation he appeals to - not His mercy, nor His grace - but to God's Own reputation," Adam said profoundly, taking in his own words, as though they were not his own. He quickly added this point to his notes. "It is worth noting, that intercession is not convincing a reluctant God to do something for you, but rather for Him! It is His reputation that is being upheld, not ours!"

"Go on!" Gertie encouraged, laying aside her afghan for the moment.

"In verse 13, it is the promise to Abraham, Isaac, and *Israel* - not Jacob, as is normally the case, that Moses reiterates. This sinful bunch of disobedient children dancing around a golden calf, that Moses hasn't even seen yet, are still the heirs of a promise that God has made by His own name. Moses is praying a prayer of intercession based on the faithfulness of God to His Own Word and reputation. Intercession is not that we might help others save face, but rather that God's name is not slandered. This hits at the motivation of our praying," Adam summed up drawing a breath, and turning toward the couch for a response from his Gertie.

"So what did God do in response to Moses' prayer?" she asked, though she knew the answer already.

"Well, King James says 'He repented', the NIV says 'He relented', and the NASB says, 'He changed His mind about the harm which He said He would do to His people.'" he read from each of the open translations.

40

"But what does that mean? Did Moses change God's mind or will?" she asked honestly.

"It doesn't say that Moses changed anything. It says God changed Himself. God is Sovereign in these matters. But what I think we are seeing is a sovereign God looking for someone to stand in the gap created by sin and say, 'I know it looks bad, but You are greater than all this. You are not dependent upon man for Who You are, man is dependent upon You for who he is. Be faithful O Lord, even when we are faithless. Don't let anything damage Your reputation - not even us!' When such a prayer is lifted to the throne, God can respond to man's repentance with a new course of action. That's when conditions begin to change. God hasn't really changed from His purpose at all. He always wanted to bless the nations through Israel - Moses just reinforced God's reputation for doing that, in spite of their sin," Adam concluded with a smile.

"So then, perhaps I need to pray more for God to show Himself strong on behalf of others, like Carey Eldridge, not because they may be going through difficult times, but because such problems can overshadow God's purpose and Honor in their midst. In other words, if I pray that God be magnified, then the problems will take care of themselves," Gertie surmised, returning to her afghan.

"Whenever we seek first the kingdom of God, and His righteousness, everything else always falls into its proper perspective," Adam added returning to his books.

As he turned the pages of the lesson guide, the panpipes began to blow Gertie's favorite hymn, and she began to sing with the tape, *"When peace like a river, attendeth my way . . . "*

————

"Mom, . . .it's me, Karen," she tried to speak above the hallway chatter after the lunch bell. "I'm at the school, and, well, I got this job interview this afternoon, if that's OK." She thought about mentioning the grounding, but thought, if her mother didn't bring it up, why muddy the waters. Like Tasha said, "let them fight it out!"

Donna tried to sound encouraging, and at the same time, was weighing the decision in her own mind. She was not aware of Howard's verdict from the night before, but knew he would like to be part of a big decision like this. Perhaps she should have Karen call the church office to talk to him about it. On the other hand, Karen was a big girl, and could use this kind of opportunity. Maybe it would be just the thing to bring some order to the household. Maybe Howard would respect her initiative a little more, and loosen her reins just a bit. It was not an easy call, but if she had to shoulder half the burden of parenting, then she should be able to make some decisions on her own.

"Honey, that sounds great. You go ahead, I'll save you something to eat when you get in," she replied as chipper as possible.

"Thanks, Mom," she yelled back, in order to be heard, "I'll see you around suppertime." Karen hung up the phone and squealed with delight. She had to find Fernando and tell him the good news. Even though she didn't have the job yet, she suddenly felt a great burden lifted from her shoulders. She hadn't felt this good since that summer camp she went to three years ago at Oceanside. She stood by the phone reminiscing about the bus ride up, the singing, the guitars, the bon fire on the beach, the Bible study, and . . . Suddenly, her mind snapped to the present. What had made her think about that? She was fourteen and stupid, then. What could she have known about real life? But all in all, she did remember what it felt like to have a heavy burden lifted, both then as well as now.

———

"Happy Birthday to you! Happy Birthday to you! Happy Birthday dear Dadddddy. . . Happy Birthday to you!" the trio sang in two-part harmony and one part off key. The boys then sang the Spanish version to the same tune ending with the verse that stated that they now wanted cake. Susan held the droopy angel food cake with the heavy lemon icing. The afternoon sun was not kind to pastry of any form, but they thought it best to start the festivities as early as possible. Carey had spent most of the afternoon on the couch, and even now found it hard to concentrate on his own celebration.

There were thirteen candles in all on the cake - four grouped on one side of the cylindrical space in the middle, and nine gathered on the other, representing forty nine years of life. Creativity was always a challenge with the lack of resources available. But Susan never failed to deliver. The boys each handed him a "home-made" card and a small gift. Since they had purchased the computer on their last furlough, crayons and glitter had given way to a high-tech publisher program with 3-D shadowed gothic letters and a host of clip art pictures. Josh's card showed a man swinging in a hammock with an umbrella drink in his hand on the front cover, along with the words, "WHEN LIFE GETS TOUGH, JUST HANG IN THERE. ." On the inside portion the message continued, ". . . BETWEEN TWO TREES - HAPPY BIRTHDAY DAD!" They all chuckled, and then he opened his gift of hammock hooks to be installed in the wooden columns of the patio. "Now all you need is a good hammock, and you won't have to sleep on the couch during the afternoon siesta time," Josh said.

"Thank you son, we'll get these put up right away," Carey said giving him a big hug.

"Bet you can't guess what this is?" Caleb said, handing him a shoebox covered in the white plastic bags they got from the market.

"I bet I can!" Carey said tearing the bag from the box. "What good are a couple of hammock hooks without a good hammock to hang from them?" he finished at the same time he opened the lid. Inside the box was the finest quality hammock made in El Salvador. The material was soft, not like the plastic feeling fabric that he saw each day at the market in town. The hoops had steel reinforcement for durability. It was indeed, the Cadillac of hammocks. Then Caleb handed his card to be read aloud. He had chosen the same picture for the front, but his message was a poem. Carey read with animation the cover page, *"Violets are blue, and Roses are red . . ."* As he continued reading the inside portion, his voice suddenly dropped, *"but if you lay here too long, they'll think you are dead!"* Susan gasped, having not read the cards beforehand. Caleb waited for the laughter that didn't come. Josh sensed something was wrong, but his father quickly recovered and smiled at his younger son. "Thank you Caleb, it is a wonderful gift. What's say we go hang these up right away?"

As the boys hurried through the den to the back porch, Carey caught Susan's eyes. She didn't know what to say. They both knew it would take time, and eventually the boys would have to know what had happened. Carey reached out for her hand as though reaching for a life preserver. He needed her more then he ever realized. She would be his help that would draw him out of the miry slough, and God would be his Way.

Chapter Five:

"The Call"

"I don't see any prior experience," the manager/owner of the boutique commented without looking up from the application. Sheila Henson was a single entrepreneur who had built her own business on experience. She had worked in specialty clothing stores through her own senior year of high school and later through her wasted university years. She had learned that her education was not going to help her ride the economic escalator. What she wore was more important than what she knew, and one thing she had discovered was that most young girls thought the same. Her eye for fashion and coordination of accessories soon distinguished her from the common clerk. She assistant managed a formal wear shop until she had saved enough to invest in her own small stock. With a convincing presentation of self-achievement and her limited collateral, she landed a modest loan and opened her own store, *Sugar 'n Spice*, on the first level of the Bay Bridge Mall downtown. She knew her trade and repaid the loan six months before it was due. She took pride as a self-styled successful businessperson that could transform the plain and simple into the hot and dazzling at a price befitting the results.

"To be honest, Ms. Henson, this is my first job," Karen said softly, then quickly added, "But I know I can do it - I'm a real people-person, and I love clothes and. . ." She stopped mid-sentence, trying to recover from what must have been a classic Freudian slip. "I mean, I feel I know clothes, and what looks good." Then changing tactic, she added, "And most of all, I'm honest!"

Sheila looked up suddenly to meet Karen's eyes. To her knowledge, no one knew that Debbie, the former clerk, had been fired for pilfering small amounts of jewelry. Sheila had felt the immaturity of the girl had led to her petty theft and gave her the option to quit quietly. But nonetheless, she was now sensitive to the mention of honesty.

"How old are you?" Sheila asked firmly.

"I am seventeen, but my birthday is only four months away," she answered honestly. Karen thought about pointing out the age of the former employee, but then decided against it, to her benefit. For a brief moment, she also thought about mentioning that her father was the pastor of a Baptist church, but wasn't sure if that would be a point in her favor or not. Sheila had smoked constantly from the time she sat down in the office, and the radio was tuned to a "new-age" music station. Karen decided this job was about her, not her father, and not his image.

Ms. Henson looked hard into Karen's eyes. What she saw was determination. This was about more than a job, it was about a young woman wanting to take that first hard independent step into the world. It was about growing a little taller in ones own eyes. It was about herself just eight years before. She liked Karen and hoped that she could teach her some things about life. In time, maybe they could become close.

"The job is yours, Karen. How soon can you begin?" Sheila smiled.

"Tomorrow I suppose. Can I call you this evening to let you know for sure?" Karen asked hoping that the dust would settle in her favor shortly after supper that evening.

"That will be fine. Here is my home phone; call when you can," Sheila said offering her one of her business cards with the home number written in by hand.

Karen placed the card in her purse and rose to shake her hand. "You don't know what this means to me Ms. . ., do I call you Ms. or Miss?"

"Why don't you call me Sheila," she said in a far less professional tone. "I would like for us to be friends."

"I think I would like that too," Karen replied. She didn't recognize all that the tone carried, but it was a pleasant change from the hostility she had been feeling for so long.

———

"That was a wonderful supper, Daddy," Gertie called from the den. "I don't think anyone can match your *macaroni-n-cheese* special." Adam tossed the empty box into the trashcan under the sink and cleaned up the powdered cheese mix that had spilled on the counter during the preparation. He ran water in the bottom of the pan and placed it in the sink next to their two plates and silverware.

"Now for your favorite dessert," he announced, "The freshest cheesecake you have ever tasted, guaranteed to melt in your mouth - and not in your hand - though I wouldn't suggest holding it in your hand."

"Ice-box cheesecake?" she asked playfully.

"Is there any other kind?" he smiled and handed her the larger slice.

Adam took a seat beside her on the couch and enjoyed the creamy dessert. He did most of the cooking since the stroke, and though he could prepare more elaborate meals, they preferred the simple dishes on the weeknights. He suddenly remembered his notes across the room on his desk and jumped up to retrieve them.

"Oh yes," Gertie exclaimed, "How is your study going on intercession?"

"Well, I have finished the second prayer in chapter 32. Would you like to hear what I have?" he replied joining her once again on the couch.

"I would think so," she said licking the graham cracker crust from the corner of her mouth.

"Well, you remember that God had sent Moses back down the mountain having informed him of what was going on, and that Moses had interceded once for them based on God's reputation," Adam recounted for her.

"Yes, and that we should always pray for God's honor and glory first and then the situation can be resolved for the best," she added laying her plate on the TV tray in front of her.

"That's right," Adam agreed, "Now we are going to see what happens when God's people see the problem for themselves." He flipped back a couple pages on his yellow legal pad and began reviewing his notes.

After several insightful moments, Adam whistled long and loud, like a descending bomb. "What did you find?" Gertie looked up from her afghan.

"Moses ordered the Levites to execute those still engaged in their idolatry as they went through the camp and three thousand died that day," Adam paraphrased, still looking intently ahead in his Bible. "But he knows that there is still more to come, so he calls on them to consecrate themselves to God in verse 29, and then tells them he is going to go and intercede for them."

"I'm not sure I follow where you are going, Honey," Gertie said sweetly.

"In this case, intercession included the activity of repentance and rededication on the part of those being prayed for. You see, intercession is 'in behalf of' someone, not 'in place of' them. Though true, Moses offered himself 'in their place' in verse 32; God corrected him in verse 33, pointing out their individual responsibility," he said looking up into her eyes.

"So then, we must pray for people, but at the same time, encourage them to get right with God," Gertie summarized.

"That's right," Adam replied approvingly.

"But dear, what if the person is not at fault, but is being attacked by the enemy, just to destroy the work of the Lord in his life? What does he need to repent of?" she asked honestly.

"Good point, my dear. It looks as though I have more study ahead of me," he said turning back to his desk. He took a deep breath and then reached up to turn the praise music back on.

Gertie smiled to herself. She already knew that there were different forms of intercession, for she had practiced them enough in her "closet". Her Adam would learn how to work them into his study. The question in her heart, at that moment, was what form of intercession was she involved in. Her prayers the night before had been directed "on behalf of" Carey Eldridge and his family. She had felt impressed to pray for some trial he was going through, and yet her spirit was being burdened for another she did not know. She wondered whether it could be intercession for some wayward believer. If so, how could she possibly encourage them to return to God if she didn't know who they were. And what possible connection could they have with Carey?

———

"I'll get it," Josh called out from the den, as the phone rang two feet from him. He picked up the receiver and heard the three short tones that meant the call was long distance and that there would be a pause before the other side would speak. He decided not to answer in Spanish, because that just intimidated stateside callers. Both Josh and Caleb spoke with impeccable Spanish accents, and more than once grandparents had hung up thinking they had dialed the wrong number.

"Hello, Eldridge family," he said, to remove any doubt for the person trying to call into a foreign country. "Who? . . . Oh yeah! Hi Uncle Billy; this is Josh." After a few costly minutes of salutations, Josh called for his father. "Dad, it's for you. It's Uncle Billy!"

Carey bounded from his new hammock and dashed to the phone. "Hey, brother, how in the Lord are you?" It was a common greeting they both used with close friends and family. It seemed a more appropriate introduction to conversation.

"We're all doing well here, big brother. We just called to give you a super birthday greeting and to remind you that fifty ain't all that bad," Bill Eldridge said strongly into the phone. He wasn't sure how good the connection was on Carey's end.

"Well, I'll have to let you know next year how fifty is," Carey replied, "As for today, I'm still in the forties, even if it is just barely. But enough about me, what have you been doing lately? I haven't heard from you since Anna came to stay with ya'll. Is everything working out all right?"

"It couldn't be better, if she were our own daughter," Billy gleamed. "She and Jenny get along just great. She's like a big sister to her. She is keeping up in her studies just fine and has even found a job at a Bible bookstore in the mall. I hope you don't mind, we let her work till 9:00 and then she takes the bus to the corner, just three houses down from where we live. We thought about waiting till she got home tonight to call you, but we knew it would be after 11:00 your time. There's two hours difference there, right?"

"No, Billy," Carey suddenly sounded disappointed that he would not be talking to his daughter on his birthday. "We don't go on daylight savings time here. We will be on Mountain Time until you go back to regular standard time, then we will be the same as Central. There is only one hour's difference between us right now."

"Gee Carey, I didn't know," Billy said, realizing the change in Carey's tone. "We could call back later, when she gets in if you want."

"No Billy, that's all right. I just had hoped to hear her voice. I've had a rough . . ." his voice broke off for a second. "I mean, we miss her here."

"Carey, are you O.K.? You don't sound like everything there is all right," Billy said showing deep concern.

"Not really, Billy," Carey started, wondering if he should mention anything on the phone. "I guess I really miss all of you guys. We didn't get to see you last furlough being on the east coast and all, and well. . ." Carey took a deep breath and continued, "There was an accident last night and I. . .I don't know how to say this easily, especially on the phone."

"Just go ahead, brother, I'm listening," Billy urged him on.

"Billy, I ran over a man with my truck last night and killed him."

There was a long pause.

"Are you still there?" Carey asked after a moment.

"Yes, Carey. I'm right here with you," the voice on the other end said soberly.

"Boy, I wish you were," Carey sighed into the phone. "I mean, *right here*! I'd give anything to have you with me for a couple of days."

There was another pause on the line, then the strong reassuring voice of Carey's younger brother, "I can be there by Saturday!"

Carey stared at the receiver for a second and exclaimed, "Do you mean it? How?"

"I'll just take a couple of days off. I have enough frequent flyer miles to go to Australia, so it won't cost me that much. The computer hacks can handle the first couple of days of next week without me over their shoulders. I'll be back by Wednesday at the latest to set things straight by the end of the week, if they mess up. No big deal. What flies into the capital there - American or Continental?" Billy said shifting into his professional voice reserved for making executive decisions.

"Either one flies in to Tegucigalpa about noon here, but you will have to leave early from where you are," Carey said excitedly.

"Fine! I'll see what I can find tonight and travel late Friday to get in by Saturday noon. Now what can I bring you guys?" Bill offered.

"Gee, I don't know. This is all happening so fast," Carey said slowing to think. "I don't suppose you could sneak Anna in a carry-on?"

"I wish I could big brother, but I'm afraid you'll have to settle for just me this trip," Billy responded.

"Well, listen," Carey said sincerely, "you don't know how much this means to me. But do tell her we miss her and that her daddy loves her a lot!"

"Roger that," Billy replied using an expression from his navy days. "I'll bring you some new Bible software we're warehousing now as well as an upgrade on your Windows."

"You don't have to do that," Carey half-objected, hoping he wouldn't retract the offer. "That stuff's expensive, and your trip is enough."

"The software is for your birthday," Billy said succinctly. "The trip is for both of us. I need a taste of mission life to help me with my new past time. By the way, could you use a case of Spanish New Testaments?"

"Why sure, but where will you find them before Friday?" Carey asked.

"In the rear of our storeroom closet. I'm now a Gideon and we have several Hispanic schools we visit. I'll bring you a case," he said enthusiastically.

"Will you ever cease to surprise me?" Carey said equally proud. "I guess you better cut this off for now. There will be much for us to talk about in two days. Give our best to Diane and Jenny. And don't forget to tell my little girl how much I miss her."

"See you Saturday by O-noon-thirty," Billy finished, and the line went dead. Carey held the receiver while the tone changed to a busy signal, and then quietly replaced it in the cradle. As he turned, he saw Susan and the boys standing in the doorway awaiting the news they had guessed at from the patches of conversation they could hear.

"Uncle Billy is coming for a visit," Carey said slowly.

The boys began to jump about the room cheering and whooping. Susan looked into Carey's eyes to see the relief that needed to be there. He smiled acknowledging her concern and then added for her benefit, "And he'll be here on Saturday!"

Howard eased the Tempo into the garage and pushed the remote on his visor to close the heavy door behind him. The door from the garage to the kitchen was near the driver's side and he didn't need the light to reach it. Normally, the sunlight through the side window was sufficient, but the sun had gone down two hours earlier and no one had turned on the garage light. He felt his way to the wall, and then found the door.

"Anybody home?" he called as he entered the empty kitchen.

"I'm sorry, I didn't hear you drive up," Donna responded from the hall making her way to the kitchen. "I left you some supper in the oven - let me warm it up for you,"

"Where's Terry?" Howard asked, dropping his briefcase on the floor beside the kitchen counter.

"He's doing homework next door at Todd's. I told him to be home by 8:30, so he should be coming in anytime now," she replied, covering the Corning ware container of lasagna with wax paper and setting the microwave for three minutes.

"I suppose Karen is sulking in her room," he asked nonchalantly.

"Well, not exactly," Donna said trying to pave the way for the big announcement. "Karen has some good news for you, and I thought I would let her tell you herself after you had eaten. But that can wait. How was your meeting with contractor today?"

Howard released a sigh, "It went O.K., I guess. He had some questions on design that I hadn't thought about, so I stayed on this afternoon to work on them before the committee meeting tomorrow."

"Why are you trying to do all this yourself?" Donna asked pouring Howard some tea. "Wouldn't it be easier if Arnie helped out, or at least attended the committee meeting to offer suggestions?"

"Are you kidding?" Howard responded with a tone of annoyance. "Arnie has had nothing but suggestions since this project started and they are all negative."

"Why didn't the church offer the project to Arnie's firm in the first place?" Donna puzzled.

"That is conflict of interest, and besides, Arnie didn't even bid. I tell you, he has something personal against me and anything I try to do in that church," Howard said blowing on the steaming plate Donna set before him. "Right now, Arnie is the last person I would go to for help."

Donna poured herself a cup of coffee and sat at the small kitchen table with him. For several minutes, neither said a word. Howard was still trying to deal with the rebuking words that Rusty had shared that morning. He knew that Rusty was not directing them intentionally at him, but they stung all the same. He also knew that something had to change between him and Karen, but he didn't know where to start. He was not used to not being in control of his life and his family, and now, this problem at the church was adding to his stress. As he finished his meal, he promised himself that he would be patient with Karen this evening, whatever this "good news" might be.

"Donna," he began quietly, "this morning, I was . . . well, I was short with you, and I'm sorry. I'm beginning to see that I need help with how to work with Karen. I need your help. I don't want to lose what I have with her or you."

"Well maybe this new opportunity will be a start," she offered. "Just listen to her before you answer."

Howard nodded, and they left together for the den. Karen was watching a video of a Tom Hanks film, but she quickly turned it off when her parents came into the room.

"Karen, I think you have some news for your father," her mother opened the conversation for her.

Karen began twirling the end of her hair and then decided that she needed to present confidence in what she was about to say. She invited her father to sit near her on the sofa. As he sat down, she began. "Dad, I know you said I was grounded for the next two weeks, but today at school a friend of mine told me of a job opportunity at the mall." She ran through the opening statement like a train behind schedule hoping he would catch her honesty about the grounding, but would miss the part about the mall. "So I called Mom and asked her if I could go for the interview, and she said yes." She paused for the first objection.

Howard looked at Donna and was about to ask if she was aware of the grounding, but he decided that question would wait till their bedroom. He was learning. He turned his attention back to Karen and asked, "So how did the interview go?"

Karen's eyes brightened and she rode the rest of the way through, "It was great! Sheila, that's the owner of the dress shop, said I could start tomorrow if it was O.K. with you guys. It is a little boutique called *Sugar 'n Spice* at the Bay Bridge Mall downtown. The bus picks up right in front of Sears and passes Appleton just one block from here. Some nights, Fernando can bring me home. . . if that's O.K.," she said, then realized she may have just crossed the line with that last suggestion.

Howard's eyes narrowed. He knew what was about to happen, but the question had to be asked. "What about Wednesday nights?"

Karen's first reaction was to jump up from the sofa. But she felt a restraining hand on her shoulder, and then a quiet voice, *"Work with him, see what you can do."* She softened her stare and replied meekly, "I'll talk to Sheila and see what I can do. She probably needs me more on the weekends anyway, though I do know the store is closed on Sundays."

Donna smiled as Howard relaxed his stance. She had gone against his wishes concerning the grounding, but she was willing to work with him, and that was a start. He had more questions, but quick reflection showed that they mostly dealt with logistics. Those things, like paper routes, seemed to work themselves out. He decided he would let her give it a try, but with a probationary clause.

"I suppose you have talked it over with Mom?" he asked glancing at Donna for approval. She nodded. "And you have considered how you will keep up with your school work?" he directed at Karen. She nodded. "Then I guess I can at least dismiss the grounding for you to start work, but on a trial period, agreed?"

"How long?" Karen asked.

"I think two weeks will tell us, don't you Mother?" Howard said trying to sound fair.

"I think so," she concurred.

Karen would have liked more leeway, but knew she was getting a good deal under the circumstances. She reached out and hugged her father in agreement. It felt warm and good, again. But in the back of her mind, she wondered how long it could last. When she pulled away, they both knew progress had been made, but neither knew exactly how much.

"I'll call Sheila and tell her the good news," Karen said leaping from the couch.

"Why do you call her Sheila, and not by her last name?" her father asked.

"Oh, she told me to," Karen said exiting the room. She would make the call from her bedroom phone. Howard felt a strange disturbance within him at those final words, but he didn't know why. Perhaps it was nothing, he thought. But he was mistaken.

―――

Luís stepped out of the cantina having not finished his third beer. He didn't feel like getting drunk tonight. His mind still raced with the image of Moncho lying on the table in his house. They would bury him tomorrow near the Catholic Church and then someone would place a cross on the road outside of town at the spot where he was found. The cross on the road would not be stone, like those found along the highway, so it would not last more than a week before it would be trampled by an ox-cart or pulled up by children. Then Moncho would be forgotten. Luís turned away from the plaza and started walking. The road to the north of town led to Las Flores. He had some friends there, so he decided he would walk the three kilometers along the moonlit road and visit them. It was early still.

As Luís walked along the road, he thought about the night before. He wondered how it could have happened. He could imagine the ambush, but how could the missionary have known what was going to happen, and how could he have overpowered Moncho? Even drunk, Moncho fought well. It had to have been some strange accident for him to run over Moncho. But most of all, where was the gun? Luís had gone back that afternoon to the site where they had waited, but he found nothing. And what about the other man that had been with them?

As he rounded the second hill, he saw a light shining from within one of the homes ahead. It was not the low flame of a kerosene lamp, but the bright light of a Coleman lantern, and it shined through the windows of the adobe house. As he drew closer to the house, he could hear the sound of singing.

"*En la cruz, En la cruz, do primero vi la luz. .*," was sung heartily to the tune of the Isaac Watts hymn "At the Cross", which had been taught to them by the American missionary. Luís realized this must be the home where his cousin and the others met for their worship services. He listened to the words of the hymn and decided to walk up to the house.

Gathered about the windows were several young boys and men looking in the windows at the girls seated inside. These were not believers, but were referred to, by the congregation as "*amigos*" (friends). Though most had no intention of ever stepping foot inside the door, they came faithfully each night to where the Coleman lantern was lit in order to watch the girls and occasionally hear the gringo preach in Spanish. They gathered in their small groups and made fun of the singing and praying, and usually left ten minutes into the message.

The service normally started at 7:00 PM on the nights that the missionary arrived, but closer to 7:20 when he was not there. Honduran time always allowed up to 30 minutes leeway before an event was considered late. The order of service was ritualistic. It began with a reading of the scriptures, usually from the book of Psalms, followed by two to three hymns from the little red paper-back hymnal supplied at a modest price by the missionary. Usually the same hymns would be repeated during the week because they only knew a dozen or so well enough to sing with the guitar.

Luís moved close to the window near the speaker. She was leading the small congregation in prayer. When she finished, an older man stepped to the front behind the small wooden table they were using for a speaking area. He greeted the visitors and gave a special welcome to the *amigos* present with them that evening. The small congregation lifted their hands and waved about the room to those standing near the door and at the windows. Luís moved back for just a moment then realized that he was standing in the shadows outside a well-lit room. No one could know it was he watching and listening. He stepped back to the window and listened.

"Brothers, we want to welcome the *amigos* tonight and invite those who wish to, to come inside and join us as we worship the Lord together," the leader began cordially. "We pray that through the worship and message from the Word of God, that you will sense God calling you to Him. Jesus said, 'I am the Way, the Truth, and the Life, and nobody comes to the Father, except through Me.' We pray you will trust Jesus tonight as your personal Lord and Savior."

Luís smiled to himself. "Those are good words," he thought, "but do they mean them?" He tried to look around the room from his window and see the faces of those both seated and standing in the small one room house. There was about twenty-five or more inside, counting the little children sprawled out on the floor, with about seven women seated. Most had small infants and were nursing them. The other men and women stood or crouched along the walls. There were about fifteen adults in all and at least ten children listening, singing and praying. Most of the faces he recognized, but did not know the people well. Some had come from above Santa Tierra, and he did not recognize them at all. He spotted his cousin, Suyapa, in the corner. She was young, single, and very attractive. Her olive skin, accented by her deep cheekbones and dark brown eyes, caught the attention of several of the young men around the windows. Suddenly, Luís felt uncomfortable around those boys, and he thought about moving towards the door. He didn't like the way the young men were looking at his cousin, and a sense of family protection began to surface.

As he reached the opening of the door, the worship leader called on Suyapa to come and lead the congregation in a chain of worship choruses. She carried a small spiral notebook to the table at the front and began to lead in three consecutive choruses written in her notebook. The congregation rose to their feet and began to clap in rhythm with the songs. The guitar player changed keys to accommodate each song as well as the singer. They sang with enthusiasm and joy, something Luís had never heard in the cantina. The first song spoke of "the one who walked on the water - is walking right here with me," followed by "Jesus is passing by here, and when he passes, lives are transformed." The last chorus sang, "There is no God greater than You, who can do the works that you do." Luís watched the eyes of some of the believers grow wide in worship while others bowed their heads reverently. There was no single response to the songs. Each person was sharing in their own private communion with their God, and he began to feel left out, literally.

He took a small step through the threshold as the final chorus came to a close. Suyapa looked up and saw Luís as he entered. She could barely contain her smile as she said, "These choruses have been sung for the honor and glory of the Lord." And with that, she stepped around the table to return to the rear of the room. She walked to Luís and took his hand and led him to the place at the wall where she had been standing. The worship leader called two of the men to come forward and receive the offering for the evening. As they passed a small woven basket among the group, the sound of coins being dropped in came from all sides. Luís thought to himself, "how can such poor people even think about giving even their change?" But give they did, and even the children found some coins to put in the basket. Prayer was then given for the offering by one of the men, and they returned to their place along the wall.

Luís had never seen one of these services, but he had heard strange stories about what went on inside their meetings. To this point, he had not seen anything strange. He had not felt uncomfortable or threatened. The mood of the house was pleasant and the people seemed happy to be there. The worship leader called for those with specials in song to come and share them. Three young girls stepped to the front holding a similar spiral notebook, and then sharing the first line of the song with the guitarist, turned and began to sing together. Their voices blended together to form the high pitch nasal tone of the country people. The song was like a ballad that carried for several verses and spoke of a man named Noah, a big boat, a mighty flood and a faithful God who saved the eight. Luís was unfamiliar with the story, but he listened to the words of the song, and thought to himself, "This is a fantastic story! I wonder where they heard it?"

When the special was finished, they also closed by dedicating the song "to the honor and the glory of their Lord, Jesus Christ." That was the second time, Jesus was spoken of as someone personal. Luís began to wonder why they weren't lighting candles and including Mary in their prayers. In fact, he noticed that Mary hadn't been mentioned once in the service. He was about to ask Suyapa why, when the older man stepped behind the table and opened his Bible to read.

Luís knew two Bible stories, one about the birth of the son of Mary in the manger, and the death of that son on a cross, but what happened between those two events, he didn't have the slightest idea. The older man announced a book and chapter for the reading and much of the small group huddled closer to the lantern, while others pulled out flashlights from their back pockets and shined them on their Bibles. Luís had never owned a Bible, and the thought that so many in one room had one was astonishing. Suyapa helped an older lady beside her find the passage and then turned back to share her Bible with Luís. He followed along as the older man began to read,

> *"When Jesus reached the spot, he looked up and said to him, 'Zacchaeus, come down immediately. I must stay at your house today.' So he came down at once and welcomed him gladly." (Luke 19:5, 6)*

Luís looked up from the Bible with a puzzled expression on his face. He did not know the story or who this Zacchaeus was. The "preacher" explained that he was both a little man and a hated man, but that Jesus loved him. He explained that the town hated him because he was a thief that stole from the people. He was the kind of man that, if he died, no one would care. But one day, Jesus came passing by (just like they had sung about earlier), and he saw Zacchaeus in a tree. He had climbed a tree just because he was curious to see what this Jesus was like. He started out curious, but he later was called. Jesus wanted to go to his house and eat with him. Of all the good people in that town, Jesus wanted to eat with a bad man, a thief. Jesus called to him to come out of his tree, and Zacchaeus did just that, and welcomed him gladly into his home. This Jesus changed his life, and he later gave his money to the poor and paid back everyone he had stolen from.

Luís shook his head. Could anybody change that much? For him, life had always been the same, and looked as though it always would. He had stolen, and fought. He had never killed a man, but he had come close. Could this Jesus change all that in his life? Was He that real? The nods of the people around him told him that something was real in their life, but could it possibly happen to him? Why did Jesus want to know this little thief? He couldn't get the thought out of his mind.

The preacher finished his sermon by saying that Jesus was standing there that night at the door of each heart that did not know Him. "He is knocking and wanting to come in and know you personally," he said. He read another verse from the Bible that said basically the same thing, so it must have been true, Luís thought. The guitar player began to softly strum a tune he did not know as the preacher asked the people to bow their heads in prayer. He asked if anyone wanted to know Jesus that night. Luís' heart began to pound within his chest, but he did not move. He knew something was pulling at him, but it was too soon - he didn't know enough, he thought. The words sounded good, and the world outside the door behind him was darker than the warm glow he felt in that small one room house. But the dark was familiar; this room was not. He wanted the glow, but did not know if he could turn loose of the dark. He wiped the palms of his hands on his pants and cleared his throat. The sounds of quiet prayers around him hovered about the room. When he glanced at Suyapa, her head was also bowed, her lips forming unheard words. Then he heard his name called. He looked around, but no one was looking at him directly. He looked back at Suyapa, who still had her eyes closed. It was not her, for it sounded like a man. But who there knew his name? This was more than he could understand or allow for one night. He let go of his cousin's hand and moved quickly for the door. No one blocked him or tried to prevent him from leaving, which both surprised and almost disappointed him. He moved quickly to the dark side of the house and stopped to take a deep breath. As he stood in the safety of the darkness, he heard the voice again, and realized that his name was not being called by the evangelicals still praying in the house, but by the object of their prayers. As his knees buckled, his head raised. His lips quivered and he stumbled on his words, but as he answered the call, the night suddenly didn't seem so dark.

Chapter Six:

"The Second Wave"

The phone rang twice before Carey could grab it. His thoughts raced with expectancy, hoping that Billy had called back with Anna this time. He answered in English and was greeted with an English response.

"Happy Birthday, Carey!" the voice congratulated, though with a slight tone of reserve. It was Albert Turney, the mission chairman. "I hope I haven't called you too late."

"Not at all, Bert," Carey replied, trying not to show his disappointment. "We were just finishing some fantastic angel food cake."

Small talk was never one of Bert's strong points, but his gentle approach to difficult subjects had won him respect among the mission family. He was not the oldest missionary on the field, but certainly one of the wisest. Three years into his fourth term meant a great deal of experience in both field and administrative duty. He had served his first two terms in a remote area as general evangelist, and could identify with the families stationed outside the capital. His wife, Helen, and he had reared their three boys and watched the youngest leave for college on their last furlough. His role as mission chairman drew many hats of responsibility, but one that he seemed to enjoy the most was serving as "pastor" to the missionaries.

"Listen, Carey," Bert eased into the conversation. "Susan called me this afternoon about the accident last night. I just want to know how you are doing?"

"Bert, I know I should have called you sooner today, but I didn't know how to tell you about it," Carey answered in a low voice. "I mean, nothing like this has ever happened in my life before, and I still don't know what to make out of it. I guess I'm still trying to put it all together in my mind."

"Susan said you did report it to the authorities," Bert said, trying to lead Carey in the conversation.

"Yes, we - Mando Ochoa and I, carried the body to the *posta* on the highway after the accident."

"And they didn't detain you?" Bert questioned.

"That's the strange part about it. I know the law is clear, but it was like the officer in charge, a Capitán at the post, knew this man, and assumed our innocence based on that knowledge. He told us we could go after less than an hour at his guard station," Carey said, realizing as he said it, how unusual the procedure had been.

"Well that is nothing short of a miracle, my brother. The Lord was looking out for you last night." Bert replied in his most positive tone.

58

"More than you know, Bert," Carey added. "The man I hit was trying to rob us, and he had a gun. When I think about what could have happened on that road last night..."

Bert let the silence work for both of them, then softly responded, "But Carey, God was with you. He knew that man was out there, and He protected you. I understand that you must hurt for what has happened, but you mustn't lose sight of the fact that God was overseeing the affairs of last night. This is not the first time something like this has happened to a missionary, and it won't be the last. If you feel like you need someone to talk to more about this, I can come down tomorrow after lunch."

Carey suddenly felt a mixed wave of emotion. On the one hand, he was encouraged by the concern and the offer of a fellow missionary, who obviously was busy with his own list of priorities, but was willing to lay those things aside to come and sit with a hurting comrade; and yet on the other hand, he suddenly felt depressed that he should need such company and attention.

"I appreciate the offer Bert," Carey began. "But that really won't be necessary. You see, I just talked with my brother earlier this evening, and he is going to be flying in Saturday. I'll be headed your way to pick him up around lunch-time."

"That's great," Bert responded. "I'll try to break away and make it by the airport to wait with you . . . if you would like."

"I would like that very much Bert," Carey said honestly.

They concluded their conversation, and Carey placed the phone back in its cradle. Susan watched him saunter to the porch and slowly mount his new hammock. He raised his arms up and placed them behind his head and swayed gently. Carey closed his eyes and tried once again to wish it all away.

———

Luís knew that something within him was changed. He didn't know the words for it yet, but it was real none-the-less. He wanted to return to the service and announce his newfound faith, but instead found himself wandering toward the road, away from the lighted house. As the small group began to sing again, he turned toward the town and saw a familiar silouhette approaching.

Most men were known by their given names, or by a variation based on their name. Few were called by a nickname based on their physical appearance, but Flaco was an exception. *Flaco* was Spanish for "skinny", and that was what the town preferred to call him. Few even knew his parents had named him Antonio Alvarez, because, from his teenage years forward, he was so skinny. He could eat his share and another's in beans and rice, but he never seemed to gain weight. Some thought Flaco had worms, but he would jokingly admit, that no worm could survive in the alcohol that he drank. Luís was one of the few men who would even associate with Flaco, but only because he liked having a drinking partner. Or at least, he used to. The last time he had drank with Flaco, they had teamed up with Moncho, and there had been a tragic accident. It seemed so long ago now, Luís thought, though less than twenty-four hours had passed.

Flaco waited till he was less than three feet away, then called to Luís with slurred greetings. "*Amigo*, why are you not in town tonight? I waited at Roberto's for over an hour, then came looking for you. Someone said you were walking this way, and now . . . here you are."

"Come Flaco, I'll walk with you back to town," Luís replied putting his arm around his skinny shoulders to steady his friend.

"I saw you at Moncho's today," Flaco started. "What a shame, to die like a dog in the road."

"What do you mean," Luís inquired.

"Moncho fell in the road and that *gringo* ran over him like a dog. He didn't even try to stop," Flaco said vehemently.

"Is that what happened?" Luís asked surprised.

Flaco began to swear profusely calling on various saints as his witness. Luís wondered how reliable his account could be, given the conditions of both the night and man himself. Even Luís had trouble making his way home that evening. He decided not to challenge Flaco's word, but rather to change the direction of the conversation. He half hoped it would not turn to why Flaco had found him outside the meetinghouse of the *gringo's* mission.

"I'll tell you one good thing that came out of all this though," Flaco said smiling. He patted his hip pocket and Luís noticed the bulge in the side of his pants.

"Now look who has the power," Flaco boasted. "They didn't find the gun, but I did, and I have big plans for it."

Luís felt a wave of caution welling up inside of him.

"What big plans do you have, Flaco," Luís asked cautiously.

"I am going north!" he said confidently.

"To San Pedro Sula?" Luís exclaimed.

"No! *Tonto*!. . .to the north!. . .through El Salvador, Guatemala. . . through Mexico. . . all the way to the North - *Los Estados Unidos!*" Flaco almost shouted.

"How are you going to get to the U.S. from here?" Luís asked incredulously.

"My cousin knows a *coyote* who will help me." he said, his voice dropping to a near whisper. "How about you come go with me? You have no family here."

"But you do, or have you forgotten?" Luís responded trying to restore logic to the conversation.

"She doesn't love me, and my kids don't even know me. I can do much better than this. So can you! What is there is *Santa Tierra* to stay for?"

Luís looked hard into Flaco's eyes. If he had asked him that question the night before, he would have been more inclined to agree with his skinny friend, pack his bag and go. But now, the world - *Santa Tierra* included - seemed a different place.

Luís had heard the same alluring stories of life in the United States. The jobs, the food, the cars, they all formed the myth of the better life. The temptation to disregard the laws, to place your total trust and finances into the hands of a stranger who traffics in human marketing, and hope to beat the odds, by being among those lucky few who somehow enter undetected and evade the ongoing network of immigration workers, just never appealed to Luís.

"I don't know, Flaco. ..", Luís started.

"You don't know anything!" Flaco countered, exasperated. He broke loose from Luís and began walking back toward town alone. He turned back in an afterthought. "You didn't get converted in there did you?" he asked, pointing with his lips toward the little house of worship from the direction where Luís had been walking.

"Why would you ask such a question?" Luís offered feebly to avoid the answer.

"Because, that *gringo* missionary is about to get more trouble than he can imagine," Flaco mumbled. "I am going to pass through Gualsince on my way through to San Salvador - it is safer that way you know, and I am going to tell Moncho's family what horrible thing has happened to him. I am going to tell them that the *gringo* missionary killed him."

The words stunned Luís. He did not know the missionary - not yet anyway, but he knew that Flaco would be stirring up trouble in his wake, and that *machete law* knew no boundaries. Luís realized it would be useless to reason with Flaco that evening. He quietly acknowledged the statement and Flaco turned back toward town. Luís decided he would try to talk with Flaco tomorrow when he was sober, and that he would try to dissuade him from involving Moncho's family. But as the waning moonlight slid from Flaco's back, he slipped into a darkness from which Luís would never see him again.

_____

"Hello, Sheila . . . it's me, Karen - Karen Pennington," she said confidently into the phone. "You interviewed me this afternoon for the sales position. You told me to call you this evening after I had spoken to my parents."

"Oh yes, Karen," the voice chimed from the earpiece. "I was just thinking about you. I trust you're calling to say you can start work."

"Yes, I can start tomorrow," Karen replied excitedly, "but I have to tell you that my Dad says this is a two week trial to see if I can keep up my grades."

"Well, I'm sure it will all work out just fine," the voice assured her.

Suddenly, Karen remembered the other stipulation her father had mentioned.

"One other thing," Karen said with less enthusiasm. "Dad would like to know if I would have to work *every* Wednesday night?" Karen knew she was hedging a little with the request, but she was nervous about mentioning why she needed that night free.

"We'll see what we can do," Sheila replied professionally. "I'm sure we can work something out."

The tone of her voice seemed to convey more than the spoken words, but Karen was oblivious to anything but the prospect of starting her first *real* job. She smiled into the receiver and quickly remembered one last important question.

"I almost forgot," she stammered. "What time would you like me to come in tomorrow?"

"Just as soon as you can after school," she replied. "I will need to take some time to train you tomorrow. Plan to come in by 3:00 and stay till closing - 9:30. Is that a problem?"

"I don't think," Karen said still smiling. "I'll tell my Mom and she'll explain it to Dad."

As she finished the conversation, she gently returned the phone to her nightstand and lay back on her bed. She pulled her favorite stuffed bear close under her chin. She had not felt this good in a long while. She glanced across the room to the open closet door. From the position where she lay, she could just see the large protruding corner of the suitcase that had caught her attention the night before. Maybe she wouldn't need it so soon after all, she thought to herself. But then she was only seventeen, and teenagers have the right to change their mind at a moment's notice.

1:47 am on the east coast is not an easy hour at which to rise. Gertie had stirred twice before she realized she was being summoned again. As Adam lay restfully beside her, his backside spooned up against her, she slowly turned over so as not to disturb him. She undertook the task of easing herself upright and lifting herself up by her walker. After ten painful minutes of maneuvering, she found herself seated once again in her rocker for prayer. She knew to pray for Carey, for his name was still on her heart. But Adam's study that morning had brought a new burden to light. She felt certain that her prayers for Carey were being directed towards his protection and his well being. But Adam had mentioned praying for those in sin and straying from God. This form of intercession is easier when you know whom you are praying for Gertie thought to herself.

"Lord, who is it I'm am praying for?" she asked aloud.

"Their names are not as important as their need," came the answer. Gertie never claimed to hear an audible voice of God, but she did know when the Spirit of God was leading her. In that way, she understood the scripture that stated, *"My sheep hear my voice and I know them and they follow Me."*

"But can you help me with the need, that I might know how to pray," she appealed in response.

"It is a family drifting apart. There is great danger ahead. Pray for the father to be the spiritual leader of his family that he should."

Gertie drew in her breath and closed her eyes. The next forty minutes were spent in earnest prayer for Carey and his unknown problem and for an unknown family and their spiritual needs. She prayed a hedge of protection about Carey, she prayed for the soon and safe arrival of her letter for his personal encouragement, and she prayed for the Lord's angels to encamp his home and protect his family in the event of his traveling away from home.

She never dozed or nodded off during the time of her prayers despite the late hour. She felt a second wind sufficient enough to match the second wave. As she prayed for the unknown family, she found herself voicing petitions for their relationships to be mended, for the father to be given spiritual discernment for his family, and for any wayward child to be guarded by the Lord. Though she prayed generally in these areas, she had no idea just how specific her prayers were being expressed. As she closed out her time in her "closet", she thanked the Lord again for calling her to Himself. Gertie always saw her prayer time as a privilege and not as a task. It was a discipline of delight and not of duty.

As she eased herself back into bed, Adam turned his face in her direction and whispered softly, "prayer time again?" She reached across his large shoulders and squeezed him close. He understood, and she loved him all the more for it.

———

As Carey eased himself into bed, Susan rolled over to face him. "I'm sorry," he apologized. "I didn't mean to wake you."

"What time is it?" she asked groggily.

"Almost 12:30," he replied. "I couldn't sleep. I know part of it is the excitement of seeing Billy the day after tomorrow, but the other part is. . ." and his voice trailed off.

"I know, honey," Susan said, offering her hand to caress his face.

He gently kissed her hand and then grabbed it with his own. Tears were running down his cheek. "I just don't understand it!" he sobbed. "I came here to help people *find life* in Jesus, not take it from them. This is not suppose to happen."

Susan chose not to talk yet. She waited for Carey to continue.

"I don't know what I'm going to do. I can't go back into that village. They must know by now what happened and who was responsible. I have lost any hope of ever having a church in that town." Carey began to regain his composure. "I wouldn't blame Mando if he never wanted to travel with me again. He's probably told all his family and friends what I have done, and . . ." His mind was spinning in a circle of regrets. Susan knew there was little possibility that Armando would use the incident against her husband, but his mind was already conjuring the worse case scenarios. She decided to speak.

"Carey, I can't offer any wisdom as to why everything happened," she began, "Or why it happened to you. But believe me when I tell you that Mando is your friend, and I don't believe he would say anything to anyone that would harm you."

"Furthermore," she continued. "I know when Billy gets here, he will help you put a lot of this into perspective. But you can't let this overwhelm you. What has happened is tragic, I know. But what has happened can not be undone. You and I have to work together through this," she said sitting up and putting her arm around him.

"I love you, and nothing can change that. God loves you, and nothing can change that. I know it hurts right now, but I'm here," she concluded pulling his head into her shoulder.

"I love you too, Susan," Carey sighed.

"And besides, today was your birthday," she added. "And I know there were thousands of people praying for you today."

"*Was* my birthday," Carey corrected looking at the clock by the bed. "It's now thirty eight minutes into tomorrow. Let's say we get some sleep and I'll face this tomorrow."

"Let's say we snuggle a little, first," she flirted. "Then we'll both face this tomorrow."

———

Flaco turned his face towards the beam of headlight as it seesawed over the ridge of the hill. He could not see the red color of the pick-up, but he could tell from its single headlamp and the roar of its broken exhaust pipe, that it belonged to Felípe, the beer and rum supplier. This was the truck they had hoped would come the night before. This truck would not have climbed over that branch and killed Moncho. In Flaco's current state of mind, he found himself blaming Felípe as much as the missionary for Moncho's death. If only he had left town when he should have, they would have robbed him and the three of them would be drinking again tonight together. He waved his arm at the truck using his hand as a signal for him to stop. Felípe recognized the lanky silhouette illuminated in his headlight and began to slow down.

"*Buenos noches, jefe,*" Flaco began cordially. "Can you give me a lift to the highway, I need to catch the early bus to Tegucigalpa?"

"Of course," Felípe smiled back. "You can sit up front if you like." Normally, hitchhikers climbed in the bed of the trucks to ride apart from the driver. But Felípe felt he knew Flaco and seemed unconcerned by the late hour of his departure from *Santa Tierra* or the fact that he carried a traveling bag. He had no reason not to trust this familiar face. As Flaco climbed into the seat beside Felípe, he shifted the position of the pistol in his pocket. He did not want his driver host to become alarmed, at least not for another five or six kilometers when they would be far enough away from the town and neighboring homes to be heard. Flaco did not want to use the gun, but he did need the truck and Felípe's money. It would be Felípe's decision as to how much "power" he would need to use.

Chapter Seven:

"The New Day"

(Friday)

Friday was pizza day at school and Terry Pennington was not about to forget his lunch money. He bounced into the kitchen with his books in tow and pleasantly greeted his mother turning bacon in the skillet. Moments later, Karen glided through the kitchen door, placed her books neatly on the table and joined her mother at the stove.

"Is there anything I can help you with, Mom?" she asked peering over her mother's shoulder. Her mother quickly looked back to find her daughter smiling behind her sincerely awaiting instructions.

"Why y y yes," she stuttered, "You can begin with pouring some orange juice for everyone. Are we all eating this morning?" she asked incredulously.

"Look's that way," replied Howard entering and taking his place at the table. He too, was impressed with his daughter's initiative and her appearance for the day. She was dressed in a plaid skirt of modest length with a complimenting pastel blouse and scarf. Her normal ensemble of jewelry had been replaced with a simple necklace and one pair of earrings, positioned in the lobes, no less.

"You are certainly looking nice this morning," commented Howard with an approving tone toward Karen.

"Thank you, Daddy," she returned in kind, "I start work today after school, and I want to make a good impression on Sheila."

"Well, I think you look just fine," chimed Donna, "And I think you will do just fine."

"Daddy, Sheila wanted to know if I can stay till closing tonight," Karen asked more in a request for permission than in a settled issue. Donna quickly caught his eye and he understood the need for latitude on this issue.

"Well, it's Friday, I don't see why not," Howard responded unreservedly. "How do you plan to get home?" Karen's face changed slightly, knowing that her next comment may kill all her chances at her new job.

"I had thought to ask Fernando from school to come by at 9:30 and pick me up," she said slowly.

"Is that the boy you were with Wednesday night?" Howard asked without changing his tone.

"Yes sir," she replied.

After a pause, her father smiled again.

"Just tell him you need to be in no later than 10:30. We're going to keep some of this 'grounding' in force - OK?" he offered.

"No problem!" she smiled. "10:30 on the dot!"

Donna set the bacon on the table and took her seat. This was truly a new day - one she had been hoping for.

"Honey, would you like to return thanks this morning?" she asked, looking longingly at her husband across the table.

"Would love to," he replied and together the Pennington family bowed their heads.

———

Adam raised the shade, allowing the mid morning sun to filter through the shears. He had pulled the shade earlier in the morning again so that Gertie could sleep.

"How was your night?" he asked easing himself beside her on the bed.

"I was up again," she yawned stretching behind him.

"I know," he said kissing her on the forehead, "I remember when you came back to bed. That makes twice this week. What's going on?"

"I wish I knew," she said sitting up. "I think there is more involved here than just the Eldridges, though. I believe I am praying for another family with problems as well."

"Who? Someone we know?" he inquired.

"I don't think so," she said pensively. "I just know that it is a family having trouble with a daughter."

Adam helped her to her feet and she endured the journey into the kitchen. Adam had prepared two small omelets and had them under cereal bowls to keep them warm. He took her hand and together they thanked the Lord for another day and prayed for the two families that God had placed on Gertie's heart.

———

Carey awoke to the sound of the boys using a crowbar to beat on the old crate that sat in the corner of their backyard. Since their last furlough, the wooden crate had served as a two-story fort, a clubhouse, and even a Honduran *McDonalds* once when Susan let them cook hamburgers on the Hibachi grill and "sell" them for a family picnic on Caleb's eleventh birthday. On this morning, they had decided to dismantle the back wall and use the plywood for a bicycle jump. Christmas toys come and go, but wooden crates serve a myriad of purposes for young boys and outlast most store bought wonders - something their Sega addicted cousins would never understand.

Susan walked in with a cup of fresh coffee. Honduran coffee is typically strong and usually tempered with large amounts of sugar. It is normally served in small "teacups". Carey became accustomed to drinking it sweet in the outlying areas where sugar was common and milk was scarce. He preferred the drip machine to the Honduran *sock* that many used to strain their coffee. He knew that most homes scalded any unwelcome germs out anyway. Susan knew just the right amount of milk and cream (something he never had away from home).

"How did you sleep?" she asked.

"Better, thanks," he replied taking the cup from her hand. "I thought I might go over to Mando's today and see how he is doing."

"I think that is a good idea," she remarked, "and while you are out, I have a small list of things we need. I need to get my materials together for my Bible class tomorrow."

"Tomorrow?" Carey asked surprised. "What time? Billy is coming in tomorrow."

"In the morning at 10:00, but don't worry, I'll be through by 1:00 before you get back from the airport," she said handing him his jeans. "I thought the boys might want to go with you."

"Oh, yeah sure," he said in a daze. "I just thought we would all be going."

"I'm sorry honey, I can't," she apologized. "I have had this planned for over a month and the ladies class is counting on me to have the devotion and the craft for their meeting. Besides, you'll have more room without me."

"I guess so," he replied half-heartedly.

Susan took his face in her hands. "You are still upset about the accident, I know, but this will be a good time for you and Billy to talk. You may even want to think about going alone, just so that you two can talk more freely. The boys can watch the house for us while I'm away and we will have a big welcome party waiting for you two when you drive up," she said in her most reassuring voice.

"Maybe you're right," he acquiesced. Carey just wasn't sure if he was ready to be alone for the ride to the airport.

———

Capitán Mendoza saw the young boy waving frantically from the road and pulled the gray pickup alongside. In broken phrases, the excited boy tried to explain that his father had found a body earlier that morning while he was carrying corn to the market at *Santa Tierra*. He and two neighbors then carried the man to the nearest home. Mendoza motioned for the boy to hop into the bed of the truck and show him the house.

As the gray Nissan pulled into the muddy entrance of the property, several young men rushed out of the adobe shack to "inform" the FUSEP officer of the assault. Mendoza pushed passed them and into the house to find the body of Felípe Cruz lying on a table in the center of the large room. A bloodstained sheet was pulled up over his chest but he was still alive. The wound was abdominal but not fatal having missed any vital organs. He needed medical attention and no vehicle had passed until now.

The young men quickly helped to transfer Felípe to the truck using the sheet as a stretcher. Two boys rode in the back with him as Mendoza drove as steadily over the gravel road as he could manage and still make good time. Within twenty-five minutes, they had reached pavement and sped on to the hospital in Choluteca. Without means of radioing in ahead, they had to locate two medical assistants on arrival to find an available gurney. Once Felípe was successfully admitted into emergency, Mendoza turned his attention to the men who had accompanied him.

"Who found him? And where?" Mendoza began.

"Santos Ochoa, I think," responded one of the men. "We met him and two others carrying the man back to Don Bent's. They said he was lying in a ditch just after the third *quebrada* before *Santa Tierra*, about six kilometers from town."

"So none of you have any idea who he is or what happened?" Mendoza asked looking at each.

They all shook their heads.

"It looked like he had been shot in the left side of his belly and the bullet came out his right side," offered one of the young men. It would take the doctors another four hours before they would determine that just the opposite had occurred.

―――――

Mando saw the red Hilux with the white camper coming down the dirt road and waited in front of his house for Carey to climb down from the cab. He walked out to his friend and extended his hand in greeting. Carey clasped it firmly and they exchanged understanding smiles. Mando knew that Carey had much to work through and what he needed most at this time was a friend.

"Something to drink?" Mando offered leading Carey into his small three-room home.

"You have a *fresco* made up?" Carey asked.

"I think Sandra has some *mora* prepared," he said, "would you like some?"

"*Mora* sounds great," Carey replied. The mora berry was the closest thing Honduras had to the blackberry back home, but it was still distinctive. Mando's wife, Sandra, always boiled their water before preparing *frescos*, or natural drinks, so Carey never feared being offered something to quench his thirst when visiting.

"How have you been, my brother?" Mando finally asked after both were served cool glasses of fresh mora.

Carey took a breath.

"It has been difficult," he started, "but Susan has helped much. I still am at a loss why we were not imprisoned till they knew what happened for sure."

"Who else would know what happened?" Mando asked. "We are our only witnesses. Anyway, I think that the Capitán knew the man we hit pretty well. He didn't hesitate to believe the story. But that is not what is bothering you today, is it my brother?"

"No, it isn't," Carey said lowering his head. "I don't know if I can go back to *Santa Tierra*. I mean, what if he had family and they know? What if they are waiting for me to return? And what about the new work? How will anyone believe we come to share God's love when the missionary takes a man's life?"

Carey paused, realizing that he had begun to babble in his questions, but Mando just let him talk. It is a wise man who knows when to listen and Mando was certainly wise for his years. After a helpful silence, Mando spoke up.

"*Hermano*, you are listening to all the wrong voices. Guilt, fear, and accusation are spearing you from every side and your shield is down. It is true you have taken a man's life, but not intentionally. In my mind, it was not even you who was responsible, but the man himself, for his own unfortunate death. He was a drunk and a thief and would have killed us both if he could, but God spared our lives and took his. You were only at the wheel."

"Furthermore," Mando continued, "you fear vengeance from the family, but you forget the protective hand that holds you. It held you that night and can hold you in the daylight as well. Wisdom and courage are both products of faith. Our faith in God allows us to follow Him where fear would hold us back. The wisdom of God is found in His direction. If we trust that direction fully, we will walk in His wisdom. God will show you when it is time to return to *Santa Tierra*, and will give you the faith to return boldly and wisely."

"One other thing," Mando said, drawing Carey's eyes to his own, "the accuser would wish nothing more than to destroy the work that has begun in *Santa Tierra*. Since he cannot prevail against the church itself, he seeks to prevail against her servants. He accuses all of us daily, trying to remind us of our sins and downfalls so that we will become discouraged and quit working. Is that what you want to do, my brother?"

Carey looked squarely into the deep brown eyes of his friend and sighed.

"How did you ever get to be so wise?" he asked smiling.

"When you walk with the wise, you grow in wisdom," his friend quietly replied.

———

"You're what?" Fernando yelled above the clamor of the cafeteria.

"I said, I'm working tonight. I just got a new job and the boss wants me to work through till closing so she can train me," Karen responded defensively.

"But it's Friday night!" Fernando exclaimed, "I thought we would go see a movie or somethin'. "

"We can still get together after I get off from work," she explained, then paused and added, "well, for an hour anyway."

"An hour?" he shouted.

"Look, I'm still on restriction from coming in late on Wednesday," Karen tried to explain calmly, but her tone was tensing with his reaction. "My Dad says I have to be in by 10:30 or I can kiss this job good-bye."

"*Mire Chica!*" he exclaimed reverting to his Spanish machismo, using an expression that demanded attention and subjection. "You work very many Fridays and you can kiss me good-bye."

Karen glared into his strong brown eyes. She would not be bullied by another male especially not one her own age.

"*Asi es!*" she replied firmly, meaning "so that's the way it", then rose from their table and marched to the door. The thought had not crossed his mind that Fernando was to be her ride home till much later in the afternoon. By then, pride had sealed her decision.

———

Santos Ochoa was a strong man for his age. Walking the hillsides between his home and *Santa Tierra*, living on rice, beans and tortillas, and working hard each season in the fields had kept him strong. Most Honduran men in the south worked hard for their families. Their days began early and ended when there was no more sunlight left by which to work. At sixty-seven, Santos was still muscular and could carry large loads on his shoulder balanced with his machete. He had nine children, fourteen grandchildren, and the same wife he married over forty-five years earlier. Most men his age were referred to as "Don", but he preferred to just be called by name without the title. He said it made him feel old.

Capitán Mendoza found him returning to *Santa Tierra* shortly after lunch with a bag of beans on his shoulder to sell in the market. Many families grew what they needed and sold what was not in order to survive from season to season. The rains had been good this year and there were beans to sell. With his oldest children in the field and the younger ones attending the nearby government school, he walked alone.

"Santos Ochoa," the Capitán called from his truck, "where are you going?"

"To *Santa Tierra*," he replied, not lowering his load, "to sell *frioles*."

"Would you like a ride?" Mendoza offered.

"Why not?" he smiled and tossed his bag into the back of the truck. As he began to climb over the tailgate, Mendoza motioned for him to come up front with him in the cab.

"Come ride up here," Mendoza called, "I want to ask you a few questions about the man you found this morning."

"You mean Felípe?" Santos asked as he closed the door beside him.

"You know who it was?" Mendoza asked surprised.

"Of course, it was Felípe Cruz from below Los Robles. He drives out two, sometimes three times a week with rum, and other drinks for the cantina in town," Santos said.

"Did you see his truck when you found him this morning?" Mendoza asked.

"No, I believe the truck must have been stolen," offered Santos. "Chances are, that is why he was robbed and shot."

"How do you know he was robbed?" Mendoza asked.

"Because Felípe bragged of the money he made running liquor and he always carried it on him, because his truck did not lock up well. When we found him, there was no wallet or money," Santos replied looking in the direction of the officer driving.

Mendoza glanced over and caught his eyes and knew he was speaking the truth.

"Can you show me the spot where you found him this morning?" asked the Capitán.

"Sure, it is just past this next *quebrada* ahead," pointed Santos. "I'll show you."

As the truck eased over the rocky terrain, Mendoza began to piece the information together in his mind. Someone had shot and robbed a liquor runner. The wounds appeared to have been caused by someone shooting from Felípe's side and slightly in front of him and to the left. But he would have to have been outside of the truck for that to happen. Perhaps Felípe had pulled over to relieve himself or to move a branch from the road. As they rounded the next curve, Santos' hand went down to the seat beside Mendoza to steady himself. As the Capitán looked down, he realized that the old man's hand was beside him in the very spot of the exit wound found on Felípe. If someone were riding in the front seat with Felípe, a gun thrust into the driver's side would come from that angle. If the driver then hit a bump and the gun went off, the bullet would enter from the right rear of the abdomen and exit through the front. For the assailant to have been in the front seat with the victim could only mean one thing. Felípe knew the man who shot him.

Chapter Eight

"The Meeting"

The Coronado Baptist Church was located on a small hill overlooking the San Diego Bay and the bridge for which it was named. The mid-size congregation was comprised mostly of middle and upper middle class families. The older generation, be it retired from military or other businesses cruised the bay on good pensions and missed their share of Sundays to the water recreation. Most people who retired in southern California did so for the weather and were seldom disappointed.

Arnie Johnson was not retired. He headed his own small construction firm that specialized in multi-level structures. He was a large barrel-chested man in his mid-forties. His well-worn CAT ball cap covered his two-thirds bald dome allowing the gray-red hair to shine from both sides. The slightest exertion or tension flushed his cheeks and forehead a deep red, giving him a strong and intimidating countenance.

Arnie had worked in the bay area for over seventeen years with just his wife and only child, Alex. They had been faithful members of the Coronado Baptist Church for most of that time. Arnie had once taught a youth class, before work demands caused him to give it over to another. He loved his family and he loved his church. Arnie had become a member under the ministry of an older pastor who worked closely with the deacons and other leaders of the church. When Dr. Pennington came, he struck Arnie as a "Lone Ranger", self-involved and arrogant. He never grew close to his "new" pastor, and not much had changed in ten years.

For almost two years, the church had been trying to raise the necessary funds to construct a new sanctuary and educational building. Arnie was not opposed to the expansion. He felt the plans themselves were short sighted and did not take full advantage of the land. He objected to the design proposed. He had expressed his disapproval at countless business meetings, but Howard's voice and opinion was always heard last and proved the most persuasive.

Diane looked up from her typing to see Arnie bustling through the doorway towards the Pastor's study. He didn't even acknowledge her, but went straight to the half-closed door and pushed it open. Howard swiveled around to see Arnie's red face across from his desk.

"So you met with the contractor yesterday and he told you the site wouldn't support the second floor!" Arnie bellowed.

"Arnie, nice of you to drop by, won't you have a seat?" Howard responded trying to maintain his own temper.

"I won't be here long enough, thank you," Arnie countered. "I just want to know if you are going to recommend to the building committee that we scrap the two story plan for one that will cover more ground and kill parking opportunities?"

"Well. . . you know, Arnie," Howard began slowly. "We've been looking it over, and . . . the best options we have seem to be . . . "

"We who?" Arnie asked accusingly. "What building experience do you have? I'm telling you, the best plan for this lot is a two story building and I can show the committee how it can be done"

"Well, thank you Arnie," Howard said rising to his feet. "I will certainly pass that information along when we meet tonight."

Howard extended his hand, but Arnie had already huffed and turned toward the door. Diane smiled up towards him politely as he lumbered out of the office. As she turned back to her typing, Rusty breezed up to her desk.

"What was that all about? As if I didn't know," he quipped.

"Just Arnie, blowing off steam again," Diane replied.

"Think it's OK to go in?" he asked looking towards Howard's door.

"Sure," she smiled, "he could probably use a friendly face right about now."

Rusty eased through the door to find Howard staring at the pictures on his desk.

"You busy?" he asked Howard.

"Nah," he said glancing up. "What would you like to change? The size of the baptistery, the color of the choir robes, maybe the carpet in my office."

"Arnie giving you a hard time, again?" Rusty said sitting on the edge of the desk.

"Nothing but," Howard groaned. "I have the committee tonight and then recommendations to take back to the contractor next week. I don't know when I am going to prepare for my messages."

"Well, good news then," Rusty said affably. "I just checked the calendar, and we have a Gideon speaker Wednesday night and that's one less sermon for you."

"You really know how to cheer me up," Howard said sarcastically.

"What do you mean?" Rusty asked.

"If there's anything more boring than a missionary and his slides, it's a Gideon," he sighed. "Are you sure it is this month?"

"This comin' Wednesday," he said confidently. "Same date as last year."

"Has another year gone by that quickly?" Howard said shaking his head. "Where does the time go?"

Rusty just looked down quietly. He did not know where this apathetic attitude was coming from, but he knew it was not healthy for his pastor.

"Listen, I have been taking some guys from the men's class with me over to El Cajon for jail ministry on Saturday nights, why don't you come go with us tomorrow?" Rusty asked enthusiastically.

"I don't know," Howard muttered. "Let me see how things are going after this meeting and I'll let you know."

"It's a blessing," Rusty added. "Think about it and let me know before three tomorrow afternoon."

Rusty turned to go, leaving Howard staring once again at the pictures on his desk. Somehow, ministering to others was the farthest thing from Howard's mind.

———

Adam carried the tray with two large glasses of iced tea and two tuna fish sandwiches neatly garnished with chips and Kosher Spears into the den where Gertie sat quietly on the couch with her needlepoint. He placed the tray on the end table between her and his recliner and kissed her gently on the forehead.

"Oh, is it lunch time already?" she asked looking up.

"Same time as yesterday," he responded kindly. "Deep in thought while you sew?"

"Deep in prayer," she smiled, "and it's needlepoint."

"How can you pray and do needlepoint at the same time?" Adam asked seating himself in his recliner and grasping his sandwich with his large hands.

"It's easy," she replied laying aside her old wooden embroidery hoop and carefully counted aida cloth, "prayer is an attitude, not a position. You don't have to close your eyes or get on your knees. . . as if I still could."

"Prayer is talking to God like He's sitting in that recliner. I talk to you while I'm doing my needlepoint, don't I?" she asked.

"Um, Hum," he replied with a mouthful of tuna fish.

"I think too many people have made prayer something mystical," she said seriously, "or something that can only be done in church. They think they have to say the right words, or talk in a language that no one uses in everyday speech. They have complicated something God intended to be simple. Prayer is just talking to Him, sharing your day and finding out what He thinks about it. We can tell him our joys as well as our fears and problems. We don't have to always be asking for something. Sometimes, I think God just wants to hear us talk to Him because we know He's there and cares."

She paused and picked up some chips.

"For example," she continued, "I just thanked Him for this food and for you fixing it so faithfully each day. We didn't stop and bow our heads and hold hands like we do so many times, but I thanked him just the same. He knows you're thankful too, though I wonder if you stopped to tell him so before you finished that first half of a sandwich."

"Oops," Adam swallowed hard, "you're right, sorry."

"Don't apologize to me," Gertie smiled, "we don't pray for other people to approve us. That's what the Pharisees did. We pray because we want to talk to our Heavenly Father. We pray because He wants to be able to talk to us. We just have to be in a constant attitude of prayer."

"Praying without ceasing," Adam added.

"That's right," Gertie said finally picking up her sandwich half. "Not with head always bowed and eyes always closed, but heart always speaking and listening."

"And what were you praying about when I came in?" Adam asked sipping his tea.

"I was praying for Carey again," she sighed, "and for that other family. They have both been on my mind all morning. When do you suppose my letter will get to Carey?"

"I don't know for sure," he shrugged, "but I would think it would be at least next week sometime. I heard once in the Brotherhood, it takes anywhere from seven to ten days for a letter to make it to an address in Central America."

"That means it could be as late as next Friday or Saturday," she calculated. "I pray it gets there in time."

"In time for what?" Adam asked looking into her eyes.

"I don't know," she said quietly, "but I haven't had peace over the matter since this started Wednesday night."

———

Capitán Mendoza knew Roberto Romero from their days in the military. They had served together during the "Soccer War" of 1969. Ironically, Roberto was an El Salvadorian immigrant who had come to Honduras to escape the political tension of his own country and found himself fighting her as a Honduran citizen. After the fighting, he sought a quieter life in the hills of *Santa Tierra*. His little cantina was not lucrative, but it was steady, and it allowed him to raise his small family under calmer conditions than they had known in El Salvador. Mendoza preferred the action of military life, but was unwilling to condone its abuses. He settled for law enforcement and unlike many of his peers, he took his job seriously. When Roberto saw

Mendoza step through the doorway into his cantina, he knew it was not for a social call.

"*Buenas tardes, Capitán*," Roberto called out because it was past noon.

"*Buenas,* Roberto," returned Mendoza. "And where is your Friday crowd?" he asked looking around.

"It is afternoon, but it is still early, my friend," he offered, "they are still in the fields."

"I didn't think your clients worked," the Capitán smirked, "at least not in the heat of the day."

"You come after all this time just to insult me," Roberto responded jokingly.

"No, my friend," Mendoza turned serious, "I have come to look for a thief and a murderer."

"Who has been murdered?" Roberto asked alarmed.

"Well, actually, no one," Mendoza began, "but a man was robbed and left for dead, and the one who shot him did not intend for him to live. He is not conscious yet and I can not ask him who shot him, but I believe he knew the thief."

"You're talking about Felípe, aren't you?" Roberto affirmed.

"Yes, do you know if he left here with anyone last night?" Mendoza questioned.

"No, he left alone, but I do know he was carrying much money," Roberto said, trying to be helpful, "I, myself paid him over two thousand *lempiras* for some back accounts. I don't know how much he had collected before he came here, but he could have been carrying more than five thousand."

"That's a lot," Mendoza nodded, "enough to kill for. Are you sure no one asked him for a ride into Choluteca when he left?"

"No *Capitán*. He left alone. I am sure."

"Do me a favor and check around," Mendoza said softly though they were the only ones in the room, "See if anyone from around town is missing. I'll check back with you in a couple of days."

"No problem," Roberto said, "I'll let you know what I find. Felípe was a good man, I hope he recovers soon."

"I do too," Mendoza said, rising to leave, "I think he knows who shot him."

The Capitán walked out into the mid-afternoon sun. The clouds were beginning to form again for rain. He didn't know which was worse, The 120°+ heat of summer or the daily rains of winter. Sometimes, he wondered if life wouldn't be better in the *"El Norte"*. Little did he realize, that Felípe's assailant was thinking the same thing.

The large bus slowed to a stop as women scooped up their woven baskets filled with rice, lard, and perhaps a live chicken or two. The bus emptied quickly - this being the final stop on this road. For many, there would be several hours walk before reaching their home. The buses could only travel by road to *Gualcince*. Those traveling to *Mapulaca* had to walk the trails from there. Flaco swung down from the rear door where others were passing supplies to their owners below. He winced at the midday sun, but realized that the temperature was cooler in the mountains than in *Santa Tierra*. He had sold Felípe's truck in *La Esperanza* and used part of the money for the bus ticket while putting the rest with what he had stolen. It would be a good start for his trip north. He turned toward the town of *Gualcince* with just a name to guide him - Reinaldo. Moncho had a mother and several brothers still living in this town. Before he left for the United States, Flaco was determined to inform them of the murderous death of Moncho at the hands of a gringo missionary.

"Did you forget anything?" Helen Eldridge called from the walk-in closet.

"I don't think so," Billy replied, tossing four knit shirts on the bed beside his suitcase. He was accustomed to packing for short business trips, but he had to keep the climate in mind. September in southern California is not yet nippy, but it is considerably cooler than September in southern Honduras. He kept to short sleeves and cotton slacks.

"How do you suppose he is doing?" Helen asked, stepping out of the closet.

"I'll soon find out, I guess," Billy shrugged. "It must be difficult though. I just pray the Lord will give me the wisdom to help him through this. I can't tell you how many times he was there for me."

"I know, Billy," she smiled. "Carey is a good brother. And Anna is sure proof that he is a good father."

"She sure is," Billy nodded. "Does she work tonight?"

"Yes, I told Jenny she could go down to the mall and ride home with Anna tonight since it is Friday. Do you think they'll be OK?" Helen asked.

"I think they'll be just fine. I do want to see Anna before I leave for the airport though. When does she get in from school?" Billy asked, zipping up his shaving kit.

"In about forty five minutes or so," Helen replied, glancing at the clock by the bed.

"Good, I'll still have about three hours before I need to leave," he sighed closing up his suitcase.

"Would you like to have prayer for the trip and for your time with Carey?" Helen offered reaching out to take his hand.

"I would like that very much," he said as they both sat together on the bed.

———

Carey left Mando to his ironwork and began the drive home. He felt encouraged by his friend's words, but more than that, he was beginning to feel at peace again. The good night's rest had helped, but he recognized this peace as that which God sends when he is troubled. It was a gentle reminder that there was no storm greater than that rest of faith when one knows that the Lord is still in control. He slipped a praise tape into the cassette player beside him on the seat and began to sing along. His thoughts wandered back to the late seventies when he had first heard those choruses. It was about that same time he was struggling in his pastorate over the question of missions.

For Carey, the matter of missions was never whether he was willing to go or not, but whether he was called or not. He had learned that the calling determined fruitfulness. As a pastor, he knew that there were many ministry opportunities that he could meet and fill, but talent and ability alone didn't constitute a call. For Carey, the calling was a divine directive that was non-negotiable. But more than that, it was the guarantee of God's grace to fulfill God's bidding. He remembered the Sunday morning service that God made it clear to him to go to the mission field. As the song carried him back to that service, he began to relive with clarity the moment he knew he was to be a missionary.

Susan sat with their newborn, Anna, glowing in the joy of motherhood. The choir had missed her sweet soprano voice, but she was too proud to leave young Anna in the nursery. Carey was expounding eloquently as ever over the faith of Abraham offering up his son Isaac, when he began to digress slightly from his sermon notes. Usually, this caused his delivery to falter somewhat as he searched for words he had not prepared, but this morning the transition was smooth and natural.

"The faith we see in Abraham on the Mount as he offered his son to God was not born that morning. It was conceived over twenty years earlier as he gazed into the stars and heard the promise of God that his seed would outnumber what he saw. It was nurtured in his obedience to go to a land he did not know simply because he was beckoned by Jehovah. He was sent and he followed. . . in faith, for he trusted the hand of the one pointing the way."

As Carey preached, he began to feel the conviction of his own words. The call to any area of ministry is not based on guilt, and Carey understood that. What he felt that morning was not guilt, but rather exhilaration and peace that was unmistakably from God. He did not know how Susan would take to the news, but he knew they needed to talk as soon as possible. To his amazement and to God's credit, her heart had also been touched during the service. Though a young mother, she was prepared to follow her Lord alongside her husband, wherever that took them.

And it had brought them to Honduras, Carey thought refocusing on the road before him. As the tape played on, he drove confidently in the knowledge that it was God and not his own sense of adventure that had brought him to this land. Whatever he would face, God would go before him and with him. He had not left the truck the night of the accident, and He would not leave him now.

―――――

Karen walked into the small boutique and looked around. The subtle instrumental music played softly over the conversations of customers browsing through the racks of jeans. Sheila was in the back room checking the invoice on some new stock. Karen glanced into the full-length mirror beside her adjusting her skirt and scrunching her hair one last time. She took a deep breath and walked into the back room.

"Reporting for work," she announced cheerfully.

"Oh, Karen," Sheila exclaimed looking up from a box of blouses. "So good to see you again. I could use a hand here first and then I'll show you around"

"Great, what do I do?" she asked eagerly.

"Just call out these numbers on the invoice and check them off when I have located them in the box," Sheila said handing her the sheet.

They finished the invoices quickly and Sheila toured the small store with Karen explaining matters of customer courtesy, helping the undecided and how to watch for shoplifters without offending honest customers. After a quick tutorial on the cash register, Karen rang up her first purchase. She complimented the teenager on her purchase and smiled as she handed her the bag. Karen liked this job and it showed. Sheila stood to the side watching in admiration.

"You are a natural," Sheila said as the young girl left the store. "I mean it, you know how to talk to young people and you are sincere. That goes a long way in merchandising. I think you are going to work out just fine."

"Thank you," Karen responded humbly.

"Did you work it out so that you could stay this evening and learn about closing the store?" Sheila asked walking around the counter to Karen.

"Well, kinda," Karen began. "You see, my folks said I could stay, but I lost my ride home today while I was at school. I kinda had a fight with my boyfriend and he was a bit peeved that I started working on Friday nights, and well, you know. . ." she trailed off.

"All too well," Sheila grimaced, but then quickly recovered her smile. "But don't worry, I'll take you home."

"Really, I mean, all the way to Chula Vista?" she asked hopefully.

"Sure," Sheila assured her. "I don't have anyone but a cat waiting for me at home, no problem. After all, we can't be putting you on a bus all the way to Chula Vista at that hour of the night, now can we?"

"Thanks, Sheila," Karen beamed. "This is going to be a great job, I can tell."

Sheila reached out and stroked Karen's hair and smiled. She was like a big sister that Karen never had. She held her gaze on Karen even after the electronic tone announced a new customer entering the store and Karen rushed to greet them.

———

Howard gathered his papers together and placed them into his brief case with a sigh of exhaustion. Diane had left the office at 4:00pm to pick up her younger sister from a music lesson. Rusty had stayed to work on his discipleship class. As Howard walked past his open office door, he tapped softly. Rusty looked up and smiled, waving him in.

"Come on in, I was just finishing my notes for class tomorrow," Rusty said.

"I can't stay, I have to get over to Ed's for the meeting on the building project," Howard said hesitating in the doorway.

"Is Arnie going to be there?" Rusty asked.

"I doubt it," Howard replied. "He said his piece at the last business meeting, and again in my office this morning."

"What is his problem?"

"He believes we are making a grave mistake in the design. He doesn't have a vested interest, because no church member was allowed to bid on the project. I truly believe that he thinks he has the churches best interests in mind, he just is a little hard headed about how to communicate his disagreement," Howard explained.

"Suppose it could have something to do with his problems at home," Rusty said casually.

"What problems at home?"

"I don't know all the details, but it seems their son Alex has been getting into trouble lately. He dropped out of the youth group over four months ago and his name has come up in discipleship class a few times during prayer requests. The youth haven't said what's going on specifically - just that the family needs our prayers," Rusty concluded.

"I had no idea," Howard said half to himself. Suddenly, he felt sorry for Arnie. He could identify with the stress of problems at home. Howard knew how a man's family life could affect his attitude towards almost everything else he works at.

"Well, I guess I had best get on to my meeting. Wish me luck," Howard said turning.

"I don't believe in luck, pastor," Rusty shouted back. "God is either in it or we are trying to do something outside of His will, right?"

Howard heard, but didn't respond. The thought that God might not want this building was not an issue to him. It had been prayed over, voted on and planned thoroughly. It was going to become a reality, in spite of Arnie Johnson.

———

"You knew Moncho well?" the elderly woman asked sadly. Her small shoulders quivered under her shawl.

"*Si, Doña Marta*," Flaco replied humbly. "We were very close. In fact, I was with him the night he died."

"Tell us what happened," flared Ricardo, Moncho's younger brother, but the oldest of the remaining siblings.

"We were walking home," began Flaco sincerely. "It had been raining and many branches had blown down from the trees. We found a large branch in the road and began to move it so that it wouldn't damage any cars coming by. I was on one side of the road and Moncho was on the other. As we were trying to move the branch, headlights came over the hill. The light blinded Moncho and he slipped in the mud rolling down the hill some. Before he could get up, the truck rolled over him like a dog in its way. I was afraid so I hid across the road. I watched them stop the truck and throw his body in the back and drive off. They made up some story and convinced the *policia* that it was an accident, but they didn't even try to stop. After all, one was a gringo and they all think we are nothing."

"A gringo!" exclaimed Ricardo. "My brother was killed by a gringo? We were not told this."

"I am not surprised," Flaco continued. "The murderer didn't even come to see the family. I don't think anybody in town knows the truth. I can not stay there anymore - it sickens me so. I have saved some money and am heading north. Tomorrow, I will cross the border at *Mapulaco* and head for San Salvador."

"We know someone who can help you in San Antonio change your money for *colones*," offered Moises, the next oldest brother. "Do you need a place to sleep tonight?"

"Yes, I do, in fact," Flaco responded pleasantly. "You all are too kind. I wish I could have done more for Moncho."

"You have done plenty," Ricardo said deliberately. "I will take it from here. Moncho's blood will be avenged - I swear it."

"Good night fellows," Howard called to the beleaguered committee members crossing the parking lot to their cars. A few just waved, none spoke. It had not been an easy meeting. Howard opened his briefcase on the hood of his car and took out his roll of antacids and popped two of the chalky tablets into his mouth. He had no idea that a building project could bring about such division. This was one time he was glad the church wasn't voting on everything. When seven men can't agree on the basics, it is certain that four hundred and fifty couldn't, even on a good night. This had been anything but a good night. Howard glanced at his watch. It was 8:15pm and he still had a twenty minute drive home.

Carey helped Susan collect the supper plates and walked with her to the kitchen as the boys switched the channels between various Spanish programs before finally deciding to pop in a video of Andy Griffith episodes that had been sent to them in the mail. As they rounded the corner away from the boys, Carey sat his dishes down carefully and wrapped his arms around Susan from behind almost causing her to spill what drink was left in the plastic cups she carried. He hugged her tight as she stood still and closed her eyes. It was good to have him reaching out again and she didn't want to discourage him. After a few moments, he lessened his grip and she leaned back and kissed him on the cheek.

"I love you too," she said softly. "How did your visit with Mando go today?"

"He wouldn't let me feel sorry for myself," Carey sighed, picking up the dishes again.

"That's because you don't need to," Susan said, setting the cups in the sink. "Besides, your brother arrives tomorrow. That's reason enough for rejoicing. I guess I have to go to market tomorrow and try to find a fattened calf."

Carey smiled. It was good to see him smile again, Susan thought.

"Bert called while you were out," she said changing the subject. "He says he plans to be at the airport by noon. He thought that would give you two some time before Billy's plane comes in."

"I guess I'll need to head out from here by 9:00am at the latest," Carey said sliding his dishes into the sink around his wife. "What do you think he'll want to talk about?"

"I suspect he just wants to see how you are doing?" she replied. "How are you doing?"

"Better," he said confidently wrapping his arms around her waist again. She turned and embraced him tightly. Neither of them heard the boys calling from the den about Barney's funny looking motorcycle. They just held each other close.

———

Luís walked with his cousin Suyapa into the little house as the other believers began to arrive from various directions. An older man took the Coleman lantern filled with kerosene and began priming it with alcohol. Once lit, the glow filled the adobe house, the children gathered first along the side walls on the floor. Nursing mothers took the front benches as the men stood in the back. The service began within fifteen minutes of the appointed hour, which was customary. Luís was not accustomed to punctuality, and neither was the congregation. Even the missionary had given up trying to start the services exactly at 7:00pm. Latin culture is more people center than event oriented. Being there was as important as what you were there for.

The service followed much of the same order that Luís had remembered from the night before. He paid more attention to the words of the songs this time and found himself singing the simpler choruses that were repeated several times. At the scripture readings, he leaned over to look on with Suyapa as she held a flashlight on her Bible. The lantern was helpful for a little more than half the house, but those who stood to the side wall had shadows fall upon the pages of their Bibles. Luís was glad he told his cousin about his experience the night before. He wasn't sure he understood all that had happened, so she had spent most of the afternoon after her school classes explaining about sin and man's need for forgiveness and how Jesus had come to provide that forgiveness on the cross. Much of it was familiar through his Catholic upbringing, but there were some new ideas presented that he had not heard before. He wanted to know more and he now felt

85

comfortable seeking those answers inside the church house instead of lurking in the shadows outside the door.

He wondered if the church would mention Moncho's funeral that had been conducted that afternoon. It was only slightly attended with less than fifteen present - most of which were former drinking partners. Even Roberto from the cantina had not attended. Luís had gone out of respect for the widow. The priest had pronounced the mass mechanically with little inflection in his voice. Even Moncho deserved a "Christian" burial Luís had thought, at the time, but now began to wonder what was "Christian" about the rite. Moncho had died in the mud and was buried alone and no one seemed to care.

"Let us pray," called out the worship leader, drawing Luís back into the service. "Heavenly Father, we praise You for Your love and grace that You have given to us freely in Your Holy Son, Jesus Christ. We pray for those who have suffered loss this week and for their families. And we pray for *Hermano* Carey, that You will let him know that there is still much to do here and that you will send him back to us soon."

As the worship leader continued praying for the sick and the spiritual needs of the community, Luís began to wonder if it would be a good idea for the gringo missionary to return so soon. There had been talk around the cantina that he had driven over Moncho on purpose. Flaco had filled many with his stories before leaving. If the missionary did come back to *Santa Tierra* any time soon, it would difficult to say how some would respond. Some people just need an excuse, and Moncho, liked or not, was now an excuse to oppose the work of the gringo.

———

Howard pulled into the driveway at 8:50pm. He knew Karen wouldn't be back yet from her new job, but already he was beginning to make mental notes of the time so that he would be ready if she were late again. They had agreed on 10:30 and he would not be disobeyed this evening. As he walked through the door, Donna approached him with a full glass of ice tea.

"How was the meeting?" she asked hopefully.

"Rather not talk about it," he said coldly taking the glass from her hand and taking a large swallow.

"Terry is spending the night at Ronnie's," she began, "and Karen is not due in for at least another hour."

"Oh, I expect she will be out for every bit of an hour and thirty five minutes," he replied looking at his watch again.

"All the better," Donna smiled slyly, but Howard did not catch the tone or the inference she was trying to make.

He dropped his briefcase on the base of the stairs, emptied his pockets onto the hall table and walked into the darkened den feeling his way for the TV remote. Donna followed behind dejectedly and turned on the light switch as he found his recliner. He had not noticed the candles in the hallway or on the landing at the top of the stairs. If he had followed the light up to the second floor, he would have found a romantic setting in the master bedroom. Instead, he began surfing the 63 channels provided by his local cable company. Donna sat quietly on the couch till Howard leaned in her direction and asked if there were any supper left that she could warm up.

Donna's own temperature was beginning to warm slightly at this point as she felt the blood rush to her cheeks. What she had prepared for was not going to happen, and what he wanted, she no longer wished to give from her heart. Howard was loosing sight of his family and she didn't know how to call him back. As she placed the casserole dish into the microwave, she began to wonder if she even wanted to make the effort. As she let the dish cool, she noticed the weekly newsletter that lay on the hall table where he had emptied his pockets. She picked it up to see what activities of the next week would keep him busy and away from the family. Among the calendar of events, she noticed an invitation for the ladies of the church to attend a weekend conference on "Being Your Own Woman". The details were scanty, but there would be guest speakers and an emphasis given to self-esteem. Donna had not attended a special conference in years, she recalled. This sounded like something that she needed at this very time. She would find someone who would listen, even if it were a stranger.

"Next Friday, Howard would have to warm up his own dinner," she thought as she carried the hot plate of chicken casserole and beans to the den. Howard took the plate without comment. Donna left the room unnoticed. "This time next week, things are going to begin changing," she said to herself as she climbed the steps to blow out the candles. Little did she realize that they had already begun to change.

———

Sheila pulled her Teal colored Le Baron out of the parking lot of the mall accelerating quickly even though there was little traffic in the boulevard. She pushed in a CD of nature sounds over soft piano music and blew a puff of smoke toward the visor. Karen had become accustomed to the smoking by now and didn't turn her head away.

"Does the smoke bother you?" Sheila asked politely.

"Oh, no. It's just that I don't . . ." Karen's voice trailed off.

"I find it relaxes me," Sheila mused. "After a full day at the store, all I want to do is unwind and relax."

Karen nodded in agreement.

"What do you do to relax?" Sheila asked.

"Oh, I don't know," Karen started. "Mostly listen to my music, maybe read some."

"You like to dance?" Sheila asked without looking in Karen's direction.

"Sure," Karen smiled. "I go to the school dances when I can. My father. . :" Karen stopped herself and thought through what she was about to say and changed her mind. Sheila didn't look like the church type and she didn't want to take a chance at offending her on the first day of work.

"Your father. . ." Sheila continued for her.

"Oh, just that my father has this curfew thing, and I try to comply."

"Have you ever been dancing at a club?" Sheila asked curtly.

"No. I'm not old enough," Karen replied.

"You look old enough," Sheila said temptingly.

For the rest of the drive home, Karen began to think of all the things she "felt" old enough for, but was still being denied. Karen was beginning to like Sheila more for her spirit of adventure and maturity. Sheila drove confidently through the city weaving her way into Karen's life.

———

Billy heard the front door open and walked out of the den to greet Anna as she locked the dead bolts behind her. Anna was a quiet girl who demonstrated courtesy and consideration for others. She was somewhat independent though she didn't drive. She had arrived in the states late in the summer and had missed the opportunity to take driver's training. Though eighteen, she had not gotten her license in Honduras and would not receive one in California till she passed driver's class. But living in both Costa Rica and Honduras had made taking the bus a common experience. In fact, it was easier in California, because there was almost always a seat and never did a person sit down next to her holding a chicken. The bookstore where she worked closed promptly at 9:00pm and the bus ride home took roughly twenty-five minutes. She seldom entered the house any later than ten o'clock, even on the weekend. She was an early riser and her work did not seem to interfere with classes. She only worked four days a week (never on Sunday) and they were usually spread out enough that she could still be active in youth activities of her church.

Uncle Billy treated Anna like a second daughter. He and Carey were only brothers and they had grown up just four years apart. When the decision came for Anna to seek schooling in the states, Billy all but insisted that she be allowed to stay with him and his family. Billy worked as a program manager for a small computer company. His wife, Helen, worked for a realty company, but was home every afternoon when their daughter Jenny came home from ninth grade. Anna was a good role model for Jenny and her presence was not a threat. Jenny knew her father's love, just as Anna knew hers. But being separated still had its moments of difficulty.

"How was work?" Uncle Billy called from the hallway.

"Busy, but then most Friday nights are," she said tiredly.

She noticed his packed bag near the door. It had not dawned on her that he would have to leave late that evening to arrive in Houston for the flight the next day to Honduras.

"You flying out tonight?" she asked.

"Got to, Anna," he replied. "The flight out of Houston is 8:00am tomorrow. This way, I arrive by midday in Honduras."

He motioned for her to come stand beside him. As she walked over, he opened wide his arms to hug her. "This is from your father," he said holding her tight. "Now, do you have anything you want me to deliver to him?"

She melted in his arms and squeezed him back. "Give him one of these for me," she said almost crying.

"I tell you what," he said, thinking out loud. "Do you work Monday night?"

"Yes, I don't get in till 9:30 or so," she said looking up at him.

"Well, I know for a fact, that there is just one hour difference between there and here now, so . . . why don't I call here at about 10:45 their time and you be waiting here by the phone so you can talk to your Dad?"

"Oh could you," she squealed, then quickly covered her mouth so as not to disturb the rest of the house.

"You just be here," Uncle Billy smiled. "I missed having you here when I called on Thursday, we'll just make up for it on Monday."

Anna hugged him again with excitement. She thanked him and bounded off to her room. Billy turned back toward the den. He still had two hours before going to the airport and didn't feel like going to sleep. He would have time for that on the plane. He had mixed emotions about the trip. He had not told Anna about the accident yet, and he wasn't sure if keeping it from her was a good idea. He wanted to talk to Carey first and see if he wanted to break the news to her himself. If not, he would tell her after he returned. As far as she knew, he was just going down for a visit because it had been so long. Billy had no idea just how important his visit was going to be.

———

Adam passed the wall clock as he ambled down the hall to the bathroom. He noticed the light on in the den. Another midnight prayer vigil he softly said to himself, though it was a quarter to one. He decided not to call out to Gertie as he passed the doorway. Her head was bowed but her lips were forming intercessions that only God would hear. He smiled and continued on down the hall. He would let her sleep in again in the morning. After all, it was Saturday - already, in fact.

Gertie prayed for over an hour before raising her head. When she did, she noticed Adam's Sunday school teacher's book on the arm of his chair. She picked it up and began to read some of his notes in the margin. She remembered their discussion over Exodus 32:1 - 14 earlier that week, but now he was covering verses 31 and 32 of that same chapter where Moses prayed for God's mercy over Israel. She noticed that Adam had written in the margin. "Prayer for is 'in behalf of' not 'in place of'; intercessory prayer must accompany a call for repentance". As she read on, she found a pencil note at the top of the next page: "Moses offered himself for punishment for their sin. We must be so burdened for the lost we would trade our salvation for theirs!" Gertie closed the quarterly and slumped back against the couch.

"Lord," she began, "I'm confused. Am I praying for Carey because of sin or because of attack?" She closed her eyes and sat still. Before long she was reminded of the other family for which she was praying. It became clear she was praying for both needs. One family was under attack, and one family was in sin. She knew she did not know all the details, but God did. He would reveal what He needed, when He needed. She had been summoned to pray and she continued faithfully.

Chapter Nine:

"The Brother"

(Saturday)

The roosters began singing as early as 3:00am in *Gualcince* calling to one another from each side of the town. Flaco was used to the crowing and slept soundly till nearly 4:30am when the women of the house began stirring to prepare the masa for the morning tortillas. Flaco pulled the sheet around his neck. It was colder in the mornings here than in *Santa Tierra*. The family had given him one of the beds, consisting of a frame covered with tightly woven strips of straw upon which to lie. The sheet had been taken from the bed of Moisés. Flaco had used his backpack with his clothing for a pillow. He had been careful to take the pistol from his pocket and place it in the backpack before lying down.

As Flaco stretched, he heard whispering from the other side of the adobe wall. He lay still and listened as Ricardo firmly advised his mother of his decision to go to *Santa Tierra* and find the man that had killed her son.

"I don't want you to go," she said through tired eyes.

"Mamá, this man kills your son - my brother - and you say let him go?" Ricardo exclaimed raising his voice. "I can't let it go. He must pay for what he has done."

"But I need you here," she pleaded. "The rains have started and we must plant now or we will lose our corn. You are the oldest - you must stay."

"I can start the planting, but Moisés is old enough to finish it with the others," he said lowering his voice calmly. "He can show them what to do after I show him. I will work till Monday, but then I will go to find this murderer and avenge our brother."

"It won't bring him back," she said, showing the sorrow once again in her voice.

"Maybe not, but it is justice Mamá," he said with finality in his.

Flaco realized he had just condemned a man to death by his story. It was not a lie, he told himself - just most of the truth. There was no need for Moncho's family to know that he died a drunken thief who would have committed murder that night had he had the chance. Flaco did not know the missionary and therefore felt no sorrow for him. He was just another rich *gringo* that had come to his country to take from their land or change their ways of living - both of which he disdained. The only reason Flaco wanted to go to their land was to rob back from them part of what they had taken.

He rose from the bed and stepped outside into the fading twilight. The pale blue of the morning sky would lighten even more before the sun would ever peak over the high mountain ranges to the east. The walk to *Mapulaca* was all down hill and there he would find the narrow *Lempe* River that separated Honduras from El Salvador. He would wait till the tortillas were ready and have a good breakfast and coffee before starting his journey. He would need his strength for the walk and the long bus ride to San Salvador.

––––––

"How about some pancakes this morning," Adam called from the kitchen.

The teakettle shaped clock read 6:40am and Adam had already showered and shaved. There was no sleeping in for the Baxter's, even on Saturday. When Gertie did not reply, Adam stepped towards the doorway and called a little louder in the direction of the bedroom. There was still no response. He set down the mixing bowl of Biscuit and briskly walked to the bedroom door. He tapped lightly and opened the door to see Gertie huddled in the comforter on her side of the bed. He called again, but she still did not respond. He stepped around the mahogany posts of the bed frame to her side and bent down close to her face.

"Honey," he called quietly, "Gertie, are you OK?"

Her eyelids fluttered gently and she focused on his face.

"Oh, Adam," she said, "Could I have just a few more minutes? I don't know when I got to bed this morning, but it hasn't been that long."

"Sure sweetie," he smiled and sighed. "You just stay in that bed as long as you want. I'll have some pancakes ready when you are."

"Thanks, dear," she yawned. "I'll let you know when I'm ready."

Adam tip toed out of the room and closed the door softly behind him.

"This makes three nights in a row she has been up late," he thought to himself. "Whatever this burden is, I hope it is resolved soon. She's not as young as she used to be."

He walked back to the kitchen and placed a lid on the mixing bowl and put it in the refrigerator. He would settle for toast till she got up. It was no fun eating pancakes alone. He picked up the morning paper and glanced at the weather forecast on the front page. A cold front was heading their way. He opened to the expanded report to see just how low the temps would be getting for Sunday morning. He did not want to miss his class, but he needed to be careful about getting Gertie out. If it was too cold, she might best stay in, especially if she had not been getting her sleep and her resistance was down. He worried about Gertie, but he knew he could never dissuade her from her prayer time. He would just have to leave her in the Lord's hands. In his heart, he knew there was no better place for her to be.

When the sun did finally rise in Choluteca, Josh and Caleb ignored it completely and covered their heads with lightweight blankets. Saturdays were for sleeping in. Homeschool classes may finish earlier in the day and demand less "busy work" in the afternoon, but it was still school and Saturdays were still Saturdays.

Susan started her day gently rocking with a cup of Honduran coffee and her devotional. She enjoyed the quiet of the morning before the boys began their displays of energy. She had to admit that having teenagers in a third world country had its advantages. Most of their activity was directed toward the home instead of away from it. They still shared the exciting details of their lives with their parents and enjoyed "family time" together. But she still treasured the early mornings when she could be alone.

Carey entered the room without disturbing Susan, knowing how much she valued these moments to herself. He walked past her to the kitchen and found the biscuits still warm in the oven. He prepared a light breakfast of fruit and biscuits and sat at the kitchen table to eat. He picked up the Bible that one of the boys had left on the table and instinctively opened it in the middle to read from the Psalms. The binding gave way easily to the center section and the pages parted at Psalm 64. Carey began to read quietly to himself from Josh's New International Version:

[1] Hear me, O God, as I voice my complaint;
protect my life from the threat of the enemy.
[2] Hide me from the conspiracy of the wicked,
from that noisy crowd of evildoers.
[3] They sharpen their tongues like swords
and aim their words like deadly arrows.
[4] They shoot from ambush at the innocent man;
they shoot at him suddenly, without fear.
[5] They encourage each other in evil plans,
they talk about hiding their snares;
they say, "Who will see them?"
[6] They plot injustice and say,
"We have devised a perfect plan!"
Surely the mind and heart of man are cunning.
[7] But God will shoot them with arrows;
suddenly they will be struck down.
[8] He will turn their own tongues against them
and bring them to ruin;
all who see them will shake their heads in scorn.

[9] All mankind will fear;
they will proclaim the works of God
and ponder what he has done.
[10] Let the righteous rejoice in the LORD
and take refuge in him;
let all the upright in heart praise him! [1]

The words leapt with pertinence from the thin paper on which they were printed. This was not a happen chance scripture reading. This was the Word of God for Carey Eldridge. Suddenly, the events of two night's prior fell into focus. An evil man had devised a "perfect plan" that God Himself had turned against him. But it was not over. Carey must still face those who would be speaking out against him. Truth may be on his side, but truth not believed is as good as a lie to those you try to convince. How could he make the people of *Santa Tierra* believe the truth? Should he even try? As he was pondering these questions, Susan walked in with her empty coffee cup ready for her day.

"Good morning, sweet heart," she said cheerfully. "Excited about Billy coming in today?"

"Yes," he said hesitantly, still reflecting over the scripture he had just read.

"You don't sound very excited," she mused.

"Oh, I was just still thinking about this passage in the Psalms I was reading."

"What does it say," she asked pouring him a cup of coffee.

"It talks about how God watches out for us when evil people try to set traps against us and how many times, they fall into their own snares. I guess that is what happened to me on the road from *Santa Tierra*. God was watching out for Mando and I, and the man who laid a trap for us fell into it himself." Carey said the last words slowly and with deliberation reliving the moment in his mind.

"I think you are right," she said understandingly. "When Billy gets here, I think you should tell him everything you are feeling and not try to pretend that everything is OK. He is your brother and he knows you well enough to offer some solid advice on what to do at this point."

She handed him the coffee and he looked up into her eyes. This was not over and what lie ahead may be more difficult to face than the body he had carried to the authorities. Carey looked back down at the Bible and whispered a silent prayer.

---

[1] *The New International Version*, (Grand Rapids, MI: Zondervan Publishing House) 1984

"Lord, I need Your grace to face the town again."

———

Moisés walked with Flaco to the river's edge. The *Lempe* River was not swift. It was a narrow physical border between El Salvador and Honduras. Merchants from both countries waded across this spot to carry blankets and pottery to sell on the other side. It was not considered an immigration threat since most returned to their prospective country that evening or the next day - it was just business. But it was also unpatrolled and that gave Flaco one less border hassle. He would follow the footpath on the other side to Victoria, a small pueblo. From there he would ask directions to *Sensiente Peque* where he could find a bus direct to San Salvador. On Saturday morning, the busses would be full and there would be less chance of a police stop checking resident papers. Flaco would exchange some of his currency for Salvadorian *colones* in *Sensiente Peque*, but he would wait till he got to San Salvador to buy dollars with the rest. Dollars would buy him currency in each of the countries he would pass easier than the exchange of the neighboring country. Flaco figured he had enough lempiras from the sell of the truck and from what he stole from Felípe to convert for almost two thousand dollars. This would be more than enough to get him all the way to the United States.

As he rolled up his pants legs, Moisés held his backpack. They had not spoken much during the long walk down to the river. Moisés was a young man of twenty-three, yet still unmarried. He had finished more schooling than either of his older brothers. He aspired to leave *Gualcinse*, but not the way Moncho had, fleeing in the night to escape the machete of a family bent on vengeance. He wanted to go to the city of San Pedro Sula and learn a trade that would earn him enough money that he could live well and still send support to his mother. Moisés was a dreamer.

"Your pack is heavy, amigo," Moisés said, trying to make conversation. He was unaware of the gun inside.

"All I own is in that bag," Flaco responded, taking it from him and strapping it on his back.

"Do you know which way after you cross the river?" Moisés offered helpfully.

"I take that path there," he pointed with his lips. "And then follow the people coming and going till I get to Victoria. From there I will ask directions."

"*Está bien*," he nodded. "I guess I will head back then."

"Thank you for bringing me this far," Flaco said sincerely, extending his hand for Moisés to take. He then casually asked, "Did I hear that Ricardo is thinking about going to *Santa Tierra* to find the gringo that killed Moncho?"

"Yes," he said disturbed. "I wish I could go, but Mamá needs me here to see to the planting."

"Just as well," Flaco said. "Vengeance is best in the hands of the elder."

Moisés did not reply, but he thought to himself, "I would not be afraid to avenge my brother - not even with a gringo."

———

The Pennington house did not stir much on Saturday mornings. Howard guarded that time for himself. He didn't even like to start home projects until late in the morning. Donna didn't prepare a breakfast, because she knew her crew would eat, sometimes, hours apart from one another. Terry played video games in his room because he felt too old for the cartoons. Karen made a point of sleeping in.

Donna found herself in a quiet kitchen staring blankly at the pastel designs in the wallpaper while cradling a mug of coffee. Her gaze panned down to the table where the newsletter announcing the upcoming retreat lay on the kitchen table. She picked it up to read again. There was a phone number to call in order to register that she did not recognize. It was not the church office number. She studied the description of the retreat again. First Baptist Church of Coronado was large enough that Howard would not necessarily know about all of its activities. Rusty had probably scheduled these speakers and promoted this retreat, she thought to herself. She fingered the newsletter and then gently folded it in half and placed it in her skirt pocket. She sipped the warm coffee and began to smile. The day was looking better already.

———

Flaco asked if he could pay for his meal in *lempiras*. Being a border town, *Sensiente Peque* was used to doing business with both Hondurans and El Salvadorians. He wanted to wait till he was in the capital before converting enough *lempiras* to *colones* to make the trip through El Salvador. He would try to find a moneychanger that would give him dollars for the rest. Dollars would be easier to exchange in both Guatemala and Mexico. The farther he got from Honduras the less his money would be worth. He figured he had enough *lemps* to buy between $1,500 and $2,000 in US currency. That would be more than enough for the journey north. Getting out of El Salvador would take about $150 including the coyote. His bus ride from *Sensiente Peque* to San Salvador would take a rough three hours but would only cost about $10.00 worth of *colones*. He would probably be able to pay in *lemps* for that ride as well. From San Salvador, he would find a direct bus going to *Ahuachapan* along the Pan American highway. Though probably the easiest leg of his journey, it would be one of the most dangerous because checkpoint stations would sometimes board busses to check everyone's passport. He was traveling without papers and with a gun. That was not a good combination in any country. After *Ahuachapan*, he would find a smaller bus on a back road to *Agua Fria* where he could cross the border with a coyote undetected.

Flaco walked out of the little *comedor* where he had eaten and began navigating through the market toward the smell of diesel where the busses gathered to spill their morning travelers and gorge themselves with those anxious to head for the capital city. He found one two thirds full that would be leaving as soon as the driver felt he had enough passengers. There was no hesitation or question when Flaco offered the driver's assistant fifty *lempiras*, which when exchanged in the capital would be twenty *colones* more than the fare. Flaco found a seat near the back of the bus where he could nestle up against the window and go to sleep. He had nearly a week of traveling ahead of him and with a little luck, he might just make southern California with enough dollars to start a new life. As the bus rumbled and began to vibrate it's way out of the market; he looked back at the hills across the *Lempe* River to *Mapulaca* and said good-bye to Honduras. Who would have thought that only three days ago, he lived in a nowhere town, without money or work, drinking beer with friends that had no prospects of ever being more than they were that night. Now, one was dead, one was bound by his own apprehension, and one was free to make his life rise above the hand he had been dealt. With Moncho's gun and Felípe's money, nothing stood between Flaco and his dream. So he turned away from the Honduran hills of his home and looked northward.

———

As Carey maneuvered the curves through the mountains between the south of Honduras and its capital, Tegucigalpa, he began to feel the anticipation of seeing his younger brother again. Carey glanced at his watch and made a mental note of where he was on the mountain. He had made the trip so many times he could calculate within three minutes when he would pull into the airport parking lot. He was trying to arrive by 11:00 so that he and Bert would have plenty of time to talk before Billy's plane set down. He had not spoken with any of the other families in the mission, though he felt confident that the others around the country had heard by now. Like Carey, not all the missionaries had access to email, but all had phones and the mission prayer chain was set up for just this kind of crisis. The fact that no one had called in the last two days was more due to deference than indifference. They were waiting to hear from Bert about how Carey was doing first.

Carey pulled into the airport at 10:58 and saw Bert's Tercel parked in the shade of a large Famosa tree. Bert stepped out from the front of his car where he had been leaning and walked toward Carey's pick-up. Suddenly, Carey felt a wave of anxiety sweep over him as he found himself unable to open his own door. Bert took the lead and climbed up into the cab of the truck and extended his arm. Carey unbuckled his shoulder harness and let Bert give a sympathetic embrace. After an eternal moment, the two men straightened up and wiped their eyes.

"It's been a long three days Bert," Carey began. "I don't know what I would have done without Susan. Thanks so much for your call also."

"I wish I could have gotten with you sooner, but I knew you needed a little time also. I am just so glad this meeting isn't taking place in a jail cell. I still don't understand that one," Bert said shaking his head. "That in itself is nothing short of a miracle."

"I know," Carey replied taking a deep breath.

For the next twenty minutes, Carey painfully relived the ordeal on the mountain road. Bert took mental notes so that he could accurately relate the details to the mission board. There would not be a formal inquiry, but a report would need to be given. When Carey finished, Bert paused for a few additional moments of silence to allow for closure. Then he lifted Carey's face slowly to look him in the eye and said slowly, "Now I want to share something you may not have known."

"Four years ago, while you all were on furlough, Mike had an accident returning from Bible classes in *Trujillo*. A drunk walked right off a bridge into the path of his truck. He was an elderly man and was hospitalized through the night, but didn't make it. Mike was held nearly two days until witnesses came forward and shared that the man stepped out in front of his vehicle."

Bert paused to take a breath.

"We don't hide these things," he went on. "We just don't rehearse them over and over – if for no other reason, than for our own sake. The rest of the mission was made aware and we had a special time of prayer and comfort for Mike and Peggy at our next gathering. He had a tremendous time working through it and almost left the field. By time you all returned, it was no longer talked about. What I am saying, Carey, and hear me clear, is that you are not the first, nor will you be the last that this type of tragedy will befall while on the mission field."

Carey lowered his eyes. Although the words were meant to encourage, his heart was saddened to think that a friend of his and colleague had gone through the same horrible experience. Bert read his face and took a deep breath.

"What's more Carey, I know what I am talking about because. . ." Bert paused and straightened up. "Because I had a similar tragedy in Mexico before we transferred to Honduras."

"You?" Carey responded in disbelief. "I never. . ."

"Many don't," Bert added. "And those that do know, don't bring it up. Maybe we need to more than we do – I don't know. What I do know is how you are feeling right now, and what confusion you are in. You are doubting everything from your purpose in being here to your very call as a missionary. You feel like both the victim and the criminal and you aren't sure if you can go back to *Santa Tierra* and face the people there again. You question God and maybe yell at Him some for letting this happen to you and then you feel guilty for that. You're probably depressed to the point of wanting to just go back to the states on the same plane your brother is coming in on, but deep down you know you still belong here. Carey, I can't tell you what God's will is for your life, but I can tell you this. It didn't change that night on a muddy road. Whatever God has for your life and whatever His call for you was last week, it has not changed because this man has died."

Bert stopped to let the words sink in and realized Carey had been caught up in Bert's passion as he spoke. No one had talked firmly to Carey yet, and that was something he needed to hear.

"So what do I do now?" Carey asked sincerely, hoping Bert would be equally wise in his counsel with him.

"I'm afraid I can't answer that one for you. You have some things to work through. But I believe God has not forsaken you and will give you clear direction."

"He started this morning during my quiet time," Carey began and continued by sharing the Psalm he had read at his breakfast table.

"I'm beginning to see the accident in a different light. That helps with the guilt, I guess, but I'm still struggling with the reason and what will happen because of it."

"Are you worried more about the work or your own safety?" Bert asked.

"I'm not sure. . . both I suppose," Carey responded honestly. "I mean, I know there will be folks in *Santa Tierra* that will not understand and will hate me for what has happened, not the least, his family. There may be physical danger involved there, I don't know, but I think I fear most for the small congregation there. It doesn't take much bad publicity in a small town to kill a work."

"Then we will make that a matter of prayer, as well as your personal safety. Do you mind if I share the details of the accident with the mission and your concerns for *Santa Tierra*?"

"Of course not," Carey affirmed. "I know they will understand, and after what you have shared, perhaps they will understand more than I thought. Have them pray for Susan and the boys as well. I have yet to sit down with Josh and Caleb to explain everything. I'm hoping that having my brother Billy will make it easier for the boys."

"I understand, and totally agree." Bert looked toward the western hills surrounding the capital where the planes usually appear first. "And it won't be long now, will it?"

"No, thank the Lord," Carey sighed. The two men sat quietly in the truck watching the clouds begin to breach allowing the sun to fill the cab with both light and warmth. Both were greatly appreciated.

———

Luís had slept in late for a Saturday. He knew there was work he could be doing in the fields above *Santa Tierra* with his cousins, but he wasn't in any hurry to join them. The recent rains had made the ground soft and the pulling of weeds from the corn stalks would be easier. But the sun had come out and the humidity would be heavier today because of all the rain and he knew that by mid morning it would be slow going even for those used to the heat.

He chose to visit his uncle the carpenter instead and see if he had some work he could do around the shop. When he arrived, he noticed his cousin *Suyapa* preparing masa for the tortillas that would be served with lunch. As she ground the lime-soaked corn kernels, Luís stepped around the corner of the adobe home to greet her.

"*Buenos dias, prima*, (cousin)" he called from behind.

Suyapa turned, startled at first and then smiled. "Luís, what brings you here?"

He stepped around the grinder and greeted her with a light kiss to the cheek.

"I thought I would see if your father could use some help today. To be honest, I didn't want to go to the fields."

"It is going to be hotter today," she replied returning to her work. "I wanted to tell you that I am glad you are coming to the services at the church. What do you think about them?"

"They are good," Luís replied more enthusiastically than Suyapa had anticipated. "I enjoy the singing and the messages also."

"You know we have Bible study on Sunday mornings around 10:00. Would you like to come and learn more about the Bible? I know you had many questions yesterday that I couldn't answer."

"I think I would like that," Luís responded positively.

"Usually the missionary comes on Sunday morning, but we are not sure if he will come this Sunday." Suyapa let her words trail off though each knew why he might not come. Luís knew more than his cousin, but he was not prepared to talk about it. Suyapa only knew what rumors had floated around the small town.

"Even if he doesn't," she quickly added, "Hermano Carlos, who has been preaching is good and knows much about the Bible."

"Is that the older man who preached?" Luís asked.

"Yes, he has known the Lord for nearly 30 years."

"Then he must know a lot of the Bible. I think I would like to come and learn some more stories," Luís smiled. "Now where can I find your father? I better find some work today."

Suyapa pointed to the house across the yard from them. "He is making a door for the Garcias. You can help him there, I think."

"Thank you, Suyapa. I will see you tomorrow at the little church up the road."

Luís stepped over the loose strand of barbed wire that separated the properties and looked for his uncle. This was looking like a good day after all.

––––––

"Sis, it's for you!" called Terry from the hall. "Telephone!"

Karen looked at the clock beside her bed. "Who could be calling at 10:30 on a Saturday morning?" she thought to herself. She reached for the Snoopy phone on her nightstand and gave a groggy greeting.

"*Buen dia, mi amor,*" began the Latin voice. "I trust you slept well."

"Fernando?" Karen countered. "What are you doing up? And why are you calling so early?"

"I wanted to catch you before you took off for your new job. You are working today also aren't you?"

It was the tone of the "also" that opened Karen's eyes.

"Yes, I work today ALSO, but not till this afternoon," she replied coldly.

"Then you work again, TONIGHT?" he exclaimed. "I thought we were going out tonight?"

"Change of plans, I'm afraid," Karen replied matter-of-factly. She was not making this any easier and her voice revealed she was not interested in trying to work it out.

"That's fine," he said with a sharp sense of finality. "I will be making other plans myself then."

"Fine!" she snapped back. She didn't wait for him to hang up in her ear, but resolutely placed the receiver back into Snoopy's hand. She rolled back into her covers and tried to release from her anger. But she couldn't.

———

"I thought you were going to stay in bed all day," Adam gently said to Gertie as she pushed her way into the den. "In fact, you gave me quite a scare this morning when I couldn't rouse you at first."

"I'm sorry sweetheart," she sighed, easing herself onto the couch. "I was up very late again last night, I'm afraid."

"Do you want some pancakes?" he offered. "I saved the batter. We could have a late brunch if you would like?"

"That would be nice. But don't stop what you're working on."

"I was just finishing up my lesson for tomorrow on Moses and his prayers of intercession. Would you like to hear what I found this morning, while you were sleeping?"

"You know I do," she smiled.

Adam shuffled through his legal sheets until he found the notes he was looking for. "Here it is," he said, pulling out the yellow sheet and scanning it with his bifocals.

"In Exodus 32:32, Moses prays for God to forgive the great sin of Israel, and if necessary, to 'blot me out of the book you have written'".

"That's serious," Gertie observed.

"That's right. Intercessory prayer is a serious undertaking. Moses was willing to trade places with the people he was praying for - his burden was that great. I don't know if I have ever been burdened enough when praying for others, that I would be willing to take their punishment."

"But that is exactly what the Lord Jesus did for us," Gertie pointed out. "When he prayed for Jerusalem and their unbelief, he was just a couple days from giving his life for the city he was praying for."

Adam laid his papers down and looked into the eyes of his bride.

"Gertie, when you pray, are you putting yourself in the place of those you pray for?"

"Like you pointed out in your study, we can't pray "instead of", we can only pray "on behalf of", but if we are not willing to be involved in their lives and the outcome of those lives, we are simply mouthing rituals. I hurt for Carey and I strive in prayer for this other family not knowing what the details in either case are. I give up my sleep because my master asks me to. If I am to be spent in prayer for others, I have been spent well, don't you think?"

Adam swallowed hard and walked to the couch to hug his Gertie. She was the living lesson he could only try to communicate through inadequate words the next morning. It occurred to him that the world would never know the mighty army of prayer warriors that waged a spiritual affront from their closets. In that sense, the church could use more "closet Christians".

———

The hardest part of meeting arrivals at the Toncontin International Airport in Tegucigalpa Honduras is waiting outside the door while family and friends figure their way through immigrations and customs without the benefit of knowing the Spanish language. For the first time traveler it could be intimidating. Fortunately, Bill Eldridge had traveled abroad before and knew how to find the non-resident line for immigration and then reclaim his luggage and proceed to the waiting customs inspectors. Also in his favor was his proficiency in packing light. He had one small suitcase and one carry-on filled with Spanish New Testaments. He had unpacked them from their box so that they could be carried easier. When he opened the bag for the customs inspector, he realized the quantity might appear suspicious. Without hesitation, he offered one to the customs agent, who looked at it carefully and then opened it to find his own language. He glanced up with a pleased smile and began to hand it back to the North American. Billy shook his head and pointed to the man's shirt pocket.

"I brought them to give away. Please keep it," he proclaimed with gusto in a language the agent couldn't understand. But his smile conveyed the message clearly.

"Gracias, Señor," the agent replied as he found it fit comfortably in his breast pocket.

With his passport processed and his luggage claims stamped, Billy grabbed his bags and exited the airport doors to be met by a throng of Latin faces waiting anxiously behind a four-foot metal banister. Standing behind the crowd head and shoulders over most of them beamed the smiling face of his brother Carey. Billy made his way around the railing and dropped his bags at their feet while the two men joined in a long needed hug.

Before Carey could warn him, a twelve-year-old boy grabbed up his bags offering to carry them to the truck. Carey started to take the bags away from the boy, when Billy assured him it was OK. They walked together to the truck and as Billy took the load from the young man, he opened his carry-on and took out another New Testament. Reaching into his wallet, he slid a folded dollar bill into the small Bible and handed it to the boy. Before they could open their doors to the front of the cab, six young boys gathered around Billy asking for money, some in broken English, while some in Spanish. Some asked for dollars, while the younger ones just used the local expression for twenty cents in their own currency. Carey smiled and let his younger brother stutter to the growing crowd in loud slow expressions. When it was apparent the situation was going to get out of control, Carey stepped in with his firm yet polite command that there was no more need for help and no more money to give. He ushered Billy quickly into the passenger door and closed it behind him. None of the boys followed Carey to his side, but rather clustered at the window of the "new gringo" knowing that he would feel guilty if he didn't roll down his window and give them all something. Billy looked into their eyes and began to discern between need and greed. As Carey inched the truck carefully away from the persistent group, Billy looked back to see the young luggage carrier showing his friends the new Bible.

"Did I do something wrong back there?" he asked innocently.

"You never do wrong when you plant a seed. You just have to recognize the difference between soil and birds."

"I guess it takes a while," Billy said settling back in his seat. "They all look needy when you first get off the plane."

"I know. Man, it is good seeing you again," Carey exclaimed, changing the subject.

"Roger that, brother. I wish I could have gotten here sooner."

"Susan is going to be so glad to see you. And the boys, I guess you haven't seen them since . . ."

"Josh was eleven and Caleb was nine!" Billy completed for him. "And that was just for a short time during the holidays while you guys were on furlough on the East Coast."

"That's right, they didn't come in with me when I brought Anna to you all in California last year. That reminds me, how is my precious baby?" Carey beamed, turning into traffic and heading for the road south out of town.

"You have one fine daughter there, big brother. She has never argued once with us or with Jenny. She is extremely well mannered and seems to be doing well with her classes in school. She has a job working at the Bible bookstore at the mall near our home. One of our deacons runs the store and gave her a job. Let's see, what else . . ." Billy paused teasingly. "Oh yes, she misses her family more than she will say, but I can tell, she really misses her Dad."

Carey stared ahead at the road to fight back the tear. "You tell her I miss her too and give her a big hug for me when you see her again."

The two reminisced as the Hilux wound its way through the mountain curves. Billy commented how few American-made vehicles were on the road. It seemed most drove Japanese makes. After about twenty minutes of casual conversation, Carey took a breath and began.

"I guess you would like to hear about the accident on Wednesday night?"

"Whenever you feel ready to talk about it, Carey," Billy replied. "I want you to be comfortable. It can wait if you prefer."

"No, I think I would rather get to it before we get home," Carey said thinking out loud. "I still haven't told the boys about everything and I would rather you be fully aware of the details before I try to do that."

"Like I said on the phone, brother, I'm right here with you."

"I am so glad you came," Carey said looking across the seat at Billy. "Where do I begin?"

For the next thirty-five minutes, Carey relived that night again. It had helped to share the story with Bert earlier, but Carey had to take more time to explain things that Bert already understood about the area and the culture. Billy listened without interruption and sighed with Carey when it became difficult to talk. Billy knew how hard it was for Carey to repeat the events and noticed his tenseness as he drove. After Carey concluded, Billy let a few moments pass before speaking.

"Have you been back to the area yet?" Billy asked

"No!" Carey sounded surprised by the question. "I'm not even sure if it is safe for me to return."

"How do you intend to find out?" Billy was already trying to pull Carey past the accident to the present.

"I hadn't thought about it much. Like I said, I've been kind of stunned and a bit numb the last couple days."

"Have you been depressed?" Billy was cutting to the chase.

"I think so. Partly out of guilt and partly out of fear," Carey confessed.

"Both of which are working against you and not for you."

"My friend Mando told me the same thing."

"He's wise. Is he the same man that was with you that night?" Billy asked.

"Yes. At first I thought he would not want to associate with me any more, but it was just the opposite."

"The devil's lies are usually just the opposite from God's truth," Billy pointed out. "We tend to let our imaginations dictate our circumstances more than the truth. Chances are, Mando is ready to go back to *Tierra Santa*. The question is – are you?"

"I don't know," Carey sighed honestly. "I don't know what I would do there if everyone thinks of me as a murderer."

"Well, you won't know till you go, but I have a rather unusual proposition for you to consider."

"What would that be little brother?"

"Go first to the widow and apologize for the accident and offer some kind of restitution for hers and the family's loss."

Carey didn't respond for nearly a full minute. He was processing his brother's words. To this moment, the thought of going to the widow had never crossed his mind. He realized that it should have, but he had mostly been thinking of his own fears than their needs. The suggestion was not unreasonable, in fact, it was the most conscientious thing he could do next.

As he allowed the words to sink in, his eyes trained on the approaching curve. Out of habit, Carey edged his car toward the shoulder when suddenly two semi-tractor trailers appeared head-on approaching them on the downgrade. The one to their left had five of his eighteen wheels on the opposite shoulder. Beside him, straddling the centerline, was a second rig carrying a refrigerated trailer of fruit from the coast. The sight of the two large trucks caused Billy to grab the front of the dash and stare wild-eyed through the passenger side of the windshield. Carey casually eased his two tires completely onto the shoulder and rounded the curve as the passing truck continued between the two vehicles. When the two trucks had passed safely, Carey eased back into his lane and continued uphill.

"Does that happen often?" Billy asked hesitantly.

"More than you might wish to think," Carey replied nonchalantly. "The unwritten rule is: 'if there is room for three, there is room to pass'. The trick is, everyone tends to expect it, so it doesn't catch you by surprise. As long as the two outside vehicles make room, the passing vehicle will be able to make his move and nobody gets hurt."

"What if there is three trucks?"

"That can be touchy," Carey smiled.

As they continued on up the hill, Billy looked to the side of the road and asked, "And what if there are people on the shoulder."

Carey glanced over to his brother with a serious look.

"Then the driver has a difficult decision to make."

Chapter Ten:

"The Challenge"

Perhaps the most noticeable characteristic that Anna Eldridge possessed was her pleasantness. It was seen through her courtesy and manners, and through her smile. Her bright auburn hair was just a shade less red than her father's was in his prime. Her friendly green eyes sparkled with an openness of spirit that could be readily seen in her countenance. She was comfortable around all age groups, and in spite of the many differences between herself and girls her own age at school, she had become popular there as well. Most of her friends gravitated to her experience of having spent most of her life in a foreign country. She could play soccer like the best of the boys, but still make herself presentable for the mall. She was a good student and could still hold down a part time job. Carey would be proud of his daughter.

Anna waited her turn to board the downtown bus. She tossed her coins into the spinning machine and took her usual seat three rows back from the driver. She had learned not to sit to near the end of the bus for safety, but not in the first couple rows either where the diesel fumes would rush in with each opening of the door. She smiled reminiscing over the busses she had ridden in Honduras. At least SDTA didn't have passengers with live chickens sitting next to you. She looked out her window and thought of the many Honduran merchants who would run to the sides of busses with snacks and drinks tied to long sticks that they would thrust up to the windows to sell. She remembered the boys that would jump on the back of the bus and ride clutching the ladder that led to the roof. At times she missed Honduras.

Uncle Billy had helped her get a job through a friend in their church that ran a Bible bookstore called, "The Lion's Den". Located on the second level of the mall near the food court, it received a fair share of foot traffic. Anna had worked most of the summer full time, but had cut back to twenty hours at the start of school. She didn't have to work Wednesdays and the store was closed on Sundays. The store carried a wide selection of both Spanish material and music in the store and Anna became very helpful in working with the Hispanic customers. She did have to reacquaint herself with the new Contemporary Christian artists in the music field, but she was a quick study.

As she rode the escalator to the second floor of the mall, she could see the Saturday afternoon crowds begin to mobilize and form ranks around their favorite stores. The Movie Plex was filling as teens tried to decide which film was worth their four dollars for the afternoon. Parents chased their children around the colorful tables as French-Fries and pizza slices began to cool and lose their attraction. Anna bravely passed the aroma of fresh pretzels and chocolate chip cookies as she walked toward the "Lion's Den". Rounding the corner, she glanced over the railing down to a window of a store on the first level. The sign declared in bold red letters – "Fall Liquidation Sale: Up to 75% off". Anna made a mental note; on her dinner break, she would give a little visit to the small clothing store.

———

"Here they come!" Josh yelled from the front yard. He ran and opened the large gate and Carey eased the Hilux into the driveway.

"It's Uncle Billy, It's Uncle Billy," Josh exclaimed, as Caleb and Susan hurried from the front door to greet them. They exchanged warm hugs and kisses while even Oso ran from the back to meet the visiting relative. At first, his size and strength intimidated Billy as he did most Hondurans who ventured close to the yard, but Oso soon proved to be more family pup than watch dog.

The boys carried the luggage into the house while Billy pulled off his windbreaker. Even southern California wasn't this warm in mid-September. Carey explained that the cooler temperatures didn't come till around late November after the rains had stopped and the breezes began. They would average in the low to mid nineties most of the year.

"It was cooler at the airport," Billy commented.

"If it weren't for the air conditioning, you would have been able to tell when it got warmer as we came over the mountain, "Carey explained. "It's just that you stepped from one altitude to sea level without the benefit of feeling the change."

"Those mountains were something," Billy said turning to Susan. He started to ask if Carey always drove like that, when he realized that the subject might be too sensitive at the moment. So he quickly changed tactic. "We see the Santa Anna Mountains from a distance, but I don't think we have views as nice as the ones we came over."

"They are pretty during the rainy season," she replied. "They are so green. Let's get you out of this heat though and find you both something to drink."

As they all gathered around the dining room table for some fresh squeezed lemonade, Billy gave all the greetings from Helen, Jenny and most of all, their precious Anna. They talked about school, her grades, her job, her help around the house and how she and Jenny were getting along so well. He pulled out a recent photo he had taken of the girls together and

Susan began to cry. Carey steadied her with his large arm as he fought back his own tears.

"I wish we could talk to her more often, but it is just so expensive," Susan sighed.

Billy smiled to himself. He felt he would keep the Monday night phone call a surprise until that evening. Anna knew to be near the phone and he would charge the call to his own credit card and let Carey and Susan talk to their hearts content. As the sun began to wane from behind their fence, the five of them continued to share experiences across the dining room table. For the first time in three days, Carey was smiling again.

—————

The phone rang three times before Howard realized he was home alone. Karen had left for work, Donna had run to the market and Terry was riding his bike with some friends through the canyons near their housing complex.

"Pennington's residence," Howard answered formally.

"Bro. Howard, this is Rusty, did I catch you at a bad time?"

"No Rusty, not at all, what can I do for you?" he said cheerfully.

"I was just calling to see what you decided about the jail ministry trip this evening?" he said enthusiastically.

Howard had completely forgotten about the invitation Rusty had extended the day before. He glanced at his watch. It was four o'clock. He remembered that Rusty had asked him to call by three.

"I am so sorry for not getting back to you," Howard stammered. He glanced around the living room where he had been resting on the couch watching an afternoon ball game. He had muted the TV when he answered the phone.

"The truth is, I was doing some last minute studying and making a few changes to my message for tomorrow. I hope I didn't cause a problem by not calling." The convenient lie was not his practice, and it pained him to deceive his associate pastor. He just didn't feel like going to some holding cell and putting on his evangelical smile for men who could probably care less that he had come.

"Not at all," Rusty replied. "We don't leave for about another hour. I just wanted to know early enough to see if we all wanted to ride together. Don't worry, we'll be fine. Like I said, it is a blessing to go – well, maybe next week, OK?"

"Next Saturday would be better for me, I think," Howard lied again. "Just remind me sometime next week while we are at the office."

"Will do!" Rusty confirmed. "Have a good evening and don't study too hard."

"You too!" Howard said half-heartedly.

When he hung up the phone, he felt terrible. Most of his day had been unproductive and now he had lied to a fellow worker in order to avoid ministry. Howard was bordering on depression and knew it. The building project was overwhelming him, but he was too proud to admit that it was more than he could keep up with. He knew relations were somewhat strained at home, but he didn't realize to what extent. Donna had been distant most of the day and hadn't even come to tell him she was leaving to go shopping. Karen hadn't spoken to him all day. He didn't even know when she was expected home from work. As he laid down the phone, he felt the words swim through his mind, *"You are all done – don't you think this would be a good time for prayer?"*

Howard paused. He looked around the room, and then shook his head. He reached for the remote and unmated the announcer who was shouting about the Padres Home Run. As he settled back on the couch, he noticed that the stadium's cheers seemed distant.

———

"I'll be back after I eat," Anna called to her assistant manager. "Would you like me to bring you something?"

"No thanks, Anna," she replied. "I'm fine."

As Anna walked around the corner to the food court, she remembered the sale on the first floor. She decided to make it a quick burger and fries so that she would have a little time for shopping. She found a short line and ordered a complete meal. The medium drink was more than she would need, but it worked out cheaper than ordering the same food and a smaller coke. As she ate, she looked around the tables at the families and young people scattered about. She would often try to see their life as it was presented in that one moment. Anna studied faces and was sensitive to joy and pain in others. Fifteen years in a third world country had taught her to recognize the difference between contentment and charade. Poverty didn't always mean misery. Some of the closest friends she had grown up with lived in homes with dirt floors. Contentment rises above and even through one's lot in life. Children with little or nothing could still have barefoot fun with a small plastic ball and rocks for goals as they played soccer in an empty lot. Most Hondurans would never see a shopping complex as elaborate and embellished as the two level Bay Bridge Mall. But then nor would they have need for most of the wares that it offered. Simplicity with contentment had always attracted Anna more than the harried affluence she had found in the United States. The faces of many displayed their discontentment, even as their arms bulged with packages. Sometimes, Anna really missed home.

She emptied her tray into a wide mouth receptacle for trash and walked to the escalators. She pondered what possible irresistible bargains would present themselves. As she stepped into the store, the electronic bell announced her entrance and the young sales attendant quickly turned her attention from the jewelry counter she was straightening.

"May I help you," the young girl asked politely.

"I saw your sign and was wondering what items you had reduced for liquidation," Anna inquired.

"Mostly those would be the items on the first two racks against this wall," the young girl said leading Anna. "But we also have some scarves and part of the jewelry in the case by the register that are greatly reduced."

"Thank you," Anna smiled. "I'll just look around then, thank you."

"If I can help you with anything, feel free to let me know," recited the young girl as she backed towards the counter she had been straightening.

Anna turned her attention to the two racks and their variety of tops and skirts. She checked a couple pieces for her size, but wasn't greatly impressed with any of the selections. These were definitely in need of being liquidated, she thought. She felt she had wasted her time completely by coming. She glanced at her watch and thought she would look quickly at the scarves. As she walked toward the case, the young girl stepped beside her.

"Interested in seeing some of the scarves?" she offered. "These are 50% off." She pointed to a small selection folded neatly on their shelf.

Anna noticed a simple scarf of hunter green with tiny squares of beige and burnt orange. She asked to see it and the clerk assisted.

"It really goes well with your eyes and hair," the young girl said encouragingly.

"Do you think so?" Anna replied accepting the compliment. "I like the colors. I guess I will take it, thank you."

The young clerk smiled and stepped back around the counter to ring up the sale. Anna had to hurry back to the upper level to clock back in. She thanked the girl for her help and quickly exited. As the clerk recounted the bills and placed them in the register, her manager stepped from the back.

"Who was that in such a hurry?" Sheila asked.

"Just a bargain hunter," Karen replied, her smile disappearing and her demeanor changing.

"Is there something wrong?" Sheila asked.

"Not really, I guess," Karen stammered. "I got a call from Fernando this morning, and . . . well, I think he's calling it off between us."

"I see," Sheila said putting her arm around Karen affectionately. "Boys can be such a pain. They think our whole world evolves around them, or that it should. Since my father ran off, I haven't known a man yet that was worth the time of day."

"When did you lose your father?" Karen asked.

"Oh I didn't lose him," she said smugly. "In fact, I didn't even miss him. He wasn't there even when he did live in our home."

"I hear you there," Karen sighed.

"Now that sounds like a different problem," Sheila remarked.

"I guess it's all related. But listen, I don't need to unload on you. I mean, thanks and everything, but we have work to do before the evening crowd gets here. I still have to straighten these counters."

"You need a ride home again tonight, then?" Sheila offered.

"That would be nice," Karen replied, feeling a little better.

"My pleasure," Sheila smiled.

———

"What is eight!" Gertie called out.

"What is eight what?" Adam yelled back from the kitchen.

"It was a Jeopardy question, 'how many people were saved from the flood?'" she replied. "I am cleaning up on this Bible category. Why don't people know these things? They are simple Bible questions."

"Now honey," Adam said calmly, carrying two bowls of hot chili into the den on a tray. "You forget – most of these people weren't raised like you and I were, and they know as much Bible as they have seen in the movies and that ain't much."

Gertie laughed out loud. Adam returned to the kitchen to bring them both some tea. It was good to hear Gertie laugh he thought. She had been so tired lately with the long nights in prayer. He sprinted back to the den before the next question, which turned out to be about foreign import cars.

"Would you like to return thanks," he asked as he set her glass down beside her bowl.

"Yes, I would," Gertie said while reaching for the remote to turn down the volume on the set. They bowed their heads and Adam stood beside her to hold her hand.

"Dear Lord, we want to thank You for another beautiful day. We want to thank you for the fine weather and the pretty leaves that are turning. We want to thank you for this food also. I pray you will continue to watch over Carey and his family. Keep them safe from the evil one and I pray for this other family who You know more about than I do. I pray you will begin working in their lives for Your honor and glory. I ask these things in the name of our Lord and Savior, Jesus Christ."

"Amen," Adam added and took his seat. "Excuse me for asking, but what other family were you praying for, or am I not supposed to know?"

"I told you before," Gertie said blowing on her spoon of chili. "I don't know who they are, or even where they are. I just know that they are going through some problems and it is between the father and his daughter."

"How will you know when to stop praying for these folks?" Adam asked.

"When God has worked His purpose, He'll give me peace over the matter. As long as I keep waking up in the middle of the night, I believe the battle is still going on."

"Well I hope He works things out quickly – I don't know how much lack of sleep you can take."

"Don't worry about me, sweetheart," she said reassuringly. "Whatever God calls us to do – He gives us the strength to do it. That's His grace."

"I know you're right," Adam replied. "I just hate to see you not get your rest."

"But honey," she said, looking across at him, "when I am with the Lord, I am at rest."

———

Josh and Caleb offered to clear the dishes from the table as the grownups finished their coffee. Billy had tried some of the Honduran coffee that Carey had brought him, but he never was sure how to prepare it. It was definitely stronger than stateside blends. Often labeled as a European quality, it was rich and black, but with a sweeter taste because sugarcane was added while being processed. That didn't stop most North Americans from cutting it more with their own milk or sweetener.

Conversation had run its course through dinner from Anna, school and family, to Billy's job and new work with the Gideons. Billy jumped up suddenly and retrieved his carry on bag. As the boys returned to the table, he pulled out a small wrapped package and handed it to them. Excitedly they tore through the paper to find the newest version of their favorite video game with all-new levels and challenges. Uncle Billy was careful to stay away from the violent fantasy games and looked for the simple "save the princess" adventures with animated characters that simply run, jump and knock things out of their way. He then reached into his bag and took out two unwrapped boxes of computer software and handed it to Carey.

"I would have brought you a modem, but I knew you didn't have access to an Internet server way down here," Billy said.

"They have them in the capitol, and if I wanted to get on line, I guess I could, but it would be a long distant call each time to connect."

"I bet it would still be cheaper than a phone call to California," Billy reasoned.

"You may be right, there. That's something I can look into."

"If you decide you could use a modem, let me know and I'll get you a good one," Billy said. "In the meantime, here is the latest upgrade for your Windows and I brought you a good office program to go with it. We'll see about installing it in a little bit."

"I don't know how to thank you, little brother," Carey said humbly. "It was really just enough to be able to see you again."

"Same here."

The boys had run off to the den to connect the video game while Susan offered more coffee to the two brothers. Billy waved her off politely.

"I already have an hour on you two, I don't need to do anything that will keep me up into the middle of the night here," Billy chuckled. "Which reminds me, what are our plans for tomorrow. I was hoping to see some of your work and what better day than Sunday to see my missionary brother in action."

Carey looked to Susan for support and then turned back to Billy.

"Billy, like I said on the way down here, I haven't been back to *Santa Tierra* since the accident. I don't know what to expect there. It could even be dangerous to return so soon."

"What Carey is trying to say," Susan interjected, "is that sometimes family members take vengeance for the death of a loved one. It's called 'machete law' and we aren't sure if it is safe for Carey to go back yet."

Billy looked down at his coffee cup for a second, then resumed slowly, "Carey, I know we didn't get to finish our talk in the car, but maybe now would be a good time. I really think you need to return to *Santa Tierra* as soon as you can for a couple reasons. One, you need to let the people of the congregation there know what happened. Chances are there are a ton of rumors already running around that town. They need to hear from you. Now I realize that may be dangerous, especially in light of what Susan has just told me, but I also can't help but think that you will not be going there alone. I for one will be with you and I believe God will be with us also."

"Don't forget Mando," Susan added.

"Your traveling companion who was with you that night?" Billy asked.

"Yes," Carey replied reluctantly.

"And he would go with you two tomorrow," Susan suggested.

"Is that true?" Billy pressed.

"I suppose so," Carey responded half-heartedly.

"Then, there you go. A three strand cord is not easily broken."

Carey recognized the scriptural significance to his brother's statement from Solomon in Ecclesiastes 4:12, where the verse read, "Though one may be overpowered, two can defend themselves. A cord of three strands is not quickly broken."

"It doesn't say that it won't be broken, it just says it won't be quickly broken," Carey pointed out in a satirical response.

"Then we're going?" Billy asked confidently.

"I suppose you're right," Carey acquiesced.

"You mentioned a couple of reasons," Susan inquired. "What other reason did you have in mind?"

"As I was mentioning to Carey this afternoon. I believe he needs to speak to the widow and if possible offer some kind of compensation for the death of her husband. Perhaps help with the funeral costs or something of that nature. We didn't get to pursue the idea much this afternoon. We were interrupted by a couple of big trucks heading at us on the mountain."

"I see," Susan half smiled. "Did Carey give you a Honduran driving lesson?"

"To say the least. I don't think I will carry that lesson back home with me though," Billy replied, sipping his coffee.

"Susan, what do you think?" Carey started. "I mean about us going back and then me talking to the widow?"

"I believe Billy is right," she replied simply. "You have to go back sooner or later, and maybe sooner is better. You have truth on your side and there is always strength in truth. As far as seeing the widow, I know that would be the hardest thing for you to ever do. The money is nothing, it is facing her and her children."

"Billy, I believe this is going to be one of the greatest challenges I have ever faced," Carey began resolutely. "But with you beside me, I believe I can go through this. I will go by Mando's early in the morning and see if he can go with us. Can you be ready to leave for Sunday School from here by, say, 8:30? I know you have already lost one hour by just arriving."

"No problem, big brother, you just knock on the door 20 minutes before you want to bug out and I'll be ready," Billy said confidently.

"I doubt Carey will have to knock on your door," Susan said collecting the coffee cups. "Our neighbors on your side of the house have chickens. They'll start singing to each other about 4:30am. If you are lucky you'll sleep till 6:00."

Billy looked at Carey somewhat dazed. "Chickens?"

———

Donna cleared the table and Terry ran off to the den to start the Saturday night line-up of his favorite TV programs. Howard sat quietly as she removed his plate. He was still sulking from his wasted day.

"When is Karen coming home from work tonight?" he asked breaking the silence.

"I'm not sure, I can only guess that she will be in after the store closes and that could be 10:00pm."

"Well, so much for her grounding," he huffed.

"You knew the job would be more demanding on the weekends," Donna countered. "Let's just be glad that she doesn't work on Sunday."

"How does she get home that late?" he asked. "I don't like the idea of her trying to catch a bus that late at night."

"She called to say she would be riding home with Sheila, her boss, again," Donna said arranging the dishes in the dishwasher and setting the timer.

"Have you met this Sheila yet?" Howard asked strongly.

"No, she just let her off last night," Donna replied. "She had driven away before I realized Karen was in the house."

"What time was that?" Howard asked.

"I want to say about 10:30. You were in the den watching TV and I was upstairs reading."

Howard huffed again to himself. He wasn't about to lose this battle. Karen had been pushing against the fences and he had to maintain some degree of control. He didn't like the idea of this job, but he knew she needed the experience and the responsibility. He didn't like the familiarity that Karen demonstrated concerning her employer, but he didn't know how to object rationally. All the same, she needed to demonstrate some discipline and respect for his authority. It seemed like he had been losing more and more influence in the past two years, and he didn't really know how to recapture it.

"Well she better be in before 11:00 tonight. Tomorrow is Sunday and I will not allow this job to interfere with her ability to attend church!" he exclaimed definitively.

"That reminds me," Donna said changing the subject. "I saw where there would be a women's retreat next weekend. I think I would like to go. Where can I sign up tomorrow?"

"What retreat?" Howard asked. "I don't know. It must be something Rusty is doing with the young married class."

"I saw it announced in the newsletter you brought home," she said.

"Well, check with Rusty tomorrow, he must have the sign up list." Howard still sounded bothered, so Donna thought it best not to say any more. She grimaced slightly behind his back. Howard was getting so caught up in his problems; he didn't even pursue the purpose behind the retreat. Donna was beginning to feel more and more alone. Maybe this retreat would giver her back some of her own identity. Something had to change.

———

Flaco listened carefully to the directions and then thanked the two men by buying them each another beer. He was a little concerned about trying to reach his contact at night, but the bus from San Salvador didn't arrive in *Ahuachpan* till just before sundown. From *Ahuachapan*, Flaco was careful to find a ride with a fruit truck that would not be taking the Pan American Highway towards the border. He found a driver willing to carry him to *Agua Fria* for 100 *colones* and no questions. He had to eat and carefully ask around for information on how to get across the border. He was now traveling without legal papers and could be turned back at any junction in his journey. He had to decide who he could trust to talk to and be willing to spread a little of the money around if that was what it took. He had a name from his cousin, but that proved to be old information. He was no longer in *Agua Fria*. But the two men in the cantina told Flaco of an auto mechanic with an ATV that could get him to *Santa Rosa* in Guatemala. Flaco was prepared to pay as much as $100 in US currency, knowing that American dollars carried more value than the local *colones* and the *coyote* could up his exchange and fee by just holding onto the money for a month.

Flaco was growing in his confidence in dealing with strangers. He gravitated toward the type of men who would know the people he needed to find. His comfort in cantinas was an asset to the image he was trying to convey. In *Santa Tierra* he had been nothing more than a skinny weakling with an aversion to hard work. He had joined with Moncho because few others would have anything to do with him. But he had learned how to act tough and Moncho's gun gave him the added *machismo* he felt he needed. *Agua Fria* was close enough to the border and far enough from the main road to draw ruthless men, but Flaco wasn't afraid. He did not look like a man carrying nearly two thousand dollars in cash on him.

He walked resolutely through the poorly lit streets doubling back only once to find the mechanic's garage with the large beer sign over the door. Beer companies offered to print the name of a business on a decorative sign as long as they could advertise their product beneath the name of the business. The same was true of several soft drink companies. It was no surprise to Flaco that the mechanic, Rafael Alvarez, would choose *Corona* over *Tropical*, the local fruit drinks, to advertise his shop. The shop doors were closed, but lights from inside the large shed were still on. Flaco took a deep breath and walked through the door beside the large garage entrance.

"We're closed!" called a voice from behind the raised hood of small Datsun B210.

"I haven't come about a car," Flaco began firmly. "I need a four wheel drive for a very short trip northward."

"How short?" the voice called back.

117

"Just across the border," Flaco replied a slight bit softer.

"The bus runs that way each day from *Ahuachapan*," came the response from behind the hood.

"I don't like crowds and I don't wish to see the sights, especially at the border."

A grease smeared face peeked around the hood for a moment and then returned to its place over the motor.

"Do you need a driver also?" came the voice behind the hood.

"It would be better, I don't plan to come back by this way," Flaco said finally being understood.

"I have much work for tonight and I have Mass tomorrow with my family. How soon do you need to go?"

"Whenever it is most convenient for the driver," Flaco smiled.

"And what are you willing to pay for this short trip?" the face appearing once again from behind the hood.

"I have $75 American dollars," Flaco replied holding back some for negotiating.

"I'm afraid you do not have enough!" Rafael replied, slamming the hood down on the little car. "I make that trip for $100."

"I can give you $90, but that is my eating money as well," Flaco lied convincingly.

Rafael thought as he stared into Flaco's eyes. After a few moments he smiled.

"You don't look like you can go without too many meals, so my wife will cook for you tonight and tomorrow. I will carry you towards *Santa Rosa* by way of the river and leave you one mile from the road. We cannot leave until Monday in the early morning. The heavy traffic at the border on Monday will occupy most of their men and fewer will be patrolling the river. I know of a shallow place where my vehicle can get across. But it will cost you $90."

"*Esta bien*," Flaco agreed, knowing that he just saved $10 on the deal. He didn't mind the delay and the thought of resting on Sunday seemed right to him.

Rafael showed him a hammock that he kept in the garage for slow days and invited him to stay the night. Flaco thought that peculiar since the mechanic did not know him and there were obviously many tools that Flaco could take if he had the mind to. He soon discovered that Rafael planned to stay the night with him in the shop. When he brought Flaco a plate of rice and beans, he also brought his own cot. It later occurred to Flaco that Rafael was more concerned over losing a client than a set of screwdrivers and wrenches.

"Are all Saturdays that rough?" Karen asked counting out the coins in the register.

"Hopefully," Sheila responded as she lowered the metal mesh into its place and closed the glass doors behind them. Her and Karen would exit through the back of the store into an employees alley that would carry them to the rear of the parking garage where a mall guard supervised the departures of the store owners. Many left with deposits and the additional security was comforting.

As they drove out of the parking lot, Sheila veered her La Baron towards the downtown area instead of the direction of Karen's home.

"Which way are we going home?" Karen asked inquisitively but without alarm in her voice.

"I need to make a quick deposit and it's closer while we are at this end of town."

Karen set back and glanced at the LED clock on the radio. She knew she could squeeze in by 11:00 without much hassle, but she didn't want to push it. Sheila weaved in and out of the Saturday night traffic with the precision of a stock car driver. Karen admired Sheila for her independent spirit and was drawn to the sense of adventure she felt when they were together. As they turned onto a brightly-lit boulevard of clubs and restaurants, Sheila began to slow down.

"I wanted you to see this place I was talking about last night," she said while pointing out Karen's window. The colored lights spelled out *"The Night Light"* and advertised dancing till 3am. Karen knew she could not go in because of her age, but the idea intrigued her. Sheila looked at the clock on the dash and swore to herself.

"I guess it's too late to check it out tonight, but maybe some time soon. Think about it," she said smugly while pulling back into the traffic. Karen looked back at the club as they drove on down the boulevard. She would think about it.

As Sheila let her out in the driveway, Karen glanced quickly at her watch. It was only 10:50. There shouldn't be any yelling tonight. And if they asked, she would simply say that they had to make a deposit on the way home. Then it occurred to Karen. They had not stopped at the bank.

Gertie sat silently on the couch. Her chin resting softly on her chest and her eyes closed serenely, Adam didn't want to disturb her. He glanced at his watch and winced. He had fallen asleep watching a nature special while she knit and prayed. It was hard to tell if she was still in prayer or had drifted to sleep herself. He eased beside her on the couch and gently slid his arm inside of hers to take her hand. She did not raise her head, but squeezed his hand. Together they passed into the next morning in prayer.

Chapter Eleven:

"The Widow"

(Sunday)

One of the busiest days for the market is Sunday morning in Choluteca as women, children and a few considerate men scurry about the fruit and vegetable stands for their day's supply of victuals. The freshest vegetables were available on the weekends as the merchants brought potatoes, carrots and lettuce from the mountain areas. Few could store fresh foods for more than a couple of days, so modest quantities were purchased and carried home in plastic woven baskets on the heads of daughters and wives.

Carey drove Billy through the market as he snapped 35mm shots of Honduran culture. Choluteca had a larger market than other villages nearby, so many came by bus from early in the morning and would bag their purchases in 50-pound grain sacks to carry back on the top of the bus. Colorful hammocks, straw mats and curbside grills interested Billy, but the biggest impression came from the copious assortment of bananas. There were small "finger" bananas, large yellow bananas and dark green "plantanos" that were much tougher than bananas and were fried in strips or coin size disks.

"I can't believe how warm it is for this time of the year," Billy commented, pulling the camera back into the truck.

"It doesn't get cool until around December and then we're talking only the mid 70's."

"I guess that's why they can harvest these fruits year round," Billy observed.

"Just one of the perks of missionary life," Carey replied.

They pulled into Mando's yard and blew the horn. Mando ran out to the truck and jumped into the back seat. The double cab pickup normally had plenty of leg room in the back but both Carey and Billy had pushed their seats all the way back to sit comfortably. Fortunately, Mando was of average height for a Honduran and didn't require much leg space.

Carey took a moment to introduce his brother in Spanish to Mando and then to translate Mando's greeting to Billy. Billy tried some of his southern California Spanish, but his pronunciation was painful. Mando responded with his few learned expressions from Carey, including a strained "y'all" which Carey had taught him as a joke.

As they traveled from the city, Carey resorted to conducting two separate conversations in each language. Mando wanted to know how much Billy was aware of and the possible dangers that awaited them in *Santa*

Tierra. Carey assured Mando that Billy completely understood the situation and it was at his urging that Carey was even making the trip this morning. Mando smiled realizing that he himself had tried to convince Carey of the importance to return, but that sometimes it takes family to help us "hear".

Billy wanted to know about Mando, his background and his family. Carey shared of Mando's conversion account at his gate and his faithfulness to the ministry and his friendship to Carey.

"I don't know of a man who works as hard for his family to provide while being a strong father and husband. Then when you and I would be kicking back for some time to ourselves, he wants to know when he can go with me to a mission or to help conduct a service. The man is tireless."

"We have it so soft in America," Billy sighed. "We do two days at the church and think that's it. There are just so many distractions that bid for our time and we welcome them. We're losing sight of priorities."

"Not everyone, little brother," Carey countered. "I just heard of a computer salesman who started giving up some of his time to tell churches about the importance of God's Word getting into hands and homes around the world."

"Thanks, but you know what I mean," Billy smiled. "We all could be just a bit more conscious of our Christianity during the day and not just on our way to worship services."

"Well, one thing is for sure," Carey added, "most folks don't have the kind of ride to church you and I are about to have." Carey turned the truck off of the pavement and scattered gravel as he started down the road that led to *Santa Tierra.* In his rear view mirror, he could see the police post where he and Mando had carried the body of Moncho. His breathing quickened as the truck lumbered over the dirt and rocky road.

———

The First Baptist Church of Carrolton was an old structure with two floors to its educational building. Adam never thought he would ever use the elevator that had been put in for handicap access, but staying up with Gertie the night before had worn him down. He hoped that she would sleep while he was at service, but most likely she would be knitting before the televised service from the previous week.

The Senior Men's class Adam taught was called "The Barnabas Class". All of the groups in that department had biblical names over the door to their room. They chose the name "The Barnabas Class" to be an encouragement to one another. Most of the men were retired like Adam, but still dabbled in activity beyond walking the malls and drinking breakfast coffee at the local fast food restaurant. Some worked in their homes, while some were still working on their homes fulfilling endless "honey-do" lists.

Adam unloaded his arms full of Bibles, legal pads and teacher's book onto the heavy podium he used to speak from. Though comfortable with the material, he never got comfortable speaking before groups. He grasped the sides of the wooden stand most of the time he spoke. His seventeen years as a Sunday School teacher were performed out of his love for the Lord and His Word and not from a love to be heard by others. His genuineness and sincerity was what brought these men back each week, even in cold weather.

As one of the men performed the secretarial duties of taking the roll and collecting the offering envelopes, another shared announcements and led in the prayer requests. Adam enlisted as many as possible to share the class responsibilities so that the men would interact more and not just look to him to do everything. After the classroom preliminaries were completed, Adam usually had between 35 and 40 minutes to teach his lesson. He knew he needed more time than that to adequately share about intercessory prayer, but he would just have to do the best he could.

He directed the class to the passages in Exodus 32 and 33 and began sharing from his notes and his heart the things he had rehearsed with Gertie through the week. He cited Ezekiel 22:30 as God's call for intercession and then Psalm 106:23 as Moses' example. Throughout the study, he gave examples of his Gertie and her devotion to prayer. This was a lesson being lived out in his home this week.

As he approached the scripture in Exodus 33, he began to realize something he had not studied. Moses' prayer was for more than God's mercy on the people for His sake. It was more than offering himself as a substitute for the sin of the people as they had read in the previous chapter. In chapter 33, God had stated He would not personally lead the people lest he destroy them for their stubbornness. Moses then prayed (verses 12 –16) for his own personal guidance as well as for the guidance of the people by God Himself and not just an angel.

"Intercession sees the need for God to be personally involved with our lives and not just to dictate the circumstances," Adam began. "It's easy to say that God allows things to happen and then sends His angels to work everything out or correct situations. But, we need to remind ourselves daily that we have a personal God Who involves Himself in our lives. We need His direction and not just the assurance that He is overseeing our decisions from a heavenly advantage point. The thing that jumps out at me here is how God affirms Moses' request by saying (verse 17) 'I know your name'. Maybe it is more important for us to realize that rather than, as monumental as it was for Moses to learn the name of God, Yahweh, it was infinitely more important for him to learn that God knew his name, Moses, and used it."

Adam glanced at his watch. He was not going to be able to get to the final passage in Numbers 14:11-20 as he had hoped. He decided to close with a personal word.

"My wife is not able to join us in service when the weather is this cool. But she has found her place in the service of the Lord in her prayer closet. She has been praying for a missionary and another family this week. She is not even sure whom the other family is she is praying for. Would you join me in prayer that the Lord will direct her prayers and the lives of the families she is praying for? After all, He knows their names." Adam closed his Bible and bowed his head. The "Barnabas Class" joined him as they prayed for Gertie and then for the ones she was interceding for.

———

Howard was seldom a patient man, but it seems Sunday mornings brought out the worse in his temperament as he rushed anxiously around the house getting ready for worship service. He had been tempted many times to take his car to the church early and let the family arrive when they could, but that made going out to eat awkward after service. He was still trying desperately to maintain the "family" image. As Karen got older, the bathroom time and morning arguments began to grow.

"Come on Karen," Terry yelled at the bathroom door. "I still need to get ready too, you know."

"I said I would be out in a minute!" she shouted back.

"Mom! Karen won't get out of the bathroom," he yelled toward the closed door of the master bedroom.

Howard rolled his eyes while tying his tie. "Your turn," he said toward Donna glibly.

Donna huffed and laid down her make-up brush. She walked silently passed Howard and through the door. Without raising her voice, she instructed Terry to walk downstairs and use the bathroom next to the guestroom. When he objected that his toothbrush was in "their" bathroom, she squinted her eyes, knowing he had no intention of brushing his teeth. He took the body language at "face value" and turned quickly toward the banister.

Donna returned to her mirror walking stonily past Howard. He noticed the coldness and straightened his tie.

"Everything OK?" he asked cautiously.

"It's under control," she replied emotionlessly.

"I'm not just talking about the kids," Howard added sincerely.

Donna paused for a moment in her make-up. Was this the right time, she thought. Did he really want to talk or just feel comfortable about leaving his house and his problems at home? She thought she would test the waters.

"What are you referring to?" she asked calmly.

Howard walked into the bathroom and looked into the mirror at her.

"I'm talking about everything," he started slowly. "Karen. . . you. . . us . . . is everything OK?"

"Not really Howard," she said gently, trying to ease into the conversation. "I don't really know how to start, but, . . ." her voice trailed off.

He took the cue and moved closer turning his gaze from her reflection to her face that had lowered from the mirror.

"Just start where you are and then work back."

"I'm confused," she began tearing up. "I know we are important to you, I just don't feel like we are."

"Honey, what are you saying?" came his pastoral voice. "Of course you are all important to me. You are my family. I love you and the children more than anything. I have just been going through some stressful things at the church that has distracted me some, you understand."

It was as though she expected each word to sound exactly as they did. Her neck began to flush with anger.

"HOWARD! I'm not one of your church members, so don't talk to me like that! Your words say, 'I love you', but it isn't you saying them. You're right, you are distracted, and you don't even see what's going on around you at home. WE ARE NOT OK, HERE!"

Howard stood dumbfounded, staring into the enflamed eyes of his wife. His first thought was that her timing was incredible. Forty minutes before he was to preach and she was lambasting him over a subject he couldn't even defend – her perception of his performance as a husband and father. His back bristled as he stood erect against the bathroom counter. He knew better than to lash back verbally, but at the same time, he did not wish to simply buckle under the accusation. Fortunately, the bedroom door was closed and they were two rooms away from the children. Howard chose his next words with care.

"I'm sorry," he started humbly but ambiguously. "I didn't mean to sound mechanical or uncaring. I was just trying to respond calmly."

"You weren't responding at all, that's the problem" she countered. "You were defending yourself with an answer. I want you to respond to me."

"I'm trying to respond to you," Howard said exasperated. "Maybe I don't say it just right . . . I'm sorry. But this is not really a good time to be bringing all this up, don't you think?"

Donna looked at him with years of penned up pain and held her tongue. She picked up her make-up brush and turned back toward the mirror. Howard looked down at his shoes and waited for a conclusive word from his wife. When it didn't come, he slowly turned back into the bedroom, picked up his coat and walked downstairs to wait.

Donna allowed the bedroom door to close behind him before she began to cry. She was not upset over how she had handled the conversation; she was upset for the direction it took and the doubts that had been lifted. Howard could not recognize the seriousness of the moment enough to set aside his church schedule. He had chosen the morning service over the urgency of his wife. He had chosen wrong again.

———

Carey was not sure how he would respond as the red Pickup neared the grade where the accident had taken place. It helped to be driving. He could concentrate more on navigating the hill than reliving the event. Billy noticed how quiet the truck became as both Mando and Carey looked silently forward. He decided against asking for the moment. For the final few minutes of the trip, the three men rode solemnly as *Santa Tierra* came into sight.

Billy was genuinely impressed with the sight of the small Honduran village. The blend of stucco and adobe and red tile roofs was just what he expected from an old Western. There was a noticeable absence of cars around the town. A few horses were tied to the fence around the plaza. Most had loads of beans, rice, fruits or some other purchase tied down behind the saddle. These were the early risers who had already been to Choluteca and the morning market. They most likely had left by four in the morning to arrive at the market by six. They had made their purchases and returned before nine. Billy was amazed by the stamina of the people.

As the red truck followed the road out of town, Luís followed its movement. He knew where it was headed. He had planned to attend the worship service that morning with Suyapa, but a twinge of fear began to surface. There was uncertainty among the members of the congregation as to whether the missionary would be there this morning. Some were hoping he would come, others were fearful for his life. Luís was not sure what would happen. He began to think that it might be a good idea for him to attend. He had heard Flaco's story, as had many in the town. Maybe this would be his chance to see if it were true or not. He glanced at his watch and decided to begin walking back up to where the church was meeting. He still had twenty minutes before the service and they seldom began on time anyway.

As the truck crossed the *quebrada* where Carey and Mando had waited so long that night, Carey glanced up into his rear view mirror at Mando seated in the back seat.

"Remember how long we sat here, brother?" he asked in Spanish. Mando nodded.

"Whoa!" Billy protested. "You don't talk for twenty minutes and then decide to speak up and leave me out of the conversation."

"I was just asking Mando if he remembered how long we waited back there before we could cross the river the other night. That was the reason we ended up going through town so late at night. We sat there waiting for the river to go down for over four hours."

"Over four hours!" Billy exclaimed. He quickly looked out his window towards the sky. "It's not going to rain today is it?"

Carey laughed. It helped to have Billy along.

"No little brother, we won't be getting stuck today."

Mando asked what was so funny and Carey explained. Mando was glad to have Billy along also. He had not expressed it to Carey, but he was also nervous about their trip this morning. His wife had advised him not to go, but his devotion to his friend and brother was too strong to let him face any danger alone. After all, an unruly response to Carey's visit might require his presence to "talk" to the people. Carey knew Spanish, but Mando was Honduran and there was a difference.

As they pulled into the small lot beside the adobe house/ church, the few that had arrived early came out of the home to greet Carey, Mando and their guest. Billy stumbled through the greeting Carey had taught him as the people shook his hand and smiled. It was as though nothing had ever happened. The warm response encouraged Carey and they walked into the small room for the service. In the back of his mind, he knew what he needed to do after the service. Then would be the time to worry.

———

Karen sat near the back of the sanctuary with a few of her friends. She used to sit near the front, but she somehow had convinced her father she could hear him just as well in the back and argued that none of the youth sat near the front. As in many churches, the young people sat collectively, sometimes to listen, sometimes to pass notes or make fun of the traditional trappings of the predictable aspects of the services. They knew who prayed the longest, which stanzas would be left out of which hymns and how the announcements would be repeated for the benefit of those too lazy to read them for themselves. Karen had once listened intently to her father's messages, but now she tended to block them out. She could remember a time when she enjoyed reading her Bible. She could remember the close fellowship she once enjoyed with a small youth Bible class, but when her girlfriend's father was transferred, she quit attending and now, Sunday school was the only spiritual training she received, and the teacher was seldom prepared for class. For Karen, church had lost its appeal.

Donna sat in the choir. Her image as the cooperative pastor's wife was to be maintained, no matter how furious she felt with him that morning. She stared at the back of his neck and felt the heat on the back of her own. She only hoped that no one would ask if she were having some form of allergic reaction to something that she had eaten that morning. She opened her church bulletin and skimmed through the announcements for the third time. She reread the information on the retreat scheduled for that weekend. She would most definitely look up Rusty after the service.

Howard tried to concentrate on his notes. There were times when a message just flowed with the same enthusiastic inspiration he had experienced in his study while preparing, but this was not one of those times. He found himself using clichés and fillers between his points for lack of material. He completely left out one illustration that he had planned to include. It was obvious to the congregation that his mind was not on the message. There is nothing more pathetic than a minister trying to preach in the power of the flesh. He glanced at the small clock he kept on the pulpit. He had nine more minutes to go. He would be glad when the hand shaking was over for this morning.

Rusty sat concerned for his pastor. He knew something was wrong, but he had no idea what the problem could be. He remembered Bro. Howard's voice on the phone Saturday and realized that the excuse for not going to jail ministry was probably not really for sermon preparation - at least not for this sermon. Rusty glanced around the congregation to assess the response of the church. He saw troubled stares, lack of interest, and an occasional sleeper. Then he noticed one man smiling. Sitting straight up with his arms folded and enjoying the obvious embarrassment of his pastor was Arnie Johnson.

Arnie sat alone on the outside end of the twelfth pew. He had come without his family to church again. He quit attending his Sunday School class and only came for the worship service. He seldom spoke to anyone afterward. At one time he had been a strong active member. Now he seemed bitter and strongly against the pastor. Why he had not left and found another church was a mystery to many. He was definitely a thorn in Howard's side. As the preacher stumbled over his final point, Arnie glanced around the rear of the sanctuary till he found Karen. She was talking to the girl sitting beside her completely ignoring her father's message. His smile left and he grimaced. When he turned back toward the front, his countenance had changed completely. Rusty noticed the forlorn in Arnie's eyes. He doubted it was conviction, but it was definitely remorse.

———

Above *Santa Tierra*, the worship service in the home was coming to a close. Billy had asked for a couple minutes at the close of the message to share with the congregation with Carey translating. He was greatly impressed with the simplicity and devotion of the small group. He was also impressed with his brother's command of the language and ability to preach passionately in a foreign tongue. There was no doubt in Billy's mind that Carey was in his element and called to do what he was doing.

As Carey introduced his brother to the smiling group of believers, Billy retrieved a small box from the corner of the room where he had placed it. He stepped beside his brother and the resemblance became noticeable. These two men were truly brothers in both sense of the word.

"My brother, *Guiermo* (the Spanish equivalent for Bill) has a special presentation that he would like to make. He knows that in heaven we will all speak Spanish, but he just hasn't learned any yet." Carey paused for the soft laughter. "So for now, I will have to interpret for him."

"I'm not sure how my brother just embarrassed me, but I forgive him," Billy began, as Carey translated each phrase. "I bring greetings from many believers in California."

Most of the congregation had never heard of California. Some knew of Miami and New Orleans, where most flights went to from Honduras, but from there the geography and size of the United States was relatively unknown. Nevertheless, they smiled and acknowledged his gracious greeting.

"I work for a company that makes computer software and distributes it to other companies," Billy began nervously.

Carey glanced at him and whispered, "They don't know what a computer is. I'll just say you are a factory worker."

Billy smiled humbly.

"But not only do I have a good job to take care of the needs of my family," Billy paused for the translation. "I also have a job with God giving out His Word wherever I can. I have brought small New Testaments for you to carry with you for wherever you go."

Smiles appeared on every face in the crowded house. Billy had even brought enough for the children who could read to have one. Most families present had at least one Bible in the home, but it was usually shared by all and kept by the father or mother. Carey helped to get the people into an orderly group so that Billy could pass between each row handing out the pocket sized brown covered new testaments. The teenagers were especially excited about receiving the little Bible and Carey had to be watchful that they didn't move around in order to get more than one. Billy began to hand out the New Testaments along the back wall where many of the men stood.

"*Muchisima Gracias,*" came a low voice from along the wall.

Billy looked up and into the red eyes of Luís. He did not understand the impact this gift was making on a man who had only recently come to know the Lord. But he did understand that there was more than mere gratitude on his face. Billy had handed out thousands of these Bibles in schools and prisons, but he had never seen such an eagerness for God's Word. It was as though he had given a feed sack of grain and rice to a starving man.

"You're so very welcome," was all Billy could say in English.

"*Con mucho gusto,*" Carey said behind him. Carey knew that the usual response of "*de nada*" was too little, meaning only "it is nothing". He expressed Billy's heart that was near bursting at this point.

Luís quickly opened the little New Testament and thumbed through the different books he had heard referred to in the few messages he had attended. He recognized the names for *John* and *Romans* in Spanish and decided that would be a good place to begin reading. A twinge of guilt and shame pricked at him as he thought back to the road outside of town just four nights ago. He looked into the gentile eyes of the two *gringos* and realized he had been wrong about the missionary. He had not come to take from his village, but rather to give. As the large man passed on to the next person beside him with hand extended for the little brown Bible, Luís knew he had found something that was real for his life. He joined the believers around him singing a familiar chorus led by one of the young women as Billy and Carey continued passing out the Bibles. Luís lifted his head as his spirit moved from shame to resolve. This was where he belonged and in a most ironic way, it was because of the man whose life he had almost threatened. He couldn't help but think how things could have been different if he had stayed on that muddy road that night; perhaps Moncho would still be alive and this missionary dead or at least too frightened to ever return to *Santa Tierra*. Now he felt indebted to the missionary. There was no way for Luís to realize just how entwined their lives would soon become.

Capitán Mendoza snaked his way through the crowded hallway following directions to the hospital's small ICU where he was told that Felípe was recovering from his gunshot wound. The hospital always seemed more crowded on Sundays. Family members brought small tin pots of rice and beans for their relatives. Without these meals, the patients would go without food over the weekend. The hospital didn't provide meals, just a bed and meager treatment. Some beds had no sheets and the halls were lined with minor emergencies awaiting outpatient attention. Felípe had been critical through Saturday afternoon, but as family prayers were lifted during the evening Mass, Felípe regained consciousness.

According to the doctor with whom Capitán Mendoza spoke, Felípe Cruz had been extremely lucky. The bullet had passed smoothly through the ileum, the larger of the pelvic bones, missing the spinal cord. He would need hip surgery eventually but he would not be paralyzed. Somehow, it had caused only minor damage passing through the small intestine, missing both the right kidney and colon. After three hours of surgery and the removal of a small portion of the damaged intestine, the prognosis looked favorable. There was infection from bile, but most of the problem had been caught in time. Felípe was attached to an IV of antibiotics that would remain at his side for several days. The bullet had exited just one inch to the right of his navel. His children would some day joke with him about having two belly buttons, but at least they would have him to joke with. He was far from well, but it looked as though he was going to live. As Mendoza stepped through the door, he quickly located which of the six beds belonged to Felípe. It was the one with eight rejoicing family members surrounding it.

"*Mire*, Capitán" called Juanita, Felípe's wife, for Mendoza to come see. "Felípe is awake and the doctors say he is going to get better."

Mendoza smiled and joined them. Though his interest in Felípe was purely police related, he could not help but join in the joy of a family that had just learned their beloved father and husband was not going to die. Mendoza stepped between two of the older sons to see Felípe face to face.

"It is good to see you awake my friend," Mendoza began. "I know your family is glad to know you will be fine."

"Do I know you?" Felípe asked puzzled looking at his uniform.

"This is Capitán Mendoza," Juanita explained. "He brought you to the hospital after you were shot. He visited us at home to ask questions. He is trying to find the man who did this to you."

"Flaco," Felípe sighed in a tired voice.

Mendoza was confused. He had been called many names by angered offenders, but he never had been called thin. His wife had been helpful in his weight, but his main problem was lack of exercise.

"Excuse me?" Mendoza responded.

"Flaco," Felípe repeated. "He is from *Santa Tierra*. He shot me in my truck."

"Do you know his last name?" Mendoza quickly asked. He did not want Felípe to tire and lose consciousness.

"No, I see him in the cantina sometimes. Did he take my truck?"

131

"Yes, but we have your plate number and are looking for it," Mendoza took a notepad from his pocket to jot down the information. "Do you remember who he is usually with in the cantina?"

Felípe closed his eyes as though trying to see his face. After a torturous stab of pain shook his body, he reopened his eyes.

"Moncho!" he said painfully.

Mendoza's eyes narrowed. In less than five days, two men from *Santa Tierra* had been brought to his attention. One had been killed and the other had nearly killed and both were close friends. Did one have anything to do with the other? He gently placed the pad back in his pocket. He knew he could not push Felípe for any more information. He had enough to warrant another trip to *Santa Tierra*.

———

Anita heard the pickup in front of her house, but did not stop her washing to see why it was there. It was not till one of her young sons came to her in the back yard calling that she even looked up from the soap covered rock where she was scrubbing out her dresses. Since Moncho's death, she had no more heavy jeans to wash and the children's clothes did not take that long. She had hoped to finish in time to start their lunch. She snapped at her son for the interruption when she noticed the three strangers passing around the side of her adobe dwelling to where she stood. All three were dressed nice and two were tall and foreigners. She pulled her loose fitting blouse together and tried to make herself presentable for her guests.

———

Adam cleared the dishes from the table as Gertie reached for her walker. He rinsed them off and carefully placed them beside the breakfast plates in the dishwasher. After supper he would run the cycle and clean the day's worth of dinnerware. By the time he reached the den, Gertie had already begun to pray. He stood in the doorway for a moment feeling as though he were intruding on a private conversation, when he suddenly felt the urge to join her again on the couch. It was time to be a doer of his lesson and not just a teacher. During his class that morning, he had stressed that whenever the disciples asked Jesus to teach them to pray, he responded by saying, "When you pray…" meaning the best way to learn to pray is to begin doing it. Adam was not foreign to prayer, he was just new to intercessory prayer for specific people. It complicated things for him when he knew one for whom he was praying, but did not know his specific need and yet to know the specific need of another, but not to know the person. He decided that part of praying in faith included the faith that God knew better than he did for whom and for what he was praying and that His will was being accomplished whether we had all the information or not. His faith was in the God of prayer, not necessarily in what he was praying for. Neither he nor Gertie were called to be all knowing, just prayerful.

———

Little talk took place in the Pennington car on the way home from church. Karen sensed the tension between her parents and knew better than to stir the coals by provoking either one. The best defense was a wise silence. Terry took the cue from his sister and refrained from asking about fast food on the way home. Howard decided without discussion on a drive through hamburger stop. There was no verbal objection from the front or back seat as the food was carried home.

Once in the house, they went in four different directions with their sacks of burgers and fries. Karen carried hers to her room while Terry opened his bag on the floor of the den in front of the TV. Howard poured himself a cup of tea to have with his meal and failed to offer a glass to Donna. She left her food on the kitchen table and went to their bedroom closing the door behind her. Howard sat on a stool at the breakfast bar and huffed. What else could go wrong today, he thought. He had no idea.

———

Flaco thanked Rafael for the plate of chicken and rice. He noticed a slight difference in the spices used in El Salvador with the rice than those used in Honduras. He also knew he would have to soon prepare himself for the spicy food of Mexico. Flaco offered extra money for the meal, but Rafael politely declined. Rafael had noticed Flaco's gun as he was unpacking for bed the night before. He didn't think Flaco was dangerous, but he still thought it best to treat him well all the same.

"When will we be able to leave?" Flaco asked.

"We will head for *Agua Fria* tomorrow early, around 4:00am so that you can be almost to *Santa Rosa* in Guatemala before the borders open and the police are patrolling the river area. From *Santa Rosa* you should be able to find a bus to *Las Margaritas*. If you pretend to be asleep at the *postas*, they should not bother you. If anyone does ask for your papers, give them this with a $10 bill in American money attached to it."

Rafael handed him an official looking document with various stamps and seals covering the bottom of the signatures.

"What is this?" Flaco asked. "And how did you know I had more American dollars?"

"You would have to in order to get through Mexico," Rafael replied confidently. "But you bargained well enough I didn't push you for the $100. You're going to need all you have to get where you're going. As for the document, it is just something a friend of mine at the border got me. It doesn't really say anything, but it has all the stamps that they use on this side. That and a good bribe should get you through local police stops. Just avoid the national police and the military."

"Thanks," said Flaco.

"By the way, I noticed your pistol last night. Have you ever used it?"

"Yes," Flaco said, trying to sound impressive.

"Do you need any more bullets for it?" Rafael asked, hoping to make a little more money off of this client.

"No," Flaco replied quickly, surprising even himself. "I have plenty for what I need to do. It is mostly for protection during the trip."

"Have you ever killed a man," the mechanic asked directly.

Flaco had not pondered that question yet. He remembered leaving Felípe bleeding on the side of the road. He had not considered himself a murderer until that very moment. With a calm resolve he stared back into Rafael's eyes.

"Perhaps."

———

Anita offered the men coffee and some hard bread she had left from breakfast. She knew one of the men was Honduran and suspected that one of the foreigners couldn't speak Spanish because the other was explaining the introductions to him. She then realized that the American who spoke Spanish must be the missionary that had been coming to their town. She had never seen him, but she had heard of his red hair. She sent her children out to the yard and pulled up a chair alongside the Honduran.

Mando began to explain who they were and the reason for their visit when Carey interrupted him. Contrary to the Honduran custom to handle business and difficult situations through a mediator, Carey felt the responsibility to share what was about to come.

"Señora Peréz," Carey began, using the name she introduced herself by. "By now, you must know who I am. I am the man who was driving the car that killed your husband." He was careful not to say that he himself had killed Moncho, but he had to acknowledge his actions thoroughly.

"I and Mando," he continued, motioning to his national companion. "We were returning from a late service when my truck was blocked on the other side of the *quebrada* by the storm. We waited there about four hours until we could pass. After we passed through *Santa Tierra*, we came to the hill just outside of town. It was there we believe that your husband tried to stop us and rob us by pulling a branch across the road. I drove over the branch and your husband tried to run after the truck. Going down hill, he slipped and fell as our truck began to slide and he was accidentally run over by the back wheel. I promise you that we did not run over him on purpose. It was something that happened completely out of our control."

It seemed to help Carey to have Mando present and to include him in the narration. Mando had agreed to share responsibility for the actions taken and also served as a witness to the things that Carey was saying. With each statement, Anita glanced toward Mando for a nod of confirmation.

"We walked back to his body and checked for signs of life, but he was already dead. We then placed him in the back of the truck and carried him to the nearest *posta* and gave our report to the police. We left the body with the police at that time." Carey paused to take a deep breath.

Anita took in his words soberly and to Billy's surprise, there were no tears.

"And why have you come to me today," she asked cordially.

Carey glanced at his brother for support. This was the hardest part. They had talked extensively the night before about his need to seek forgiveness from the family, but then to take even a further step towards finding that point of overcoming his own guilt and self-condemnation.

"For two reasons," Carey began. "The first is because I wish to ask you personally to forgive me for taking the life of your husband. Whether it was an accident or not, I have brought injury and loss to this house and I ask you to forgive me. I am responsible in part for the loss of your husband and your children's father."

Anita understood fully what he meant by "in part". If there was blame to be placed for that night, Moncho should shoulder the greater part. She did not hold anger or hatred for the man before her, and yet she understood why he was asking forgiveness and the importance for her to extend it, if for his sake alone. Her life, in all honesty, would be easier without Moncho.

"Señor Carey," she began slowly. "I do not hate you and my children do not know that it was you. I can not blame you for what Moncho brought upon himself. I believe your story completely because I know the man I was married to. If you are asking me to forgive you for taking a human life, only God can do that, but if you are asking me to forgive you because I no longer have my husband, then I do that."

Tears welled up in Carey's eyes. He knew where he stood with God, and now he felt one step closer to a clear conscience. He knew there were a few more steps to take and that they would not be without risk, but for now the first step was made and he stood on a stronger ground than he had felt in several days. He glanced at Billy who was sharing in his joy. As their eyes met, Billy gave him a nod to continue.

"As I said," Carey started with a renewed strength in his voice. "We have come for a couple reasons. Another reason is to say that we wish to help you and your family in this time of loss."

Carey reached into his pocket and took out an envelope. He gingerly handed the package across Mando to Anita's trembling hands. The white business letter envelope was filled with sixty-five 100 *Lempira* bills. Six thousand and five hundred *Lempira* was more than Moncho could earn in two years if he worked steady which he seldom did. It would pay for schooling, food and help them find a new home with plenty to spare. The amount was equivalent to $500 American dollars. Though the idea was Billy's, Carey and Susan had decided upon the amount after prayer. A moneychanger in the market had made the transaction possible on a Sunday.

Anita's eyes grew wide before them. Then they began to fill with tears. She had no words. She had thought that she would ask for some money to help with the funeral that they had conducted, but this was so much more than what was spent. She wanted to hug the three men, but sufficed to express her thanks repeatedly as she looked for a place to hide the money. Even the children could not know how much they had. She was so glad they had done this in private. Her first purchase would be to find a more secure home, or to return to her parents till something could be found.

"I have one other matter, I need to ask you," Carey added. Anita turned to give him her full attention. "Do you know what village Moncho is from? I would like to go to his family's home as well and ask forgiveness from them, but I understand that he is not from this area. Do you know where he is from?"

Anita's smile suddenly left her. She realized the missionary was sincere and caring and was only thinking of doing what was right, but he did not understand machete law and that to direct him to Moncho's family would be to send him to his death.

"I don't think that would be a good idea," she said seriously. "Moncho has three brothers still at home who could hurt you. You must not go."

Carey took a deep breath as he began his next step.

"I understand your concern. My companion Mando has explained to me about your custom and the danger of family members taking vengeance upon me for the death of their brother. I must believe that if God is directing me to do this that He will protect me in the way. I don't ask you to understand all of my reasoning, but please help me locate them. It is important to me, just as it was important for me to see you."

Anita looked hard into Carey's eyes. She saw a genuiness and strength that she could not resist. This man was willing to face death to do what he believed was right. Perhaps his God could protect him. He certainly demonstrated more faith and courage than she had ever known or seen.

"Moncho is from *Gualcince* in the department of *Lempira*. His family name is Reinaldo and his mother and family still live there. Do you know where *Gualcince* is?"

"I can find it, I'm sure," Carey replied confidently.

"We can find it," said Mando. Carey turned to his friend.

"You don't have to do this Mando," Carey objected.

"I haven't left you yet," he smiled. "I don't intend to when you will need me the most."

Billy did not understand the details of their conversation. He would be informed during the drive back to Choluteca. This was not a trip he would be able to make anyway, his return to the states was scheduled for Tuesday. Carey was already making plans to stay the night in the capital and start his trip to *Gualcince* early on Wednesday morning.

"I can't let you do that, Mando," Carey objected again. "You will be needed here on Wednesday night for the evening service. We can talk more about this on the way home, brother."

Anita looked at Mando. "What time does your service begin on Wednesday night?

"We try to start by 7:00, but it is usually a little after," he replied distracted by her question.

"May I bring my children?" she asked.

"Of course, we have many who come."

Carey smiled as he realized that Anita might soon be coming to the Lord through this contact. He knew that Mando would come Wednesday, just to make sure that Anita made it to service. After all, if there was to be danger in *Gualcince*, he didn't want to involve Mando. He would trust the Lord to protect him.

Before they dismissed themselves, Billy gave Anita a New Testament and used his memorized Spanish to say, "God bless you". She thanked the men for coming and thanked Carey again for the gift. As they rose to leave, Carey offered to pray for her and the family. Anita welcomed the opportunity.

"Dear Lord," Carey began in Spanish. "We turn to you at times of difficulty for both grace and peace. We thank you for your Word and the copy that Anita now has to read. We pray she will find You and Your Son through it. We thank you that you have a special place in your heart for both the widow and the orphan and that you have promised to become a father to the fatherless. We pray Your blessing upon this household today and give them direction through Your care. Protect them in the days to come. In Your Son's Holy name we pray, Amen"

"*Igualmente*" Anita prayed softly before opening her eyes.

Billy whispered to Carey, "What does that mean?"

"It means, 'the same to us'," Carey explained. "She is asking God to protect us in the days to come as well."

"Roger that," Billy replied.

Chapter Twelve:

"The Warrior"

Alberto Reinaldo had fathered six children before abandoning the family and moving to *La Esperanza* to live with a younger woman. He was shot over a gambling debt of less than 100 *lempiras*. When news of his death reached *Gualcince*, his oldest son Ramón swore vengeance. At the time, he was only fifteen years old. But vengeance seethes with years and when Ramón was nineteen, he recruited three other friends and they journeyed to *La Esperanza*. It took two days to locate the woman his father had moved in with and discover the name of the man who had shot him. Though Ramón's mission was successful, one of his friends had been shot and wounded by the man. When the deed was done, Ramón took his gun for a prize. Ramón would grow more violent through the years, wielding "the power" and killing again, until it would be necessary to flee his home in *Gualcince*.

Ramón's brother, Ricardo had admired him for his manliness, but till the news of his brother's death, Ricardo had never considered taking a life. As the oldest surviving family member, it was his responsibility to avenge the murder of Ramón, known to his friends as Moncho. Ricardo knew that his mother strongly objected, as she had when Moncho killed their father's murderer, but he also knew there was honor at stake. One could not allow death to go unpunished, especially for a family member. If what Flaco had told them was correct, the man who ran over his brother was not even held by the police. He must have paid a bribe to gain his freedom, Ricardo thought. He swore he would accept no such bribe to spare this man's life.

Moisés walked with Ricardo from the fields where they had been working. Mass was optional in the Reinaldo family, but work on Sunday wasn't. The threatening rain clouds overhead punctuated the need for them to get their planting in so that the life crop of corn would get a good start that season. Ricardo would not jeopardize the family's need for the family honor, but the work was nearly done. Moisés, the younger brothers, as well as the sisters, could finish getting the crop in by Tuesday without him. It was now late afternoon and they were out of corn seed. The beans could be planted tomorrow.

"Are you still planning on going to *Santa Tierra*," Moisés asked as they walked.

"Yes, I plan to leave early tomorrow so I can make *La Esperanza* and try to find a bus that evening if possible."

"How long do you think it will take you to get there?"

"What's the matter, little brother. Are you afraid I will not come back to help finish with the crop?"

"No," he said softly. "I'm afraid you may not come back."

Ricardo stopped and looked at his brother whose head was low.

"What do you mean, not come back?" he asked. "Do you fear for my life?"

"No, I fear you will find a life there that you will want more than here like Moncho did and will not want to come back."

"Why would I not come back here? My family is here."

"But there is nothing for us here," Moisés replied strongly.

Ricardo recognized the yearning in his brother's voice.

"You are not worried about me, you are worried about what YOU would do if you had the chance to leave *Gualcince*."

Moisés looked up surprised. But his brother was right.

"Yes, I would leave if I could," Moisés responded. "Do you blame me. I am twenty-two with no hope for a good job. I want to have a family, but I have nothing to offer but a small piece of ground that is getting harder each year. What is there for me here?"

Ricardo looked sympathetically at his brother and placed his hand on his shoulder.

"You may be right. I know I would like to leave, but it just seems like this is all we will ever have. You can get angry about it and try to forget it drinking like many do, or you can work hard and make it more till someday you have something that will support a family. Life is not given to you. You must work hard for what you get. Or you must steal for it. You decide."

"What do you plan to do when you get to *Santa Tierra*?" Moisés asked to change the subject.

"I will first find Moncho's widow and then see who knows this missionary and when he comes to their town. Then I will wait for him. I hope it doesn't take more than a week. I need to get back here, but you all can finish getting the crop in from here."

Moisés nodded.

"How do you plan to get to *Santa Tierra*?" he asked.

"I have a little money I can use for a bus to Tegucigalpa. I will try to catch a ride from there south and then find a truck or someone going into *Santa Tierra*."

"That could take two or three days in itself," Moisés noted.

"Two, if I am lucky and can get into Teguc. tomorrow. I will leave before sunrise and hopefully find a truck that will get me into *La Esperanza* before lunch. I can leave there as late at 3:00 in the afternoon."

"How will you deal with the *gringo* when you find him?" Moisés tried not to refer to him as 'the missionary'.

"I will see when I get there."
Moisés nodded his approval.

———

Susan had fixed a typical Honduran lunch to impress Billy, though they would not be returning to the house till nearly 2:00 in the afternoon. Carey had explained that they would be stopping over to visit Moncho's wife after the service. Susan had prayed at the noon hour for the meeting and then began preparing the meal of chicken and rice, with fried platanos, refried beans with sour cream, fresh fruit from the market and even some fried tortillas. She and the boys normally accompanied Carey to Sunday morning services, but with Billy and Mando going, there would not be room. With the men stopping after the service to visit the family, Carey had insisted that his sons not try to go, even though they could have ridden in the back of the truck.

After lunch, Billy installed Carey's new computer programs and brought him up to speed on the current technology. For Carey, the ability to write letters and perform simple databases was more than enough. Such marvels as email, voice typing, and video conferencing was beyond him completely. It would be years before southern Honduras would have such access. Till then, he would rely on snail mail and monthly phone calls.

"You know, email from the capital is not unreasonable for you here," Billy explained. "I'm sure they have a net server there. You would just need to make a long distance call to get your mail. With a good modem, you wouldn't be online more than a minute or two. How much is a long distance call to the capital?"

"About 14 cents a minute."

"That's a little more than we pay, but how much is a postage stamp?" Billy questioned.

"About 52 cents," Carey smiled.

"There you go," Billy said excitedly. "You could be sending and receiving five or six letters by email at less than a third the cost of sending just one letter by the post office."

"How much does it cost to connect to the net?" Carey asked.

"Usually about $20 a month. I don't know about here. But listen, it is worth it when you think about instant communication. How long does it take you to get a letter to or from the states?"

"Seven to ten days usually," Carey confessed.

"There you go again," Billy exclaimed in his salesman voice. "What would it be worth to you to have mail answered the SAME DAY you sent it?"

"I could write Anna every week and get a letter every week instead of this once or twice a month exchange we have going," Carey began to think out loud.

"I would even set her up with her own email address, so you could be as private as you want to be."

The idea of being able to communicate on a weekly basis with his daughter was appealing. Maybe computer technology was not so bad after all.

"OK, I'll look into it the next time I'm in the capital, but no promises until I talk to them and understand everything," Carey acquiesced.

"You won't be disappointed, big brother, I promise you."

Susan brought in some fresh squeezed lemonade.

"What time do you guys need to leave for evening service?" she asked politely.

Carey looked at his watch and jumped up.

"Oh my goodness, is it that late already. I better get changed." He turned to Billy. "You going back with me tonight aren't you?"

"Wouldn't miss it brother."

———

Donna came out of the bedroom and walked downstairs to pour herself a glass of ice tea. The shadows in the kitchen told her it was already late afternoon. She had slept most of the time since church. Howard heard her in the kitchen and stepped out of his office. He was still in his suit clothes from that morning. He glanced at the clock on the kitchen wall.

"Don't you think you should be getting dressed for church," He suggested. We'll be leaving for Discipleship Class in less than thirty minutes."

"I'm not going tonight, Howard," she countered coldly. "I'm not feeling too well and I think I'll just stay home tonight."

Howard stared at her for a moment. He knew she was upset, but nothing had ever kept her from going to church before.

"Are you sure, honey?" he started.

She turned and glared at him with the pitcher in her hand. He quickly understood and began to back pedal.

"I mean. . . of course. If you aren't feeling good . . . you should stay home."

"Thank you," she said simply.

"Who's staying home?" Karen asked, walking in the room and noticing the tension.

"Your mother isn't feeling well and will be staying home tonight from church," Howard responded informatively.

"Can I stay also?" Karen risked. "I have a major project due tomorrow and I haven't had much time to work on it."

"Is your job already interfering with school?" Howard snapped, taking his frustration out on Karen.

"Don't fuss at her," Donna interjected. "We told her she needed the responsibility. If she needs to adjust a little till she can handle both, I don't see a problem."

Somehow, Howard knew best not to object at that moment. Whatever problem Donna was having did not need to be compounded by engaging in a power struggle between him and Karen at this time.

"OK," he said throwing his hands up. "I just hope this doesn't become a habit."

Karen looked at her mom appreciatively, but did not receive the comforting exchange she had hoped for. What she saw was pain. Whatever her mother had just done was not for her, but against him. Suddenly, Karen felt alone in her own kitchen in the presence of both of her parents. It was not a good feeling.

————

Flaco walked inconspicuously around the small town of *Agua Fria*. He wondered if the name referred to the river water being cold. According to Rafael, he would not have to ford the river. The ATV was high enough to cross. Up to now, he had not felt lonely, but even the brief friendship with Rafael and his family would be short lived and he would be on his own again soon. He was beginning to miss the familiar faces of *Santa Tierra*. He told himself that he didn't miss his family, but that wasn't completely true. What he had left behind was his responsibility to them not his thoughts for them. He told himself he was going to the North to make a better life than he could have had in *Santa Tierra*. Someday, he may even return for his family. And if he did return, he would return a better man with enough to be noticed. Someday, he would be respected for what he was doing. And yet, all of his dreams could not fill his loneliness in the little town of "Cold Water" that night.

————

Carey, Billy and Mando arrived at the evening service above *Santa Tierra* in time to visit with some of the believers before the singing began. Mando helped the local leader with the Coleman lantern while Carey introduced Billy to the families arriving. Luís watched them step from person to person speaking. Luís had had a restless afternoon thinking about whether he should speak with the missionary or not concerning the night of the accident. He knew he was not directly involved, but he was there, and possibly could have kept Moncho from trying to rob Carey, or could have warned Carey before they reached the top of the hill. There were so many things Luís could have done, and yet he ran. Had his cowardliness cost Moncho his life? Luís was struggling with what to do when Carey stepped in front of him to present Billy. Carey did not know Luís by name and had only seen him for the first time that morning, but he treated him like an old family member. Luís sensed a true love from these two brothers and decided they needed to hear the truth.

"*Hermano*," Luís began. "May we speak outside for a moment before the service?"

Carey sensed the seriousness in his voice and asked Billy if he would excuse them while they spoke together in Spanish. Billy smiled and nodded not thinking at all about being left to himself alone without an interpreter. He walked over to where the young musicians were tuning their guitars and watched.

As Carey and Luís walked around to the dark side of the house, Carey began to feel a little uncomfortable. It occurred to him that he did not know this man and had only assumed he was a new believer. Perhaps he was a family member from Moncho who had not been as forgiving as Anita. In his effort to speak with the man in privacy, he had just made himself vulnerable to attack. His pulse began to quicken and he nervously looked to each side to determine the availability of help should the need arise.

Luís looked down at his work shoes and began to speak humbly.

"*Hermano* Carey, I need to tell you that I know what happened last Wednesday night on the road from *Santa Tierra*. I was there. I didn't see the accident, but I know what was going to happen. At least what was supposed to happen."

Carey began to fidget, but decided to hear more.

"You see, I was a friend of the man who died on that road," Luís said calmly.

Carey felt a lump form in his throat. He watched Luís's hands carefully, but he saw no weapon. . . yet.

"We had been drinking that night and ran out of money. We went outside of town to wait for the liquor salesman so that we could rob him. But you came by instead."

"So you WERE there," Carey said, thinking he had caught the man in a lie.

"No, when I saw it was your truck coming instead of Felípe, I told Moncho I would not be a part of the robbery. I left then through the ravine back into town. I was there only till you came, then I left. That is why I say I didn't see the accident."

Carey began to relax his stance and listen to the man who was making no threatening moves or statements.

"I know about the branch that Moncho had us pull across the road."

Carey suddenly caught something that pierced him with fear again.

"Us?" Carey asked.

"Yes, there was another there that night. His name is Flaco. He was across the road from Moncho waiting."

"But we didn't see anyone else there," Carey said curiously.

"He was there, *hermano*. He took Moncho's gun after you left. He must have been hiding when things didn't go as Moncho planned."

Carey let that sink in as he tried to recreate the scene in his mind. Their attention had not been on the left side of the road. It was possible he could have been hiding there.

"Then he knows it was an accident," Carey suddenly realized.

"Unfortunately, he is not telling the story that way," Luís said soberly. "He is telling people you ran over Moncho like a dog. Those who know you here at the mission know better, but the village people who don't know you want to think the worse of strangers. They accept Flaco's story."

"Where is Flaco?"

"I don't know. He came to me last Thursday with plans to "*go wet*" to America. He asked if I wanted to go. I told him no and I haven't seen him since."

Carey recognized the expression meaning that Flaco was planning to enter into the United States illegally.

"Does he have family here in town?" Carey asked.

"Yes, but he didn't tell them he was leaving. He doesn't care about his family. He could be all the way to Guatemala by now."

Carey thought for a moment, then asked the obvious question.

"Where would he get enough money to do that?"

Luís had been so pre-occupied with his new found faith and his study of God's Word for the past three days that he had never made the connection between Flaco's leaving and the assault on Felípe's truck on Thursday night. He lifted his head and Carey saw the look of concern in his eyes as the tone of his voice changed from informative to distress.

"He must have robbed and shot Felípe."

Carey was unfamiliar with the crime that had occurred over the weekend. He wasn't sure he wanted to know much more than he had already been told. He had just discovered a second assailant was on that road and he

145

was now armed and dangerous and spreading a damaging report about him to townspeople. Suppose Flaco did not head to the states, and was waiting for the missionary to return to *Santa Tierra* to take vengeance himself. Would he and Billy be ambushed that very night on the way home? Carey was losing control to his imagination when a soft voice rose from his inner most being - *"I have not given you a spirit of fear, but of power, of love and of self-control. Trust me with your steps."*

Carey heard the praise choruses begin from within the house. He thanked Luís for sharing the truth with him. He put his arm around Luís' broad shoulders and they walked together to the light of the worship service. As they stepped inside, Carey looked around for his brother. He finally spotted him seated between to musicians on a bench to the left of the table from where Carey would preach . Billy was playing the guitar while the small congregation sang. Without a translator, without written music, he was worshipping with a group of believers who loved and worshipped the same God he knew and loved. Carey smiled as he walked to the front. Yes, he thought, God IS in control.

———

Howard could feel the emptiness of his own soul as he preached a perfunctory message from his sermon files. He looked out over the faithful who had gathered to be fed and felt like a hypocrite. He was no more prepared to teach the Word of God that evening than if he had just opened the Bible and begun to shoot from the hip.

Among those who noticed most were Rusty and Arnie. Both caught each stuttering mistake, but only one was amused. Both had noticed the absence of Howard's family, but only one understood the reason. Both knew something was wrong, but only one suspected what it was. Both were deeply interested in why, but for differing motives. One had been there, and still was.

———

Karen decided to take a break from studying and find some munchies. Donna had come down from the bedroom and was sipping warm tea at the kitchen table alone. Terry had gone to church with a friend from school. Since the rest of the family was staying home, he thought it was a good time to accept a long-standing invitation. There had been no objection from his parents, which surprised him, a little. This left the house nice and quiet for Donna.

"I didn't know you were down here," Karen said walking into the kitchen. "Feeling better?"

"I'm fine, thank you," Donna replied, cradling her mug. "How is your study coming?"

"OK, I guess," Karen replied, opening the kitchen cabinets above the stove where the chips and cookies were stored out of reach of Terry. "I guess it wasn't as much as I thought it would be."

"How is your job going?" Donna asked.

"I like it a lot," Karen said, reaching for some milk to dip her chocolate chip cookies into. "I like Sheila a lot. She is good to work for and I'm learning a lot about clothes and accessories."

"The basics of life," her mother offered cheerfully extending her cup upward as in a toast.

Karen smiled and sat down beside her mother. It had been a long time since they had sat and talked together. Karen realized it had taken an argument with her father to put them on the same side.

"Do you think you may want to do some work with clothing some day," Donna inquired. "I mean like designing clothes or something like that."

"I don't know," Karen answered honestly. "For right now, I just enjoy putting combinations together for people and helping them find what looks good for them. You know, not everybody can wear the same thing and look good doing it."

"Tell me about it," Donna lamented. Since Terry was born, she had not been able to return to the dress size she liked. She was continually comparing herself to slimmer women in the church.

"Mom, you look great," Karen responded, sensing the self-inflicted insult.

"Does Sheila have any children?"

"No, she's not married," Karen replied dipping a cookie in her milk. "In fact, I don't think she even has a boyfriend. But she has a cat."

"How old is she?" Donna asked.

"I'm guessing mid to late twenty's. I'm not sure."

"And she has her own business already? That's impressive," Donna said. "Maybe she can teach you some things after all that will be helpful."

"Hope so," Karen said with her mouth full. Neither fully understood the impact of their simple conversation and the direction it would take Karen in the days to follow.

―――――

"Going to bed so early?" Adam called to Gertie from the den.

"It's past 8:30," Gertie replied jokingly shuffling her walker down the hall toward the bedroom. "Besides, I never know when I'm going to get back up to pray. I best get some rest while I can."

Adam turned the volume down on the TV so that Gertie would not be disturbed. He reflected over the lesson he had taught that morning. There was so much more to intercessory prayer than he had first thought. Most of all, he was learning that it was part of a greater conflict. He had once read that prayer was like a walkie-talkie used for calling in resources to fight the battle, rather than an intercom system for ordering more snacks from the kitchen. As a WWII veteran, he could identify with that. Gertie was as much in the throes of war as those in the trenches. Her limitations in this life were insignificant to her participation in the spiritual warfare of the kingdom of God. She was a mighty soldier from whom he could take lessons. She was a warrior with a walker and Adam respected her greatly.

Chapter Thirteen:

"The Letter"

(Monday)

"This is as far as I go," Rafael declared.

Flaco strained to see beyond the small beam of fog lights that Rafael had attached to his truck and was using in place of his headlights. The amber glow provided him enough vision without drawing too much attention from the highway about a kilometer away.

"If you walk about ten minutes in that direction, you will come to the road three kilometers up from the border and about two kilometers outside of *Santa Rosa*. From there you can find a bus driver who will take you to *Antigua*. I would suggest getting some breakfast first and walking around the market listening to the *muchachos* who work on the busses taking the money. Talk to a few and feel them out about the trip. Find the one who will take your money, but don't show dollars. Buy about $25 dollars worth of *Quetzales,* the currency used in Guatemala. Eat on part of it and then offer about four times the normal fare to one of the boys and explain that you do not wish to be disturbed, especially at check points for papers. He will understand and shield you from any police stops. Talk as little as possible, your accent is different than theirs."

Flaco made mental notes while nodding at each instruction. It was still an hour before sunrise. He looked again into the direction Rafael had told him to walk. It didn't look too difficult.

"You need to go now," Rafael encouraged him. "I need to be back across the border before day break. They begin patrolling then."

"You're right," Flaco acknowledged. "I better go."

He climbed down from the big truck and walked around to Rafael's window.

"Thank you, *amigo*," Flaco said extending his hand.

"You be careful and all will go well. *Buena suerte,*" Rafael replied wishing him luck.

Flaco began walking quickly in the direction Rafael pointed. He looked back once to see the big truck maneuver around a tree to head back to the river. That would be the last time he would look back.

———

Carey had thought to let his brother sleep in after two trips to *Santa Tierra* the day before. He forgot about the neighbor's chickens next door.

Billy stumbled into the kitchen where Carey sat sipping on his second cup of coffee and reading the devotional that Billy had brought him.

"Sleep well, little brother?" Carey asked without standing.

"Like a baby," Billy replied pouring himself a cup of coffee.

"The chickens didn't bother you?" Carey taunted.

"What chickens?" his brother replied sarcastically. "I just thought it was the busy traffic of this great metropolitan city you live in."

"Ready to see some of this 'great metropolitan city' today, plus some of the other areas where we have work going on?"

"Sounds like a winner to me. How much time do I have to scrap my face and wash off the top layer of dust?"

"Drink your coffee, and take your time," Carey said motioning for Billy to sit down and relax. "We don't have a schedule today. Remember, you are in Latin America now. We go at our own pace. Have yourself some breakfast and we will go whenever you are ready."

"What is Susan doing today?"

"Homeschooling. The boys start classes about 8:30 and go till around 2:00 in the afternoon. We'll have time with them when we get back."

"I don't want to miss an opportunity to spend some time with the boys while I'm here," Billy explained.

"They know that. They are looking forward to spending time with you also. We'll have some time this afternoon, OK?"

"Roger that," Billy replied sipping carefully the strong Honduran coffee.

———

The battle-gray pickup truck usually meant someone was in trouble. FUSEP did not normally patrol *Santa Tierra*. It was just too far off the main highway. There had to be a reason for a police officer to visit the same home twice in less than one week. Capitán Mendoza had no trouble finding the house and pulling into the yard, especially since the mud had dried. Mendoza traveled alone this time. Although he was involved in an official police investigation, he was following some personal hunches and did not want to have to explain his every move to another officer. He also felt that Moncho's widow would be more responsive to him, if he came alone. He smiled at the playing children in the yard as he walked toward the open front door.

"*Buenos dias*," he called to the house.

Anita stepped to the doorway with a child in her arms.

"Señorita Peréz," he began using her maiden name. "I am Capitán Mendoza. I was the one who brought the body of your husband last week here to the house. May I come in?"

Anita had no objection and invited the police officer into her home.

———

Little Ramón was twelve, but he was the oldest of Moncho's sons. He earned money by helping on small jobs around town. Today, he was straightening bent nails for Luís and holding them till he needed them. Luís was hammering the final board completing the window frame for his uncle. Once the frames were completed, the adobe block could be laid on its next level across the top of the windows. The frames were used to support the layers above the window. Luís enjoyed the carpentry work and was glad to be doing something productive with his hands again. While they worked, Luís noticed that little Ramón was especially excited.

"Why are you so happy today?" Ramón asked playfully.

"Because we will be moving to a better house soon," little Ramón said cheerfully.

"Who says you will be moving?" Luís asked.

"Momma said that the missionary gave her enough money to move into a better house."

Luís stopped hammering. He looked down at little Ramón who was busy pounding a bent nail with a rock.

"When did she tell you this?" Luís asked seriously.

"Just this morning, she is very happy also. She didn't tell the other children – just me."

With good reason, Luís thought to himself.

"Listen to me, little Ramón," Luís said firmly.

Little Ramón stopped his pounding and looked up at Luís on the makeshift platform above the window. He seemed so big and high up.

"You must not tell anyone else about this money, it is not safe. Do you understand me?"

Little Ramón nodded. Luís climbed down from the scaffolding and laid his hammer next to the boy.

"Use this for a while, I am going to go visit your mother for a minute."

Luís walked around to the front of the house where his uncle was working on the front door.

"*Tio*," Luís called addressing his uncle. "I have to run an errand for a minute. I will be back as soon as I can."

His uncle nodded nonchalantly and Luís trotted through the back lots to Moncho's house. He saw the gray pickup in the front yard and stopped. Why were the police at Moncho's again? He began to reconsider going to the door. Did the missionary report what he told him? Even so, he could not be held responsible, he had left before anything had happened. But he could not prove that he had left. Then again, no one could prove he had been there. As the whirl of thoughts began to cloud his thinking, he closed his eyes. Suddenly, prayer seemed the most logical course of action for him to take. He had been learning that a child of God should seek wisdom from God when he didn't know what to do. He simply asked God if he should go into the house. Though this was new for Luís, it seemed so natural. Within moments, Luís sensed calmness in his mind. He walked to the door and knocked. Anita came to the door, as Capitán Mendoza sat at the table.

"Anita, may I come in," Luís began. "I knew Moncho. We were friends, and. . ."

"Please come in," came the authoritative voice of the police Capitán.

Anita stepped aside and Luís walked into the front room. She showed Luís a chair and then rejoined them.

"Capitán Mendoza was just saying that there was a robbery outside of town last Thursday," she explained.

"But Moncho was killed on Wednesday night," Luís objected.

"Oh he wasn't suspecting Moncho. In fact, Capitán Mendoza is the officer who brought Moncho's body back to *Santa Tierra*."

Luís looked confused.

"Felípe, the liquor supplier for Roberto's cantina was robbed and shot last Thursday night," Mendoza began. "The truck was stolen along with a good bit of money. Felípe is in the hospital in Choluteca. Yesterday, he regained consciousness and told me the name of the man that robbed him. He was a friend of Moncho's. I was hoping Señorita Peréz could help me locate him."

Suddenly Luís felt weak. Not only had he been involved the night of Moncho's death. He knew who had robbed and shot Felípe.

"Capitán Mendoza," Luís began slowly. "Was the person who shot Felípe a skinny man?"

"Why yes, in fact his name was . . ."

"Flaco!" Luís completed his sentence for him.

––––––

"Ricardo!" his mother called out toward the fields below their house.

Moisés could hear her from where he was working. He knew that Ricardo had slipped out of the house before she had awakened and could stop him. She must have assumed he rose early to come to the field. When he had not returned to the house for breakfast, she first thought he was delayed by some problem, like a tree that needed removing. Moisés knew he would have to be the one to tell his mother where her son had gone. He thrust his machete into a fallen log where he could find it and walked back up to the house.

"Ricardo is not here," he told his mother. "He left early this morning to go to *La Esperanza.*" He hoped she would assume it was for purchases and would not pursue the matter.

"Where does he plan to go from there?" she asked deliberately.

Moisés hesitated before answering, but realized she already knew.

"Momma, he is going to *Santa Tierra*. He is going to find the man who killed your son."

Señora Reinaldo turned away, but not before Moisés saw the pain on her face. He wasn't sure if it was for the death of Moncho or for the action of Ricardo to avenge his death. In either case, it both saddened and angered Moisés. A mother's pain is not easily dismissed.

———

Sometimes problems just seem to fade after a good night's sleep. Such was not the case in the Pennington home. Terry made a point not to complain about Karen in the bathroom, while Howard limited his morning conversation to the polite necessities. Donna appeared to be in no better mood than that of the night before. Karen marched about her morning routine with little to say. The overall demeanor of the household was cordial at best.

Each one prepared their own lunch and provided for their own breakfast. There was no smell of bacon or toast in the kitchen. Karen left first, soon followed by Terry. Howard made a pot of coffee while he skimmed the morning paper. He had hoped that Donna would come down and join him. He wanted to talk about what was going on. He worked through a couple approaches and introductions in his mind. It would be easier, now that that children were both gone. He sipped his coffee and waited.

Donna stood before the mirror in their bathroom brushing her hair. She had heard the door slam twice and knew that the children had gone to school. She was hoping to hear the door open and close a third time, but it hadn't. Not yet. She felt the tears in her eyes, but pushed them back. She wanted to be back in Texas. She wanted to see her family. She wanted to sit down and talk to her mother and tell her the aches of her heart. She wanted to know what to do when you didn't feel loved anymore.

Howard put down his paper and looked at his watch. He was aware of two appointments that morning plus the staff prayer meeting. Many pastors took Monday off because they wanted the refreshment from Sunday and they felt the break gave them a good start on the rest of the week. Howard tended to rest on Saturday. This week would be less rigorous since he did not have to preach Wednesday night. At least, he thought there would be less pressure this week. Howard had no idea that this Monday marked the beginning of one of the hardest weeks he would ever have to endure. What would transpire by the end of these next six days would change the course of his life forever. He was not getting off to a good start.

———

"What do you know about Flaco," Mendoza asked.

"Moncho, Flaco and I drank together at times," Luís stated carefully. He wasn't sure how much he should say.

"Were you three drinking together the night Moncho died?" Mendoza asked taking a pad from his shirt pocket for taking notes.

"Yes, we were."

"Did Flaco have a gun?" Mendoza asked.

"Not before that night."

Capitán Mendoza looked up from his pad and scrutinized Luís' face.

"Tell me about that night," Mendoza said slowly. Anita leaned forward to hear better. Luís looked at Anita as though to apologize for the story he was about to tell.

It took about four minutes for Luís to give all the information he knew concerning the events leading up to the accident. He was careful to point out that Moncho had the gun before the accident.

"How do you know that Flaco had the gun after the accident?" Mendoza asked.

"He showed it to me."

"And when was this?" Mendoza continued.

Luís took a breath.

"On Thursday night. He said he was going north – *wet* – and asked if I wanted to go with him," he said nervously. At this point, Luís knew he was giving testimony against Flaco. And yet, telling the truth seemed to be the only reasonable thing to do.

"Did Flaco have the money to go north?" Mendoza pondered out loud.

"I doubt it. He said he had a cousin that could help him, but he didn't tell me how much money he would need. From what I have heard, he would have needed at least over twenty thousand *Lempira*, and a way to convert it to American dollars."

"If he robbed Felípe and sold his truck, he would have more than enough," Mendoza concluded. "Did he say which way he was going to leave the country."

"In fact, he did," Luís found himself offering. "He said he was going to go through the department of *Lempira* and cross at *Mapulaca*."

"We have no police at that point that I can contact," Mendoza thought. "Chances are he would drive the truck as far as *La Esperanza*. That is the last place he could find someone with enough money to buy it. It would be a waste of a good part of his money to hire someone from around here to drive him."

"My guess is, if he left *Santa Tierra* on Friday, he is already out of Honduras and probably through *El Salvador*. You will never catch him now," Luís shrugged.

"Maybe not, but we can at least recover the truck for Felípe," Mendoza replied putting his notepad back into his pocket. "We have the license number from Felípe's records and a description of the truck. We should be able to locate it. Thank you for your help."

The Capitán rose from his seat and thanked Anita for her cooperation. He had hoped only to find the name of Flaco's wife, so he could question her. The chance arrival of this friend proved to be more information than he had hoped. He now had a solid lead. He didn't know how soon something would turn up, but he could at least contact the FUSEP office in *La Esperanza*.

"Oh, one other thing," Mendoza suddenly remembered. "What is Flaco's real name?"

"Antonio Alvaréz," Luís replied after careful thought. "But you won't find anybody that knows him by that name."

"God knows his name," came the reply, but not from anyone in the room.

———

The familiar red Hilux with the white camper was a welcome site to many of the villages around the mountains of the southern Honduras. Carey's fourteen years of Church Planting had been instrumental in the formation of over a dozen congregations in the rural area as well as almost eight more churches in the large city of Choluteca itself. Most all of these congregations now had their own pastor or lay leader. They conducted their own services, paid their own bills and some were even building their own additions. Carey provided resources and services like access to literature and Bibles, theological training and leadership training workshops. The goal of the missionary was to be the catalyst of a new work and then to turn it over to the congregation as quickly as it could stand on its own. The goal of Carey was to start as many congregations that could support and govern themselves as possible. As they began to reproduce themselves, he could move to other areas. Billy had seen a young mission in formation. Now he was seeing what full-grown churches had become after Carey left.

"I had no idea you were involved in so many churches," Billy said impressed.

"I have had my hand in many, but most of these I don't even need to visit anymore," Carey corrected.

"How many churches have you started since arriving?" Billy asked.

"None!" Carey responded quickly. "I may be part of a movement of the Holy Spirit in a town like this, but there are usually believers here before I arrive. God saves the lost and calls out the leaders. I am just a tool He uses to proclaim His gospel and disciple His children. It's His church that you see before you."

"Point well taken," Billy said. "I meant, how many churches have been formed since you came to the south of Honduras to serve?"

"I have been involved with about thirty congregations. Some are strong self-sufficient churches, some are struggling, some didn't make it and some are just getting started. I look for the day when there will be enough trained nationals in the south that I won't be needed."

"Kind of like working yourself out of a job," Billy observed.

"Exactly," Carey confirmed. "In mission work, that's the goal to shoot for, because there is always somewhere else to go and more work to do."

"So you don't see yourself here forever?" Billy inquired.

"Only for as long as God wants me here."

———

Flaco tried to sleep on the bus, but the road was bumpier than he expected. He had no trouble finding a young man who would take extra *Quetzales* and assure him an undisturbed ride to *Antigua*. As Flaco glanced around the bus, he realized that Rafael was correct. The brightly colorful dress and Indian features of the Guatemalan people marked a stark contrast between Flaco and the majority of the people around him on the bus. He pulled his worn straw hat over as much of his face as possible to hide the difference. The last thing he needed was to draw attention to himself. He would make a point of eating away from the other riders when they stopped midday at the *comedor*. He shifted his weight and turned his face toward the window. He still had two more hours on this bus till it would stop for lunch.

———

Howard stared at the same page of his commentary for over four minutes. He had hoped to talk out the problem with Donna before leaving for the church, but she never came down to join him. He glanced at the mail from Saturday, but didn't open any of it. He didn't even notice the first knock on his door.

"Bro. Howard, are you coming to the staff and prayer meeting?" Diane called through the partially opened door.

"Yes, Diane," he replied, as though interrupted from deep thought.

He tossed the commentary onto his desk and slowly walked to the door. Rusty was waiting at Diane's desk. He caught the concern in Rusty's eyes as he walked slowly past him. Howard was not so naïve to think his countenance and performance in the pulpit the day before did not indicate problems. He knew Rusty was aware of his struggle, but he did not know the reason. Howard was not about to share his family problems with a single young staff member, and especially not at a staff prayer meeting.

The staff and prayer meetings were held in the lounge of the youth department because there were more couches there than any of the offices. Most brought their coffee or diet cokes with them to the meeting. They would discuss any difficulties in any of the departments or classes. Each staff member was responsible for overseeing an area of ministry and reporting any problems in that area. Once a month, the chairman of Deacons was invited and the family ministry program was discussed. Afterward, prayer was shared for each area as well as the current hospital list. In the afternoon, both Howard and Rusty would make the hospital visits. Sometimes, they would travel together if the list was small and at the same location. Sometimes, only one would make the trip.

They found their favorite places and took turns reporting. The Youth Director reported on the increase in attendance for their "fifth quarter" meetings on Friday night after the local high school football games. This activity was held whenever there was a home game. He repeated the scheduled events for the coming month and stressed the need for more prayer for the young people of the church.

As each report was given, Rusty watched Howard nod assent but refrain from comment. It was apparent that he was not giving the meeting his full attention. After the prayer requests were given, Howard called on Rusty to lead in the prayer. This was the first time anyone could remember Howard not taking the lead during the prayer time. As they bowed their heads, Diane passed a concerned glance toward Rusty.

As they paraded back to their offices, Howard informed Diane that he did not wish to be disturbed till lunchtime. He closed the door fully to his office and slumped onto his couch. He wanted to just close his eyes and wake up to a new day. He felt totally drained of strength. He lay back on the couch and pulled his arm up over his face. He had counseled people in depression before. He should have seen the symptoms before now, but he hadn't. What's more, he didn't care.

Sheila tossed the small pile of mail on her desk and pulled off her sweater. She took out a stick of gum and mentally cursed the "smoke free" policy of the mall. As she swiveled up to her desk, she began sorting between the envelopes. The consumer circulars were quickly filed in the small can to her right to await emptying that evening. She flipped through the business letterheads till one caught her eye. She quickly opened it with a nail file she kept by her phone and skimmed past the greetings to the announcement. Her eyes shot up to the large calendar on the wall and she quietly cursed. She quickly scooped up her sweater and called for the sales attendant that was re-hanging blouses near the front of the store.

"Amber, I just realized that today was the day of the big bazaar at the fair grounds at Oceanside. I need some help."

The young woman nodded.

"Can I get you to stay till Karen gets here this afternoon and then let her watch the store this evening. It's Monday and usually slow, I'm sure she can handle it. I can't possibly get back before the store closes because I have a dinner with one of the designers. Could you come back in at . . . say 8:30, let Karen go home and then close down the store for me?"

Again, the young woman nodded.

"You're a peach," Sheila said kissing her on the cheek. "I have to run. I'll see you tomorrow and make the deposit then."

Amber just waved her on and watched as she lightly trotted out the door and out of sight.

"Does it always take this long at the bank?" Billy asked.

"Patience, brother," Carey smiled, shifting his weight to his other foot. "Remember, things move slower here. Part of it is lack of technology and part of it is that Latin America is more people-centered than event-centered. That means they look at encounters as opportunities to meet people and not just get things done. I have made several friendships while standing in line."

"I'll remember that the next time they fail to open an extra check out register at the grocery store when I get back home."

Billy paused in his thinking for a moment, then changed the subject.

"You don't think of the United States as home anymore do you?" he asked Carey.

"Not really," Carey responded. "I mean, don't get me wrong. I will always think of 'back home' when referring to either mine or Susan's family. But for myself, I don't think of 'back there' as home. You can't when you are only there one out of every four or five years."

"When do you come back to the states again on furlough?" Billy asked trying to calculate in his mind.

"Just under two years," Carey replied. "We will return of course for Anna's graduation and stay long enough to help her with her college plans. We can take up to a month for vacation during the year."

"That reminds me," Billy said. "I have told Anna to expect us to call her tonight around 9:00pm her time. I plan to put it on my calling card, so I don't want to hear any objections. It's the least I can do for her not being home when I called on your birthday."

Carey smiled broadly. "You're too good to me little brother."

"Nonsense," Billy replied. "I know how much it means to her also and I made her a promise. She's a wonderful girl."

"You don't have to tell me. She's the one thing I miss the most from the United States."

The teller motioned for Carey to step up to the window. He transacted his exchange and they headed to the post office.

———

Receiving mail was one of the little joys of mission life that Carey relished. Their mail varied from mission correspondence, family and friends, birthday and prayer cards from unacquainted but supportive church members, to crayon drawings from youngsters studying missions back in the states. The Eldridges tried to respond to each letter. If it were directed to one of the boys, Susan would help them answer the questions and write back as a school project. Carey kept most of the letters in a file. He enjoyed quoting from them in his presentations during furlough.

Once a month, the stack in the post office box was larger than normal because the boat mail would bring in the magazines and state papers all at the same time. Those were the days when the mail was celebrated and sorted around the kitchen table. It was not that time of the month, but there were still a good number of cards in the box for Carey.

"Looks like some late birthday cards arriving today," Carey said, handing the stack to Billy as they remounted the truck. As Carey began to drive back toward the house, Billy began sorting the letters and cards.

"I count about seven cards and three letters to you, some official looking envelop for Susan and nothing for the boys. They are going to be disappointed," Billy said arranging the cards according to size.

"Where are the letters from?" Carey asked while driving.

"Let us see," Billy replied, pulling them from the bottom and checking the return address. "You have one from Wake Forest, North Carolina, ... it looks like a seminary alumni notice."

"Next!" Carey said. He wasn't being disrespectful, he was just interested in personal letters first.

"You have one from your bank in Virginia Beach. Probably a monthly statement."

"It is, but it is at least six weeks old. I have to balance my check book by faith," he joked.

"Don't we all," Billy agreed. "And the last one is a real letter from a real person."

"Well, don't hold me in suspense, who is it from?"

Billy tried to read the town and had to examine the postmark to make sure he was correct. His eye for detail caught something interesting.

"Didn't you tell me that it takes between 7 and 10 days for a letter to make it here from the states?" Billy questioned.

"Normally, but some take longer. Depends on holiday schedules and strikes. How long did that one take to get here?" Carey asked jokingly.

"It was mailed from Carrolton, VA on September 18th. Isn't that your birthday, big brother?"

"Yes, but that was just last Thursday," Carey replied. "How in the world did it get here in . . ."

"Five days!" Billy finished the calculation for him. "Looks like God wanted you to get this letter sooner than usual."

Chapter Fourteen:

"The Bus"

Rusty knocked softly on the door to Howard's office. At first there was no response. Then Howard mumbled from behind his desk loud enough for Rusty to interpret as permission to enter.

"We were about ready to go get some lunch, would you like to go with us?" Rusty offered as congenially as he could.

"I don't think so," Howard replied in a tired voice. "I need to do some more reading and preparing for Wednesday night."

"Have you forgotten again, we have the Gideon speaker Wednesday. You don't have a mid-week service to prepare for. You have been closed up in this office since the staff meeting this morning. You need to get out," he encouraged.

Howard looked up from his desk with lifeless eyes. He was in no mood for conversation. He did not want company for lunch and he lacked the energy to hide the way he felt. He knew Rusty was observant, sharp and concerned. But he was not ready to unburden his soul. The voice he had ignored so often in recent days began to speak again. *Go with him for lunch. You two can go somewhere private. Rusty can help you. Go with him, now.*

"Thanks, but no thanks. I need to run by the hardware supply to check on some things for the building committee. I'll just grab a bite while I'm over there." It was not a complete lie. He did have a list from the contractors he wanted to compare prices on."

"Then I'll come with you," Rusty replied undaunted. "I'm interested in seeing how things are coming along."

"You don't have to do that," Howard objected. "I mean, I'm not sure when I will get back and you have visitation this afternoon."

"Just one hospital, and it is over near the supply company. We could both make the visit."

Howard was too tired to fight. Reluctantly, he closed his book and grabbed his sweater. They walked out to the parking lot and Rusty clicked off his car alarm. Howard had hoped to drive, but again, he did not resist. He climbed into the Corsica and buckled up.

"How does a salad bar sound?" Rusty asked.

"Sounds healthy. I guess that will be OK."

They drove in silence for a while. Rusty purposely left the cassette player off. He was looking for an opening.

"I noticed Donna wasn't at church Sunday night," he started innocently. "Is she OK?"

"She wasn't feeling good," Howard responded. "Karen had a school project, and Terry was at a friend's church," he added to cover all the curiosity.

"Is she doing better this morning?" Rusty continued. "I mean, you have seemed so preoccupied this morning. I thought maybe there was something wrong at home."

Rusty was careful to crouch his comments around the question of health, but inwardly, he was hoping that Howard would take the opportunity to open up. Howard sat quietly for a couple street blocks. He knew that Rusty was hinting at more than a simple headache that Donna may have experienced the night before. He also knew that he should be talking to someone, but pride was choking his words. He looked at his hands and huffed.

"I guess things could be better," he started with difficulty. "There has been some stress around the house lately."

"We're not just talking about Donna not feeling well, are we?" Rusty said quickly to get his foot in the door.

"I guess not," Howard replied in surrender. "I don't know how much I feel comfortable getting into this."

Rusty let Howard take the lead.

"It isn't anything really serious," he started. "I mean, it's not like we have drugs or anything like that in the house."

Now Rusty was confused. "I don't follow you, Bro. Howard. Are we talking about Donna still?"

"Yes and no. My biggest problem is not with Donna and yet it is affecting us. I have been having some real struggles with Karen lately. I guess it's just that teenager thing and the power struggles that goes with it, but lately I have just felt so distanced from Karen. Donna has picked up on it and. . . well, to be honest, I don't know what HER problem is, but she seems so defensive about everything. Then add to that all the pressures of this building project and I have just been drained of all my energy."

"It's starting to show," Rusty said diplomatically.

"I just need some time to regroup and rest a little."

"Personally, I think you need more than that," Rusty said boldly. "I think you need some time away with your family. I think you need to put some priorities into perspective and right now, your family is priority."

"But when do I have time to do that?" Howard asked. "I have building project meetings most of this week."

"Take a short weekend Friday/ Saturday and get away. You can take the family somewhere, or just take them out here somewhere. Go to the zoo or Sea World or something fun."

Howard thought hard about the suggestion. It made sense, and it couldn't hurt. He didn't have to prepare for Wednesday night, so he could work his Sunday messages earlier this week and be ready by Friday afternoon to take off when the kids came in from school. It sounded like a great idea. The more he imagined them being together, the better it sounded. By the time they pulled into the restaurant parking lot, Howard was already making mental plans on how he could put together a great mini-vacation for the weekend. It completely slipped his mind that Karen might have to work or that Donna had already made her plans for a woman's retreat. It never occurred to him that he should consult their schedules first. He was already two steps ahead, making his plans, and expecting everything to fall into place. He was doing it again. Things were about to fall, but not into place!

———

Karen sat alone in the cafeteria nibbling on a tuna fish sandwich. She had sworn she would never buy the pizza at school again, but she was not crazy of tuna fish either. It was just the quickest sandwich she could fix. The tension around the house that morning and the day before was enough to squelch her appetite anyway. She looked around the tables to take her mind off of her lunch. She began to make mental comparisons beginning with what they were eating.

Karen was one of the few seniors at NCHS that didn't have a car. She had been shuttled to school activities and games for her first two years of High School. When she turned sixteen, her parents had finally let her date and she could begin to get rides with friends and boyfriends. Until this last week, Fernando had been a reliable ride and a fun guy to be around. They had dated a few times with others in a group and a couple times alone. Karen knew the facts of dating and how many of her classmates had already experimented with sex. She was not naïve, but neither was she experienced. She had set personal limits and had kept them. Perhaps that was the real reason Fernando was quick to bring their relationship to a close. He saw the job as too much competition in an already difficult "game". Karen huffed to herself with a sense of gratitude that he was no longer an intricacy to her life. She didn't need Fernando anyway, she had a job, she had Sheila, and Sheila had made it in life. Sheila had things, money, a place of her own and she had done it herself. Sheila had told Karen that she had not finished college, but had taken only one year at a Junior College before realizing she could start in the business world without formal schooling. Karen was beginning to see Sheila as more than an employer. She was a role model who could help her after this year to get out on her own, to find the freedom she longed for from the rules of her father, and to start getting the things she really wanted out of life.

Karen took another bite out of her sandwich. She began to think about going to work that night. It became the only thing she looked forward to during the day. She looked around the tables again. Suddenly, all the comparisons seemed meaningless. These were just kids. Karen was preparing herself for the real world.

Donna set the timer on the microwave. She was re-warming the burger from the night before that had been dutifully placed in the refrigerator. She removed the clothespin from a bag of potato chips and poured a handful onto her plate. When she finished pouring her tea, the buzzer sounded and she took out the warm burger with the chewy bun and sat at the breakfast table. Lunch was lousy which matched her feelings exactly.

A Christmas ago, Howard had bought her a copy of Oswald Chambers "My Utmost For His Highest". It sat on the breakfast table under the recent copies of "Reader's Digest". Donna had had high hopes of beginning a morning devotion with the family and reading from it to start their day. As with most of her "hopes", this too had been laid aside. With a sense of defeat and surrender, she picked up the book and flipped past the unread pages to the devotion for that day. The title surprised her. The top of the page read: "The 'Go' of Renunciation". The scripture came from Luke 9:57-61. As she read the passage, she began to quiver. The devotion spoke of three men who came wanting to follow the Lord and His response to each. In each case, there were strong words to the men concerning commitment. The words of Oswald Chambers that followed cut deep into her soul.

> *"The one who says – 'yes, Lord, but...' is the one who*
> *is fiercely ready, but never goes. . . When once the call of*
> *God comes, begin to go and never stop going."*

Her heart cried as she recalled a promise she had made to the Lord when she was sixteen years old. She began to weep outwardly as she felt the weight of the personal responsibility for what she believed to be her own failure. She knew what God had asked of her and she had not followed it. Instead, she had given her life to a man who was following his own calling, and worse, was leaving her behind in it. She had always thought that the ministry was the ultimate manner in order to please God, especially for one brought up in the church. But now she was alone. Worse, she felt she had disobeyed God and was now separated from Him, also.

She looked again at the words of verse 61: "Let me go back and say good-by to my family." Maybe the way for her to go back was to cut ties here and return to Texas. Maybe she could find a way to keep her promise.

Maybe there was hope yet. Maybe God could still use her. Her bewildered mind resorted to "maybes" that had no basis in either the Word she had just read, or the leadership of God's Spirit, but God had gotten her attention and that was the first step.

———

"Watch your step," the bus driver said politely. Anna stepped gingerly onto the sidewalk and waited for the bus to pull away. She looked up at the sky and hoped it would not rain before her trip home. She glanced at her watch. Only six more hours till she would be home again. It was not her custom to look forward to work being over before it began, but it was not everyday that she would be talking to her family by phone. She hoped nothing would keep her from being home in time for the call.

———

Antigua was the perfect name for the old Guatemalan city that was a blend of picturesque Latin antiquity and quaint tourism. Before the earthquakes, it had served as the country's capital during its colonial period. It was also the perfect place to change busses and routes because it was such a hub for foreigners. It was the one town where Flaco would not stand out. He meandered through the merchants' shops near the rows of busses that lined up like taxis in line for fares. The signs above the windshields identified their destinations, but many had their cities painted proudly on the sides. Guatemala showed more character as a country than he was used to. His route from the border had carried him through the mountains. Rafael had suggested *Antigua* because of Flaco's ability to convert more dollars without going through Guatemala City. From *Antingua*, he could double back to the south towards *Escuintia* where he could find a direct bus to *Las Margaritas*. Flaco had decided he would travel as close to the Pacific coast as he could, but this small detour would be necessary. Though a greater distance, it would prove to be a quicker route due to the availability of busses going out of *Antingua*. He would take the Pan-American Highway south of Lake Atítlan avoiding the mountains and skirt back toward the west on a slower national highway to *Las Margaritas*. With any luck, he would reach the small border town by late nightfall. There he would have to locate a coyote that could get him across the *Suciati* river into Mexico.

Flaco indulged himself with local food and beer and even took an hour to browse the many shops. There was more craftsmanship, color and cultural identity in the garments and carvings than what he was used to seeing. He knew the world outside of southern Honduras was different, but he was beginning to see the immensity of that difference. It would be easy to become overwhelmed, but Flaco saw his New World through eyes of adventure. He couldn't wait to see what Mexico looked like.

———

"Thanks Rusty," Howard said getting out of the car. "It was a good lunch, a good hospital visit and a good afternoon. I appreciate the advice."

"Can I make one more suggestion?" Rusty offered. "When you meet with the committee tonight, try to find a way to delegate some of this leg-work. You really are trying to do too much on this building project."

"I will certainly try," Howard assured him. He walked across the parking lot to his car while glancing at his watch. There was not enough time to drive all the way home and come back for his meeting. Howard decided he would make use of the time in his office working on his Sunday message and try to free up the weekend like Rusty suggested. He walked past Diane's empty desk. He didn't realize it was already past four. As he threw his coat on the sofa, he began thinking about where they could go for a family time. His heart was in the right place, but his mind was on the weekend. By the time he remembered to call home about not coming in for supper, the lasagna had gotten cold and so had Donna.

———

Karen strolled briskly into *Sugar n' Spice*. She had noticed that her mother had been unusually quiet on the drive over. She was relieved that she would be getting her ride home from Sheila. Things were getting just too tense around the house. She looked around the shop and figured Sheila must be in the office doing paperwork. Amber met Karen at the register.

"Sheila told me to stick around till you got here. She had to drive up to Oceanside and would be gone till late tonight. I'm supposed to come back around 8:30 and relieve you and close down the store."

"8:30?" Karen asked puzzled. "But, I usually work till closing."

"Something about you not being out so late tonight," Amber reasoned. "Besides, I need to be here at 8:30 to start closing things down anyway. No sense in both of us being here, right?"

"I guess not," Karen said disappointed. "Wait a minute? How do I get home? Sheila has been giving me a ride home each night?"

"The same way I get here and back," she replied smartly. "Take the bus. Where do you live?"

"Just off of Hilltop Drive in Chula Vista," Karen said.

"No problem, the bus runs all the way down Hilltop Drive from West G street down to Palomar. You don't live below Palomar do you?"

"No."

"I didn't think you looked Mexican. That's about all there is down that way."

"Yeah, well lots of my friends live down there," Karen replied defensively.

"Whatever!" Amber shrugged. "All I'm saying is that the bus will get you home, so I'm out of here. See you around 8:30. You OK with the register an' everything?"

"Yes," Karen huffed. "I've been working since last Thursday. Sheila has checked me out on everything."

"I bet she has," Amber said under her breath while turning to go.

Karen put her things away in the back and returned to the sales area. The store was empty of customers and she had time to straighten the racks. She didn't realize how disappointed she was that Sheila wasn't there till she was all alone. She had hoped to have the chance to talk to her again about her problems at home. She always felt a little better after their time together. Now she had three and half hours to spend re-hanging dresses, waiting on the few customers who might chance by to browse on a slow Monday night, and to feel sorry for herself. The majority of her time would be spent in the latter.

It was times like this Karen felt like no one really understood her. Her father couldn't acknowledge that she was no longer a little girl. Her mother didn't recognize her need for more independence. Fernando had mistaken a relationship for ownership. It seemed the only person that knew what Karen wanted was Sheila. Now even Sheila wasn't around. Karen felt unusually lonely.

―――

"It's about time you guys got home," Susan chided as the Eldridge brothers kicked the dirt off their shoes. "I was about to send Joshua and Caleb out to Mando's to see if you were over there."

"It was my fault Susan," Billy apologized. "Carey was showing me some of the mission works and I asked to see a mountain church. I had no idea the work was so spread out."

"What's for supper sweetheart?" Carey asked kissing his bride on the forehead.

"I thought I would go with spaghetti, since we have already had the typical food."

"Typical food is good," Billy encouraged.

"But spaghetti is better!" Carey quickly added. "You haven't tasted her garlic butter on fresh loaf bread yet. It is to die for."

"Did you get the mail, while you were out?" Susan asked.

"Yes, and you'll never believe it, but we received a letter from Virginia in FIVE DAYS!" Carey said excited.

"That's incredible," Susan responded stirring the sauce. "Anyone we know?"

"I think so," Carey said. "I mean, she surely knows us. Her name is Gertie Baxter. Does that name ring a bell?"

"Gertie Baxter?" Susan repeated the name. "I can't say that it does. What town was it from?"

"Says Carrolton, Virginia," Billy said holding up the envelope.

"That must have been one of the churches near the Chesapeake Bay we spoke in," Susan said trying to make a mental image. "That was three years ago and we spoke in so many, I just don't know."

"Well she is a real prayer warrior, you should read her letter," Billy said tossing the envelope on the kitchen table.

"I will, but for now, put it with the rest of the mail on the desk and set the table."

"Roger that!" Billy said compliantly picking the letter up from the table and handing it to Carey.

Carey walked into the den where the mail was kept on his desk waiting to be answered. There was a small stack already sitting by his devotional Bible. He pulled the sheet out from the envelope and looked at it. Billy had read him the letter in the car and he had not seen the delicate handwriting. He was struck by the familiarity of the message. This was a person who sincerely cared for his well being. The tone of the letter seemed more urgent than the general notes that missionaries receive from prayer groups. Then he noticed something that Billy had not read. In the top right corner of the page was the date. But under the date there was a time. There was no mistake, Carey read the numbers and choked.

———

"You could have at least called," Donna snapped. "I knew Karen would not be here, but I at least expected you to join Terry and I."

"I know," Howard said discouraged. "I wasn't thinking. I got back to the church late in the afternoon and didn't think I had time to eat at home and be back for the building committee meeting."

"Like I said, you could have at least called," she repeated, driving her point home.

"I said I was sorry. What else do you want to hear?"

Terry turned up the music in his room so that he wouldn't have to hear the arguing.

"I just want you to be more considerate," Donna replied. "You are so wrapped up in this building program. You don't even notice what's going on around here."

"I know that we have not been OK lately," he tried to say calmly. There was no reason to add to the argument with attitude. He wanted to get to Rusty's suggestion without it sounding like an attempt to just cover over things.

"Howard, you have no idea how long things have not been OK," Donna answered. "I have tried to explain to the children why you are short with them. I have tried to excuse your preoccupation and distance by saying it will get better when you get past this urgent phase, but you just seem to move farther and farther away from us. I have felt abandoned, and . . ." Her voice trailed off.

Howard saw the opening and thought it would be a good opportunity to raise the suggestion. He stepped closer to Donna and reached out for her hand. She gave it reservedly.

"I know I haven't been there when I should have been. I know I have been a little hard on Karen and I haven't been spending time with Terry like I should. Why don't we make up for lost time this weekend?" He tried to inject some enthusiasm into the proposal. "We could go to the zoo, or Sea World, or take a ride out somewhere. What do you think?"

Donna pulled away and stared at Howard, who had no idea what he had just ignited. He could see her face contort from hurt to anger. He was totally unprepared for what was about to come.

"You are really incredible, you know that!" she started. "You have absolutely no idea what is going on in this family do you? You think Karen can just take off from a new job on the weekend? You don't even remember about the Ladies Retreat I signed up for this weekend after we talked about it Friday and Saturday?"

Howard vaguely remembered the mentioning of a retreat, but had totally dismissed it. He knew better than to suggest that he did not think she was serious.

"You honestly believe we can all just drop everything we have planned for this weekend and go see some monkeys or sea lions?" she continued sarcastically. "Once again, you are not even thinking about your family. What is the matter with you? You are living in some private world out there that doesn't even include us. I can't believe you were thinking about just packing us all up and going off without checking to see if we had made any plans. That is mostly inconsiderate to Karen. She just got this job. She can't be running off on weekends especially."

There was that word "inconsiderate" again. Howard was losing a downhill battle and there was no where to run. Rusty had meant well and his suggestion was not bad, but Howard had just failed to think it through completely. A quiet retreat was his best defense at the moment, but he had to be careful not to appear uncaring.

"You are absolutely right," he said softly recalling his many messages on Proverbs 15:1. "I wasn't thinking about the family's schedule. I'm sorry. I just thought we could use some time alone for a change." He wanted to mention it was Rusty's suggestion, but thought that might look like he was shifting the blame. The truth was, he didn't think about their plans and that was the problem.

"What I think we could use is some time alone, but not together," Donna said in a low and serious tone. "I would like to just go on this retreat Friday and work through some things. Maybe when I get back, we can talk more about how to work on things here at home." In her mind, she wasn't sure if matters could improve or if she even wanted them to, but she was willing to talk after she got back.

Howard nodded.

"I understand and maybe you're right. I know I have to get some things worked out in my own life and this schedule thing is one of them." He wanted to say more, but felt restrained. This time, he knew when to quit. Surrender and yielding are closely related and not always the result of weakness. God had just gotten Howard's attention.

———

Karen walked out of the mall entrance and glanced around for the SDTA sign that marked the bus stop. She found a small group huddled around a concrete bench and saw the sign above their heads. As she approached the group she began to feel a little uncomfortable. Four of the boys wore similar colors. She knew of gangs but had never tried to learn very much about them. Some of her Latin friends at school had brothers in a gang, but these boys weren't Latin. She looked for an inconspicuous place to stand as she glanced at her watch. It was 8:40 and the bus for Hilltop Drive was due in five minutes.

"You look lost," came a voice from behind her. "Are you waiting for the bus?"

Karen turned to see a young girl about her age. Her bright green eyes were warm and reassuring. Her red hair was tied up behind her head and held with a scarf that Karen recognized.

"Why yes, are you waiting for the Hilltop Drive bus?" Karen asked.

"Yes, it should be by soon. Is this your first time to take the bus?"

"Kinda, does it show?"

"Not really, it's just that I ride it pretty regularly and I haven't seen you ride before. But you do look familiar. Do you work in the mall?"

"Yes," Karen answered. "At *Sugar n' Spice*."

"That's where I've seen you. I bought this scarf there last weekend and I bet you are the one who helped me pick it out."

"I think you're right. I thought I had seen that scarf before. My name is Karen Pennington, what's yours?"

"My name is Anna Eldridge," she replied extending her hand.

The two girls talked shop about mall work and food court diets till the bus pulled up in a cloud of warm diesel air. They sat together and chatted about school and homes, when Karen began to change tone. Anna was sensitive to the change and wondered if she should probe.

"What are things like at home?" Anna asked innocently.

"Well," Karen sighed. "Could be better I guess. If my Dad would just lighten up some. He's a preacher and sometimes he treats me like a member of the congregation and not his daughter."

"How do you mean?" Anna replied, deciding to learn more about Karen before sharing who and what her father was.

"I mean, like curfew for instance. He goes absolutely ballistic if I'm just a few minutes late on a school night. I guess he will be overjoyed I will be in by nine tonight, that's thirty minutes early for me."

"I'm sure he's just looking out for you," Anna started to offer.

"No, he's trying to control my life. And to be quite honest, I'm just about sick of it. I got this job just this past week and for the first time, I'm starting to feel some real independence. If things don't get better at home, I don't know. I might would find a place of my own and just drop out of school. I can make it - - like Sheila."

"Who's Sheila?" Anna asked cautiously.

"That's the lady I work for. She started her own business and didn't even finish college," Karen said proudly. "I bet she would help me find a place, or maybe even let me move in with her for a while."

That was the first time the thought occurred to Karen, and as radical as it sounded, it didn't seem too improbable. Karen needed to vent and since Sheila wasn't there, this stranger who enjoyed talking would have to do. Anna was beginning to feel uncomfortable with Karen, but her stop was just two blocks away.

"Before you do something that drastic, try talking to your Dad," Anna appealed. "You might be surprised to find out just how he feels. Dads have a way of sounding tough when inside they are really learning just as much about being the father of a teenager as we are about being one. Neither one is an easy task."

Karen let the words slip in, but she wasn't prepared to accept them completely. Anna felt sorry for Karen. As she pulled the cord to announce her stop, she turned back to Karen and extended her hand.

"I work at the Bible Book store on the second level," Anna said quickly. "Anytime you want to talk, feel free to look me up. We could go to lunch sometime if you want."

"Thanks," Karen said politely. "I may just do that."

As the bus continued on passing beneath the streetlights of Hilltop Drive, Anna whispered a prayer for Karen. God was getting her attention.

———

"Are you sure?" Susan asked.

"Look at the date," Carey said. "It says she wrote the letter on Thursday, the 23rd."

"Your birthday," Billy added.

"Right, but she also wrote in the time," he said pointing to the note. "It says 2:55AM, not PM! She wrote this in the early part of the morning on my birthday."

"So she couldn't sleep," Billy said.

Carey looked at Susan carefully.

"2:55 Eastern Standard Time, is 12:55 Central Standard Time. That is within five minutes of the time of my accident in *Santa Tierra*. She was praying for me while those men were plotting against Mando and I."

"I was up praying around that time also that night," Susan realized.

"Wow! That's incredible," Billy exclaimed.

"Not for God," Carey laughed.

"Are you going to write her back and tell her what happened?" Billy asked.

"I think I will. Could you carry it and some other letters out with you tomorrow and mail 'em from the states? It will get to her quicker than from here."

"Sure thing, big brother. By the way, don't let the time slip up on us. I told Anna we would call the house around 9:00 their time, and it's almost that now."

"Let me get the boys up," Susan said. "They haven't talked to their sister in over a month."

"The more the merrier," Billy replied. "We'll give her a little extra time to get home. She's usually in by 9:00 on the bus, but it could be running a little late. You have time to get them stirring."

Carey sat the letter down. This was almost too much excitement. First, a letter of prayer support at a time when he needed it had come, and now he was about to call his daughter. His cup was overflowing.

———

Anna let herself into the house and was greeted by Helen. Jenny had already gone to bed and Helen had a bowl of microwave popcorn finishing up. Helen invited her into the kitchen for a light snack of popcorn and Diet Cola. Anna put her sweater over the chair and sat down.

"Did you have a good night," Helen asked, offering her a small Tupperware bowl of popcorn.

"It was OK. Not too busy. Monday's usually aren't," Anna replied popping a small handful of popcorn into her mouth. "But 1 did meet someone interesting on the bus ride home. It was a girl my age that was going through some problems at home. I feel kind of sorry for her."

"Does she go to your school?" Helen asked, sipping on her drink.

"I don't think so, we would be in some of the same classes I would think."

Helen and Anna snacked and chatted till the phone rang. Helen just looked at Anna and nodded toward the receiver. They both knew who it was and Helen wanted Anna to be the first one on the phone. She snatched it off its cradle.

"Hello!" she almost squealed.

"Anna?" came the tender familiar voice of her father.

"Oh, Daddy!" she cried. "I'm so sorry I missed you on your birthday."

"Me, too, baby. How are you doing there?"

"I miss you guys all the time, but Uncle Billy and Aunt Helen are great. He reminds me a lot of you."

"How are you getting along with Jenny?" Carey asked, trying to prolong their time together.

"She is nice," Anna replied. "Like having the sister I always wanted."

"Speaking of which, I'm going to pass you around to your brothers, but save the last dime for me, OK."

"I will. It's good to hear your voice, Dad."

Anna took turns with Josh and Caleb who each had little and mostly the same thing to talk about. She then talked with her mother about her studies and boys and her lack of time for both. Susan was relieved to find she had chosen studies over boys. They talked of her work and how she was adjusting to life in the US. Uncle Billy took the phone for a quick chat with Helen. He gave her his flight times for arrival the next evening. Finally, the phone was handed back to Carey.

"Sounds like you are staying pretty busy with school," Carey started. "Have you settled on an area of study you like yet?"

"I kind of like English and composition. I enjoy writing. I have been keeping a journal and I write in it every night."

"I wish you could send it down here, so I could catch up on all the things we haven't been able to do together. I really miss you *'mija'*".

"Mija" was a pet name he had for Anna. It was a common Spanish expression for a daughter, though usually found around Mexico. It was an abbreviation for *Mi Hija* meaning, "my daughter".

"I really miss you too, Daddy," she said clearing her voice.

"I want you to know how proud I am of you. You are everything I always wanted in my little girl."

"Thank you, I wish every girl could have as good a relation with their father as we have had. I met a girl tonight on the bus ride home that is having a real hard time with her father. Her name is Karen Pennington and her Dad is a minister, but she isn't happy. She and her father don't get along at all. She says he's too busy and doesn't try to understand her."

"Sometimes ministers lose sight of what's most important," Carey admitted.

"You never did," Anna reassured him. "You always found time for you and I to be together. I remember us riding in the truck and playing our music together. Would you remember Karen in your prayers? I plan to. I think I will see her again at the mall. That's where she and I both work, only we are in different stores."

"I sure will, *Mija*," Carey replied. "Anything else I can do for you. Do you have enough money? I can send some with Uncle Billy when he comes home tomorrow."

"I'm just fine. I make a good check and Uncle Billy treats me like one of his own daughters. That's the only thing that makes this work so well."

"I know you are in good hands," he said, smiling at his little brother. "I guess I better let you go. This call is on him also. I sure do miss you, sweetheart."

"I miss you all too! Give mom a big hug for me."

"You know I will. Ask Aunt Helen to give you one for each of us. We're planning to make it in next May for your graduation and then we will be back for furlough shortly after you start college. Keep me posted on your plans. By the way, if your Uncle Billy can get it set up, I may be able to start that email stuff down here and you can write me on the computer."

"That would be great, then we wouldn't have to wait so long between letters or calls," Anna said choking up.

"You better go now, I just want you to know again how much I love you and am proud of you. Take care and dream about us when you can. I will always be as close as your heart."

"I know, Daddy. I love you, too, very much."

Carey held the phone and swallowed hard.

"Goodbye *Mija,*" he said softly.

"Goodnight, Daddy."

Anna handed the phone to Helen so she could hang it up. Then Anna reached out her arms for the first of four long hugs.

Chapter Fifteen:

"The Farewell"

(Tuesday)

Ricardo Reinaldo was awakened by the early market merchants opening the shuttered windows of their small wood frame businesses. The market dogs followed the meat vendors to their prospective shops in the vain hope that some portion of beef would miraculously fall from the large hind quarter hoisted upon the merchant's shoulder. The smell of small wood fires melting lard in metal pans preparing for breakfast beans and tortillas filled the narrow alley area where Ricardo had spent the night.

Ricardo had arrived in *La Esperanza* too late to catch a bus into Tegucigalpa. His limited funds prevented him from renting a room for the night. He would need all he had to make bus fair from there to the capital and from the capital to Choluteca. He had just enough for meager meals along the way. He hoped to find hospitality in *Santa Tierra,* perhaps from Moncho's widow, and gain a little money for the return trip. He was determined not to let the lack of *lempiras* prevent him from his mission. He was going to avenge his brother's death, just as his brother had avenged their father. It was a matter of honor and duty and family.

He walked among the old women huddled over their dark iron *comals* smelling the beans and wondering how much he could afford for breakfast. The sun had not risen completely and he appeared as a mysterious unfamiliar figure weaving through the market area. Perhaps that is what caught her eye. Juanita was preparing the breakfast for her grandmother who was sick at home. The young girl was responsible for preparing the food, selling the meals, washing the plates and returning to the house before going to school. Her older sister would prepare the lunch at the market.

Juanita's young smile and bright eyes caught Ricardo's. He walked over to the small grill where she was stirring the beans and rolling out the tortillas. He noticed the small bag of eggs at her feet. Ricardo was both attractive and strong. He was not clumsy in his actions or his speech. After just three minutes of conversation, he was filling a handful of tortillas with eggs and beans and washing it down with strong black coffee. Juanita prattled about school, her family and her dreams. Ricardo was only interested in breakfast.

After a "pie crust" promise to someday return and take her away with him, Ricardo began looking for the busses to the capital. He asked about arrival times and realized that he may not find a bus out of Tegucigalpa heading south that late. This trip was taking longer than he had hoped. It would be Wednesday before he could make it to *Santa Tierra*.

―――

Flaco's time in *Las Margaritas* was not much unlike his stay in *Agua Fria*. He had arrived early enough the night before to tour the local cantinas and find a reliable coyote to get him across the *Suciati* river. This man preferred to work nameless and without the cordial treatment Flaco had received from Rafael. Flaco agreed to meet him at the Plaza around 3:30am with $150 worth of *Quetzales* that he had exchanged in Antigua. He did not let this man know that he was carrying US dollars. Though there may be honor among thieves, Flaco did not trust this man.

The coyote's truck was not like the ATV that Rafael had used, but then the river was less than a foot deep where they crossed. The border of Mexico was not as heavily patrolled as that between El Salvador and Guatemala. To make the trip worse, Flaco had been deposited more than two miles from the highway. Fortunately, there were not many trees to obscure the lights of *Tapachula* in the distance. As he worked his way through cornfields and open meadows, Flaco watched the orange spears of the rising sun outline the mountains to his right. This was the dawning of the lonely part of his trip.

―――

Susan rolled over. Her arm found an empty gap in the bed where her husband usually lay. Normally, she rose before he did, but his brother was returning to the states that day and Carey couldn't sleep. He was at his desk re-reading Gertie's letter. He wanted to respond so that Billy could carry it with him and mail it from California. He wanted her to know just how timely her prayers and letter had been. Unfortunately, the last person to receive a handwritten letter from him was his mother while he was in seminary. Once he bought an electric typewriter, he nearly forgot how to write cursive. He either printed or typed, and all letters were typed. He booted up his computer and began pecking.

Carey started with a gracious greeting and quickly moved into his appreciation for her thoughtful correspondence. He took careful pains in recounting the accident in terms of timing and how her prayers for him were lifted at the very moment of danger. The words came easily as he related the events – in fact, more easily than he had expected. It was as if she already knew. As he started to close his letter, he heard the words of Anna

177

requesting prayer for Karen and realized that this would be a good person to pass a prayer request on to.

"Mrs. Baxter," he wrote. "I realize that you will not know the young girl I am about to mention, but my daughter in California knows her and has asked for prayer for her and her family. They seem to be going through some difficult times. The girl's name is Karen and her father is a Baptist minister. He has been confusing his priorities and his daughter is drifting away from him. Again, I realize that you do not know these people, but I know that they would greatly appreciate your prayers."

Carey looked at his letter, and decided to add the following.

"One last thing. I plan to visit the family of the man who was killed in the accident. I would greatly appreciate your prayers for this meeting. I should see the family sometime this week. Should you receive this letter by the weekend, I ask you pray for them and me. In Christ, Carey Eldridge."

He checked her envelope again for the return address and printed it on his own. He left the stamp off deliberately since his brother would be mailing it from the states and would not need a Honduran stamp. Billy could mail the letter from the airport when he arrived and it would be delivered much sooner than if mailed from Choluteca. With any luck, it would reach Virginia Beach by Friday. Carey had no idea how important the timing of its arrival would be for Karen, her father, and himself.

———

Gertie read her devotional at the kitchen table. The change of scenery from the couch in the den was pleasant and the warm sun came through her large bay windows. Adam had picked some late blooming hibiscus from their hedge and placed the red blossoms in a small Mayonnaise jar on the table. He had slept well and never knew when she rose and made the difficult trek to the den. This had made six nights in a row she had awakened to pray. The burden had not been lifted. For Gertie, that could only mean that the need was still present.

"Did you sleep well, Pumpkin?" Adam asked walking into the kitchen.

"Not as soundly as you did," she replied with a smile. "You had the same drone when I came back to bed as when I left," she said referring to his snoring.

"You were up again last night?" Adam questioned. "That makes almost a week of prayer for these families."

"Don't forget," Gertie said seriously, "Our Lord prayed forty days once. So what's a week?"

"Pretty long for someone your age," Adam replied in a voice of concern.

"God never calls us to do what He is not prepared to do through us. I pray in His strength, not mine. I feel great this morning. What would you like me to fix for breakfast?"

"Not so fast," Adam laughed. "I'm still the chief cook and bottle washer around here. You just finish your devotion and I'll scramble us up some eggs."

"That would be nice," she said, returning her gaze through her bifocals. "I was just about to get to the birthdays for today."

"Well, let's hear them. There may be someone today we both know."

Gertie began reading the names of the missionaries around the world celebrating their birthdays. Though each would be remembered that morning for their special day, the name of Carey Eldridge would be added to the list. Even without the names that would soon be sent to her in the mail, Gertie would also pray for the unnamed father and his daughter that she had been *shown* to pray for. As the sun warmed their small kitchen, God began warming their hearts in special time of fellowship and communion.

———

Moisés finished his breakfast first and grabbed his machete. There had been very little wood for the breakfast fire. He decided he would cut some small limbs and carry them back to the house so that his sisters would not have to gather any for lunch. Moisés was now the oldest at home and had to look out for the family. He knew his mother made the decisions, but he had to provide. Till Ricardo returned, he was in charge. The family's needs, their protection, and their honor was up to him. He took the file from the porch and began sharpening his machete. He was now the man of the house. He had to show initiative and strength. He would have only three days to prepare for the greatest test of his manhood as well as for the honor of his family and he didn't even know it. But God did, and like Moisés, He was already at work.

———

"But it seems like you just got here," Susan sighed. "I mean, I knew it was going to be a short visit, but I hardly had any time with you at all."

"This will not be my last trip to Honduras," Billy promised. "Now that I know how easy it is to get into the country, I'll just keep my passport up to date. Who knows, maybe next time I will be able to bring Helen and Jenny."

"Don't forget Anna!" Carey quickly added while packing a thermos for them to carry.

"You do plan to be back this afternoon don't you?" Susan asked Carey.

"Yes. If I'm going to make that trip to *Gualcince* on Wednesday, I need to get back here and take care of some things."

"Who is going to take the service at *Santa Tierra?*"

"Mando is going to go up for me. He said he would take the bus and spend the night and come back the next morning. Work is a little slow at the welding shop this week," Carey explained.

"Speaking of Mando, isn't that him now?" Billy asked looking out the front window.

Mando was one of the few Hispanics that *Oso* the dog would allow inside the gate without taking great issue. Mando carried a small package under his arm and stepped up to the door to knock. Susan opened the screen door and invited him in. Mando gave his greetings and then asked Carey to translate for him as he presented Billy with the gift.

"Mando wants me to tell you that he is so glad you came," Carey began as Mando spoke in slow choppy phrases. "Your visit came at a very needful time. My friend and brother in Christ was very *desanimado*."

Carey paused having used the Spanish word by mistake. He then explained, "That's a Spanish word that means that the person is without much strength or extremely discouraged, and he is right. I was."

Mando continued to share.

"You have helped him with both direction and faith to go on," Carey continued translating. "Here, Bro. Carey has taught us that faith is like a hammock. You place yourself completely in God's hands and you rest in Him. You have helped Bro. Carey to find his place in God's hammock again."

Mando's message was simple but pointed and both Carey and Billy felt the impact. Carey found himself translating words that he also felt from the depth of his heart. He was glad that Mando had chosen to "say" them through him. Billy opened the plastic grocery bag to find a hammock from the marketplace. It was not the quality of what Carey had. In fact, it was the simplest style available, made of the colorful strands woven on the side of the roads they had passed together during their travels.

Billy held it up proudly and thanked Mando in Spanish, something he knew he could do on his own. He then asked Carey to translate for him.

"I will never forget my trip to your country. The people are so friendly. I used to worry about my brother being down here, but now that I have met you, I know he is fine. Please help take care of him and his family, especially when he travels. I thank God you were with him that night."

Again Carey echoed the words and the feeling with which they were given. It was as though God was speaking to both of the men through Carey. Carey found himself both embarrassed and yet relieved to be able to relay the messages. He knew he was blessed to have both a friend and a brother who cared so very much for him. God made sure that nothing was left unsaid.

Carey invited Mando to ride with them to the capital, but he politely declined in order to finish some matters around town so that he could take the two days in *Santa Tierra.* They circled in prayer and Carey prayed in both languages thanking God for their friendship and love, and then praying for the situation in both *Santa Tierra* and *Gualcince.* As much as he would like to take Mando with him, he knew this trip had to be made alone. Billy also worried about the trip, but trusted Carey's sense of leadership from the Lord on this matter. He would be praying for him also during the trip. As the circle prayed, the petitions of an elderly woman at her kitchen table in Virginia gently joined with theirs.

———

"So this is Mexico," Flaco thought to himself. It didn't look much different than the last hundred kilometers or so of Guatemala. He had eaten in *Tapachula,* and then re-boarded for the next four hours of travel. He leaned against the sleeping woman beside him. This would be longest part of his journey.

After a while, he looked out the window as a heavy thunderstorm began to come up from the sea to his left. Rain always made bus travel harder because the windows had to be pulled up and body heat would soon cause the windows to fog and the humidity rise inside the bus itself.

"Best not go to sleep," came a call from behind him.

"Why not?" replied Flaco.

"We will be coming to *La Ventosa* soon and there is an inspection station. We will all have to get out while the police check our luggage and our papers."

Flaco swallowed hard.

"How soon?" he asked nervously.

"Let me see," the voice thought aloud. "We just passed *Tonala.* I would say within the next half hour."

Flaco slumped down in his seat. He had no papers and he was carrying a gun in his travel bag. He suddenly wished he were outside in the rain.

———

Karen listened for the sound of normality in the kitchen. Terry was fixing his own pimento cheese sandwich and her parents were nowhere to be found. This was unusual. At least her mother should be about, fixing toast or some other breakfast food to pass on to the family. Karen was beginning to feel the uneasiness of her parent's disagreements. It was OK at first when it took the attention off of her, but now she was getting worried.

"Have you seen Mom or Dad this morning?" Karen asked her brother.

"Dad was up when I came down, but he is in his study with the door closed. Mom hasn't come down at all that I know of."

Karen poured herself some orange juice and sipped on it while she looked through the refrigerator for something to carry to school. Cold chicken or sandwiches was about all the choice she had. She closed the door and looked in her purse. There was enough money for the school lunch. She squinted her eyes and tried to think what was served on Tuesdays - potato bar and salad. That wasn't too nauseating, she thought.

"Tell Dad I went early to the bus stop. I need to see someone," she said, throwing her purse over her shoulder and grabbing up her backpack.

Terry doubted his father would even come to the kitchen before he had to leave, but he nodded. It wasn't really lying if he didn't know it was a lie, he told himself. Terry found himself feeling alone in the kitchen. He wanted to cry, but knew he was too old. Ten-year-olds only cried when they got real hurt. But deep down, he felt real hurt.

———

The drive to the capital seemed longer than usual. Carey had most of the landmarks timed out in his mind, but even the clock seemed slower as they climbed the hills toward Tegucigalpa. They both needed to talk, but neither wanted the visit to end and the conversation they would begin would eventually have to bring them to his flight back to California.

"So you planning to try to find the family of the man this week?" Billy began.

"Yes, I plan to start out in the morning. I won't try to make it in one day; it's just too long a trip. I'll stay the night somewhere between the capital and there, then arrive fresh the next day. As long as I am home by Saturday at the latest, I'm OK for services. I might even stay over in the capital on the way home and do some grocery shopping for Susan. What are your plans for the rest of the week?"

"Well, first off, I need to kiss some special girls and let them know how much I missed them," Billy said with a degree of enthusiasm. "Then it's back to work tomorrow to straighten out whatever glitches may have been caused during my two day absence."

"Oh, surely they can get along without you for a couple days," Carey said sarcastically.

"I hope so. Then I have a meeting in Fresno on Friday, but I'll be back the same day. Oh yeah, I have a Gideon presentation to make this Wednesday night in a church near the bay."

"I'm really glad you are involved with them, and thanks again for the Bibles you brought."

"My pleasure, really. I'm looking forward to getting the pictures developed that we took of those folks getting their New Testaments."

They drove the next three kilometers without conversation. As they rounded the top of one of the mountains, Billy turned toward Carey.

"How are you doing now?" He asked seriously.

"I'm much better than when you and I talked last week. God has used several people to show me that what happened was not my fault. But more than that, he has showed me how I can reach out to the families. I must admit, I was afraid to go to the widow's home at first, but now I know that God is in control. I don't know exactly what I will face at his mother's home, but I believe God is going before me and will prepare the way. I'm not really afraid to go alone."

"I'll be praying for you on Thursday for sure," Billy assured his brother.

"Pray that I have wisdom. And that whatever I face, I will face it in the strength of the Lord."

"Have you ever thought about losing your life on the mission field?" Billy asked.

"I didn't till last week," Carey confessed. "I don't know that it is something you consciously think of till danger presents itself, but to be honest, it is a question we should deal with before we ever step on foreign soil. This whole ordeal has caused me to look at that issue more. I don't know for sure what to tell you. One thing I do know; I can think of worse ways and reasons for one to lose their life."

"Well . . .hey. Let's talk about next year. Are you all going to be able to make it for Anna's graduation in May?"

"You can 'Roger that one' little brother, and 'take it to the bank' and 'bet your sweet Bippy' and . . ."

"OK, I get the picture," Billy laughed.

They wove the mountain roads retelling old jokes and reliving past experiences of their days growing up together on the East Coast. Carey made a point of driving slower than he had ever done. He knew the plane schedule, but arriving two hours before the flight was just a suggestion by the airlines, not a law. He would stand in the line joyfully with his brother, if it kept him from the upper floor waiting room where Carey couldn't follow. He would wait till the plane had risen above the city heading north. He would drive across the street to the Pizza Hut, order enough pepperoni pizza for the family and carry home a treat to be reheated for supper. By the time he reached Choluteca, Billy would nearly be in Houston. Carey hated farewells.

―――

La Ventosa meant the "strong windy area" and was so named for the powerful jets of air that crossed literally from coast to coast of Mexico at that point where the joining of the Americas was at its lowest and narrowest. Large trucks had been known to blow over on this section of road. It was also the site of a checkpoint for the authorities to review the papers of travelers. The heat from within the bus was stifling, but that was not the reason that Flaco had sweated through his shirt.

As the bus approached the checkpoint, Flaco's pulse raced. He wondered if he should consider fighting. Maybe he could be taken and bribe his way out. His concentration was drawn to wild imaginations and scenes of shoot-outs. He became oblivious to his surroundings. He didn't notice the people around him, the heavy rain outside his window, or the fact that the bus was not slowing down.

"Guess they don't care to get wet today," came the voice from behind Flaco.

"What?" Flaco responded, bewildered.

"The police. They must not have wanted to get out in this rain," the voice explained. "They just waved us through. Maybe we'll make good time after all today. You can relax and take your nap now. We have another hour before our next rest stop and then six more hours before we reach Acapulco. Is that where you are headed?"

"No, I'm going a little farther north than that," Flaco sighed settling down against the large back of the sleeping woman beside him. "I'm just passing through this area."

―――

Howard sat at his desk most of the morning staring at the framed copy of the building blueprints that hung proudly on the wall. He had been so pleased when the contractor had first presented them to the church. They had been displayed for the first three weeks in the hall across from the choir entrance. There had been so much enthusiasm for the church expansion. Now the building fund goal had been reached for the first stage to begin and Howard had nothing but headaches over opinions and plans. The long meetings, the inevitable changes in costs and substitutions of material, the disagreements over minutiae all took their toll on Howard's brow. It was showing in his messages and it was showing in his home. Something had to change and change soon.

Howard glanced at his calendar. He had another meeting that evening with the building committee. He grimaced and took no comfort in the fact that, at least, he didn't have to preach on Wednesday. He wanted to call Donna, but decided he didn't know what to say. She had hardly spoken five words to him all morning. Perhaps the best course of action was to give her space for the time being.

He reached across his desk and picked up his Bible. Howard needed a word from the Lord. As he had learned from grade school, if he opened his Bible to the middle, it would settle in the book of Psalms. Since he had no other direction in mind, he allowed the Bible to open to Psalms 128. Reading from his new translation, he found the short Psalm potent with application.

> *¹ Blessed are all who fear the LORD,*
> *who walk in his ways.*
> *² You will eat the fruit of your labor;*
> *blessings and prosperity will be yours.*
> *³ Your wife will be like a fruitful vine*
> *within your house;*
> *your sons will be like olive shoots*
> *around your table.*
> *⁴ Thus is the man blessed*
> *who fears the LORD.*
> *⁵ May the LORD bless you from Zion*
> *all the days of your life;*
> *may you see the prosperity of Jerusalem,*
> *⁶ and may you live to see your children's children.*

Howard was taken aback by the impact of the six brief verses. It was as though God was placing his hot lance directly to the boil of Howard's life. If the man "who fears the Lord" has a family that is blessed, then perhaps what Howard lacked was a genuine fear of the Lord. The phrase intrigued him, because he had known of it most of his life, but had never examined it. He was sure that a study of the language would reveal something significant to it's meaning and after forty minutes of researching was not disappointed. In fact, the more Howard poured over his Bibles and reference works, the more he was convinced he did not have the remotest idea of what the "fear of the Lord" actually meant to his life. All this time, he had referred to the "fear of the Lord" as though it were an aversion to punishment. In truth, he found two distinctive words for "fear" used in the Old Testament. The first spoke of a serious dread that trembled at the prospect of impending punishment. The second found synonyms among "honor", "respect", and "reverence". The two different words were contrasted between the horror one experienced in the face of certain disaster, and the respect one held for another of revered status.

As Howard jotted down notes and references, Rusty knocked on the door.

"You up to some lunch?" Rusty asked.

Howard looked at his watch. He had not even noticed the time.

"Sounds good," he replied. "Let me finish this last reference."

"What are you working on," Rusty inquired, "seeing you don't have a mid-week message tomorrow night?"

"It started as a personal study, but I may use this on Sunday. It's on the 'fear of the Lord'"

"Good material," Rusty said. "Have you checked out Exodus 9 around verses 29 and 30? It's about Pharaoh asking Moses to stop the plague of hail. There's a neat verse in there that says something like, 'I will do this to show you that the earth is the Lord's, but I see that neither you nor your household FEAR the Lord.' You see, Pharaoh was afraid of Moses and his God, but he didn't 'fear' or respect Him. Fearing God is not being afraid of what He can do to you when you mess up. The fear of the Lord is the respect you have for Him that keeps you from wanting to mess up in the first place. God used the plagues to get Pharaoh's attention, but that kind of fear only made him straighten up till the plague was gone – it didn't change his heart towards God or His people. Hence, three more plagues."

Rusty motioned for him to get his coat. They could talk more about the fear of the Lord at the restaurant. Rusty could see the hunger in Howard's eyes. He took full opportunity by offering to drive as well as buy the lunch. Howard was finally in a position to listen.

———

Donna pushed her shopping cart through the grocery store half dazed. She had looked at the same item on her list three times before realizing she was in the wrong aisle. She looked around to get her bearings and then worked her way around the stock girl putting out cereal. As she walked by the young girl, she thought of Karen. This girl looked no older than her daughter did and yet she wasn't in school. Chances were, she had a small child at her mother's home while she tried to work to support the baby. There was no ring on her finger. This could be Karen if things didn't change, she thought to herself. She tried to smile at her as she wiggled her cart past the boxes in the floor, but the best she could muster was a sympathetic glance. Donna tried not to make eye contact for very long. She rounded the corner and forgot again what she was going after. Her mind raced to wild imaginations of Karen pregnant and without a home. She tried to imagine Howard's reaction and couldn't. She tried to project her own response to the prospect of Karen leaving school and making grave mistakes with her life. She had been so involved with her problems with Howard, Donna realized she had also been neglecting her children. Donna was not usually given to depression, but she began to feel like she was drowning in the soup aisle. Fortunately no one was there to see her tears. Something had to be done and soon. If Howard would not take responsibility for the family, then she may have to. Like Terry at the table that morning, she felt real hurt deep down.

———

Karen passed the day in school as though she was on one of those walking escalators at the airport. She just seemed to breeze by her classes and her friends. She had her eye on the clock and her mind on the mall. She couldn't wait to go to work that afternoon. There was nothing for her at home. She couldn't wait to clock in, to talk about clothes with customers. She couldn't wait to see Sheila. She knew that Sheila represented everything Karen wanted to be – free, independent, successful, and the shaper of her own rules. To Karen, each day at work was another step away from home. In her hurry, she failed to see the friends as well as family she was leaving behind. But there was one that wouldn't let her go so easily. There was one friend that she had made many years before, whom she had grown very close to and then let slip away. There was one friend who was watching from a short distance for that right moment to step in and remind her of their relationship and hopefully bring her back to her senses. For now, Karen was in a hurry, but that would soon change.

———

For those who had never traveled into the capital, the sight of Tegucigalpa was overwhelming. As the bus rounded the final hill and began it's descent along the mountainside overlooking the city, Ricardo was speechless. He had always thought *La Esperanza* was a large town. He had marveled at the size of *Comayagua* and *Siguatepeque* as they passed by, but nothing could compare to the tens of thousands of homes filling the saucer shaped valley of Tegucigalpa. Even from the great distance, he could see the national Cathedral. It's large columns and tall windows reflected the western sun beginning to set over the ridge before him. The city was actually two separated by large rivers, one being the center for political and commercial growth and the other, *Comayaguela*, her sister city, where the business district had overflowed and the coarser elements had gathered.

Ricardo knew he would have to spend the night in Tegucigalpa, but he wasn't sure where. He figured there would be a place near the bus station to eat and possibly a room for the night, but he had to watch his money. Maybe he would just find a corner of the station to rest in if it stayed open.

He began to think about what he would do when he reached *Santa Tierra*. He would first go to Anita, and then find someone who knew where the gringo held his meetings. With any luck, the missionary would be coming to town that night. There were evangelical churches near *Gualcince*, and he had noticed they met almost every night. He never thought ill of the evangelicals. Once, a group of them had brought some North American doctors to *Gualcince* and they stayed for several days. In the daytime, they saw the sick and in the evening they preached in front of the school. His cousin had been given medicine for her fever that week, when there was no medicine at the health center. He remembered that his mother also went and was given something to help her cough. He had forgotten about these things until now. As the bus began to navigate the narrow roads leading toward the downtown area, Ricardo dismissed the thoughts of the good work done by the doctors years ago. No amount of medicine could make up for this missionary running his brother down in the road like an animal.

As Ricardo looked out the window, he saw more vehicles on one street than he had seen in his whole life. He wasn't sure if he was ready for the big city, but he could go no farther. He would have to stay the night. The gringo would have one more night with his family.

Chapter Sixteen:

"The Pieces"

The afternoon passed quickly as Howard and Rusty went from lunch to hospital visits. There had been two members scheduled for surgery that Rusty had discovered the day before. He was relieved to find that Howard was more than willing to make the visits with him. The members of the church had grown accustomed to seeing Rusty in pastoral duties, but always preferred the visits from Howard. There was something about seeing *your* pastor during times of distress. Rusty never felt slighted.

As they began leaving the hospital to return to the church, Rusty took advantage of Howard's new refreshment of spirit in order to probe.

"You are certainly doing better today than the past couple days, is everything OK?

"I don't know that everything is OK," Howard responded honestly. "But, I believe they are looking up."

"Anything you care to talk about?" Rusty asked innocently.

Howard didn't respond immediately. He was weighing the prospect of sharing personal family problems with another staff member who was also younger and not experienced in marital difficulties. But Rusty had been a friend before he was staff. Howard believed Rusty could be trusted not to share whatever information he may decide to divulge.

"You know I've really been worked up over this building project and all the committees and everything."

Rusty nodded keeping his eyes on the road.

"Well, it has been bleeding over into my family life as well, I'm afraid. Lately, I seem to have less patience with Karen, less interest with Terry and. . . well Donna and I have had a few 'discussions' lately about how I'm doing. I have been feeling like my life is falling to pieces. I try to do what I think is necessary for the work of the ministry and yet it is never enough or at best, inadequate. I have little energy left for the family and when I try, I mess things up because I have forgotten something important."

Howard took a breath.

"For example, remember your suggestion about taking the family somewhere this weekend?"

Rusty quietly nodded again.

"It completely slipped my mind that Donna had already made plans. Karen has this new job and I wasn't thinking about her getting off from work, and well. . . needless to say, Donna didn't take too well to the whole suggestion."

"Ouch!" replied Rusty. "I didn't realize I was starting a battle at home."

"It wasn't your fault - it was mine. I was the one who wasn't thinking. I haven't been thinking much lately. It's like there are times I know what I should do, and I just don't let myself do it. I don't know, call it pride or whatever, but sometimes I just feel the hair on my back bristle and I don't want to back down."

"So what changed that today?" Rusty asked getting a better grasp of the situation.

"Today, I opened the Bible. I know that sounds trite, but it was the one thing I was not doing. I was trying to solve all my problems on my own and getting deeper and deeper into a mess. This morning I opened to the Psalms and the verses just jumped out at me."

"About the fear of the Lord?" Rusty added.

"Yes, exactly. I guess I was trying to keep my life together myself and it was just getting worse. Then I saw how a man who fears the Lord has his life together. Not because he has everything under control, but because the Lord brings everything together."

"So what have you learned about the fear of the Lord?" Rusty asked.

"I'm still learning. But one thing I got out of today. It is not the fear of punishment - Pharaoh had that and still didn't fear God. It is the awesome reverence of being in His presence."

"Amen." Rusty affirmed.

"I need to do some more study, but I believe God can put these pieces back together. I don't know how, and it won't be easy, there are some major breaches in my family right now, but I believe He can do it."

"That's the Howard I remember hearing in seminary," Rusty replied enthusiastically.

Howard thought about that for a moment. His walk with the Lord was deeper during his seminary days. His zeal was brighter, he remembered. What had happened? How could he have gotten so far from the Lord and now from his own family? How much time did he have to get it back?

"Oh Lord," Howard prayed silently. "Help me get back to You and then help bring my family back around the table."

The bus had gotten crowded around *Pinotepa* as they went through *zona negra*. The Mulattos were a community of Africans whose ancestors had survived a slave shipwreck and colonized on the western coast of Mexico. Through the years, they had maintained their cultural identity. Those who had intermarried had relocated leaving a virtual pure race of Africans. Flaco had never seen so many black people in one location and he couldn't help but feel uncomfortable. It was not their color as much as their size and strength that intimidated him so. He felt that at any moment they could demand to take over the bus and rob the passengers. His fear of their presence was matched only by his misjudgment of their character. The Mulattos were a quiet and gentle people that wished to live peaceably and to keep to themselves. Because of their difference, they simply appeared menacing. Fortunately the rain was behind them and the windows were wide open. Unfortunately, the road had gotten worse and the bus was traveling slower. Flaco did not sleep at all as the bus lumbered along the rough road to Acapulco for the next three hours.

As the bus driver announced their approach to Acapulco, Flaco became excited. He had seen TV shows and commercials of the beautiful beaches and hotels. To his dismay, what he saw was quite a contrast to the tourist image. The commercials never showed the poor shanty houses that were built on the opposite side of the hills in front of the beach. The bus didn't pass through the wealthy sector. In fact, if he had not been told he was entering Acapulco, Flaco would have thought this was just a large pueblo of poor Mexicans. He slumped down in his seat disappointed.

———

Karen was relieved to see Sheila hanging some new dresses as she ambled through the door. She was hoping she wouldn't have to ride the bus again that night.

"Karen," Sheila called out. "How was your day at school?"

"Sad!" Karen replied using an expression for lousy and pathetic. "Sometimes I wonder if the teachers even care if we're there or not. They just give us a bunch of work to keep us busy."

"Are you keeping up OK with your studies?" Sheila asked. "I mean, is work interfering any?"

"Oh no," Karen replied confidently. "I get it all done in study hall - no problem. Schoolwork comes easy to me. I make pretty good grades too," she added proudly.

"Have you thought about what college you may go to after high school?"

The question took Karen by surprise. She knew that Sheila had never gotten a degree.

"I'm not sure I even want to go to college," Karen said putting her things in the back room.

"Why's that?" Sheila asked.

"I mean, you know. . . school isn't everything. I may just see what I can do first."

Sheila smiled.

"I admire your determination," she said simply. "Sometimes you need to just discover what life is all about before charging off in some direction. There is always time for school when you know who you are and where you want to go. There is so much we need to learn about ourselves first."

Karen smiled back.

"That's exactly what I think," Karen agreed. "I need to find out who I am first."

"Well, right now, you are a clerk on the clock, so why don't you grab that box over there and help me do some hanging."

"You got it," Karen said enthusiastically.

Tonight was going to be a good night.

———

Carey helped Susan clear the dishes from the table as the boys raced for the Sega to play the new game Uncle Billy had brought them. The dinner had been quieter than during the past couple days. It was apparent Carey had much on his mind. As they reached the privacy of the kitchen, Carey gently placed his plates in the sink.

"You know, I haven't sat down with the boys yet and told them about the accident," Carey said.

"They know you had problems that night, but I think you're right, I think you need to let them know what all happened," Susan agreed.

"I was thinking I would talk to them before going on my trip tomorrow so that they would understand why I would be away a couple days."

"I think that's a good idea."

"Would you have prayer with me before we call them in?"

Susan nodded and reached over to take Carey's hands. They prayed for wisdom and sensitivity as they would together share with Josh and Caleb about the accident. After their prayer, they called the boys back into the kitchen, and sat together around the table. Carey had to remind himself that the boys were twelve and fifteen and probably not as unaware of what had been going on around the house as they used to be. They knew something had happened, they were just waiting to see how it would affect them.

Carey began with a simple narrative of the evening. The boys nodded in understanding about the *quebrada* and the wait for the rain to go down. They had been there before with him. As he began to describe the scene of the ambush, he could tell they were both disturbed and relieved that their father had not been hurt. But when he related the accident, they weren't sure how to respond. Caleb wanted to cheer that the bad guy had been killed, but he knew that no one else seemed happy about it. Josh looked tenderly at his

192

father with an understanding of his pain. Carey explained how Uncle Billy had come to help him get over the bad experience. One thing that Uncle Billy had done while he was there, was to help their father know what he could do to help relieve the feelings of guilt for the accident. He made it clear that he was not guilty of murder, but he had been responsible for the death of a man and that he needed to face the family about that. Carey told of his visit to the widow's home and the money that he had given her to help her and the children. The boys agreed that that was a good idea.

Carey then explained that he was going to take a short trip to the place where the man's family - his mother particularly - lived and apologize for the loss of her son. Josh asked if there were other brothers at home.

"Probably," his father answered honestly.

"Do you think they will try to hurt you?" Josh asked with equal honesty.

"I don't know. But I believe this is something God wants me to do, so I believe that He will be with me and not let anything happen."

"Can I go with you?" Josh asked.

"No, honey," Susan interjected. "We still have school, and besides. . . like your father says, he will be fine." The words barely comforted her, let alone the boys.

"That's right," Carey quickly added. "God will go before me and be with me while I'm there. If I didn't believe that, I wouldn't be going."

Somehow, there was assurance in their father's words. They joined hands around the table and Carey led in prayer.

"Father, we thank you that you love us greatly and that you care for us always. I thank you for sparing my life the other night, and ask you to go with me as I go to the family. May your angels go before me and protect me while I am there. May they encamp this home also while I am away. We trust you with our lives and commit those lives to you completely for your glory. Now give us rest through the night and strength for the next day. In your Son's Holy name we pray, Amen."

Each of the boys gave their father a warm strong hug for the journey. Susan would save her embrace for later that evening.

———

Getting five young children ready for bed in *Santa Tierra* is not easy. Normally, doing so as a single parent would make the task more difficult, but Anita actually found it easier without Moncho to threaten either her or her children. The oldest son, little Ramón helped out considerably by seeing to it that the two youngest children were bathed after their supper. His sister cleared the table and washed the meager dishes while her mother helped the middle child with his schoolwork for the next day. They had learned quickly how to function without a father and perhaps even better than when he had been around, though none would make that comment.

Anita had not told the other children yet about the money. Ever since Luís mentioned that it would not be a good idea to talk about it, she had worried that others already knew and that she could be targeted for a robbery. Luís had waited till Capitán Mendoza had left her home to speak to her about it. She had wished now that she had not even have told little Ramón. She would need to be looking for a new house soon so that she could get the *lempiras* out of her house.

Her mind drifted from her child's writing assignment as she remembered the gentleness with which Luís had warned her. He was truly concerned for her safety, she thought. Luís had lived most of his life in *Santa Tierra* and to her knowledge had never been married. She looked around her small house and began wishing.

"I am through with the babies," Little Ramón announced. "I put them in their hammock. Can I go out for a little while? At least till you are finished with Pedro and his homework?"

"Don't go far," Anita said cautiously. "I need you around here."

Little Ramón nodded with understanding.

"Would you rather that I stay home? I don't have to go out."

Anita smiled.

"You are my man of the house now," she said. "But you are also a young boy still and you need to play also. You have worked hard today, so go spend some time with your friends. Just come in before too late."

Ramón opened the door and was startled by a large man standing near the doorway. In the dark, he could not tell who it was. The man stepped closer to the doorway and was illuminated by the glow from the oil lantern next to Anita on the table.

"It is Luís!" Little Ramón yelled to his mother.

"Come in Luís," Anita called quickly.

Little Ramón noticed the enthusiasm in his mother's voice and smiled up at Luís as he stepped politely through the door.

"I was just passing by," he started. Anita looked at his belt and saw his machete attached to his side. Usually men wore their machetes only when they would be traveling, returning from work or preparing to stand guard for the night.

"Going somewhere this late?" She asked, looking at the long leather sheath.

"Not really . ." he began stuttering. "I mean, I plan to be around the town tonight."

She looked at him puzzled.

"What I mean is, I thought I would keep a watch on your house some this evening."

Anita offered him some coffee. Her eyes thanked him.

———

Donna looked through the shear curtains to see Howard's headlights pull up into the driveway - late again. Most of the day, she had recounted his past month's failures in her mind fueling her antagonism toward him. She relived his actions of neglect and inconsiderateness until they seemed like character traits that would never change. She had not saved him supper and was ready to debate the issue heatedly should he raise his voice once in objection. With her guns loaded and triggers cocked, she stepped away from the window and took her stance as he unlocked the front door and stepped in.

"Donna! What a pleasant sight to see!" Howard exclaimed as he closed the door behind himself and wiped his feet on the rug. He dropped his briefcase and stepped over to kiss her on the cheek.

She stood erect and stunned, but did not resist his show of affection.

"I expected you much earlier," she began, in a tone several decibels lower than she had prepared for. "I didn't save you anything from supper, because . . ."

"Don't worry, I had a large lunch and will probably just make myself a sandwich anyway," he said, cutting her off and smiling. "Can I get you something, while I'm in there?"

Donna cocked her head curiously. Was this the same man who normally walked in with a list of demands and a short sprint to his easy chair in the den? She couldn't respond before he snatched up his briefcase and headed for the kitchen.

"Let me make you a BLT? I haven't done that in a while. Has it been long since you all ate?"

"Karen is still at work and Terry and I had spaghetti around 6:30," she replied numbly.

"Why that was two hours ago," Howard exclaimed. "You could handle a sandwich and some chips now couldn't you?"

Donna followed him into the kitchen where Howard was washing his hands in the sink before opening the refrigerator. This was a first.

"I don't think so, but thanks anyway," she said softening. "Did you have a good day today?"

"Much better than the weekend," he bragged. "Rusty and I spent most of the day together and I really got a great deal done. How was your day?"

Donna was speechless. She couldn't remember the last time he had asked her that question. Most of their evening conversation was centered on his problems, his messages, or his "sheep". She thought of just shrugging off the question, but then decided to test his sincerity.

"Well, I did several loads of wash, wrote a couple letters, went out and paid the light bill and the phone bill. . . let me see . . . I got some groceries for this weekend, and then helped Terry with Social Studies and Physical Science this afternoon. I started supper around 6:00 – we ate, and for the past couple hours, I've been waiting on you and watching a little TV."

To her surprise, Howard looked at her the whole time she spoke.

"I'm sorry I didn't call. Our visits this afternoon took me right up to the time of the committee meeting at the church," he said, apologizing.

"Another committee meeting on the building. You just had one last night, I thought," she started to sound agitated.

"I know, we had to get some quotes after yesterday's meeting and two of the men brought their bids in tonight. I forgot all about it this morning."

Howard was trying to be congenial. He knew that they hadn't spoken to each other hardly at all since Sunday night.

"By the way," he added. "What were you saying about groceries for this weekend?"

"You haven't forgotten again already," she sighed. "I am going on a retreat with the church this weekend. You have the home Friday afternoon and night and most of the day Saturday. Now Terry is talking about spending the night with some friends on Friday, but I'm not sure. I should be home sometime late Saturday afternoon."

"Yes, yes, yes," he repeated reminding himself. "I remember now. That should be fine."

He cut his sandwich and took a large bite.

"You sure you don't want one of these?" he asked with a drop of mayonnaise in the corner of his mouth.

The sight helped Donna relax her guard. She smiled, took a napkin and gently wiped his face.

"No thanks," she said softly. "I'm glad you're home. By the way, I almost forgot. I did get a call here for you sometime this afternoon. I guess someone called the office while you were out with Rusty. Anyway, Diane must have given him your home phone, because he called here. Said something about the Rotary."

Howard looked puzzled as she turned and walked to the hall phone where she had left the message.

"The Rotary?" he replied. "I haven't had any dealings with the Rotary Club."

"Wait a minute," she called from the hall. "My mistake, it wasn't the Rotary, it was another group. Here it is."

She walked back into the kitchen with a small florescent post-it sticker on her index finger.

"It was the Gideons. I knew it was one of those groups."

Howard smiled to himself.

"He said he was coming tomorrow night to speak and wanted to know what time the service began," she explained. "I didn't know anything about it, but I told him that normally services began at 7:00pm on Wednesday night. He said he would try to come a little early to meet you."

"Yes, we are having a Gideon speaker tomorrow night. I imagine it will be like every other service we've had with them," Howard said reluctantly. "Did he leave a name?"

"Yes, I wrote it down."

Donna focused on her note and read her writing slowly.

"His name is Billy Eldridge."

Chapter Seventeen:

"The Mission"

(Wednesday)

Comayaguela, the sister municipality to the capital, was the first city that Ricardo had ever visited, let alone stayed overnight in. He had found a small hospice near the bus station that charged what he could afford. Throughout the night, he could hear the sound of taxis blowing their horns calling out to streetwalkers. Around 3:30am, he had been awakened by the sound of gunfire. He had gone to his window and seen several walking nonchalantly by. There were women in high skirts, a trio of drunks helping each other walk, and children sleeping against the buildings. This was a different world from *Gualcince*, and Ricardo didn't care for it. He slept very little that night.

Ricardo was accustomed to rising before the sun, but here, it was as though life had never rested. He cleaned up and dressed. When he stepped out onto the sidewalk, the light blue/gray glow of the heavens silhouetted the cluttered skyline around him. Though the buildings were not more than seven or eight stories high, they were the largest structures he had ever seen. The city did not hold the lure or attraction he thought it would. He shook his head sadly and turned his thoughts toward his mission. He must locate the bus to the south and then find a ride into *Santa Tierra*. Once there, he would need to find the church or house where the missionary would be holding services. He would first try to locate Moncho's widow and tell her how he had come to avenge the death of her husband. In his mind, it was a mission of family and honor. The thought of God had not entered into the picture at all - yet.

———

Luís heard the heavy board being removed from its brackets behind the doorway. The only security that Anita had for her house was a four-foot length of a rugged 2x6 that Moncho had stolen from a lumberyard. It fit squarely between two fairly strong braces and held the front door closed during the night. Luís made sure that no other protection was needed. He napped periodically near the entrance with his machete close at hand. As he rose and stretched, Anita opened the door.

"Can I get you some breakfast before you go?" she asked.

"That would be nice," Luís smiled.

Anita invited him in where she had already prepared a fire to cook tortillas and beans. They let the children sleep as they whispered. Anita poured him some coffee she had reheated from the evening before.

"I really thank you for watching the house last night."

"I don't think it is a good idea for you to have so much money in your house. Especially if others know," Luís said strongly.

"I don't think others know. I have talked with Little Ramón and he will not say anything to anyone else," she replied.

"That is not enough. You must be careful how you spend it also. Too much at one time in one place will draw attention. You should put it in a bank until you are ready to do something with it. Little Ramón says you are thinking about getting a new house."

"Yes," she said, stirring the beans in lard. "I am thinking of moving to another town also."

She noticed a look of alarm in Luís' eyes. She may have been mistaken to mention the move at that time.

Luís sought to change the subject.

"I am going to the worship service tonight. Would you care to join me?" he asked.

"What about my children? I can't leave them alone in the house with all that money."

"Bring the children with you. . . and if you would like, I can hide some of the money at my house to get part of it out of yours," Luís offered hesitantly. He knew that she did not know him well enough to trust him with such a large amount of money, but he was sincere and hoped she would see that.

"I don't know," she replied.

"I understand," he said quickly, trying to relieve her of the embarrassment of explaining.

"I'll think about it," she responded. "In the meantime, thank you for the invitation."

"I have been going for almost a week now, and except for missing last night, I have been almost every night. I am learning much about God and His word. I am also learning how to live better."

Luís did not know how to put his newfound faith into words yet. In fact, Anita was the first person with whom he had even tried to share his new life. It felt right. As he thought about it, he had not been back to the cantina since the night of the accident. There was a difference in his life and he was beginning to see it. He hoped that she would also. She did.

———

Flaco did not want to get back on the bus. He had not slept much in the small room near the bus station. He expected more from being in Acapulco, but he couldn't chance moving too freely around the streets. He would have to settle for his view of the ocean along the highway.

During breakfast he heard talk of the danger during the next leg of the trip. High-jackers were known to set up roadblocks along the six hour stretch between *Acapulco* and *Tecoman* and rob bus riders. How ironic, Flaco thought. This whole adventure had begun because of an ambush that went bad. Now he was facing the prospect of his own highway robbery. Flaco glanced around him. He carefully opened his traveling bag and removed fifty dollars from his money pouch hidden at the bottom of his bag. He would need to buy some more pesos before getting back on the bus. He thumbed the still thick stack of dollars. He was doing well. He knew the largest amount would be needed to actually cross the US border, but he should still have close to two thousand dollars to work with by that time. He rearranged his clothing to cover the money. He felt around for the gun. It was still there. Should he ever need it, it was still there.

———

Carey wasn't sure how many changes of clothing to carry. He did not plan to go all the way to *Gualcince* that day. The whole trip would take over twelve hours. He could make it in one day, but it would put him arriving late in the afternoon and possibly after sundown. Carey would rather spend the night in *La Esperanza* and get an early start the next morning. He would feel safer approaching the family in the daytime. It would be best if he could get in and out in the same day. Then if he could leave *Gualcince* by mid-afternoon Thursday, he could get back to *La Esperanza* and sleep over. He would then have to decide if he wanted to pass an extra night in the capital on the way home or not. Susan could always use some groceries and he could bring pizza home for the boys on Saturday. Carey looked at the slacks folded neatly on his bed. He would be safer to carry three pairs and to be prepared to stay over on Saturday. He walked to the closet and selected three dress shirts to match his pants.

Susan walked into the bedroom with his shaving kit.

"I think I have everything in there," she said softly.

They had not spoken about the trip all morning. There was never a time that Carey left the house that Susan didn't realize that he might not return. Most trips to churches outside of Choleteca were far from home. Carey usually didn't travel at night unless he had someone with him like Mando. In her mind, she would have felt better if he were going, but in her heart, she knew Carey was right to go alone – this time.

"Did you get my razor?" Carey asked.

"Yes, and I threw in an extra one just in case it was getting old."

Carey thanked her and took the kit. He was in no hurry to leave, but he knew he should be on the road no later than 9:00am.

"When do you think you will be back?" Susan asked.

"I could make it back by Friday," Carey replied. "But I'm thinking of staying over in Teguc. on Friday night, so I can go by the grocery store for you. I think I may try to see Bert on the way back and let him know how it went. I'll probably see if I can just stay over with him and Sandy."

"I'll be glad when you are back home and this is over," she said emotionally.

"Me too, honey," he replied taking her into his arms. "I wouldn't be going if I didn't believe the Lord was in this. Billy is right. I need to make the effort to apologize to both the wife and the mother. I may not receive as cordial of a forgiveness from the immediate family as I did from the widow, but I need to at least face them. I am trusting the Lord to go before me."

"I will be praying for you each day of the trip," she promised. "When do you expect to be in, . . . where is it?"

"*Gualcince*," he supplied. "I hope to be there around lunch time tomorrow."

"Then the boys and I will take a special break from school and pray for you at lunch time tomorrow," she said, pulling on his collar, and drawing his face closer to hers.

"Why don't we have prayer now, and then I will go down and say good-bye to the boys," Carey suggested.

They knelt together and took their places beside the bed where they had prayed many times. Carey led and prayed for God's safety and wisdom for the trip. He prayed for Anita and the family he hadn't met yet. He prayed for Mando and the service he would be leading that night in *Santa Tierra*. After he closed, Susan prayed for God's angels to protect Carey both on the road and in the presence of Moncho's family. When she finished, she waited before closing out her prayer. She wanted to sit with him and hold his hand just a few moments longer.

———

The eastern seaboard was beginning to feel the mid-autumn chills. Adam had placed an additional comforter on the bed the night before. He noticed that Gertie had wrapped herself in it and was still asleep. Maybe she had finally gotten a full night's rest he thought. Then he noticed her walker was at the foot of the bed. Normally it was parked in front of the nightstand. He remembered seeing it there when he turned out the light. She must have been up again. He placed it back in front of the nightstand so that she could get to it easier when she awoke.

Adam had learned to quit worrying about his Gertie during these prayer vigils. This was not the first time the Lord had her devoted in prayer for someone over a period of time. He recalled once how she interceded for a couple from their church for two weeks while they faced marital problems. They reconciled and now serve as dorm parents for a children's home just outside of Norfolk.

Since her stroke, Gertie had struggled with feelings of inadequacy. Her ability to attend worship services had abated. Her potential for ministry outside the home was extremely limited. Gertie wanted to remain in the warfare of the kingdom, and found her weapon of prayer mighty. Lives had been greatly altered when Gertie prayed. Adam knew this was her service to the Lord and that God was faithful to perform through her all that He ever required of her. So he had learned to pray for her and with her during these times.

Adam poured himself just a half of cup of fresh coffee and sat alone at the kitchen table.

"Whose lives are being changed this time?" he thought to himself. "What would that change involve? Would they ever hear about it when it was over or would God just carry them on down the road and they never know the outcome of their intercession? Was it really important that they know the outcome?"

Adam had more questions than answers. But then obedience doesn't wait for the answers to obey. So he sipped his coffee and opened his Bible. It was not a coincidence that his morning devotion had come to Galatians 6. He read the familiar words, but found strength as he reached verse nine.

> *"Let us not become weary in doing good, for at the proper time we will reap a harvest if we do not give up. Therefore, as we have opportunity, let us do good to all people, especially to those who belong to the family of believers."*

"Give us strength, Lord," Adam prayed aloud. "Please help Gertie to rest in You as she sleeps. I know she rises throughout the night and prays, but please renew her during her hours of rest."

"Amen!" Gertie added as she slid her walker through the doorway. "Thank you honey."

Ricardo was awakened by a large wicker basket sweeping across his shoulder carried by a larger woman getting on the bus. He looked around and tried to determine where he was. He had never traveled to the south before and didn't know the towns. He asked the young man across the aisle.

"We're at *Pavana*, about halfway between *San Lorenzo* and *Choluteca*," the young man responded.

"How much longer to *Choluteca*?" Ricardo asked.

The young man looked up toward the bus driver who was accelerating to pass as many cars as he could on the long stretch of straight road.

"At this speed, I would say about ten minutes."

Suddenly, Ricardo's mission seemed imminent and real. He was speeding toward the town where the murderer of his brother lived. He needed only to ask directions to *Santa Tierra* and he would be hours away from facing Moncho's killer.

He rode the final kilometers seated erect looking forward out the windshield. As the bus passed the factories at the edge of town, Ricardo began to gather his bag of clothes that he had stuffed under his seat. He felt around till he found the handle of his machete. Those around him did not feel threatened to see such a weapon carried on a crowded bus, because the two-foot blade was also the tool of the Honduran workman.

Ricardo stood and weaved his way to the front of the bus indicating his desire to disembark at the posta ahead. The driver pulled right in front of the FUSEP officer standing in the doorway of the security building. Ricardo walked up to the uniformed officer and greeted him for the morning.

"*Buenos Dias, Jefe*," Ricardo called to the officer.

"*Buenos*," he replied. "Can I help you?"

"Yes, I'm looking for *Santa Tierra*. Do you know which way I should go?"

"Just a minute," the young officer said. He turned to call inside the small building. "Capitán Mendoza, do you know the road for *Santa Tierra*?"

Mendoza stepped through the doorway and looked hard at Ricardo.

"You looking for *Santa Tierra*?" Mendoza asked.

"Yes," Ricardo replied. "I was told that I could find the road that leads to *Santa Tierra* from the pavement here."

"That's right," Mendoza said pointing across the highway to the gravel road with his eyes. "You take that road to the second fork. Stay to the right at both of them. But if you wait around at the entrance, you can usually catch a truck going that way."

"Thank you very much," said Ricardo.

He grabbed up his bag and machete and began walking across the street.

Mendoza walked back into the police shelter. There was no phone in the shack, but there was a radio. Mendoza picked up the walkie-talkie style radio and called into the station in *Choluteca*. It took a couple tries for him to raise someone on the other end.

"Base in . . . over!" squawked the voice through the static.

"Base, this is Mendoza at the entrance of the city. . . over!"

"Yes Mendoza, what do you need? . . . Over!"

"Have you heard anything on that stolen truck from last week? . . . Over!" Mendoza asked.

"As a matter of fact we have. The tags were traced to a truck that was pulled over for speeding just last night . . . Over!"

The Capitán's eyes widened. From the last report, Felípe was recovering well. Mendoza wanted to oversee personally the return of his truck.

"Do you have that location? . . . Over!" Mendoza asked eagerly.

"Just a minute," came the reply.

After a long pause, static crackled again over the walkie-talkie.

"It looks like *La Esperanza* on the report. . . . Over!"

"Which department? . . . Over!" Mendoza demanded.

"*La Paz*. . . Over!" came the response.

"Are there plans for recovery of the vehicle? . . . Over!" Mendoza inquired.

"Not yet. We are booked solid today. Doesn't seem to be a hurry. . . Over!"

"Tell Sergeant Fuentes that I will go after it early tomorrow . . . Over!" Mendoza ordered.

"You don't want to send someone later this week when we can spare the man?"

"No!" the Capitán shouted before the young officer could finish his transmission.

"Copy, sir . . . Over!" came the intimidated voice on the other end.

Mendoza put down the radio. He may just be able to recover a stolen vehicle and solve a shooting. He hoped the man driving the stolen truck could give him a lead as to where he could find Flaco. He had no idea the skinny thief was already five days and almost two thousand miles away.

———

The morning has passed smoothly for Howard. Donna had been downstairs for breakfast and in a good mood. Karen hadn't balk when he reminded her of Prayer meeting that night and that she needed to be there. And there had been no calls all morning concerning any problem with the building project. Howard had just settled back into his study of the fear of the Lord when Diane buzzed his intercom.

"Dr. Howard," she began courteously. "You have a phone call from a Billy Eldridge."

"Thank you, Diane," he replied to the speaker.

Howard picked up the phone and greeted Mr. Eldridge professionally.

"This is Dr. Pennington, may I help you?"

"Yes, Dr. Pennington," the friendly voice replied. "This is Billy Eldridge, and I believe I will be speaking to your church this evening."

"Yes, that is correct," Howard responded without comment.

"I was just wondering if we could get together for a little bit before the service, so that I could get to know you and maybe a little about your congregation. I know the Gideon office set up the engagement with your church, but I would like for you to know a little bit about me before I share in your pulpit."

"That's thoughtful of you, Mr. Eldridge, ..."

"Billy," he interrupted. "You can call me Billy."

"OK," Howard continued, still sounding distant. "As I was saying, I appreciate your sensitivity to the situation. I should warn you, our Wednesday night crowd may not be as large as Sunday evening, but then this was the only time we could schedule you in."

"Size doesn't bother me, Bro. Pennington," Billy said with a flare of familiarity that Howard was not prepared for. "Like I tell my wife, I speak to the eyes, not the size of the congregation."

"That's just fine," Howard responded unamused. "How early where you wanting to come by?"

"I don't know. Service begins at seven. Would six fifteen be too early for you?"

Howard stiffened in his chair. He couldn't think of any reason that a Gideon would need to talk with him for thirty to forty minutes before a service. After all, the program would be identical to the year before – statistics, testimonies of passing out bibles in the prisons and the schools, some verses on the importance of God's Word and then how the church can contribute for more Bibles to be given out. The only consolation is that Gideons hadn't started showing slides like the missionaries.

"I suppose I could be here that early," Howard said hesitantly.

"That would be great," Billy said excitedly. "That will give me a chance to get to know you, and also share some exciting things that I was a part of just last week."

"And where were you last week?" Howard asked humoring him in the conversation.

"I was visiting my brother in Central America where I had a chance to pass out some Spanish Bibles."

Howard pursued the conversation politely, but began looking for a way to bring it to a close. If he was going to meet with this man for forty minutes before the service, he didn't want to tie up his morning with him on the phone.

"And what does your brother do in Central America?" Howard asked.

"He's a missionary!"

"Great!" Howard thought to himself. "I now have both."

———

In spite of his restless night, Flaco found it difficult to sleep on the bus as it cruised along the ocean front highway toward *Tocoman*. The trip was beginning to take its toll on him. First the scare of the check point, then the large black men, the sleepless night, and now, the fear of being robbed and possibly killed over the dollars in his bag was more than Flaco cared to endure. He was tired of the bus and the same ocean scenes from the highway. He still had a couple days to travel and he wanted desperately to find another way to do it. Tractor-trailer trucks were plentiful along the highway also, he thought, but they were also stopped regularly at weigh stations and checkpoints. He had to think of a way to travel that didn't pass the road side stations and yet, didn't take him so far out of the way that it added days to his journey. The longer he was in the country the more of the dollars he was spending.

Trains. He had noticed train tracks leading into and out of Acapulco. They had to travel north also, he thought. Perhaps someone around him could give him some information on the trains and how he could board one up the road. Anything would be better than the cramped conditions on the bus. He glanced around to find most of the passengers near him asleep. He would approach someone when they stopped for lunch – if they weren't stopped themselves by thieves. He began looking out the window again in hopes that he could spot trouble early enough and have his gun ready just in case. It seemed strange to him how the thought of being robbed was now a fearful thing. He had both stolen and shot a man, possibly killed him, and yet, he felt nothing for his own crime. When put in the position of the victim, it was different. Flaco rode on under a cloud that wouldn't leave him alone.

———

Carey drove into the capital to eat at his favorite "American Fast Food" restaurant before beginning the six more hours he would travel that day to reach *La Esperanza*. He could remember when just one US food chain was in the capital and how they would travel the two hours just for an American hamburger on Saturdays with the boys. The country had changed greatly in the fourteen years on the field. A great many things had changed and many of them for the best. It used to be, Carey would not have been able to reach *La Esperanza* in one day and the last twenty kilometers to *Gualcince* would have to be ridden on mule or horse. As he remembered the journey, he let nostalgia carry him back to his early days on the mission field. Though much had changed, in so many ways, so much had stayed constant. He remembered the first time he had ever flown into this city. The hillsides seemed gray and without life. The housing had already begun to run along the inner edges of the crater called Tegucigalpa. The mission was small, and only two families had met them at the airport. The work in the south was barely begun, and nothing was well organized. Carey had been used to begin planting churches wherever a group of believers would meet and grow. He had not visited much of the northern coast, except to see other missionaries, but he had been to *Gualcince* before. His last trip was over five years before when he went with another missionary from that area to conduct a ten day Bible class for some students that were training to be leaders.

Carey reflected fondly over his missionary career. He and Susan had made mistakes, but the Honduran people had been kind and patient. He realized that much of what he had been feeling for the past week had been accusations from the "evil one" as to his fitness and calling to be on the mission field. As he replayed the memories of his service over the years, he realized that he was exactly where he needed to be. What had happened on that muddy road a week before was tragic, but it had not changed who he was, or what God had called him to do. The calling was not affected by the accident. His life belonged to God and so did his ministry. Carey was not naive enough to think he was invincible, but as long as God was using him, he was shielded. God had made that clear on that muddy road a week before. Carey would face Moncho's family in the confidence that his life belonged to God.

––––––

Luís looked for an excuse to walk past Anita's on his way to lunch. She was at the back of the house washing clothes at the *pila*, a square concrete above ground cistern used to collect water when it came through the town's PVC system. She noticed him also and waved. He took the invitation and walked over.

"Do you ever run out of clothes to wash?" Luís asked jokingly.

"No, just time to wash them in," she replied in good humor.

"Have you thought any more about this evening?" he asked.

207

"You mean the church service above town," she recalled. "I was thinking I would try to go."

"Good," Luís replied smiling. "Would you like me to come by and pick you all up, so you won't have any problem finding where we meet."

Anita noticed two things from his question. First, he was already identifying himself with the congregation. To her knowledge, he was just a former drinking companion to her late husband. What caused him to take on identification with an evangelical group so quickly. Secondly, he must know that everyone knew where the group met, because it was the only house with a bright lantern above town. In many respects, it was truly the only "light" in the night above *Santa Tierra*. Since he must have known she knew where the house was, then he also must have wanted to walk with her. That was what convinced her most to go.

"Will the missionary be there tonight?" she asked.

"No, he is on his way to *Gualcince* to meet with Moncho's family." Luís said matter-of-factly.

"You don't suppose he will meet with trouble there, do you?"

"I hope not," Luís responded concerned. "We must remember to mention him in our prayer requests tonight. I'm not sure the rest of the congregation even knows what he is doing. His companion from *Choluteca* will be with us tonight."

"Wasn't he the other man who came to my home?" she questioned.

"I'm not sure," Luís replied honestly. "He was with Bro. Carey and his brother this past Sunday. His name is Mando."

"I believe that was the one," she said thinking. "He didn't go with the missionary to *Gualcince*?"

"No, Bro. Carey felt he would be safer here. He may be right."

Neither Luís nor Anita could have known just how much danger awaited Mando that night in *Santa Tierra*. If they had, they would have begun praying that afternoon.

Chapter Eighteen:
"The Service"

Two hours in one place seemed discouraging to Ricardo. Few trucks had stopped to offer rides to the group huddled around the small refreshment shack at the edge of the gravel road. When one did stop it was quickly loaded by young men with grain sacks hoisted on their back. Ricardo waited patiently to board a pick-up without offending one who may have been waiting longer than he had. He used the time to learn which roads he needed to get to *Santa Tierra*. Though he didn't ask specifically about the mission, he did learn about the cantina and figured he could find the information he needed from there.

The sound of sliding tires over gravel caught his attention. He swung his empty coke bottle onto the ledge of the shack and ran to the lowered tailgate where several young men were climbing to stand behind the cab of the truck. Ricardo knew that the greater dust would swirl around the rear of the truck, but by the time he reached the pick-up that was all the space left available. He slid into the back as far as he could sit and dangled his calves over the tailgate. It would be a long bumpy ride to *Santa Tierra*.

––––––

Sometime after lunch they had passed the fishing village of *Zihuatenejo* and then the high rise apartments of the tourist area around *Ixtapa*. As they made their way slowly toward *Tecoman*, Flaco became more vigilant. He looked nervously out the window. He did not know where the local banditos preferred to lie in wait, but he could pick out several ideal places as they drove over the poorly paved road.

Suddenly Flaco felt a sharp pain on his neck as though someone had stuck him with a pin from behind. He slapped behind him suddenly and jerked his head around. There was no one even near him. The woman seated behind him was nursing her baby and the man seated beside her was asleep. He turned back around and within minutes felt the same prick on the underneath part of his arm. He slapped at it as he had his neck, but found nothing. He wondered if it was a spider, but he could not find any trace of any insect.

"No seeums," came the comment from across the aisle. The expression was in English and totally unfamiliar to Flaco.

"Beg your pardon?" Flaco replied in Spanish.

"No seeums," echoed the unknown informant.

"What does that mean?" Flaco questioned.

"It means you can't see them," came the Spanish response.

"Can't see what?" inquired Flaco.

"The tiny gnats that are biting you. We are approaching the swamp areas and they are plagued with little gnats you can't see. In English they say, 'no seeums', so that is what they are called around here."

"How long will they bother us?"

"All the way to *Compostela*," came the disheartening answer.

"Great," Flaco complained to himself. "If the bandits don't get us, I will be eaten alive by bugs I can't see."

The decision was settled. As soon as they reached *Escuinapa*, he was looking for a train.

———

Howard glanced at his watch. The afternoon had passed quicker than he thought. He didn't have enough time to drive home for dinner and return to the church in time for his meeting before the service with the Gideon speaker. It would be another fast food roast beef sandwich for supper. He called Donna to explain and detected a slight coldness. He had hoped to be making headway with her, but this would prove to set them back. He would bring her home some special ice cream as a peace offering.

He wasn't really looking forward to the meeting. It would be hard enough enduring the presentation that evening, he was now being asked to listen to stories before the service – and possibly missionary stories at that.

———

Donna hung up the phone firmly. She caught a glimpse of Karen with sweater in hand heading for the front door.

"And where are you headed?" she called.

"I have to go to work," Karen replied.

"But it's Wednesday," Donna exclaimed. "I thought you weren't going to work on Wednesdays."

"I can't help it," Karen replied defensively. "One of the girls called in sick and Sheila called me this afternoon. She needs me from 6:00 – 9:00."

"Karen, you know your father won't be pleased with this," Donna said with slightly less conviction in her voice. "What's he going to say when he gets home tonight and you aren't here?"

"I'm sure you will be able to smooth things over for him," Karen said smiling.

"Don't get smart with me young lady," Donna snapped. "I have enough problems with your father right now without getting in the middle of you two."

Donna was letting more frustration surface than she intended. Her emotions had been rocking up and down. At times she thought things were getting better between her and Howard and then she would begin to feel estranged again. At times she wanted to take sides with her daughter against her husband and at other times she didn't want to be involved at all. This was one of those times.

Karen rolled her eyes and took a deep breath.

"Are you saying I can't go to work?" Karen asked defiantly.

"No, that's not what I'm saying," Donna stammered. "I just mean. . . your father is not going to like this, and you need to be prepared for that. I understand when a boss is in a tight place and needs an employee to fill in, but you are forgetting what happened last Wednesday you didn't go to church and came in late."

"But I won't be in late. I'll be in by 9:30. I promise."

Karen lessened the intent of her gaze.

"I promise, Mom," she repeated as sincerely as she could.

"OK," Donna acquiesced. "Just try to get home as soon as you can."

"I will. Thanks, Mom," Karen said, her smile returning. "I'll see if Sheila can bring me home. It's quicker than the bus."

"Just get home as quick as you can."

Donna watched her bounce out the kitchen door. The last comment about Sheila didn't set well though. It seemed that Karen's relationship with her employer was getting too familiar and Donna was uncomfortable about that. It wasn't something she could put her finger on specifically, but it just didn't set well. Perhaps that was the clearest thought she had had lately.

———

Roberto's Cantina was nearly empty. Ricardo had arrived in *Santa Tierra* by late afternoon and found his way first to the cantina. He spent nearly half his food budget on beers before asking Roberto about Moncho's family. Roberto had heard Moncho speak of his wife, but he was not very helpful with directions. After another beer, Ricardo began to ask about the mission.

"I understand a group of evangelicals meet around here somewhere," Ricardo said casually.

"Yeah," Roberto answered. "It's just above town about a kilometer or so. In fact, I think they are meeting tonight."

"How will I know where to go?"

211

"Just follow the road out of town. Look for the house with all the people hanging around," Roberto said reluctantly. "In fact, things will be a little slow around here tonight because of them."

Ricardo smiled to himself. After he was through, several people would probably need a drink.

———

Howard was startled by the light rap on the doorframe. Since Diane had left for the day, he had left his door open. He stepped from around his desk to greet his visitor. Billy stepped into the room and extended his hand. He was dressed nicely and Howard took note of his firm grip. Most Gideon speakers he had met were older men with ill fitting suits. Howard was impressed with Billy's professional presentation.

"Dr. Pennington?" Billy asked.

"Howard," he offered cordially. "Please come in and have a seat."

They both took chairs in front of the desk.

"I hope this wasn't too much trouble to meet with you before service," Billy apologized.

"Not at all. I have been spending a lot of time at the church since we started our building program."

Billy looked confused.

"You're building?" he asked. "I didn't see any construction going on outside."

"It hasn't started yet. We are still getting the plans together. Lot's of meetings, committees, you know. . ." Howard chuckled.

"I suppose so," Billy replied uncomfortably. "I've never served on a building committee before."

"Let me show what we're planning to do," Howard said enthusiastically. He walked to the bookshelf and picked up the blueprints.

For the next eight minutes, Howard shared his dream with Billy. His pride for the project was evident. His part in the planning was emphasized. The church would have a building to be proud of – just as Howard would be.

"What's the cost for something like that?" Billy asked cautiously.

Howard gave him a multi-response including a breakdown of the existing church funds, members pledges, as well as the loans and their interest rates which they had secured from the bank. When he finished, he beamed with self-approval. Billy shook his head.

"That's a lot of money," he said slowly.

Howard detected a tone of disapproval, and began to roll up the plans.

"You think that's too much to spend?" he asked as though it were a challenge.

"I was just thinking how many churches that much money could build in Honduras."

Howard sighed, bracing himself for the lecture and the plea.

"And I suppose you know what a church costs to build in Honduras."

"Well, as a matter of fact, I was just there last weekend while visiting my brother," Billy commented.

"Oh, yes. You did say on the phone you had a brother who was a missionary."

Billy detected a tone of coolness that he couldn't quite identify. He wasn't sure if the pastor was being sympathetic or sarcastic. It reminded him of the tone he had heard from a state professor while he was in an ethics class who took issue with Christians and their stance on absolutes.

"Do I gather that you are not impressed by missionaries," Billy probed.

"Oh, don't get me wrong," Howard reacted politely. "I have nothing against them, and to be quite honest, I suppose I admire their commitment and sacrifice."

"But. . ." Billy said, leading him to continue.

Howard took a deep breath. He didn't want to offend the man who was about to fill his pulpit, but at the same time, he felt he had a valid point to make. He believed this educated Gideon would be able to understand and appreciate his opinion.

"I went to seminary with several men who told me they were called to the mission field. I found myself preparing for the same ministry and taking the same classes. We learned Greek and Hebrew, philosophy, Biblical studies including Theology, Hermeneutics, and Homiletics. I use that education weekly. They are down in some third world country filled with poverty and illiteracy and to be quite honest, wasting a tremendous education on people who could never understand a fraction of what we were taught."

Billy refrained from responding. He sensed Howard had more to get off his chest.

"Now I don't know your brother, he's probably an incredible guy. Like I say, I admire the sacrifice they make to do what they do. But what kind of sacrifice is it? They spend their lives denying themselves and their families to get some little village church started somewhere where it will probably die out as soon as he leaves to work somewhere else. Or worse, he spends years spinning his wheels and finally gives up to try in some other village. I've heard the glowing reports of many that come back and talk about the hundreds of conversions, but how many of them really end up in churches. I mean so many of those stories are padded with numbers to impress the folks back home and keep them feeling good about giving their missions offerings. If they were really growing churches, we would see slides of buildings like the one I just showed you wouldn't we?"

Howard paused to let his comments sink in. Billy sat quietly waiting on the Lord for his response. Howard took the silence as permission to continue.

"And one more thing," Howard quickly added. "It can't be healthy to raise children overseas. How are they expected to adjust and fit in this culture after they have spent most of their lives living sub-standardly. How can they possibly know how to socialize and merge into the work force here. They are the products of two cultures and they don't really belong to either one."

Now he had hit a nerve. Billy could excuse the shallowness of his opinions, but he would not let him degrade the life and legacy of his niece.

"May I ask you a couple questions, Dr. Pennington?" Billy reverted to formality on purpose.

"Certainly."

"First of all, what do you know of the missionary call?"

Howard paused for a moment, then ventured a reply.

"I suppose it is like any other calling to full time Christian service. Some feel they can function in the ministry better overseas than here."

"Do you see any difference in a call to missions as, say, a call to the pastorate?"

"Not really. They are both forms of ministry." Howard responded confidently.

"Do you find the call to be a 'missionary' distinctive in the Bible?" Billy asked.

"Well, I'm glad you brought that up. You see, the word 'missionary' doesn't even appear in our Bible. We have Paul and Barnabas going on journeys but nowhere are they ever called missionaries."

"Did I understand you to say you took Greek in seminary?" Billy asked rhetorically.

"Yes, I did, as well as Hebrew."

"Did you take Latin also?" Billy continued.

"No. It wasn't required for a Master of Divinity."

"By chance are you familiar with the Latin word, 'mittere'?"

"Can't say that I am," Howard admitted.

"It means 'to send'. You see, 'missionary' is a Latin word, not a Greek word. It means, 'one sent'. Do you know what the Greek equivalent for that word is Dr. Pennington?"

Howard knew the answer, but was hesitant to say it.

"Yes I do," he finally responded. "It is 'apostolos'".

"That's correct. You see the Bible does speak of the missionary and his work. It just uses the Greek word instead of the Latin. It says in Ephesians 4:16, 'And He gave some to be . . .'"

"Apostles," Howard completed the verse for him.

"That's right and then later is listed, 'pastors and teachers'. So you see, the calling to be a missionary is distinctive than the call to be a pastor. Primarily, because it involves different gifts and approaches to ministry."

"What do you mean?" Howard asked.

"For one thing, cultural adaptation. God's grace makes it possible for a family raised in one culture to make the move and adjustment to another. By the way, that kind of cultural adaptation becomes a plus for the children," Billy was careful to include his defense for Anna early. "Children raised on the mission field acquire a larger world view, and find adjustment to other cultures, even their own, easier because they see the value of the culture first. They tend to be more patient and mature. What factors in our culture are increasing the maturity level of our young people?"

Howard took that comment like a sting. There was no way this stranger could know of his difficulty at home and how immature his own daughter was acting.

"Another aspect of the calling is seen in cross-cultural ministry. You talk about how a missionary's education is wasted when he can't use it on the field. I have found that my brother has had to draw on all he has ever learned and then add to it principles of anthropology and sociology to clothe that information into a culture that is totally different from his own. It is a challenge few men can step up to plate to meet. Pastors in this country rely on other men's notes. The missionary has to learn how to rewrite the book without doing damage to the message. If you ask me, that takes more education than he ever got in seminary."

Howard took the point well. He sensed that Billy was not through.

"As for sacrifice. That too, is part of the call. But maybe you need to understand what sacrifice means to those who go to the field. It is not giving up. It's giving over. The things we feel we can't live without here aren't really the issue. When it comes down to it, we adjust to where we are, whether it's economical, social, or even physical. You can always adjust to heat, poverty and learning a language to survive – if you have to. That's not sacrifice. Sacrifice is declaring to God, 'I'm Yours – completely and without reservation. My life is for Your Glory. Use me or take me home, I'm Yours.'"

Howard nodded silently. He knew he was hearing truth. He just didn't know how to respond to it. Billy sensed the receptivity and calmly made his final statement.

"Dr. Pennington, I don't say these things because my brother is a missionary. I say them because I believe God calls men and women like him to a special task – a task distinctive from that of the pastorate or any other form of ministry. Being a missionary is not a super spiritual calling. I could tell you all about my brother's feet of clay. He's a man no different than you. He probably has no more faith in His Lord than you do. But I can tell you this. He has not thrown his life away or run off to the mission field because he couldn't 'cut the mustard' over here in the states. He is not running or hiding – he's serving. God called him there, placed him there and will leave him there till He is through with him. He has not wasted his life. He has given his life."

"I'm sorry," Howard started sincerely. "I didn't mean to imply anything negative about your brother or his work. I guess I have had an impression about missionaries that wasn't warranted. Thanks for sharing those things with me."

"I hope I didn't come across too strong," Billy replied, smiling.

"Not at all. In fact you made two strong impressions."

"What was that?"

"Well, before you came, I kind of put missionaries and Gideons in the same boat," Howard confessed. "You have shown me that I was wrong about both. You can be extremely passionate and convincing in your presentation."

"You haven't heard me talk about the Bible yet. If there's anything I have a stronger passion for besides missions - it's the Bible."

"I'm sure you will challenge our hearts tonight," Howard said. "By the way, since you feel so strongly about missions and since your brother is a missionary, why aren't you serving on the mission field?"

"To put it simply, Bro. Howard, God didn't call me like He did Carey. I have been on short-term trips, but God has chosen to use me here at home. I'm sure you understand."

Howard nodded. At least he thought he understood.

———

Karen just didn't understand. One day her Mom was on her side and the next day, she was biting her head off. If it weren't for work, she thought that she would go crazy. She began telling Sheila about her problems at home between customers and Sheila seemed interested. She never made Karen feel like a teenager. She always treated her as more mature than her parents did. She never belittled her and even praised her for good ideas she had for displaying merchandise. Sheila made Karen feel good about herself.

"So you need a ride home again, tonight?" Sheila asked while folding some blouses that had been left near the dressing room.

"If it isn't any trouble," Karen said apologetically. "I mean, I know it's out of your way, but it would really help me out."

"Why didn't you tell me before that your father was a preacher?" Sheila asked.

"Oh, that! Well, I guess I didn't think it would matter about me getting the job."

"It's not that," Sheila said. "It's just I never pictured you as a . . . well, you know, a preacher's kid."

Karen hung her head slightly. She wasn't sure how to take the comment. In a way, it hurt. As much as she resisted being labeled a "PK" (Preacher's Kid), she still hoped that it would show a little. She wasn't rebellious against the church, just her Dad's control. Neither was she ashamed of her relationship with God. It just hadn't been a central part of her life lately. In some ways, Sheila's words felt like an indictment and Karen felt embarrassed by them.

"I guess Preacher's Kids can be just like everyone else," Karen said half joking.

"I guess you're right."

Sheila seemed slightly distant the rest of the evening. Karen knew how Sheila felt about lying and hoped she didn't think that her new employee was going to be a problem. Karen really needed this job to get away from her family. Why, with a little encouragement from Sheila . . . Karen couldn't think about that. At least not for now.

———

Carey settled into the small room. It was still early, but there was nothing to keep him awake after such a long drive. At least the hotel was clean and at least two blocks away from the nearest "disco" where the music of the late night band could be felt along the street. He would try to get a good night's rest and start early the next morning for *Gualcince*. He read a couple chapters from the Gospel of Mark and then laid his marker in the place were he stopped. He removed his glasses and began a time of prayer.

"Lord, thank you for the safe journey this day. I pray that you will prepare the way for tomorrow. I ask your protection along the road and when I arrive. I don't know what to expect, but I know that nothing will surprise You. Help me to be ready."

"Lord, I also wish to pray for my family while I am away. Watch over them especially through the night. Be with Susan and the boys and be with Billy as he returns to his family and to our Anna."

Carey remembered Anna's request.

"Lord also be with that family that is going through problems at home. I know it is tough keeping the family a priority in the business of the ministry, but just give Bro. Pennington a little reminder of Who You are and what Your priorities are."

"And Lord, be with Mando tonight as he is probably in the middle of the service at *Santa Tierra*. Let the people hear him and respond to Your Word, Your love, and Your Son, Jesus Christ. And may he be protected by Your angels this evening."

————

Mando had enjoyed the music and the specials. He was hoping there would be a couple more when the worship leader sat down and motioned for him to take the front for the message. Mando didn't consider himself a preacher, but he had sat under Bro. Carey and accompanied him enough that he had a solid understanding of presenting the gospel. He could also relate Bible stories with relevance to the people. He wasn't an orator, but God used him when Bro. Carey couldn't attend a service.

Down the road from the home where the congregation met, two men sat against a large rock near the side of the road. They had been discussing the condition of the fields since the rain the week before. They saw the lone figure walking up the road towards them but couldn't make out who it was. He was tall and brandished a longer machete than was normally used for work.

Inside the small building, Mando began reading from Joshua chapter 1. He wanted to set the stage for the story of the "fall of Jericho". Luís opened his Bible to the New Testament and Suyapa reached across him and flipped the pages back to the Old Testament. He looked up and smiled and then leaned towards the young lady on his other side.

"I guess there are still a lot of things I need to learn," he said sheepishly.

Anita smiled back. This was her first time in an evangelical service and she felt completely lost.

When Suyapa pointed out the verse, Luís quickly moved the Bible across his lap towards Anita to show her where Mando was reading.

Outside, the stranger stepped up to the two at the rock and lowered his machete to his side. He looked around the building lit up just ahead of them and then turned back to the two watching him closely.

"Is this where the evangelical group meets?" Ricardo asked sternly.

"Yes, right up there," answered one of the men pointing towards the house using his lips as was the Honduran custom.

There was no vehicle near the building. Ricardo looked disgusted. He looked back at the two men.

"Doesn't a gringo come to hold services here?" he asked.

"Usually," the other responded, "but I haven't seen him around tonight. He drives a red pick up with a camper on the back."

"But that man who usually rides with him is here," added the first.

"That's right," replied the second fellow. "I saw him go in earlier. He's probably the one preaching. He does that sometimes when the missionary can't come."

"Do you know if he was with the missionary last week?" Ricardo asked.

"I think he was," one said looking at the other. "Wasn't that the night Moncho was killed?"

Ricardo flushed with anger. He didn't wait to hear any more. He turned towards the house and walked deliberately raising his machete as he stepped.

"God told Joshua not to be afraid," Mando declared firmly. "In verse nine he said clearly, 'Be strong and courageous. Do not be afraid, the Lord your God is with you wherever you go'. Joshua had been one of the spies who knew the size of the people in the land. He knew what he was up against, but God was telling him to have faith and not to fear. The opposite of faith is fear. When we are afraid, we are not able to trust God."

Luís would not have recognized the resemblance between Moncho and his brother because of the difference in their years and how they had lived. But he did notice the stone cold stare of Ricardo when he stepped through the doorway. He turned his attention back to Mando briefly and then felt the urge to look again at the visitor. He was no longer in the doorway, but was inching his way along the wall towards the front. Luís was not accustomed to getting messages in his spirit, but he felt something was wrong – very wrong. He followed the stranger, expecting him to find a place near a window and stop. Many took positions near the windows when there was no place to sit in order to feel some of the night breezes, but this man passed two windows without stopping.

Luís stepped up from his bench scooting passed Anita to reach the opposite wall. He was not noticed because many men moved about during the service, especially as body heat began to grow in the small building. Luís mirrored Ricardo's movements along the opposite wall.

Mando had not noticed the movement of either man. He was explaining the strength that comes from knowing God and knowing that he was the provider of all grace for living. Ricardo had not been paying any attention to Mando's words. He was focused on one aim. He had taken assessment of the room as he stood in the back. He knew the women would cause confusion and there was a doorway behind the area where Mando was speaking that he could push his way through. Once outside, it would be easy to be lost in the darkness around the house.

Luís had come to the side bench where the musicians were sitting. Ricardo had reached the same point just in front of the first bench filled with nursing women. The children had left the front of the preaching area now that the music was over and the message had begun. Luís watched him step forward and for the first time saw the large machete in his hand.

"*Moncho*" came a voice in Luís' head. Suddenly, he knew who the stranger was. Worse, he knew why he was there. Mando kept looking forward as he expounded on the goodness of God in His provision, His care, and . . . His protection.

Luís ran his hand along the wall and felt the neck of one of the guitars.

Ricardo tightened his grip on the machete. The determination burned from his eyes as he glared at Mando. He watched and waited for the preacher to move away from the table so that he would have a direct line of attack toward him. This man was worse than the gringo. He was a Honduran who gave consent to a murder of one of his own. This man deserved to die and die as an example to others that they must not allow their own countrymen to be murdered by foreigners and continue to support them. He would strike down this dog and put the fear into the rest of them. This congregation would never forget this night.

"Be strong and courageous!" Mando repeated, stepping back from the table to make his point strong. "The Lord your God is with you!"

Luís watched the machete slowly rise from Ricardo's hip. Like a reflection, he lifted the guitar to his own shoulder. The musician seated beside him glanced over to see what he was planning to do.

Ricardo gave a yell that stalled him long enough for Luís to step forward first. As the two men rushed toward the center of the room, Ricardo wielded his machete high in the air intending to bring it down squarely across Mando's neck. Luís gripped the neck of the guitar with both hands like a piñata stick and prepared to swing upward toward the descending blade. The sight of both men startled Mando such that he stumbled backward out of the way. In a synchronized swing, the two instruments collided in mid-air and the machete buried itself deep into the wide base of the guitar. Ricardo was halted in his swing and caught off balance by the counter swing of Luís. The machete was ripped from his hand embedded in the wooden shell. Luís followed through with his swing by tossing the guitar and machete to the rear of the room, where it was immediately recovered and held by two other men near the back door. Ricardo stumbled into the bench of women who scattered frantically with their infants. Before he could recover to his feet, five large "brethren" of the church including Luís surrounded him.

———

Flaco was beginning to feel the fatigue of the trip. The anxiety over the highway bandits did not ease until they had past the turn off to *Guadalajara*. He wished he was heading inland, but he kept to his course to snug the shore. He reached *Compostela* by nightfall, and dragged himself to the nearest hotel. He was just glad to get off the bus. The ride into *Escuinapa* would be a short two and a half hours early the next morning. He would leave as quickly as he could in order to find a train he could board to *Mexicali* that morning if possible. He was willing to pay handsomely to keep from riding anymore busses.

As Flaco locked himself into his small room for the night, he began to think about *Santa Tierra*. The small town seemed years as well as miles away. It was hard to believe so much had happened in just one week. He suddenly realized that it was the same night of the accident. He wondered if the Gringo missionary had returned to the town yet. He wondered if anyone from Moncho's family would really make the trip to avenge their brother's death. He wondered if he had done the right thing by telling them. In a way, he felt responsible for the Gringo's destiny, should it come to that. That placed two possible deaths on his soul. He was starting to wonder how God must have been feeling about him. Was there even a God? Flaco was not a very religious person, but that night, he had trouble getting to sleep in spite of how tired he felt.

———

"Who are you?" one of the men from the church demanded.

Ricardo held his silence while three men held him against the wall of the mission. Mando had tried to restore order, but too many on-lookers from outside the building had come in to discover what was going on. Most of the women had retreated to just outside the front door. The small room was filled with men both from within and outside of the congregation.

"You are not from this area are you?" one commented.

"No, he's not!" yelled a man from near the doorway. He was one of the two from the rock down the street. "He was asking questions about the missionary. He was looking for him. When we told him that his traveling companion was inside, he suddenly left us to come here."

"Is that true?" questioned another. "Where you looking for Bro. Carey?"

Luís stepped toward the man held quietly against the wall and looked at him carefully.

"You are Moncho's brother, aren't you?" Luís asked calmly.

221

Ricardo looked up at him. His eyes showed the answer to Luís' question.

"You came to avenge his death, didn't you?" Luís continued.

Ricardo nodded slowly. A quiet murmur spread toward the back of the room.

"You think the missionary murdered your brother, don't you?"

"I know he did," Ricardo responded, speaking for the first time.

"How do you know this?" Luís asked in a steady tone.

"Because the man who saw him murdered told us." Ricardo spit back.

"Was this man tall and skinny?" Luís toyed with him.

"Yes." Ricardo acknowledged.

"Was his name Flaco?"

The room began to repeat bits of the conversation towards the back. The name of Flaco was heard in all directions.

"Yes, that was his name. How did you know?" Ricardo asked.

"Because I was with Moncho and Flaco the night Moncho was killed." Luís confessed.

The room began to relay the news of Luís' involvement.

"Flaco didn't mention anyone else being with them. He said they were alone when Moncho was run over."

"That's correct, I had just left them moments before the missionary arrived because I didn't want to be a part of what they were going to do." Luís replied.

"What do you mean, 'what they were going to do'?" Ricardo asked, loosening his body against the pressure of the other three men.

"Flaco didn't tell you that he and Moncho had set a trap for the missionary and were going to rob him?" Luís asked.

"No! that's not true. Moncho was resting on the road and the missionary ran over him like a dog and didn't even stop." Ricardo argued.

"Is that what Flaco told you?" Luís asked. He motioned for someone to bring Anita into the room. "Would Moncho be sleeping face down in the mud?"

Ricardo suddenly looked puzzled.

Anita was brought in before the group surrounding Ricardo.

"This is Moncho's widow. Maybe you will believe her."

Luís turned his attention to Anita who seemed frightened.

"Anita, who brought Moncho's body to you?" Luís asked.

"Capitán Mendoza of FUSEP in Choluteca," she replied.

"And how did he come to find the body?" Luís continued.

"He said that the missionary brought it to the posta the night before."

Ricardo looked shocked. Flaco had told him that the missionary had never even stopped.

222

"And was the body and clothes muddy?" Luís probed.

"Yes, but just one side," she answered.

"Which side?" he pressed.

"The front. He had been laying face down in the mud when the car ran over him," she responded with difficulty.

"Did Capitán Mendoza tell you how he was run over?"

"Yes, he said that Moncho had been trying to rob the missionary. He slipped in the mud and fell under the truck."

Mando listened but did not interrupt. If given opportunity, he would confirm, but he saw himself as the object of opposition for the moment and not likely to be believed.

Ricardo dropped his eyes. He had no trouble believing that his brother was trying to rob someone, he just didn't realize that it had brought about his death. He had no reason to not believe the widow.

Luís turned to Ricardo who had ceased his struggle completely and sat motionless against the wall.

"Do you still believe that the missionary or this man right here killed your brother on purpose and left him in the road?"

Ricardo lifted his head and then looked toward Mando. He did not see hatred for his deed reflected in Mando's eyes. Nor did he see fear. There was calmness, a peace that he didn't understand. He had just tried to kill this man and he was looking back at him as though he himself was in an accident and needed help or medical attention. Ricardo realized that Luís was telling the truth and he felt ashamed for trying to kill an innocent man. Mando had been the victim – again.

"I am sorry," he said toward Mando.

"The question is, do you want forgiveness?" Mando responded.

"I don't know what you mean," Ricardo said confused. "I said I was sorry."

"I'm not talking about forgiveness from me," Mando was quick to add. "You have come here with murder in your heart. I suspect that is not the only sin you harbor there. Your brother lived a hard life and he died the way he lived. That was unfortunate. What is more unfortunate is that he died before he knew that he didn't have to live that way. That he could be forgiven for his sins and God could give him a new heart. It begins with forgiveness and then goes from there to a new life. I ask you again, do you want forgiveness? – from God?"

Ricardo looked around. He was not the only one listening. Many who had come in from the outside was looking at Mando and attending to his words. It was not a sermon, it was a simple, genuine invitation to a man who almost committed murder to be forgiven, cleansed and given a new chance at life. Suddenly, many were interested.

223

"You don't understand," Ricardo cried out. "I almost killed you!"

"You don't understand," Mando replied softly. "They DID kill Jesus! And yet, He is the one who stands before you tonight offering forgiveness. All He asks is that you give Him your life along with your sin. He will forgive you and make your life better."

Ricardo dropped his head. He felt the heavy conviction, as did others around him. He had expected to be lynched for his failed effort to strike down their preacher. Instead, he was being offered something he had never considered before – a chance to live above the reputation of his father and his brother. He had come to *Santa Tierra* out of a pretense of duty to his family, but in reality, he was trying to measure up to the standard that the men of his family had set. He had come to show he was as tough as the other's before him. Now he was being offered a new life, a new family, and a new standard by which to be measured. Ricardo saw strength in the peace that Mando possessed at that moment. That was the strength he wanted for his life.

"What do I need to do?" he said in surrender.

As Mando explained, others gathered around, removing their hats and kneeling near Ricardo. As the word of what was happening filtered to the women just outside the door, the sound of singing could be heard around the house.

Maybe it was just Luís' imagination, but it seemed that the light from within the small room seemed to grow brighter, though no one had adjusted the Coleman lantern above their heads.

———

Gertie paused in her prayer time. She felt warmth deep within her soul. Adam had already gone to bed. She would like to have shared the moment with him. Instead she began to sing softly to herself. Something was happening somewhere. She thanked the Lord for His goodness and grace. She sang several stanzas and quietly drifted to sleep on the couch.

———

Karen slid into Sheila's car and sighed.

"That was a busy night," she said exhausted.

"Wednesdays can be like that," Sheila replied revving her motor and shifting into gear. "You would be surprised how many people don't go to church on Wednesday night."

Karen detected a slight jab with the comment, but didn't feel it was directed toward her. She glanced at her watch. They were making good time. She should be home before curfew at least.

"Are you able to work tomorrow?" Sheila asked.

"I should be able to," she replied. "As long as I don't get in trouble for being out tonight, but I should be OK. We're going to make it back by 9:30 and that is what I told my Mom that I would try to do. Hopefully, she will run interference with Dad for me."

"You have much trouble at home?" Sheila asked.

"Not any more than most girls my age, I guess," Karen replied, trying to downplay her situation and feelings.

"Have you ever thought about moving out?"

The question seemed bold being spoken out loud. Of course she had thought it, she just didn't express it. Somehow that seemed like a step closer to doing it.

"Sometimes, but I'm still in school and, well, you know . . ."

"All too well, Karen," Sheila said slyly. "Listen, if you can work tomorrow, then tell your folks, I'll bring you home again – about the same time tomorrow night. Will they mind that?"

"I guess not, why?" Karen asked.

"It's a surprise, OK?" Sheila taunted.

Karen giggled.

"OK, a surprise. What time do you need me to come in?"

"5:00 is early enough, and dress smart," Sheila added.

"Sounds interesting," Karen said excited. "I'll be there."

They drove on towards Karen's home, but in reality, they were headed much farther down the road.

———

The service continued well into the night. Instead of people getting tired and going home, they went and found more neighbors and returned. The singing moved into the room, but the space was getting small. Luís invited Ricardo to join him and Anita just outside the door. It was apparent that Ricardo was not going to try to run away anymore. He was beaming with his newfound faith. Luís led the other two away from the sounds of the elated congregation.

Luís took on a serious look and began asking Ricardo more questions.

"You said something earlier about 'us', when mentioning Flaco. Was he in your home?"

"Yes, he came through on his way to El Salvador," Ricardo answered.

"El Salvador?" Anita asked.

225

"Flaco is headed to the United States," Luís explained. "That's why he robbed Felípe"

"I wondered where he was going to get the money to go all the way to the US," Ricardo commented. "I am really beginning to feel deceived."

"When he told your family, did they send you to avenge Moncho?"

"Not really," Ricardo admitted. "In fact, my mother was against my coming, but my other brother Moisés felt I was doing the right thing."   .

"You have another brother?" Luís asked alarmed.

"Yes, but since I am the oldest, it was my duty to come. I'm just glad I learned the truth before I really hurt someone."

"But your brother thinks the missionary murdered Moncho." Luís stated.

"Yes, but he won't be coming here," Ricardo replied smiling. "And when I get home, I will tell them all the truth."

"You don't understand," Luís said tensely.

Anita looked into his eyes and understood.

"Brother Carey is headed to your family's home to apologize."

"We must stop him. When does he leave?" Ricardo said, understanding the urgency.

"He left yesterday for the capital, and he should be arriving in *Gualcince* tomorrow by lunchtime."

"We can't possibly get there by then," Ricardo said. "It took me two days to get here myself."

"What will your brother do if he shows up there?" Luís asked, knowing the answer.

"Exactly what I tried to do tonight, only there will be no one there to stop him."

Anita looked at both of the men and spoke slowly and deliberately.

"Maybe there is a way."

Chapter Nineteen:

"The Family"

(Thursday)

Carey had slept soundly through the night, in spite of the "disco" music two blocks away. He knew he had about four hours travel, if the roads were good. He hoped to arrive around lunch and try to find Moncho's home. It shouldn't be difficult in a small town, he thought to himself. Carey ate a light breakfast of beans, tortillas and a hard fried egg. He drank the strong black coffee wishing he had a couple bags of creamer in his truck. After breakfast, he started out of town passing another red pick-up that sat inconspicuously next to the police station. Carey had no reason to recognize the truck.

———

Capitán Mendoza had not planned to spend the night in the small town eight hours from his home. He had hoped to drive in and out the same day, but the paperwork had not been done on the stolen vehicle and even his rank didn't seem to expedite the process. He arrived in *La Esperanza* by midday the afternoon before in hopes of claiming Felípe's truck, finding a driver and getting all the way back to *Choluteca* before very late. What he found was an incomplete report on the purchase of a stolen vehicle and an uncooperative Sergeant. He called his wife by nightfall and surrendered to the reality that he would not make it home till the next day (if even then).

He had risen early with hopes of intimidating the new shift into action. As he stood in the doorway of the FUSEP office, he caught a glimpse of the red Hilux with the white camper shell pass by. Though the color and make of the truck was common, the tall redheaded driver was not. He paused long enough to follow the truck with his eyes as it squeezed down the narrow road and turned towards the road out of town at the end of the street. Mendoza thought it strange. That road did not lead to the main highway that would take him back to the south, but rather to the long dirt road winding itself up towards the mountains of the department of *Lempira*.

"The missionary must be on an important journey to be this far from his home," he thought to himself. Mendoza turned his attention back toward the young officer working hard at his typewriter.

"I don't wish to spend another meal here, let alone another day," he barked.

"*Si Señor*," replied the officer. "We just lack two more signatures, and you can take the truck, sir".

The Capitán huffed to himself totally unaware of the divine nature of his delay.

_____

"$100!" Flaco exclaimed. "Train tickets don't cost that much!"

"Not to ride inside on the seats with other Mexicans," came the taunting reply of his "travel agent". "But for you, I have a quiet private car where it will be easy to sleep, since you won't have much of a view of the countryside. For that and no questions, the ticket is $100."

Flaco knew he would still have enough to reach the United States, he just didn't know how long he could live on the remainder of the funds. He hoped to find a job soon after arriving, but if not, he still had the "power" to survive – even in America.

Reluctantly he paid the dollars and followed his guide to an enclosed storage car two-thirds the length of the train from the engine. They waited till no one was inspecting the cars and then the coyote slid open the heavy door and instructed Flaco to jump in.

"This is a storage car that brings crates of goods from Mexicali to this region, but it always returns empty. There is a crawl space between the last crate and the wall of the boxcar. When the train stops, hide in the crawl space, because they may inspect the car for stowaways. While the train is moving you can stretch out in one of the empty crates. You won't have much light, but then you should only have two stops, one in *Culiacan* and one in *Hermosillo*. The trip usually takes 20 hours. You will be in Mexicali by 6:00am Friday morning."

"How do I get off the train?" Flaco asked like a nervous child.

"I have a worker in the train yard in *Mexicali* who will let you out. That is why the price is so high. You are paying two men to risk their jobs, Señor."

Flaco didn't appreciate the sacrifice as much as he could. He felt he was the one taking most the risks. He was also not fond of the idea of placing his full trust in strangers. As he thought about it, his whole journey had been trusting strangers from one leg to the next. Though the trip had been uncomfortable, it had not been distressing. He had not been robbed or fallen sick along the way. He felt he had been lucky. He still didn't realize Who was traveling with him.

_____

Susan didn't usually worry about Carey when he traveled, but this was different. She tried not to look worried as she prepared the boys for their schoolwork. She did make a point of insisting that they begin their day with prayer for their father as he traveled.

Caleb led in prayer.

"Heavenly Father," he began. "Please be with Daddy as he travels. Keep his truck safe on the road. Keep him company while he is away from home, and help him tell someone about Jesus today. And should he ever feel afraid, remind him that You are right there with him. Bring him home safe, we pray. In Jesus name – Amen."

———

Moisés was glad it was almost the weekend. The crop was almost planted and he would be able to be with his friends on Friday. He thought about Ricardo and wondered if he would see him again soon. He wondered if Ricardo was able to go through with his mission. The next question would be if Ricardo would return to *Gualcince* or not. Moisés wasn't sure if he would return if it had been him who left. The ground was hard, the crop was unsure and life had no prospects for improving. At least in the city (or better yet, the capital) he could do something exciting with his life.

Moisés realized that he was now the oldest at home. He did not want the new responsibility. The more he thought about it, the angrier he felt. It was all that *gringo* missionary's fault. He was the one that killed Moncho and then caused Ricardo to leave home. He was the one that hurt his mother so deeply and caused her to weep. He deserved to die. Moisés hit at the dirt vicariously with the edge of his shovel.

———

Carey maneuvered the pickup along the difficult road leading up to *Gualcince*. As he drove he reflected over the advise he had received during the previous week. He remembered Mando's calm assurance that God was still in control.

"You fear vengeance from the family, but you forget the protective hand that holds you. It held you that night and can hold you in the daylight as well. Wisdom and courage are both products of faith. Our faith in God allows us to follow Him where fear would hold us back. The wisdom of God is found in His direction. If we trust that direction fully, we will walk in His wisdom," echoed Mando's words in his ears.

He remembered his conversation with Bert before Billy's plane arrived and those penetrating words, "Carey, I can't tell you what God's will is for your life, but I can tell you this. It didn't change that night on a muddy road. Whatever God has for your life and whatever His call for you was last week, it has not changed because this man has died."

Carey replayed many of his talks with Billy in his mind as he drove. The most meaningful included his advice to visit both the widow and the family of the man whose life had been taken. Visiting the wife had been far easier than he had expected because of the manner of husband he had been, but going to the home of the mother would be different. No matter what a man does, his relationship to his immediate family seldom changes. Given the fact that he had been gone from this home for many years would only make it more difficult. They would remember the good in him more than the bad.

All in all, Carey still felt he was doing the right thing. He had not felt the leading of the Lord in trying to dissuade him from the trip. In some respects he felt like Paul on his way to Jerusalem when all those around him only saw catastrophe. Carey knew that, like for Paul, the safest place to be, was in the center of God's will.

He glanced at his odometer and made the calculations. He should be arriving in *Gualcince* in less than twenty minutes.

———

She was known to most of the village as *Doña Marta*. It was an expression of respect, though she was the only one of the family afforded such. Her husband and oldest son had both been murderers. She had tried to raise her children (primarily her sons) to rise above the *machismo* that had led to such violence, but for the most part had been unsuccessful. She knew Ricardo had left that week to take the life of a man and it broke her heart. She wasn't sure how to respond when she saw the red Toyota with the white shell drive up in front of her house. Flaco had described this truck to them before he had left.

Carey had only had to ask two others directions in order to find the *Aguila* home, where Moncho had grown up. He turned off the engine, set his brake, and whispered a prayer.

Doña Marta watched him carefully as he climbed down from the truck. Her first thoughts were that another one of her son's was dead and this man was somehow involved again.

Carey walked around the truck and introduced himself as though he were completely unknown to this woman. As far as he knew, he was. He extended a hand that she did not move to accept. He tried to continue undaunted with his introductions.

"*Doña Marta,*" he began slowly. "My name is Carey Eldridge."

He paused as she responded with a nod.

"You do not know me," he started again slowly. "But I come from the Department of Choluteca. I am a missionary in the south among the evangelical Baptist churches."

Her eyes narrowed as she recognized exactly who he was. She was not making this any easier. Carey had thought he would be invited into the home by now, but she sat stoically in the small frame chair next to her doorway. Carey felt the awkwardness of the moment stretch into what felt like several minutes. He stepped toward the house keeping his hands in view and his eyes fixed on hers. He knew they were aware of the death of Moncho, he just wasn't sure if they were aware of his involvement or not.

"I'm not sure if you have been told or not, but I was involved in the death of your son, Ramon," Carey stated timidly. He felt the direct and honest approach to be the best given the situation. She was not about to take the time to get to know him first.

To his surprise, *Doña Marta* nodded again never taking her eyes off of him.

"I feel very bad about what happened," he started again nervously. Carey wished she would respond verbally in some manner. Her silence was more difficult to deal with than he had anticipated. "It was an accident. We were on our way back from a worship service above *Santa Tierra*. It had been raining, and we had been stuck on one side of a swollen river bed for several hours."

"WE!" came a young man's voice from the side of the house.

Carey turned to his left and saw Moisés taking long strides toward him. In his hand was a tightly gripped machete.

"And did WE kill my other brother also?" Moisés nearly screamed.

Carey now gave his full attention to the man approaching him. He was not as tall as Carey, but more muscular. Though young, his boyish features were lost in the intensity of his glare. He paused in his approach giving Carey a chance to respond.

"I don't understand," Carey said confused. "What other brother?"

"Ricardo!" Moisés replied, still screaming. "He went to find you, and he hasn't returned, but you are here!"

Doña Marta stood from her chair, but still did not speak.

Carey glanced at her and then faced Moisés bewildered.

"I never met your other brother, I left from Choluteca on Tuesday."

Moisés allowed his statement to penetrate and he quickly calculated the time. If the *gringo* were telling the truth, then Ricardo would not have reached him. The quickest he could have arrived would have been sometime Wednesday.

"If you didn't meet my brother, how did you know to come here?" he asked as a challenge.

"I asked Anita, Moncho's wife, where I could find you," Carey explained calmly. He was beginning to find strength in his answers. He realized that God was with him and that he was not facing this danger alone.

"You spoke with Anita?" came a gentler voice. *Doña Marta* now stepped between Moisés and the missionary.

"Si Señora," Carey responded politely. "I went to her just as I wanted to come to you. To tell you what happened and how terribly sorry I am for it happening."

Moisés was still unmoved by the words of the *gringo*.

"I came to ask your forgiveness," Carey continued humbly.

"For murdering her son?" Moisés accused.

"No, it was an accident!" Carey replied addressing him, and then quickly looking back at her.

"I don't believe you!" Moisés replied, and took a step around his mother toward Carey. "You ran over Moncho like a dog in the road, and you left him there to die. We know! Someone who was there has been here and told us everything."

Carey did not know how to respond. He knew the young man was gravely mistaken, but Carey did not know how to make him listen. Carey began to feel fear.

"Fear not, for the Lord God is with you wherever you go" came another voice that only Carey was able to detect.

"I don't believe it was an accident," Moisés continued, his own voice now showing the strain of adrenaline. "I don't believe you. You come alone. You have no one with you to support what you say. You ask us to forgive you and say it was an accident. You forget whose land you are in now. Your American passport means nothing way out here. Do you not think I will avenge the death of my brother, just as Ricardo went to do. You may have escaped him, but you haven't escaped me."

As Moisés finished his speech, he raised the machete above his head.

Doña Marta turned to stop him, but her son had already maneuvered around her. Carey braced himself and closed his eyes.

———

Neither the missionary, nor his assailant noticed the gray truck hurriedly approach. Capitán Mendoza leaned on the horn as he slid the truck to a stop on the gravel in front of the house. Moisés stunned by the sudden commotion, pivoted in place to see Ricardo leap from the back of the truck and run toward him yelling.

"Stop Moisés! Stop!

232

Gertie lifted her eyes from prayer. A single tear followed the crease that had been formed through years of smiling. She could taste it at the corner of her mouth when Adam walked into the room.

"Are you OK, Sweetheart?" he asked, stepping over to her side at the edge of the couch.

"I'm fine," she smiled. "I'm just fine."

Gertie could never explain the peace she felt when she sensed her prayers had been answered. It was a shared moment between her and God alone.

Capitán Mendoza helped *Doña Marta* back to her chair. Carey stood in disbelief as the passenger door opened and Mando and Luís stepped out of the police truck. Ricardo was still talking rapidly to Moisés as he gently took the machete from his hand.

"I don't understand," Carey exclaimed. "What are you guys doing here?"

"It's a long story, *hermano*," Mando stated. "But it is worth hearing."

For the next fifteen minutes, Luís and Mando took turns explaining the parts that each knew. Carey looked over and noticed that Ricardo was smiling through most of the story, but was saving his part for the end.

"Then when we realized that you were headed here and that Moisés was prepared to avenge Moncho, we had to get here right away."

"So you got Capitán Mendoza to bring you?" Carey concluded.

"Not quite," Mendoza responded. "I was already in *La Esperanza* because of Felípe's truck. I had stayed the night, as you had. I even saw you leave town early this morning just about thirty minutes before these three arrived."

"Wait a minute," Carey interrupted. "If you didn't bring them and they did not discover about Ricardo till last night, how in the world could you all have arrived in *La Esperanza* by early morning. It took me two days to get here."

"As it took me two days to get from here to Choluteca," Ricardo confirmed.

Carey looked to Mando for the explanation.

"Both of you spent the night somewhere," Luís spoke up. "We traveled all night long."

"But how?" Carey inquired. "There are no buses that travel direct through the night like that."

"You are right, my brother," Luís continued. "but we hired a truck to bring us to *La Esperanza*, and we prayed we would find early transportation that would get us here in time."

"But hiring a truck to take you all the way from *Santa Tierra* to *La Esperanza* would take nearly a thousand lemps."

"We found someone who would do it for only 800," Mando smiled.

"800!" Carey exclaimed. "But even that is more than you have to spend, Mando."

"The money was given by Anita," Luís said proudly. "It was her idea."

"Anita?" *Doña Marta* repeated. "Where did she get that kind of money?"

"From the missionary," Ricardo said firmly. "When he visited her, he gave her money to live on because she had lost Moncho. She offered what was needed to get us here. She said that the missionary had given her more than money – he had given her a new life. She wanted to try to help save his."

Carey now felt a tear of his own eyes.

Doña Marta brought out lemonade in small glasses. There was no ice, but at least it was wet. The Renaldo family had invited those near their home to come and meet the missionary. Ricardo shared his testimony of the night he almost killed Mando, while Moisés relived the events of just the previous hour in his mind. Ricardo then related his personal prayer for forgiveness and his subsequent new life in Jesus Christ. Moisés listened intently.

"I had believed a lie and had almost taken a man's life," Ricardo stated. "What I didn't realize, was that I had believed a lie most all of my life – that I could be a man without God in my life. On the trip up here, Mando explained that God made us with the ability to know Him and that is what makes us special. Sin destroys that ability to know God and makes us less than what God intended. Jesus came to die for our sins and to give us back what we lost. We don't take life in our own hands, we place ourselves in God's."

Carey looked at Mando and smiled.

"He's a natural-born preacher."

"He's a fast learner, too," Mando added.

Moisés watched his older brother and saw how the people held on his every word. He saw a difference in him that did not exist before he had made this trip. Whatever it was Ricardo had found in *Santa Tierra* – Moisés wanted.

A second hour passed and Capitán Mendoza whispered to Mando that he needed to be heading back to *La Esperanza* to pick up the truck. Most likely, he would have to stay another night, because it was already too late to get there before 5:00, and the trip on to Choluteca would be another eight hours. He was happy that they had avoided a tragedy with the missionary and he felt that they would be safe enough now.

Carey realized that he needed to get word to Susan that everything was all right. He asked Mendoza, if he would be kind enough to call her at their home when he arrived in *La Esperanza*. He, Mando and Luís would be staying the night in order to hold services. The Capitán assured him he would get the message through. Carey thanked him again for bringing the three men the rest of their journey.

"I did not know what you were doing out this way when I saw you this morning," Mendoza explained. "All I knew was that I was not going anywhere else till that truck was processed. A man, whose signature that I needed, didn't show for work this morning. They were going to take all day again. When I saw Roberto's truck, I knew something was wrong. Nothing but an emergency ever gets him out of *Santa Tierra*."

"You mean, not even money?" Carey asked.

"Not even money. I have known Roberto since the war. He doesn't do anybody favors – not even for money."

"Why do you suppose he made the trip?" Carey wondered out loud.

"If you ask me," Mendoza replied, looking in the direction of Ricardo. "I think something special is happening in *Santa Tierra*."

Mendoza climbed into his truck and left Carey pondering his final statement.

———

Howard was having trouble relating to Donna. All morning, she was distant and yet not antagonistic. They had spoken casually at breakfast without mentioning Karen once. He sensed that Donna was hiding something that she didn't want to talk about, but he had no idea what it could be. He had hoped he could share some of the exciting truths he had been learning about the fear of the Lord. Unfortunately, he had forgotten her plans to attend the women's retreat that weekend. In her present state of mind, she was not going to remind him again. Howard left for the office troubled. Donna just watched him go.

———

Karen drifted in and out of concentration during her morning classes. She was excited about going to work that night. She wasn't sure what Sheila had in mind, but she was just eager to do anything with her. Karen could tell there was friction at home that morning, but was just glad it didn't involve her – at least not overtly. She was ready to welcome any diversion from her family. At least she thought she was.

Chapter Twenty:

"The Explosion"

Karen stepped off the bus and walked instinctively towards the mall entrance. She didn't even notice Anna just steps behind her. The two girls took the same route past the escalator. As Karen turned left towards *Sugar n' Spice*, she happened to look back and notice Anna mounting the mechanical steps to the second floor where she worked. Karen wanted to call out to her, but the sound wouldn't rise from her throat. She stood for a moment watching Anna glide to the top. There was something about her that Karen envied. She wasn't sure exactly what it was. One thing for certain, it wasn't her clothes. She watched till Anna was gone from sight. Maybe it was the sense of peace that she always seemed to carry with her.

Karen walked into the store and was met by Amber. She was surprised since Sheila rarely worked the two high school students at the same time.

"Are you working also tonight?" Karen asked.

"What do you mean *also*?" Amber replied curtly.

"What I mean is, I'm here and you're here."

"You figured that one out easy enough," Amber chided. "I guess that means that one of us isn't going to work, and three guesses which one of us that is?"

Karen didn't understand, and she certainly didn't feel she deserved the attitude Amber was dishing out. They didn't really know each other too well, but Karen sensed a definite tension between them when they both were in the store.

"What is happening," Amber continued, "is that I have been called in to cover your shift while you and Sheila go do something."

Amber added her own huff of disgust as she turned to straighten garments. Karen was still confused, but at least she understood why Sheila had asked her to dress nice. Karen suddenly felt tingly inside as she repeated Amber's words in her head - "she and Sheila were going out to do something." She could barely contain her excitement.

———

Howard neatly cleared his desk while his secretary closed down her computer for the afternoon. He preferred working on the Sunday message at his home where he could practice portions in his own study without sounding absurd to the rest of the church staff. Rusty had gone home early.

237

As Howard finished packing his briefcase, he glanced down at the family portrait on his desk. A whimsical thought brightened his eyes. He had been very hard on Karen lately and coupled with the tension in the home between he and Donna, he mused over the idea of surprising Karen at work and then carrying home some Chinese food from the food court for him and Donna. The more he thought about it, the more he was convinced it was the perfect thing to do. He would be able to see Karen in her arena of responsibility as well as meet the woman she worked for and thought of so highly. The peace offering of Chinese food would be just the ticket for smoothing things over between him and Donna.

———

Donna whisked about the kitchen like the proverbial juggler balancing ten pie plates on spinning poles. She had begun shortly after Terry had arrived home from school. She knew that Karen would be away at work, so she didn't have to prepare supper for the whole family. She decided to go all out and create an Italian extravaganza down to the individual garlic breadsticks. She had to make a separate pot of spaghetti for Terry, because he didn't care for the cheeses in the Fettuccini Alfredo she was toiling over for her and Howard. She glanced at the clock on the wall.

"He should be leaving the office right about now," she thought out loud.

She lifted the lid of the pot and tasted the pasta. This was going to be a wonderful meal and a new beginning for them. Before she left for her retreat, she was going to make one last effort to reach him. As the heated vapor warmed her face, she failed to see the significance of the steam rising. It would prove to be a prelude to the evening that followed.

———

Flaco had grown tired of resting. Sleeping most of the day was the only way he could travel in the heat. The sun had finally set and the temperature of the boxcar had dropped about ten degrees. He figured the sun had gone down about an hour before. That meant he wasn't quite half way through his trip yet. He checked his water bottles and discovered he had done well by sleeping. He had only used one of his four bottles. He should not have any trouble making the rest last through the night. He also didn't want to overdo his drinking. The accommodations didn't include bathroom facilities and he didn't want to contaminate his living space. He still had about fourteen hours to go.

Flaco stood up in the small space and listened to the rhythm of the wheels on the rails. The swaying of the boxcar didn't affect him like he thought it would. In fact, it had helped him to sleep. He tried looking through a small crack in the wall of the boarded train car, but couldn't focus on anything substantial. He could only guess where he was, and how far away he still was from *Mexicali*. The man who had put him on the train had assured him that his partner in *Mexicali* could put him directly in touch with a "coyote" who could carry him personally the rest of the way across the border. It hardly seemed true. By this time tomorrow, he could be seeing the night lights of southern California. Flaco began to wonder what he would do if he couldn't find anyone who spoke Spanish once he was across the border. There was no way for him to know just what to expect.

The train rolled on.

———

"Where are we going?" Karen asked excitedly.

"Don't you remember?" Sheila replied slyly.

Karen thought.

"Do you remember *The Night Light?*" Sheila finally said breaking the silence as well as Karen's concentration.

"You mean the dancing club?"

"Yes. We went by it the other night," Sheila reminded her.

Karen sat back in her seat quiet. She didn't know how to feel. On the one hand, she felt exhilarated over the prospect of going out with Sheila, but on the other hand, she wasn't sure if she was ready for a nightclub.

"You're worried about the ID thing, aren't you," Sheila asked.

"I guess," Karen responded feebly.

"Don't worry about it, I have you covered. I know the owner and she has assured me you won't even be carded."

Somehow that didn't give Karen much comfort. She felt like she was being swept up into something beyond her control and possibly her will.

"Hey, don't worry!" Sheila said, trying to reassure her. "I promise I won't be keeping you out too late. Your folks won't even know you were here. I doubt anyone in your Dad's church hangs out here." Sheila smiled to herself.

"Oh, I'm not worried," Karen lied. "I just didn't realize where we were going. I'm cool. This is going to be fun."

"That a girl," Sheila said enthusiastically. "You are going to do some major growing tonight."

Karen sunk down a little lower in her seat and tried to smile. Well, at least her father wouldn't know where she was. This was not his normal traffic area.

———

Howard didn't realize how much traffic there was at the mall on a Thursday night. As he began to think about it, he couldn't remember the last time he had even shopped in the mall. Since Karen was old enough to take herself and Terry had very little interest in shops, his presence was no longer required at the two story, high price labyrinth. He had to park near the multiplex cinema because its lot didn't usually fill up till the weekend.

Inside the mall, Howard had to get his bearings. He knew which direction was the food court, but he had no idea where Karen's dress shop was located. He ambled past the arcade towards the fountain where he felt sure he would find one of those multi-colored directories that identified the location of all the shops by name. Within minutes he was snaking his way through the crowd towards the small entrance of *Sugar 'n Spice*.

The electronic tone sounded as he crossed the invisible beam. Amber looked up from the counter where she was seated.

"May I help you?" she asked reluctantly.

Howard didn't respond at first. He was looking around the small store in hopes of catching sight of Karen before she knew he was there. When he couldn't see anyone else on the sales floor, he decided that she must be in the back. He stepped lightly towards Amber as though to include her in some great secret.

"I'm Karen's father," he said softly. "I came by to surprise her. Would you mind calling her out here please."

Amber stared at him, at first confused, then a smile swept across her face.

"Oh, she's gonna be surprised all right," she said, rising from the stool she had been perched upon.

———

"Are you surprised?" Sheila asked enticingly.

"Well, yeah," Karen stammered as they walked through the door into a small-darkened corridor. Karen could hear the music and see the colored lights through the next passageway. As they approached a small window inset near the doorway, Sheila pulled out a crisp ten-dollar bill creased lengthwise and slid it through the opening in the glass.

"Evening Sheila," came a pleasant voice from within the booth. "Have a new friend with you tonight?"

Sheila just returned the smile. There was no question of age or request for ID. Karen slowly followed Sheila through the doorway and began looking around. Smoke was heavy and carried the colored lights that danced about the room. Karen then noticed the fog machine and realized it was not all from cigarettes. The music was loud, but there was no band playing – it was CD mixes. There was a bar to her right, but she tried not to stare at it. She was afraid Sheila would want to buy her a drink. Karen was beginning to feel uncomfortable.

"Why don't we find a table?" Sheila offered.

"Sure," Karen responded with a tone of false confidence.

They waded through a group of dancers, Karen following close behind Sheila. She bumped into a couple and looked up to apologize when she suddenly realized - there were no men on the dance floor.

————

Howard could feel his temperature rising as he stood in the line at the *Grand Pagoda* waiting to pay for the Chinese meal he was determined to carry home. His mind raced over the various points of attack he would take with Karen when she returned home that evening. Amber could not give details to her whereabouts with Sheila, but one thing was for certain, Karen was not at work as her parents were led to believe. She had either lied to them, or at least consented to go out without calling home. Either way she was trying to deceive them and that was the last straw.

Howard balanced the Styrofoam containers of fried rice and Chop Suey while he clenched the bag of eggrolls and Wantons in his other hand. By the time he reached his car, he was seething. It never occurred to him to be worried for her, and praying for his daughter was the farthest thing from his mind. He was gearing up for a showdown. He had been wrong to even let her take this job while she was being punished. He would correct that mistake as soon as she got home. As he drove home, he rehearsed his indignation into the rear view mirror.

————

Donna heard the car drive up and she took a breath. She wanted everything to go well that night. The dining room table had been set for two. Terry was already eating his spaghetti in the den and watching TV. She quickly lit the candles she had set out and dimmed the overhead lights. She couldn't decide on whether she should be seated at the table when he came in or to meet him at the door. She decided to quickly check on her garlic bread that was warming on low in the oven. She glanced through the stove window and then heard the front door open. She decided to meet him as he emptied his things onto the hallstand. As she rounded the corner she collided with the Styrofoam containers.

"Look out!" yelled Howard, as the top container filled with rice was knocked from his hand and rained across the hall rug. The bottom container buckled and opened in Donna's direction. Howard dropped the bag of eggrolls trying to regain control of the Chop Suey. He caught the carton, but only after half of its contents had slid out on to Donna's dress.

"For crying out loud!" Howard bellowed.

Donna stood quiescent as she slowly surveyed the results of their collision. Howard pushed by her to deposit the remaining contents of the Chop Suey on the kitchen table. She accompanied him in the kitchen not wanting Terry to hear what was about to follow.

"Why didn't you call home, if you had planned to bring supper?" Donna started.

"I thought I would surprise you," Howard started defensively. "It seems mine was not the only surprise of the evening."

Donna thought he was referring to her dinner, though he had not yet noticed the dining room settings.

"Well, I just thought you would like something special for a change," she said in a less than loving tone.

"What are you talking about?" Howard countered.

"I fixed Italian, including bread sticks," she replied almost in tears.

Howard glanced around the kitchen and then noticed the table and candles in the dining room. For a moment, a spirit of calmness came over him and a thought passed through his mind, *"I'm sorry honey, let me help you clean all this up and we can enjoy your meal together."* But once again, his pride took over.

"Well that's just great," he barked. "And what am I supposed to do with all this Chinese I brought home?" He knew the question was irrelevant because most of the meal was ruined already. He somehow wanted her to realize and at least acknowledge the effort and expense he had undergone in order to surprise her.

"I suggest you start with a broom and then finish up with the vacuum!" she retorted. She quickly turned toward the sink to clean off the sauce that clung to her dress. Howard wanted to explode, but realized that much of what he was feeling was directed toward Karen and not his wife, who had just spent a great deal of energy to do something pleasing for him. He redirected his attention to the mess in the hall. He would give both Donna and himself a chance to cool down before pursuing the conversation. He knew he had some apologizing to do, but then wasn't the time.

As Howard went for the broom, Donna stepped into the dining room and blew out the candles in a deep huff.

"You sure you don't want something to drink?" Sheila said, speaking loudly over the music.

"I'm sure," Karen replied smiling slightly. "I don't need to have anything on my breath when I go home." She didn't want to admit that the only drinking she had ever done was to sip from Fernando's beer at a ball game, and she didn't even like that.

"You're not having a good time, are you Karen?" Sheila asked.

"I guess it just wasn't what I expected it to be," she responded honestly.

"Do you feel like dancing?" Sheila asked innocently.

Karen looked around. She knew better than to ask.

"I don't think so," she replied, dropping her head.

"Then why don't we just get us a bite to eat somewhere else then," Sheila offered. "Surely you can put away a hamburger."

"That would be great," Karen brightened up.

Sheila left a five-dollar bill on their table for her drink and helped Karen out of her chair. The two walked quietly to Sheila's car. Karen felt relieved to be out of the club, but she now felt a little nervous around her employer. She wasn't sure what to think. As they left the parking lot, Sheila picked up on Karen's confusion.

"You didn't know, did you?" Sheila asked.

"I guess not," Karen stammered. "I mean, not that it matters, I just . . ."

"Of course it matters," Sheila cut her off. "It matters to me. I realize that you may be uncomfortable with it, but don't say that it doesn't matter. That's so condescending."

"I'm sorry," Karen said, slightly intimidated by Sheila's tone. "What I meant to say was . . ."

"Don't try to back pedal, Karen. The truth is you didn't really know what to say and that's OK. You come from a world of rules that have shaped who you are and what you believe, I can understand that, but I need you to know something."

Karen turned to look at Sheila, anticipating a tremendous statement of profound wisdom.

"You have rules," Sheila said firmly. "I have choices!"

Karen's mouth fell open. She had used those same words just a week earlier to her father as they argued about her curfew. Suddenly, the issue with Sheila was not about orientation, it was about the freedom to choose. Karen realized what it was about Sheila that she admired so much – her freedom to be what she wanted to be.

As they drove back towards the mall, the conversation began to lighten between them. Sheila wasn't upset and Karen was no longer uncomfortable. They talked about life and living on their own. Strategically, the subject of the club never came back up. Unfortunately, neither paid too much attention to the time either.

———

"Do you think anyone will come?" Mando asked Carey to the side.

"I don't know, but Ricardo has been gone all afternoon."

The two men sat on short tree stumps in front of the health clinic of *Gualcince*. Ricardo had gotten permission for them to use the enclosed area in front of the clinic because it was one of the few places in town that had an open area for sitting.

Señora Aguilar had fed them well. Moisés had helped locate and carry some benches to the small yard and was now hunting chairs he could borrow from nearby homes. Carey closed his eyes and whispered a prayer of thanksgiving for the day. God had not only spared his life again, he had opened the door for the gospel to be shared with an entire village. Now if only that village would show up!

"Hermano Carey," Mando called, breaking into Carey's silent prayer. "Look over there."

Carey opened his eyes and turned in the direction of the plaza. A single lantern carried by a man rounded the corner. Carey focused his eyes and made out the face of Ricardo with the lantern. Behind he could see vague shadows of two or three men. For a moment, his heart raced as he thought about the treachery of the New Guinea tribes he had read about in one of his mission books. As the men approached, the lantern illumined more of the building they were passing. More people were rounding the corner and falling in line behind the men. It was a procession led by the men and then followed by women and children. Some of the children broke ranks and ran ahead to the area in front of the clinic. More lights appeared as villagers approached with oil lamps and flashlights. Children ran ahead of the group to find a place to squat near the front. As the men reached the yard of the clinic, Carey could see that the crowd was still coming around the corner of the old building facing the plaza.

Ricardo walked up to Carey and smiled.

"They have come to hear about the man that forgives murderers and thieves and loves them enough to die for them," Ricardo said firmly. "I told them you would tell them how they could know him also."

"That's what we're here for, brother," Carey replied. "Can you help me get the lights scattered around the crowd so everyone can see?"

Ricardo took charge and soon the group was in a semi-circle facing Carey and Mando. The children gave their seats to the women with babies, and squatted in front of them on the ground so that they could hear. Moisés appeared from the back of the crowd with a small wooden guitar. He handed it to Carey who quickly passed it to Mando. As the stragglers found a place to stand, Mando quickly tuned the instrument and began teaching a simple chorus. Those who knew the words helped to teach the song to the rest. Most though had never heard the simple song of praise.

Carey motioned for Ricardo to step to the front and to share what had happened in *Santa Tierra*. At first Ricardo was shy about speaking in front of his friends, but as he looked into their eyes, he saw the hunger that he himself had known. He began with the news of his brother's death and the hatred he felt for the foreigner who had killed him. As he described the events of the service in *Santa Tierra*, he could see the faces of friends and neighbors hang on his every word. The crowd listened intently as he related his attempt on Mando's life.

When he finished, Mando shared how he had come to know the Lord through the *Gringo* missionary and how he traveled with him to tell others. He described how the Lord had given him grace to forgive Ricardo at the meeting. He told them that the same God can give you grace to put away those things that don't please Him and to desire His best for their life.

Carey let Mando share for nearly twenty minutes. When he stepped aside, Carey opened his Bible and began reading scriptures. Moisés stood behind him holding a flashlight steady so he could see. He began with the need for all men to realize that regardless of the level of sin they may have committed, all had sinned and were separated from God. He spoke of Jesus Christ in basic terms, describing Him as God who had come in the flesh to live among men. He did not assume any knowledge on their part, but spoke of Jesus as the One who had come to finally restore to man what was lost when Adam sinned. He even took the time to explain about Adam's sin in the garden so they would understand why man would even need a Savior. He tried not to add too much commentary to the scriptures, but to let them be seed for themselves in the hearts of those listening. He spoke for just about fifteen minutes and then explained how to turn from their own sin and to place their faith in Jesus Christ to be their Lord and Savior.

As he asked them to pray, he watched as nearly every head bowed. Carey began to share a simple prayer and asked them to repeat it with him if they so desired. As he spoke loud enough to be heard, he could hear the soft murmuring of repeated phrases flow like a fresh stream through the gathering. When he finished, he invited those who had prayed with him to indicate by lifting their hand. Mando gasped as nearly every hand in the clearing was lifted. One older man near the front raised both of his arms into the sky as though he were surrendering. In some respects, he was. Carey allowed a small burst of joyful laughter to explode from his lips.

"To Him who is able to do exceedingly, above all that we ask or think, according to the power that worketh in us," came the thought to his mind.

"Amen!" Carey affirmed.

"Amen!" Mando exclaimed.

"Amen!" Ricardo repeated.

———

Donna had left the mess for Howard. She retreated to the bedroom to have a well-deserved cry. After ten minutes of sweeping and vacuuming, Howard tapped on the half closed bedroom door. She quickly composed herself.

"Look, I'm sorry about the meal mix-up," Howard apologized while entering. "I should have called ahead of time. I planned to from Karen's shop, but I was so upset by time I got out of there, I wasn't thinking straight,"

"What do you mean?" Donna asked turning to face him.

"I went by that clothing store to surprise Karen and see where she works, but when I got there, she wasn't there."

"Did you go to the right shop?" Donna inquired.

"Yes, I talked to the salesgirl who was working. She said that Karen and her boss, Sheila, went out for the evening and left her with the store. She was even called in so they could go out," Howard explained.

"You mean she isn't working tonight? But she left here saying she was going to work and would be home by 9:30."

Howard looked at his watch.

"We'll know in about ninety five minutes," he said calmly.

"What are you going to do?" Donna asked in a careful tone.

"I don't know yet. I guess it depends somewhat on her story and what she tries to tell me. I do know that she best not try to lie."

Donna looked away.

"Howard this isn't just about a meal or even Karen," she began slowly. "This is about you and me."

"What do you mean?" Howard asked, taking a chair near Donna.

"Just now, you said, 'what she tries to tell ME!' You didn't consider that I was part of the discussion. You leave me out of everything! You have been leaving me out of a lot of things lately. You are so busy with that blasted building project at the church – you don't even see what's going on in your own family. You're only around for damage control and how to 'straighten things out around here'. Your life around home is practically non-existent. You don't spend time with Terry. I bet you haven't even spoken to him since you got in this evening."

"Well, we had somewhat of a collision and mess and . . ." Howard tried to interject.

"That's right, and you took the time to clean the mess, but in the meantime, your son doesn't even know you are home. Which is the greater need, Howard?"

Howard chose not to respond. He had been involved in these types of discussions before with Donna and the best thing for him to do was to let her 'air-out' before he could determine what the REAL problem was.

"I have been doing some thinking for myself these past few days," Donna continued. "And you know, I'm not sure this is what I thought being married to a preacher was going to be."

Howard took in the last statement with a sense of caution. This was the first time she had expressed concern for their marriage.

"I mean, I know you love me and the children and all that, but I'm just not sure where the church fits into your priorities. You seem more interested in building a sanctuary than a home. Something that you can point to and feel proud about. When was the last time you felt proud of Karen?"

Those words stung. Howard dropped his head as Donna continued.

"When we were in Texas, I knew what my part in the church was. Here I'm lost. It's like you started climbing some ecclesiastical ladder of success and have left me behind. I had dreams and callings too, you know."

Donna started to cry again.

"What callings?" Howard asked, trying to keep her talking.

"What does it matter now. We're here and you're building a church. I just want you to know that I'm not happy and I really don't know what to do about it."

"Donna," he tried to console her. "I know things have been rough around here lately, and I haven't been there when I should have. But this past week, I met someone who helped me see some of that. I have been doing some study for myself and I think I'm starting to see some of the things you have been mentioning. Please, don't give up on us just yet. God is doing something."

Donna looked up to see the sincerity in his eyes.

"I pray He is," she sighed. "I plan to go on that retreat tomorrow and I'm praying He will show me what I need to be doing. I strongly suggest you do some soul searching yourself. Something has got to change . . .for the family's sake."

Howard nodded.

———

"Sheila, I think I need to be getting home."

The waitress refilled Sheila's glass with more tea.

"Don't tell me you don't enjoy good seafood?" Sheila asked.

"The meal was great. I really thank you for it. Shrimp is always better than burgers, but it's getting a little late, and I really don't want to have to explain why I missed my curfew again, especially since they think I'm at work."

"You worry too much, Karen," Sheila said. "You have to learn how to relax. Just tell your Dad that I was your ride home and I got delayed in closing up. No big deal."

"I guess you're right," Karen shrugged. "By the way, what time do you want me to come in tomorrow?"

"I need you as soon as you can come in. Do you think you can come straight from school?"

"I suppose."

"I have another sale convention up the coast and I don't think it would be a good idea for me to try to get Amber to cover again. I'll have her come in the evening and close up like she did last time and you'll just have to take the bus home. Can you handle that?" Sheila asked tossing her napkin on her plate and gathering her things.

"No problem. It's Friday and I won't have the homework thing. I'll just let my folks know that I will be going straight to work."

"You're my girl," Sheila said leaving a tip on the table.

Karen looked down at the bills on the table and wondered just how to take those words.

———

Howard looked out the living room window and watched the Le Baron pull up to the curve in front of the house. This was the same room in which he had waited the week before for her to return home. Sometimes it seemed like things would never change.

Karen stepped out and waved back to Sheila. She stepped lightly across the lawn and came up the driveway giving the Le Baron plenty of time to pull away and head down the road. For some reason, she didn't want Sheila to still be there when she stepped through the front door. Before Karen could reach her key, the front door opened.

"Oh, Dad! You scared me!"

"What time is it?" Howard asked firmly.

"Uh . . . 9:40," Karen replied, looking down at her watch. She felt that the more innocent she acted the more innocent she would appear.

"I thought we said 9:30?" her father reminded letting her in the door.

"Dad, give me a break," Karen replied smugly. "Sheila had to close up the store and she had some delays before she could bring me home."

"And how was work tonight?"

"Oh, same-o, same-o. Wasn't too busy tonight. Most of the heavy business will be tomorrow night."

Howard felt his jaw tighten. He had been rehearsing what he would say for the past thirty minutes. Karen turned to face him and their eyes met. She could see the tension. He could see the lie. But neither could see the Presence that stood between them. Howard suddenly felt a wave of gentleness flow over him. As he looked into Karen's eyes, he could see Donna pleading, "something has got to change".

Howard swallowed once and began to speak.

"Well, I'm just glad you're home safe. You need to go on up and get ready for bed though, you have school tomorrow."

Karen blinked and refocused her eyes. Her father was smiling at her. She turned and slowly walked to the stairway. She looked back. He was still smiling.

"Good night, Dad."

"Good night, Karen."

Neither one of them exactly knew what had just happened. But as Karen reached her room, she began to feel bad. For the first time in a long time, her Dad was being civil and understanding and she was lying to him. What would he be like if he really knew, she thought to herself. She would probably be locked into her room. Guilt began to poison the moment for Karen. Only one of them would rest well that evening.

"Gertie, it's 1:45am. How long have you been up?" Adam asked standing at the entrance to the den with a glass of milk in his hand.

"Not long, about 30 minutes or so. I've been praying for that other family. I wish I knew more about them than just that they were having family problems."

"Well, why don't you pray for that and then call it a night," Adam suggested jokingly.

"Oh, drink your milk and go back to bed," Gertie called back.

Adam shook his head and walked back down the hall to their bedroom. Gertie adjusted the blanket over her legs and closed her eyes.

"Oh Lord, Adam is right. I would like to know a little more about this family you have me praying for. If you would please let me understand more."

She continued in prayer for another ten minutes before dozing. She spent the rest of the night on the couch. But it was a restful sleep.

Chapter Twenty One:

"The Border"

(Friday)

Carlos was the nervous sort. He didn't like the risks, but he would do it for the money. His job at the train yard included cleaning out stock cars after crates or animals were unloaded. Every so often he would receive a call from *Escuinapa* informing him of a "special cargo" in a certain car. Carlos' job was to open the car as soon as possible once the train arrived and release the "special cargo".

Flaco had awoken when the train began blasting its whistles at each crossing entering into *Mexicali*. The sun had barely risen and just slight orange slivers seeped through the few cracks in the side of the boxcar. He had mercifully slept the final five hours of his trip. Flaco gathered his belongings and squatted into his hidden corner as the train finally came to a stop.

Flaco could feel the sweat begin to run down the center of his back as he waited. His mind raced through possible scenarios of his being discovered. Next to the near police stop in *La Ventosa*, this was one of the most anxious parts of the trip. He felt both alone and trapped. The person to open the box car door would be responsible either for his escape or his capture.

Carlos had arrived two hours early for work, so as not to miss the arrival of the train. He ran to the designated car and went first to the corner where Flaco should be huddled. He beat three times on the side of the car and waited. Flaco had not been given any signal, so he sat silently. After a moment, Carlos called out to the boxcar.

"How's the weather in *Esquinapa*?"

Flaco sighed. This must be the contact.

"It was trying to rain when I left," Flaco replied.

"Well, it's going to be a sunny and hot day here," called back the voice. "Would you like to come out and see it?"

"More than you know," Flaco nearly shouted.

Carlos opened the door and Flaco quickly jumped to the ground. He looked around suspiciously before shaking hands with Carlos. After gathering his bag, he asked where he could find some breakfast. Carlos still had thirty minutes before having to report to work so he agreed to carry him to the terminal area where several shacks were busy preparing beans, eggs and tortillas.

"I was told you might would know someone who could help me get the rest of the way into the United States," Flaco asked.

"That depends," Carlos said cautiously. "How much are you able to pay?"

"I have enough to cover getting in," Flaco responded. He did not like Carlos' inference.

"But you need a travel agent," Carlos smiled.

"OK, how much do you need to find me a ride?" Flaco grimaced.

"I think $100 should be enough?"

"$100! Just to find someone!" Flaco exclaimed.

"You have come a long way, my friend. You are almost there. You can check around yourself and maybe get taken, or you can trust me to find you someone who will not kill you and just take your money. The choice is yours. I could have left you in that train, but I came for you. You should trust me now."

Flaco didn't like the idea of the extra expense, but he did have to admit that this man had helped him so far. He knew how much was still in the bag. He knew he could afford the extra hundred whether he particularly wanted to pay it or not. He was also tired and didn't want to waste time and money in *Mexicali* looking for someone.

"You have a point, but I have a limit to my funds," he tried. "I can give you $75."

"If you can give $75, you can sacrifice $25 more. The price is $100."

Flaco swore. He would have to find more money as soon as he got into the United States. He told Carlos to wait for him while he retrieved the money and then found a public restroom.

———

Carey, Mando and Luís finished their breakfast and thanked *Doña Marta* for the wonderful hospitality. Ricardo and Moisés accompanied them to the truck. It was a miracle that these five men were standing together in the same place embracing. Both brothers had tried to kill two of the other men within the past forty-eight hours. God had not only spared the lives of two of them, He had saved the souls of two others. There was no wondering among them, of which was the greater miracle. Carey had come to *Gualcinse* with the assurance that he was doing the right thing, but not the guarantee that he would return home unharmed. He had no expectation of being part of a new church start in the town. Once again, God had done exceedingly, above and beyond what he could ask or think. They would be leaving *Gualcince* in a cloud of victory as angels mounted the sides of his truck.

"*Hermano* Carey," began Ricardo slowly. "Do you think I could get some help in studying the Bible and maybe some more Bibles for some of the people who were there last night?"

"Ricardo, I will personally see to it," Carey replied, through his sparkling blue eyes. "In fact. . ., "

Carey broke off long enough to walk to the back of his truck and open the tailgate. "I still have some New Testaments left that my brother brought from the states. Let me give you the rest of them to pass out."

Ricardo gladly took the box from his arms, holding it like a treasure chest. In many ways, it was.

"When can you come back this way?" Moisés asked.

"That's up to God, but I will make sure that someone near here makes periodic trips and gets you the Bible study material you need," Carey promised.

"We can't thank you enough," proclaimed Ricardo proudly.

"I'm sorry it was under these circumstances," Carey replied humbly. "But God does have a way to bring all things together for the good. I believe that with all my heart."

"I do too . . . now," said Moisés.

"Amen," chimed Ricardo and Mando at the same time.

"Well, brothers, I hate to break up a good meeting, but I need to be getting back to *Choluteca*," commented Carey.

"Don't forget, you have things to get in Tegucigalpa for Susan," reminded Mando.

"That's right," Carey remembered. "We may only get as far as the capital today. Can you men stay over tonight with me somewhere?"

"I have no plans," shrugged Luís.

"I'm with you," added Mando.

"Then we better get started, it's still a long way to the capital from here," Carey concluded, and the three men climbed into the truck.

As the red pick-up lumbered down the cobblestone entrance of town towards the long dirt road that would carry them back towards *La Esperanza*, Ricardo put his arm around his younger brother. *Gualcince* would never be the same, and neither would they.

———

Howard slapped the alarm button on the clock beside their bed. Rolling over, he discovered Donna had already gotten up. He then could hear the water running in the shower. He pulled the covers up under his chin and decided to wait his turn.

Donna exited the bathroom fully dressed. She hurried about the room pulling items from her drawers and placing them together on her side of the bed.

"What are you doing?" Howard asked groggily.

"I'm getting my things together for tonight."

"What's tonight?" he inquired somewhat confused.

Donna turned to look at him firmly.

"You have forgotten again," she began. "I am going on a retreat later today and will be gone till tomorrow evening when the van will bring us back to the church."

"And you are packing now?" Howard asked.

Donna didn't reply but returned to the closet to pick out her outfits. She had been looking forward to this trip all week and her anxiousness showed. Howard decided to let her pack while he showered.

When he finished shaving, he returned to the bedroom to find Donna sitting quietly on the bed, her suitcase beside her. There was something disturbing about the image. It was as though she had packed for more than just an overnight retreat. There was a stoic sense of resolve on her face. She wouldn't make eye contact.

"Everything OK?" Howard asked.

"Yes, I don't think I have forgotten anything," she replied distantly.

"That's not what I meant. You just look like something is bothering you."

"Did you talk to Karen last night when she came in about what you told me?" Donna tried to change the subject.

"I talked to her," Howard began. "I didn't say what I had prepared to say, though."

"Did you confront her about the lying?" Donna asked looking up at him.

"Not really," he confessed. "In fact, I didn't mention anything. I just told her I was glad she was home and she went on up to bed. I don't know why I didn't bring it up. It just didn't seem to be the right time. Maybe tonight when I get in from my meeting."

"You have a meeting tonight?" Donna sounded surprised.

"Yes, it's at 7:00pm. I'll make sure the kids have some money to call in pizza, but I have the building committee wanting to discuss the initial groundbreaking."

Donna huffed to herself.

"Is there no one else who can oversee this project?" she asked downcast. For Donna, much of the family problems were tied to Howard's insistence to be involved with every facet of the project, even the areas where he had little experience. All the committees, all the meetings, all the attention was the wedge that widened the breach in their family. What would it take for him to understand?

"Donna, I've told you before," he started in his condescending tone. "There is only one man in the church who even comes close to having the experience to handle a project like this - Arnie Johnson, and he is opposed to most of what we are trying to do. I wish I knew what he had against me, but I don't. All I know is that he has no intention of supporting the plans. So someone has to take care of the details."

"Well, what about Karen?" Donna challenged. "Are you going to let her go to work tonight? Are you just going to leave Terry on his own till you get back from your meeting? Have you even thought about these things? I'm not going to be here, you know."

Howard paused. He hadn't thought about Karen being at work and Terry being alone. He wasn't sure he could keep Karen from a job responsibility just to baby-sit.

"I may need to take Terry with me, tonight. He'll be OK. I'll set him up with a video in the library while we meet. Karen will probably have to work anyway, since it's the weekend. Don't worry, I'll handle it."

Donna had heard those words before.

———

Billy Eldridge tapped lightly on the bedroom door of the girls. Anna looked across the room to Jenny who was still sleeping. She reached for her Bible on the nightstand between their two beds. She opened to her bookmark and proceeded to read the next two chapters of Joshua where she had been reading. She read of the monument of twelve stones that were made by Joshua to remind the tribes of Israel to share with their children how the Lord had brought them over the Jordan on dry land. It was important that the fathers taught their children about the Lord, she thought. In her prayer time, she thanked God for what her father had taught her and for the "stones" in her life that would always remind her of what God had done. She prayed for Jenny, and that she would grow to appreciate what her father meant to her and for the Christian home she lived in. She prayed for her own father on the mission field. Then her prayers turned toward the girl she had recently met who didn't have such a good relationship with her father.

"Lord, I pray for Karen this morning. I don't know how things are between her and her Dad, but it didn't sound too good. I pray you will draw her heart to him and his heart to her. I pray you will bring them together somehow that they might be closer and look to you. I pray you will raise up stones to remind them of Who you are."

Anna then slid out of bed, stood over Jenny and lightly shook her shoulder.

"Hey girl, time to get up! Good news! It's Friday!"

Karen stirred slowly. She blindly made her way to the bathroom to shower. As she became more alert, she began thinking of the night before. Who could she tell of where she had gone? What would they think? For that matter, what did she think? Then the thought passed, what would her father think if he knew? She hadn't done anything wrong and she hadn't drunk anything while she was there - she was just there. But she had lied about being at work, she thought. Did that matter? Sheila didn't seem to think so. Karen began to think more about Sheila. She was beginning to feel confused. She so admired Sheila. It didn't matter about Sheila's preferences - or did it? What was important to Karen was that Sheila was her own person. That was what attracted Karen.

Suddenly, Terry began to beat on the bathroom door. Karen had lost track of the time. She yelled back for him to be patient and quickly finished styling her hair. As she looked at herself in the mirror, she began to feel older - perhaps old enough to start making some of her own decisions about life. She finished in the bathroom and walked back to her own bedroom. Closing the door behind her, she went to her closet. There it was, still taking up space. She pulled the suitcase down from the top shelf and set it beside her bed. She stood back and looked at it for a moment. It was a crazy thought. She smiled to herself, it was just a thought, but one she would spend the rest of the day pondering.

Flaco followed the hurried Mexican from the train yard to a small business district. Carlos' time was short - he had to return to start work soon. He would barely have enough time to introduce Flaco to Don Miguel Hernandez. Hernandez was a tall barrel-chested man who stood with an intimidating presence. Flaco quickly realized that there would be no negotiating with this man. He was a businessman who merchandised in human cargo and he offered no discounts. He was never short of demand and knew he probably never would be.

In addition to being the capital of Baja California, *Mexicali* was an industrial center that boasted of its "maquila" or assembly industry. Farming was also a strong part of the area due to the rich fertile soil produced by the irrigation system connected to the Colorado River and the Morales Dam.

Commercial and farming traffic between *Mexicali* and *Calexico* was closely monitored at the border crossing. But while border patrol stretched itself thin looking for illegal aliens in hidden compartments of agriculture and commercial transports, Don Miguel had found a way to transport a double market across the border.

Carlos left Flaco with Don Miguel and hailed a taxi to carry him quickly to the train yard before he was missed. Flaco took a seat as Don Miguel stood just to the side of his desk.

"So you want to go to America," Don Miguel said sarcastically.

"*Si Señor*," Flaco responded humbly. "I have a family . . ." he began to lie, but Don Miguel quickly cut him off.

"I could care less why you want to go, I have heard every story one could tell. Mostly, because they couldn't afford my price and wanted me to feel sorry for them. I don't feel sorry for them. I am not trying to help my countrymen, I am trying to make money. Do we understand each other?"

"*Si Don Miguel*," Flaco nodded.

"Can you afford my price?" the tall man asked.

"I believer so, how much do you charge?" Flaco asked timidly.

"$1,500 American dollars! No less. For that I get you across the border, carried to *Calexico* where a van will carry you as far as Oceanside."

"But I understood that I could get all the way to Los Angeles."

"Oceanside is only about 90 miles outside of Los Angeles. There is a border check just north of Oceanside, just south of San Clemente. I can't chance my men going through that. There is less patrolling done around Oceanside and less chance of being detected once released. Trust me, I have been doing this for a while," the big man smiled.

Flaco had heard some horror stories about border crossing methods. He couched his next question carefully.

"What method do you use to get people across the border?" he asked.

Don Miguel laughed.

"I herd them over like cattle of course."

Flaco didn't like the sound of his response. He began to imagine being squeezed into a confined area and left for hours. His thoughts of the train ride only surrounded by a hundred others left him gasping.

"Don't look so worried, what I mean is I carry them over with a herd of cattle. That is the beauty of the system. I am actually smuggling two cargoes at the same time. My ancestors used to drive cattle across the border regularly. Our family still owns some of the property just to the northwest of *Mexicali*. Local *Calexico* officials mostly patrol the interstate and roadways. No vehicle can make the rough terrain from the northwest. So I use cattle and horses. The trip takes only about two hours. Then we have a cattle truck meet us on the property of one of my cousins and he handles the sale of the cattle and carries the riders to the van in *Calexico*. From there, you are shuttled to Oceanside which is roughly another three hours."

Flaco listened carefully. It did not sound either difficult or dangerous. His next question was his most important.

"How soon can I go?"

"It just so happens I have a group preparing to leave today at noon. Do you have the money?" Don Miguel asked firmly.

"I have the money," Flaco responded standing.

"You can only take what you can carry on a horse," Don Miguel added.

"No problem, this bag is all I have," he assured him.

Flaco extended his hand and Don Miguel took it firmly. Flaco had no idea just how close he was to reaching the other side of the border. By that afternoon, he would be arriving in America.

———

Karen made a point to slip out of the house for school before her father came downstairs. In part, she didn't want to face him for fear he may have had time to think about the night before and decide to question her. She had too much to think about that day than to have to face her father.

At the same time, Donna had very little conversation with Howard before he left for the office. She was tired of trying to get through to him about her feelings and fears. She knew he would get caught up in the appointments of the day and return home to find she had already left for the retreat. Maybe she would leave him a note. Maybe she would include that she loved him so he wouldn't feel bad about missing her departure. Maybe.

———

Betty Johnson was not a hard woman to please. She married a carpenter, who had built his own business into a large construction company, but their home was simple. Their needs were small because they only had one child. Her husband, Arnie, was strong and a hard worker, and tried repeatedly to instill that quality into his son Alex. But without fail, Alex would never show the initiative that Arnie demanded. As he entered high school, Alex gave less of his weekend time to help his father, until finally he announced defiantly that he would never be helping him again. When push came to shove, Arnie reciprocated with emotional distance from his son. Then came the problems. It began with minor infractions that usually included lying. When money for a building project came up missing from the office, a bewildered watchman had been fired, but Arnie often suspected that he had blamed the wrong person. Betty was perhaps the only force holding the family together. She was not a hard woman to please, but when she was upset - Arnie knew.

"When are you going to try to get some help?" Betty asked.

"What do you suggest I do?" Arnie tried to respond gently.

"I don't know, but we need help. Things have gone too far this time. He has never not come home," she pleaded, with tears in her eyes.

"I know," Arnie replied bowing his head. "I'll make some calls from the office and see if he has been around any of the places he usually hangs out."

"Aren't you even going to contact the police?"

"Betty, it hasn't even been 24 hours," Arnie tried to reason. "Let's just give it today and see if he shows up after school. He was probably just hot over my refusal to lend him the car last night. I'll even call the school and see if he has been reported absent. He probably went to a friend's house and is on his way to classes now."

"I pray you're right," Betty said. "Don't you think it's time to call Pastor Howard and see if he can help?"

Arnie bristled at the suggestion.

"Let's give it today," he responded restraining himself. In his mind, he thought how could a man help me with my wayward son when he can't control his own daughter.

————

One of the things that Adam Baxter enjoyed about their neighborhood, was that it was the beginning of the mail route. They could always enjoy reading their mail before lunch. As Gertie sat crocheting, Adam brought in a small stack of letters.

"Let's see here," he started in a teasing fashion. "Water bill . . . department store flyer . . . some promotion from some realty down the coast wanting us to come see their condos . . ."

Gertie laughed.

"Oh here's one," he said in a more serious tone.

Gertie looked up and saw the color striped thin envelope that meant overseas airmail. She sat down her afghan and held out her hand.

"It says, 'Gertie Baxter' from . . . 'Honduras'."

Adam handed her the letter and sat down beside her while she fumbled with the flap. She opened the letter and began to read aloud.

> "Dear Miss Baxter,
>   It was such a joy to receive your letter today. You have no idea how timely your words and prayers were. According to your letter, you rose to pray for me in the

middle of the night on the eve of my birthday. According to my calculations and the time you placed at the top of your letter, you were praying for me at the very moment I was encountering a tremendous trial."

"I would rather not go into great detail, but suffice it to say, at that hour, my life was in danger and God intervened in a mighty way. I can't help but believe that your prayers had much to do with that."

"Since the ordeal, I have been in low spirits. God has used two things to help me: the visit of my brother from the US, and your letter. I can't thank you enough for your prayers. I have some difficult days ahead and ask that you continue to pray for me as the Lord leads."

"One of the greatest sources of strength that the missionary has on the field is the knowledge that saints back home are praying. We covet your prayers for our protection, our work, and that God will bring harvest through our efforts. We thank you for remembering us on our birthdays, but please remember us whenever God should bring our name or face to mind."

Gertie's hand began to tremble as she read the last paragraph. She reached out and took Adam's arm.

"I realize that you will not know the young girl I am about to mention, but my daughter in California knows her and has asked for prayer for her and her family. They seem to be going through some difficult times. The girl's name is Karen and her father is a Baptist minister. He has been confusing his priorities and his daughter is drifting away from him. Again, I realize that you do not know these people, but I know that they would greatly appreciate your prayers.

In His Eternal Service,
Carey Eldridge"

Gertie turned to look at Adam as he finished the letter. A tear began to form in her eye as she smiled.

"This is the other family I have been praying for, Adam," she cried. "I asked God to let me know who they were and He did. This is them."

Adam nodded with her.

"Now we have a name... Karen," she said softly. "Karen, we are praying for you and your father. God will be with you."

Flaco refrained from talking to any of the others in the back of the pick-up as they bumped along the back road of Don Miguel's property. He was grateful for the good meal they had been served before the trip. He hoped it was included in the $1,500 fee. To be honest, it was the best food he had had on this trip. Maybe this would be a foretaste of what living in America would be like.

The truck pulled up to a small-dilapidated barn near a dry riverbed. In the distance a small herd of cattle were trying to graze among the scarce patches of grass. Most of the area was dry. As the nervous group climbed down from the sides of the truck, one of Don Miguel's men directed them toward the doors of the barn. When the group had assembled, the doors were opened and twelve saddled horses were led out into the area.

"Do any of you have any experience around cattle?" one man called out.

Most raised their hands. Flaco raised his hand though he had never worked a day in his life on a horse let alone around cattle. He figured to just stay on and stay close. The whole trip would only take two hours - he could fake it that long. He didn't want to do anything to ruin his chance of crossing the border now.

Six of Miguel's men mounted alongside the ten travelers to handle the cattle as well as to lead the way. It was assumed that the group would be too nervous to care for the herd. Flaco noticed that each wore guns on their sides. He thought about bringing his out, but then decided against it. If there was going to be a need for it, he preferred that they not know he had it.

They wasted no time gathering the cattle together and giving just two words of instruction to the group: don't stray from the group, and don't say a word to anyone they should meet along the way. There shouldn't be any contacts but sometimes young boys played or hunted snakes along the property lines. With that, the drive began. Flaco looked off into the west and could barely see the base of the Laguna Mountains. Though he didn't know what they were called, he knew that at some point they quit being mountains in Mexico and became mountains in the United States of America. He was close enough to see it. His journey was almost complete.

The horses began to trot.

Chapter Twenty Two:
"The Last Mile"

It was the longest two hours and fifteen minutes Flaco had ever experienced. After all he had traveled, it was ironic that he never knew the moment he had actually entered United States territory. The group did not talk to each other and the guides never offered the information. The horses had slowed to a brisk walk. Flaco was getting anxious. Suddenly a truck motor could be heard and several turned in panic to look at the guides. Don Miguel's men gave a reassuring nod into the direction of the sound as the canvas-covered pickup came into view. It was too ragged looking to belong to border patrol. It must be the connecting transportation that would carry them to the van. Flaco breathed a sigh of relief and then realized - he must be in America!

The group was quickly gathered together near the truck and their horses were collected. Half of Don Miguel's men were assigned to stay with the livestock. A tractor-trailer would arrive later for them. It would be easier to get the horses back into Mexico by truck. The "immigrants" were ushered into the back of the truck were benches were provided. It was not unlike some of the local "busses" Flaco had encountered in Honduras. From this point on, they would look like field workers being carried to another area of work. It almost seemed too easy. Flaco felt a slight disappointment that there had not been a greater sense of danger involved in his penetration of the great "El Norte". But he was not complaining. There was still the afternoon van drive to the location where they would be released. He still had a few more miles to cover. He leaned back and rested his head against the warm canvas covering as the truck bumped along the rough back road. He had made it.

Donna went over her notes one last time. She would be gone for less than thirty hours, but had given enough instructions to last the family all weekend. There was food for snacks, leftovers for meals, and all the clothes were washed. The sink was empty and could just receive dishes till she returned. She asked that messes be cleaned and unused food returned to the refrigerator and not left out to change colors. She tacked the sheets onto the message board in the kitchen and returned to the bedroom.

Her suitcase was packed and waiting on the bed. Her makeup kit lay beside it. The sight of the two awaiting her gave her a strange sensation. She couldn't remember ever packing for a trip without Howard. A twinge of accomplishment and independence swept over her. Though just an overnight trip, it was her first step away from his side - and shadow. Donna began to feel more excited about the trip. She glanced at the clock beside the bed. Her ride should be there anytime now. She gathered up her luggage and went downstairs to wait.

As Donna sat in the living room, she began to reflect over the feelings she had been experiencing for the past week. It was hard to determine just what she felt. She knew that she was not happy. She knew that she was experiencing mood swings with respect to Howard. She knew that she didn't feel completely satisfied with her life and what she was doing with it, but she loved her family. She felt a little distant from Karen and blamed much of that on Howard. She was looking forward to feeling better about herself at this retreat. "*Being Your Own Woman*" was just what she needed. This retreat was going to be the starting point of a new life for her. Little did Donna know just how much of a change it would bring. God was about to speak. The question was whether she was ready to hear what He was going to say.

———

The hands of the clock never went slower than they did for the last class of the day. Karen must have looked up every three minutes hoping the final bell would soon ring. She couldn't remember a single thing she had been taught that day and she wasn't paying attention in this class either. Her mind had been channeled towards one thought - was she ready to savor life on her own? She wanted to talk with Sheila about so many things. In spite of her father's mellowed response the night before, she felt it was only a matter of time before things would return to the way they were. She did not want him making decisions for her anymore. She wasn't sure if moving in with Sheila was even an option, or if she would be interested if it were. But maybe she could at least help her get set up with something. Karen was determined that her life was going to be different. She was right. As the hand of the clock slowly moved toward the sound of that final bell, God was preparing to speak. The question was whether she was ready to hear what He was going to say.

———

Howard sat at his desk rereading the final draft of his Sunday message. Because of his busy week, he had chosen to pull an old outline from his files and redress it with a few new illustrations. Diane didn't recognize the points as she typed his notes for him, but she did notice the lack of relevance the message had to the current affairs of the congregation. He finished reading the notes and felt as enthusiastic about the message as Diane did.

Rusty knocked lightly on his door.

"Am I disturbing anything?"

"Not a thing," Howard responded putting the notes away. "In fact, you are rescuing me from my own message."

"You'll get to hear it again on Sunday, anyway," Rusty joked.

"Don't remind me," Howard returned in jest. "I may just let you preach it."

"Welcome the opportunity. Maybe some other time though."

"What can I do you for today?" Howard motioned for him to sit.

"I just have a minute, thanks. I wanted to give you a days warning that I would be going to the jail again tomorrow and wanted to remind you with a renewed invitation."

"Did I say, I would go next time, when you called last week?" Howard asked half-heartedly.

"I believe you did."

"Then I'm out of excuses, I guess. What time do I need to be ready?" Howard surrendered.

"I have a youth meeting tomorrow night, so I thought I would try to go a little earlier. How does 3:00pm sound. I'll have you home by 5:00 at the latest," Rusty assured him.

"That will be good, I'll be home before supper and won't have to make arrangements for Terry and Karen," Howard reasoned.

"Where's Donna?"

"She went to that Ladies retreat today. She won't be home till that evening sometime," Howard explained.

"Then it's a date. I'll swing by and pick you up at your house," Rusty said with finality. "And trust me, it will be the experience of your life. You will never be the same."

"I'm sure you're right," Howard agreed politely.

Rusty was right. God was about to speak. The question was whether Howard was ready to hear what He was going to say.

———

"Adam, come here!" Gertie called from the kitchen.

Adam rushed from his chair in the den where he had been working on his Sunday school lesson.

"What is it Gertie?" he asked excitedly.

"Oh, I'm OK," she assured him. "I was just thinking . . . it's been a while since we have had your class over for a fellowship."

"I suppose so," Adam thought.

"Do you think they would like to come over for a prayer time followed by some homemade goodies?"

"I don't know why not. It's kinda short notice though, don't you think?" Adam suggested with his question.

"I don't think so," Gertie said confidently. "I have a feeling your class would be agreeable, even on short notice. I was thinking we could have a special time of prayer for both Carey and Karen along with her father, the minister."

"I think that is a wonderful idea," Adam encouraged. "My lesson Sunday morning is to follow-up on intercessory prayer. What better way to teach than to practice it."

Adam looked at his watch.

"It's after 5:30 now, I'll start making the calls. You know I think this is a great idea."

Gertie smiled to herself. Of course it was. Prayer is always a great idea and the more the better. God had been speaking to her and was about to speak again. The question was whether she was ready for what He was about to say.

———

The three men reached the pavement with a heavy sigh. It was a long drive on hard road from *Gualcince* to the main highway leading to the capital. It would take them another two and half hours to reach Tegucigalpa. Carey was glad they planned to stay the night. He would call Susan as soon as they arrived. He decided to splurge and stay in a regular hotel with his two companions instead of a simple hospice with a bed and a fan. They had been through a tremendous trip together and deserved a shower and air conditioning. He would take them out for a good steak meal also. They had some celebrating to do. After all, the angels in heaven were rejoicing.

"Luís, tell me about how you came to know the Lord after the accident," Carey said reopening conversation.

For the next fifty kilometers, Luís recounted of his involvement on that fatal evening and then his subsequent sense of despair over the death of Moncho. He related in detail about the service that pricked his heart with the gospel and then his hunger for all that God could show him. He shared his desire to be involved in the work of the Lord. With humility, he described the night Ricardo arrived with his intention to kill Mando.

"You know, Luís," Carey interrupted. "God is already using you in a mighty way. He not only used you to help save both Mando and I, He has used your testimony to help others in *Santa Tierra* understand the life changing power of the gospel."

"Do you think so?" Luís asked.

"No doubt about it," Carey replied.

"You know the people," Mando added. "They have seen your life before you met the Lord and they can see the difference now. The missionary and I can come to town and preach, but sometimes it takes someone they know to help them to listen and understand. You could do much to help bring the gospel to *Santa Tierra*."

"I suppose you are right," Luís began to realize. "I never thought of myself as a preacher."

"You don't have to be a preacher to share what you have found," Carey corrected. "You just have to know that what happened to you is real, and that it can happen to others. The gospel is good news and just needs to be shared - like food among hungry people. Someone once said, "Evangelism is just one beggar telling another beggar, where to find the bread.""

"Well, I can sure do that," Luís replied with a smile.

They continued on down the road sharing about the work to be done in *Santa Tierra*. Carey began to feel a renewed strength and spirit. The accident was finally behind him. He had taken the advice of his brother and God had protected him in every step. He could now look ahead to what God was about to do. Whatever it incurred, he was ready. Mando also sensed a new dynamic to the work they were about to begin. He believed that Luís would be a strong part of that work. *Santa Tierra* had begun to sense God at work, and there would be more to come. Luís rested in the satisfaction of being a part of a group that had meaning and purpose. He thought about the vast difference between these two men and the two he had been running with just a little over a week before. As the three men journeyed over the final miles into the capital, they taught Luís some new songs to go with his new life. They were right. Things were not going to be the same in *Santa Tierra*. God was about to speak. The question was, would these three men be ready for what He was about to say.

The driver of the van was experienced in making these runs. The people were situated as comfortably as possible in the back of the van, which was also conditioned with bench seats to hold a maximum of passengers. Tinted windows kept the outside world from spotting the transport. Exterminator decals had been applied to the sides of the van to avoid detection. The choice of decals seemed funny to the driver.

Flaco sat motionless squeezed between two Mexican men. Evidently, not all had had opportunity to shower before their horse ride and the cramped arrangements only intensified the odor. Flaco determined not to say a word. He was not going to do anything that would draw attention to himself or his belongings. He still had a good amount of cash in the bottom of his bag along with the gun, carefully wrapped in clothes, so as not to be easily felt by others.

The driver glanced at his watch to calculate the time of arrival. He then remembered it was Friday. The interchange to Interstate 5 from I-805 would be horrendous in just 30 more minutes as traffic left the city. He had just passed the exit to Alpine. He still had 40 more miles to I-5. His desire to avoid the slow traffic and possible detection caused him to push the speedometer slightly.

———

Officers Phil Kelser and Robert McConnell of the California Highway Patrol had only 80 minutes left to their shift. Phil's family was going to be waiting for him at Chucky Cheese for supper. He looked forward to Friday nights with the family. McConnell would return to his small apartment and watch the ball game he recorded the night before. The mid-afternoon sun had been rough that day and they were both watching the clock.

Phil was the first to spot the van in the distance as it made an irregular maneuver to pass a bus. He motioned to Robert and they accelerated their motorcycles in unison. They trailed behind for about three car lengths hidden behind a semi. Phil edged his bike around the truck to observe. The van was definitely going faster than the flow of traffic. They clocked their present speed and followed for another mile. Phil motioned to Robert that the van was definitely speeding and had made another irregular pass. They nodded and turned on their lights while proceeding around the truck.

"*Qué barbaridad*!" the driver blurted out.

"What is it?" his partner called from the passenger seat.

"*Policia*!"

"You're kidding . . .where?" cried the other.

"Coming up from our right on motorcycles," he shouted. "I thought you were watching."

"I was, I swear!" defended the other. "We did not pass anyone."

"Well they are there now. What should I do?" asked the driver.

"Try slowing down and move back towards the right to see if they stay in our lane or are looking for someone else."

The van slowed to 5 miles below the speed limit and eased over one lane to the right. Robert noted the break lights and smiled. They knew they were being followed, he thought. Hopefully, they would not try to run now.

The officers did not change lanes, but continued directly behind the van one car length behind. When the car behind the van eased to the right, the two patrolmen pulled in behind the van.

"Now what do you suggest?" asked the driver.

"Do you think we can outrun them?" his partner asked desperately.

"Not with this load," he replied.

The driver took one last look in the side mirror. They were right behind him and motioning for him to pull over. His accomplice slid the curtain that had been rigged to block the view of the benches and travelers in the back. It was their only chance. They pulled over and hoped the officers would just address them from the window.

Robert approached the vehicle while Phil called in the tags. The driver had his license and registration in hand before the officer arrived at his door.

"You know why I am pulling you over?" Robert asked.

"I guess I was speeding," the driver replied sheepishly.

"That's right and you were also making lane changes without signaling," Robert added.

The other passenger sat quietly and faced the front.

As Phil was getting the information on the plates, he noticed the rear axle of the van. He signaled to his partner to rejoin him at the motorcycles. When Robert arrived, Phil pointed out the rear of the vehicle. Robert walked calmly to the driver's window while Phil stepped up towards the passenger side. He eased the safety strap off of his gun as he stepped around from the back of the van. As they each stood at a window, Robert handed the license back to the driver and asked what they were carrying.

"Just some insecticides containers, spray tanks, and their tools," the driver nervously replied.

"Now that's funny, because I wouldn't expect that kind of equipment to weigh more than about 80 pounds tops, would you Phil?"

"No sir, I wouldn't," his partner replied from the other side of the van.

"And yet, your van is riding extremely low on your rear axle as though you were carrying a lot more weight than that, isn't it Phil?"

"A lot more weight, I would guess partner," Phil responded.

"I don't suppose you would care to open that curtain behind you and just let us glimpse back there for ourselves?"

The driver looked at his partner. Neither one had any fight in them that day. It would be their first offense each and most likely they would just be returned with the cargo they were carrying. The officers were equally relieved that the two decided to cooperate. Within a few minutes, ten "illegals" and two coyotes were seated in the grass alongside Interstate 8, just outside of La Mesa, California.

"I'll call Border Patrol on the radio and we'll just sit it out here. Guess we won't be getting off on time tonight," observed Robert.

"I guess I better call home and let them know I won't be making pizza either."

Flaco sat fuming to himself on the embankment, his eye fixed on his bag just twenty feet away. If he could just get to his gun.

———

Karen found her mother's note in the kitchen. She had also forgotten about the retreat that weekend. Karen went to her room to change clothes from school when the phone rang. It was her father.

"Karen, do you work tonight?" he asked.

"Yes sir, I was going to leave in just a few minutes to get there by 5:30. I guess I'll be taking the bus again," she said reluctantly.

"I'm afraid so," Howard apologized. "I plan to make it home by 5:00 and then turn around and head back at 6:30 for a meeting. I'll just take Terry with me, then."

"Terry said something about spending the night with a friend. He was going to ask you when you get home."

"That might work even better, because I don't know when this meeting will be over. Why don't you let me talk to him."

Karen called Terry and they worked out the arrangements. Calls would be made and Terry would be picked up at the house by 6:00. Everything was falling into place, Howard thought.

"Then I can go on to work, now?" Karen asked.

"Yes, I hope I'm home by the time you return, but if not, carry your key," Howard said.

Karen rushed through the good-byes and hurried out the door. She was anxious to get to work and Sheila.

———

"Ladies, it is a joy to have you with us this evening and tomorrow," welcomed the nicely dressed hostess. She took the first moments to acknowledge those responsible for the accommodations and more important, where necessary rooms were located. Two hundred women in one conference hall would need to know that there was more than enough bathroom facilities.

"We want you to take a moment and look with us at your program for the weekend."

Donna opened the pastel colored folder to find the schedule of activities. Her eye was quickly drawn to the seminars that would be conducted the next morning and afternoon. She half listened to the speaker introduce the conference leaders as she read the description of each session. She was quickly drawn to the conferences that would be dealing with "self-esteem" in the ministry. She needed all the build-up she could get in these two days.

"Tonight we will have the privilege to hear from one of our true heroes," stated the speaker.

Donna heard the word "hero" and looked up.

"Maybe, I should use the word heroine," she continued jokingly. "After all, she has been on the mission field for nearly thirty two years, and has been there without husband and family. She is a single missionary and her name is Marnie Hutchinson. She will have our devotion this evening and then you will see her listed among the conference speakers for tomorrow. I can't encourage you enough to make sure you sit in on one of her sessions."

Donna wasn't sure which part of the introduction impressed her more, that she had been a missionary or that she had been so while single. Donna began to wonder once again what her life would have been like if she had not married. Could she have fulfilled what she felt was a real calling on her life if she had just not settled for being a "pastor's wife". Donna took her pen and circled Miss Hutchinson's sessions for the next day.

———

"What do we have here," asked Officer Martinez of the Border Patrol assigned to San Diego County.

"We have ten illegals and two coyotes," replied Phil.

"Talked to them, yet?"

"No, we just sat them down and put their things over there," he said pointing to the pile of bags.

Officer Martinez motioned to his partner to begin going through the bags while he approached the two men separated from the group. He began to explain in perfect Spanish, who they were and what the procedure would be for returning the group to Mexico. He explained that they would be held though and their van confiscated. As he talked, the two began to regret not trying to run.

The other border officer picked up Flaco's bag and noticed the weight. He began to feel around in the bottom of the bag and stopped.

"Who's bag is this?" he called out in Spanish to the group seated on the ground watching on.

At first, no one would respond. Flaco sensed danger in the question and refrained from acknowledging.

"Let me put it this way," the officer continued. "If I don't learn whose bag this is, you will all be carried to jail."

It was an idle threat, but they did not know that, and worse, they could not imagine what American jails were like. Their imaginations caused them to turn to each other in desperation.

One of the larger men spoke up.

"It belongs to the skinny one."

All heads turned toward Flaco and began to nod in agreement.

"Is that true?" Martinez asked firmly.

Flaco did not know what to do. He was already caught and there was no chance of getting to his gun now. His true nature of cowardice and weakness surfaced. He dropped his shoulders and nodded. The power he thought he carried with him was in that bag and he realized he had no power of his own. He was just a lazy, weak man who thought he could find a better life by running away.

"I think we have a problem here," the young officer explained.

He dumped the contents of the bag on the ground and the other officers gathered around. Dirty clothes and personal items fell out first, followed by a large shirt that was rolled up. It fell particularly hard onto the ground. The young officer picked it up and unwrapped it. He held the gun with two fingers as though it was a dead fish.

"Well, this changes things a bit doesn't it?" Martinez observed.

"Not from where we stand," Robert countered. "They are illegals and that makes them your problem. Just take the gun and ship them back over the border. There's no reason to involve us."

The young officer then reached into the bottom of the bag and pulled out a handful of money. He began to straighten it out and discovered the different currencies.

"I'm not so sure," he said holding up the money for Martinez to see.

Officer Martinez examined the different bills and shook his head in disgust.

"He's an OTM!" Martinez said angrily.

"A what?" Phil asked.

"An OTM, 'Other than Mexican'," the young officer explained. "He has currency from at least three different countries here in this bag. My guess is he started in Honduras, since that is the currency farthest away from here. That means he doesn't just go back across the border. We would have to process him, contact his embassy, do at least four hours of paperwork apiece on him and then fly him back to Honduras."

271

"You're breaking my heart," Robert said sarcastically. "That's your problem, not ours, we went off shift fifteen minutes ago."

"No, that's your problem," Martinez responded as firmly as he spoke to the men on the ground. "He has an illegal gun which he transported across the border and that is a crime in this state, regardless of who commits it. By the time you finish with him, he will probably do some time here and then someone else will have to process his return to Honduras."

Officer Martinez pointed at the group on the ground that looked on wondering what the officers were arguing about.

"I'll take these nine, and those two," he said indicating the "coyotes". Then he pointed directly at Flaco. "You can have that one."

As the southern California sun began to set, Flaco watched the rest of his group loaded into the border patrol vehicles. Within ten minutes, a police car arrived and he was handcuffed and placed in the back. One of the policemen spoke to him in Spanish. He explained that he could remain silent if he wanted to. He said other things that Flaco didn't regard with much attention. He decided he would take the officer's advice and he didn't speak for the rest of the trip. When they arrived at the police station, he was quickly processed and placed in a cell with other Hispanics. Flaco tried to keep to himself. He didn't know what was happening or what they would do to him next. He began to feel afraid.

———

Karen wasn't sure how best to open the conversation with Sheila. She had arrived at the mall early, eaten a couple pizza slices for her supper, and practiced various approaches. She reported to work fifteen minutes early and Amber wasted no time clocking out. Karen began to straighten some of the front window displays that recent customers had been handling still thinking about the right words.

"Oh Karen, I didn't know you had already come in," Sheila observed. "Has Amber left?"

"Like a bat out of . . ." and she stopped herself. She didn't usually use expressions like that. "Well, you know."

"Must have a date," Sheila said reluctantly.

"You know, I don't think she likes me," Karen said.

"It's not you. She hasn't cared for the past three girls I have had working in here. Of course, the last one was a thief and I can understand that Amber is afraid I may look at her the same way. I don't know what she may have against you. She is a good worker, though, and honest. That is what I like."

Karen smiled and returned to straighten the clothes.

"I wanted to ask you how things went when you got home last night?" Sheila went on.

"Oh, it was fine. Dad wasn't upset at all. In fact, he was pretty cool - better than he had been in a while," Karen admitted.

"What is the biggest problem between you and your Dad?" Sheila asked.

"I don't know, I guess it's because he won't let me live my own life. He's always wanted me to be involved in things that I didn't want to do."

"Like what?" Sheila probed.

"Oh you know, stuff at the church, stuff at school, even projects in the community," Karen tried to sound annoyed.

"And you're not into those things, I take it."

"Well, I used to," Karen confessed. "I mean they had their place, but now I'm older and I just want to look into other things."

"What kind of other things?" Sheila asked carefully.

"I don't know. Maybe do some traveling. As long as I can remember, I have lived in some part of California. We've been down here since I was eight. Before that it was up north."

"San Francisco?" Sheila guessed.

"I wish, though I would have been too young to get anything out of it. No, it was some place called Mill Valley. Dad was finishing school. I don't remember a lot about it. I remember the first year we came down here, he took us to Disneyland and I thought this was the best place in the world, but I was young. Now I'm ready to see more of the world."

"Have you ever been to the mountains?" Sheila asked teasingly. "There are places you can go in the Lagunas that doesn't even seem like California anymore. We could take a drive to Mount Laguna. It's only 60 miles from here. You mean to tell me that your father never carried you to the mountains."

"No, weekends are usually his busiest time," Karen sighed.

"Well, we will go to the mountains tomorrow, if you want to see some of the world. It is breath taking."

"But what about work?" Karen asked.

"I'll have Amber come in at lunch. She does that sometimes on Saturday anyway. She won't mind, I promise."

"I'm not sure," Karen hesitated. Then she swallowed hard. Why not? The whole issue was over living her own life. If she wanted to see the mountains, she should be able to go. This was no longer an issue for her father to decide. She was going with or without his permission - with or without his knowledge if necessary.

———

The meeting seemed to be running in circles. Some of the committee members were concerned about parking. Some were concerned about design. Most were concerned about budget. There was little sense of unity among the members present.

Howard mentally checked out and allowed the discussion to banter about while he tried to solve some of the design objections in his mind. The voices echoed incoherently around him till he heard a name mentioned.

"I don't understand why we don't bring Arnie in on this - he's the contractor, who would know better?"

"Whoa!" interjected Howard. "What do you mean 'bring Arnie in'. He doesn't't even support this idea, let alone the design."

Howard didn't mention Arnie's idea of the multi-level structure. He just let the members think that Arnie was against the whole project. Conversation soon turned back to financial concerns. Howard listened till he felt every angle had been presented. He then readjusted his tie as an act of decisiveness and drew the conversation to a close.

"Gentlemen and ladies," he said professionally. "I think we need to commit these issues to prayer. It is obvious that we do not have all the answers yet, but I believe we can have them as we dedicate our steps to the Lord. He has brought us this far, He will see this project through. I believe that."

The committee took the cue and began to gather their things together. It was difficult to argue with spiritual advice such as prayer. For the most part, everyone was tired and wanted to go home.

As Howard locked up the office, he felt frustrated. He thought that the church would support his ideas, his design, and his enthusiasm for the construction. The church had grown under his ministry. They had trusted him in programs and growth. Now he was hitting a wall he didn't know how to get over or around.

He walked alone to his car. Even his family was not supporting him, he felt. Donna was distant and Karen was rebellious. He was not getting the respect he deserved, either at home or at the church. The more he pondered on these thoughts, the more agitated he became. To make matters worse, someone had brought up Arnie. If there was a thorn in Howard's side, it was Arnie Johnson. Sometimes, he wished Arnie would just get frustrated enough to join some other church. The drive home was bitter, and each mile got worse.

———

The phone rang three times before Mrs. Johnson answered. Arnie lay asleep in his recliner.

"Hello," she said into the receiver.

The voice on the other end identified itself. There was a pause, a gasp, and then a chilling shout.

"Arnie, wake up! Alex has been arrested!"

———

Carey held the phone close and spoke low so as not to disturb Mando and Luís who had already gone to sleep. They had driven over ten hours and just finished a good steak meal. Sleep was inevitable. Carey wanted to talk to Susan before he succumbed to the bed.

"Evening honey," he said softly and tenderly.

"Carey, I'm so glad you called. Where are you?"

"I'm in Tegucigalpa with Mando and another man from *Santa Tierra*," he answered.

"From *Santa Tierra?*" she sounded surprised. "How did he join up with you?"

"It's a long wonderful story that I will tell you tomorrow. For now, just know that all is well. We are all fine and as soon as I can get the things you need from the grocery store in the morning we will be on our way home."

They shared a moment of quiet.

"I love you so very much," Susan said.

"I love you too, and I am a lot better now. Billy was right - I needed to make this trip. But God had more in store than just helping me out of depression, He did an incredible work in both *Santa Tierra* and *Gualcince*."

"I can't wait to hear all about it," she replied excited. "Listen, the boys are still up since its Friday night. Would you like to speak to them?"

"Of course I would," Carey responded and leaned back in the hotel chair to get comfortable.

For the next ten minutes, he listened to his sons describe the days they had spent since he had left that Wednesday. Though he had only been gone for three days, it seemed like weeks. He didn't try to shorten their time or interrupt. He drank in their tales and voices and heard every word. When they finished, Carey took another five minutes to say good-bye to his wife. He knew he would have to pay handsomely for the call the next morning, but it was worth it.

Chapter Twenty Three:

"The Decision"

(Saturday)

The Pennington house seemed unusually quiet for a Saturday morning. There was no breakfast cooking in the kitchen, no TV shifting from one channel of cartoons to another, and no arguing. As he got dressed, Howard wasn't sure if he was confusing the quiet with lonely.

He showered and went to the kitchen to start the coffee maker. He had read Donna's note the night before after his meeting, but was not in too good of a mood, so he took the time to reread it. He opened the refrigerator to check out which Tupperware containers would be used for lunch and which ones for supper. He found the note with the phone number of the home where Terry was spending the night. He made a mental note to call about noon and check up on him. Howard walked to the den and put on some old country western music. As Randy Travis filled the house with nasal twangs, Howard poured his coffee. Quiet Saturday mornings could be addictive he thought to himself.

The whine of steel guitars was not music to Karen's ears. The sound had not awakened her, but it wasn't making her morning either. She hoped that by the time she had finished in the bathroom, the CD would have changed or that her father would tire of the sound. By the time she reached the kitchen, the disk player had moved on to Kenny Rogers Greatest Hits.

"Dad, you have got be kidding," she exclaimed.

Howard was startled from his trance.

"Oh, come on, you used to love this when I played his tape in the car," Howard tried to coax a smile.

"I was eleven years old and didn't have much of a choice what we listened to in the car," she countered while pouring herself a cup of coffee.

"You used to sing right along with Dottie West and Kim Carnes," he teased.

"I used to sing a lot of different songs," she admitted, ". . . when I was younger."

"You used to sing in church, too," he sighed.

"I remember," she acknowledged. "I remember you asked me to."

"Not always. There was that time after the youth group went out one summer up to Oceanside. I remember you begged to be a part of every activity going on in church. We had to stay on you to make sure you got your homework done because you were at the church all the time."

"You just wanted to make sure I could keep my grades up, so I could go to college," she said sarcastically.

Howard knew where she was headed and he tried hard to redirect the conversation.

"What are your plans for the day?"

"Well, Sheila wanted me to come in to work at opening time this morning," she said guardedly.

"They open at what? . . . 9:00am. You should be getting off by about 5:00 then, right?" Howard calculated. "I hope so, I will be gone this afternoon, but I plan to be back by 5:00 for supper. Your mother should be in shortly after that."

Karen quickly thought of her afternoon trip with Sheila and tried to determine if they would be back by 5:00 or not. She was unsure of how long they would be in the mountains. It could be longer. She was afraid to try to deceive her father again.

"Well, not really," she said.

"She's not planning of working you all day and then all night also, is she?" Howard began to interrogate.

"No sir," she began slowly. "Sheila said she would like to carry me out to the mountains this afternoon. We were going to go after lunch. I'm not sure when we will be back. I don't expect it to be much after dark if even that late."

Karen's honesty had been primed by her father's understanding the night before. She didn't want to deceive him again. She thought that by being open, he would continue to understand. She gravely underestimated his patience. She was unaware of what he already knew.

"Wait a minute," Howard started, feeling the blood in his cheeks. He had been restrained the night before from exploding, but now it was happening again. He had to confront her.

"Are you telling me that you were going to go to work and then off on some joy ride with your boss for the afternoon and let me think you were at work?"

"No sir."

"When did you plan to tell me? After you got back?"

"No, sir," Karen was beginning to feel cornered.

"Were you planning to tell me at all?" Howard questioned.

"Of course."

"Oh really, like you planned to tell me where you were Thursday night?" he challenged.

"Thursday night?" she tried to respond innocently.

"Yes, Thursday night! I went by the dress shop where you were supposed to be working and the girl there said you were out with your boss.

277

Now I don't know what you two were doing, but I do know what you weren't doing. You weren't working like you told us you were. Now you are planning on going off again with this woman? I don't think I like this one bit."

"But it's just a drive to see the mountains," Karen tried to explain. She wanted to get him off of Thursday before he asked what they did do.

"That's not the point, and you know it. The point is that I can't trust you to do what you tell me you are going to do or to be where you say you are going to be." Howard's voice had passed the level of stern discussion and he was showing his anger.

"You don't understand. I am almost 18 years old. When Sheila was my age, she was already making plans for starting her own business. She never went to college and look at her - she has her own store now and doing pretty well. I just want to be like her."

Howard looked hard into his daughter's eyes. As difficult as it was for him, he had to realize that he did not know the young woman who stood defiantly before him. Even the memories they had just reminisced were buried over by layers of rebellion that he couldn't even fathom, let alone break through. He never felt more helpless as a father than at that moment. He wanted to reach out to her, but he couldn't. In his heart, he felt it was too late. Only one person could recover the little girl who once sang in church because she wanted to - and he was not that person.

Karen turned sharply to return to her room. She didn't want her father to have the opportunity to give her an ultimatum. His hesitancy gave her the out. As she marched loudly up the steps, Howard sat down slowly at the table. She slammed her door closed behind her. She grabbed the suitcase she had lowered from the closet shelf the night of their last big argument and threw it on the bed. She would pack it and leave it to pick up later in the afternoon when her father was away, she thought. Maybe Sheila could at least put her up till she did have a place to go. At this point, she wasn't thinking too far ahead. She began pulling things from her drawers and throwing them into the open case.

Below, Howard still sat at the table as Kenny began to sing *Lucille*.

———

Teresita was the youngest of four daughters. Her mother preferred for her to stay close to the house. It was bad enough living near the main road. But Teresita was now six. She had to walk to the school with her sisters along that road. At least she should be able to go with them and get water on Saturday mornings. The town pump was located in a little ravine just off from the road. Besides, her sisters argued, she could bring one extra container of water back to the house. Hesitantly, her mother allowed her to go with them. She knew the traffic from the capital was usually in a hurry to get south and vice versa. But she agreed. After all, it looked like it would be such a beautiful day.

———

"When do we expect the class to arrive?" Gertie called from the bedroom. She was busy fixing her hair.

"Just any time now. I told them we could have them over at lunch time and I would have little sandwiches for them," Adam replied from the kitchen.

"Are you going to do any sharing before the prayer time?" she asked.

"I'll just see how the Lord leads when they get here. I don't want to take away from your time with them in prayer."

Gertie finished brushing out her hair and grabbed her walker to stand. She knew this was going to be an important day.

———

Karen left the house shortly after her argument with her father. She slipped out the side door to avoid him. She had over an hour to get to the mall, but she didn't want to pass the time at home. Her mind was spinning in several directions. She was still upset, but she was also feeling a sense of pain. She had taken a real step towards separation and she could feel the tear. She had placed the packed suitcase in her closet, ready to be picked up. In her mind, she had already left the house for good.

As she sat on the bus, she began to think about her mother and brother. Their good-byes would have to be by phone - for now. She didn't know how long it would be before she could feel comfortable enough to see any of them again. Hopefully, it wouldn't be that long. Once she turned 18, there was nothing they could legally do to make her return home.

She arrived at the mall to find most of the stores still locked up with heavy metal mesh or fencing. Several senior citizens were walking the perimeter of the stores at a stimulating pace. Karen decided to join them while she waited. She began to walk each of the store levels. The activity was good for her. It helped her take her mind off of the morning. She glanced at her wristwatch. She still had thirty minutes before Sheila would be arriving to open the store.

Karen circled the lower tier of stores twice when she noticed that some couples were using the stairs for exercise as well. Karen didn't venture much on the second level since she went to work. She decided to take the extra time she had that morning and see what new shops were up there.

She reached the top of the stairs and decided to start to her left. She walked briskly past each of the darkened stores making a mental note of which ones she would like to visit sometime when they were open. She was amazed at how many dress stores that were clustered on the second level.

As she walked along, one in particular caught her eye. It was not the fancy displays in the windows or the difference of merchandise that she noticed. For the most part, the store was very similar to the one she worked in, but with one difference. A simple computer printed sign hung near the front door: "Total liquidation sale - going out of business". Karen was taken aback by the thought that someone was losing their business. Somehow she never conceived of Sheila or anyone actually having to go out of business. It took some of the wind out of her sails as she walked. She just always assumed that having your own business was a mark of success and an ability to stay on top. She knew nothing of failed dreams and bankrupted efforts.

Karen began to walk slower thinking about what would happen if Sheila had to close her store. For some reason, the idea had never crossed her mind. She just felt that Sheila was in total control of her world around her. That was what drew Karen to want to be with her. Two walkers passed on either side of her and Karen stopped. The store beside her had its lights on. Though the chain-link fencing that slid over the front doors was still closed and locked, Karen could look inside. She saw bookcases of paperbacks, as well as cases of music along the walls. In the center were promotional tables of Bibles, book sets and various trinkets. But what caught her eye most was a portrait on the wall. It was large and well painted. The more she looked, the more she saw. It was a portrait of Jesus hugging a young girl, only the girl was not dressed in the tunic of early Palestine. She was in ragged jeans and a tank top. She was not dressed like one who would be going to church, let alone hugging Jesus. The closer Karen looked, she could make out different body piercings. She wasn't sure, but she even thought the shaded area on her shoulder was a tattoo. The girl's hair was matted and unkempt. Her face was turned ever so slightly and it looked as though she was resting the side of her head on Christ's chest. His large arms wrapped around her tightly. Then Karen noticed his eyes. They had been painted in such a way as to not reflect pity, or sternness. They were not judging her for her clothes, or anything she may have done. They saw her fully, and loved her completely. Karen had never seen a painting like this one before. Her mental pictures of Christ were filled with a distant untouchableness. He was there, but not accessible, like her father. She began to envy the girl in the painting. Then she saw something that had escaped her before. It was the tears. They were glistening across the cheek of the young girl. She couldn't tell if they were tears of pain, or joy, or just relief, but she could imagine. Here was a young girl who found someone who would hold her, let her cry and love her for who she was. The saddest part of the image was that Karen once knew what that felt like. She remembered when she felt that close to Jesus, she remembered when it seemed like He knew her very . . .

"Karen?" came the voice behind her.

Startled, she turned and saw the person who could help her most.

———

Flaco stretched and stood. He had slept on the floor to avoid as much contact with the others in the cell as possible. After breakfast, he returned to his corner. He had no idea what lie before him. What could they do to him? They had already taken all his money. Maybe he was just going to stay in jail. He knew nothing of the American justice system.

He did notice that they separated the English-speaking prisoners from the Spanish speaking though. Across the passageway, he could see other men being held. He studied their faces to see how worried they looked. One face stood out. It was a young face - almost too young to be behind bars. The young man looked bewildered and lost. He didn't look like a criminal. He looked like a boy who had gotten lost. Flaco felt sorry for the young man. He stood at his bars and watched him. He had nothing else to do.

———

Carey placed the bags in the floorboard of the backseat behind the driver. Luís scooted behind Mando, who sat up front to make more room for the groceries. Carey looked at his watch.

"With any luck, we should make it home by 10:30 and Susan will have a lunch ready for us," he noted. "Who's ready to go back to Choluteca?"

"Can you let me out at the *posta*, so I can catch a bus back to *Santa Tierra*. I am anxious to get back before service tonight. I have so many exciting things to tell them," asked Luís.

"No problem," Carey replied, starting up the truck. "I only wish I could carry you in myself and be in service with them, but I need to take this time to be with family. We also have a lot to talk about."

Mando agreed and the three men started their trip home. It would be a beautiful day for travel.

———

About eleven class members had arrived by the time Adam began to gather them together in the dining room. He had spread chairs around the wall in hopes that the whole class would eventually show up. The little sandwiches were available on the table in the center of the room. Gertie made her way in and was given the chair closest to the doorway leading to the kitchen.

"I am so glad you all took time from your Saturday schedules to come and be with us this afternoon," Adam began. "You may recall that last Sunday, I was teaching on intercessory prayer when I mentioned that my wife was my greatest inspiration. Since Gertie can't go to church when the weather is like it is, I thought I would bring you all here. Actually, she asked if you could come. I want you to listen to her as she shares something that she has been involved with for . . . over a week now, isn't it honey?"

Gertie smiled and nodded.

"It has been ten days," she began, "or I should say, nights and days."

The group took their seats and began to listen as Gertie explained how she first felt summoned to prayer. She related the burden and how she knew it was the Lord leading her to pray for these two families and then how the Lord had even used one family to reveal the identity of the other. She shared the letter she had received and sighs could be heard as the details of God's timing was confirmed by the missionary she had been praying for.

"Not a day has passed since a week ago Wednesday that I have been able to sleep through the night," Gertie continued. "I am awakened by the burden and I must pray. I have asked that you all come today to pray with me. I feel this day is important in many ways. God wants to do something mighty in the lives of those I have been praying for. Would you just bow your heads and pray with me for these two families?"

There was no hesitation. The lesson had moved into practice. Adam's class was about to learn about intercessory prayer through doing it. Adam bowed his head as well.

———

"Karen," the voice repeated. "Do you remember me?"

Karen stared for a moment.

"Uh, yes, you're Amy," Karen said flustered.

"Close. It's Anna, . . . Anna Eldridge. We met on a bus once."

"Yes, I remember now," Karen replied, embarrassed.

"What are you doing here this early?" Anna asked digging into her purse for her keys.

"I work this morning down at the dress store. You remember *Sugar n Spice* where you bought your scarf last week."

"I'm sorry," Anna said humbly. "I meant, what are you doing here at the Bible Book Store this early. We don't open for another ten minutes. Was there something I could get for you?"

"Oh, Uh, no." Karen stammered. In all her trips to the mall, she couldn't remember the last time she had been in the Bible bookstore.

"Would you like to come in while I get set up?" Anna offered.

"Will you get in trouble?" Karen asked.

"No, it's fine. The owners are real nice and besides, you work here in the mall also. So it's kinda like family."

The word "family" struck hard. Karen followed Anna into the store and began to look around.

"You said your father was a minister, didn't you?" Anna asked.

"Yes."

"What church may I ask?"

"The First Baptist Church, Coronado," Karen replied without great enthusiasm.

"Oh, I'm Baptist also. My uncle and aunt carry me to a smaller Baptist church near National City."

"Your uncle?" Karen asked. "Why don't your parents carry you to church?"

"Well, it's a little difficult for them," Anna smiled. "They live in Honduras with my two brothers"

"Honduras?!?" Karen exclaimed. "What in the world do they do in Honduras?"

"They're missionaries," Anna said proudly. "I lived there till just last year."

"No kidding? Was it neat?"

"Neat is usually a word you use to describe some place you visit. It was definitely different than here. I guess you could call it neat, but for me, it was more like home. I grew up in Central America and my brothers were even born there."

Karen was impressed. Here was a girl her age that had lived in another country.

"Are you still having problems at home," Anna asked carefully. She had no idea how sensitive the subject was.

Karen looked away for a moment and found herself staring in the direction of the painting again. She could see the details better now that she was closer. She could see the tears, and how they had even stained the white tunic that Jesus was wearing. She stepped even closer to the picture while Anna looked on.

"Lord, we pray for Karen this afternoon," said Gertie, as others whispered in agreement.

———

Anna whispered a silent prayer for Karen and then gently called her name again.

Karen began to cry. She closed her eyes and tried to hold back the tears while her head was turned away from Anna. Anna took a couple steps toward her and placed her hand on her shoulder. Karen burst into sobs. She turned and reached out for Anna. There in the quiet of a store not yet open, Karen found the open arms she needed.

———

"And Lord, we pray for her father also," continued Gertie.

———

The phone rang twice before Howard realized it. He reached for the receiver on the wall of the kitchen and answered in a low voice.

"Bro. Pennington, this is Betty Johnson. I hope you are not too busy. We need to see you right away if possible."

"Betty, I can be there in about twenty minutes," Howard replied. "May I ask the nature of the problem?"

"It's Alex, Bro. Pennington," she said regretfully. "He was arrested last night and they are holding him at the County jail in El Cajon."

Howard remembered his appointment with Rusty and thought it would be helpful to have him along.

"Would it be OK if I brought Rusty Patterson with me. He knows the jail well from his weekly ministry there."

"That will be fine, Pastor," she agreed. "Would it be better for you if we just met you at the jail?"

"That may work better, since Rusty will be coming from that direction."

"We'll see you in the lobby. Thank you Bro. Pennington, Arnie is just beside himself."

Howard hung up the phone. I bet he is, Howard thought to himself. He immediately called Rusty who was more than prepared to meet them at the jail. Howard grabbed his Bible and headed out the front door.

———

Capitán Mendoza was anxious to get south. His extra day in *La Esperanza* followed by the unexpected trip to *Gualcince* was more than he bargained for. They had finally given him a driver to take Felípe's truck back to Choluteca, but then held him over in the capital for the theft report. He had sent the driver ahead on Friday morning and stayed one extra day in Tegucigalpa on paperwork. He slept at the main station and took his time getting up Saturday morning. But he was finally on his way home.

_____

Carey and his passengers resumed their singing from the day before. Luís was anxious to learn as many hymns and choruses as they could teach him. He sat behind Mando and bellowed out, "At the Cross" each time they reached the refrain. The day was nice and many cars from the capital were making their way south towards the beaches.

_____

Teresita's sisters helped her place the water container on her head. Since she was still young, she used a small woven ring, much like a large donut, placing it squarely atop her head and using it to balance the plastic jug that contained about fifteen pounds of water. The girls balanced their loads as they worked their way up the hill from the water pump towards the road. They laughed and talked about boys. Teresita didn't care about boys, she was concentrating all she could not to spill any water from her container. She was going to show her mother that she was big enough to make these trips. They reached the hi-way and began the slow trudge uphill to their home.

_____

Carey started the second largest incline on the road heading south. It was slow for semis and some busses. His truck had the power to pass though - even on a hill, so he waited for the openings and then took the lead. He was anxious to get home, but not so rushed as to take risks. He leveled off his speed and worked the mountain with grace.

_____

"And Lord," Gertie prayed. "We also wish to lift up Brother Carey. We know you have been working through his life and we pray Your best for him

285

at this time. May he serve you fully and only bring glory to Your name where You have placed him."

———

"*Hermano* Carey," began Mando. "I can't help but believe that God has been able to use this whole accident for his glory. I know it involved the death of a man and has put you through some incredible heartache and even depression. But who would have guessed that *Santa Tierra* and *Gualcince* would respond to the gospel the way they have. In part, it is because you showed God's love in the face of tragedy. You did not let Moncho die in vain. God did not let Moncho die in vain. His death triggered an incredible course of events that have led to this."

"I must agree," added Luís. "I most certainly wouldn't be sitting here today if it weren't for what happened on the mountain that night."

Carey whispered a silent "amen" and then a "thank you Lord".

As Carey's Hilux began to round the next bend to the right, he saw the grill of a large semi rounding the curve. Instinctively, Carey eased toward the shoulder just in case another vehicle was going to pass. He remembered the words he told his brother just a week ago that day, "if there's room for three - there's room to pass". He rounded the curve in time to see the driver's arm flail wildly up and down out his window. That was the signal to someone passing, not to try because there was oncoming traffic. Carey began to slow his truck. When he rounded the curve he saw the other large truck already committed and in the center of the road. His downhill speed would not allow him to pull back. Carey prepared to ease onto the shoulder as he had in so many cases before. This was not a panic situation. Then he saw the four girls.

Teresita turned her head to shield it from the dust that the big semi was raising. She was the only one of the four to see the truck that was about to head straight toward them. Her eyes grew large as she looked into the face of the man driving the red pick-up with the white camper.

Carey's thoughts flashed in a millisecond to the second statement he had made to his brother. What if someone is on the shoulder, Billy had asked. - "Then the driver has a difficult decision to make."

Carey had no time to speak, to warn, or to even blow his horn. He could not run onto the shoulder without hitting at least two of those girls including the one that was looking at him. He felt he had only one recourse. He hit his brakes as hard as he could holding fast the wheel. He knew he could not avoid impact, but just maybe the truck would not be knocked in the direction of the girls. Mando and Luís braced themselves.

Anna held Karen for several minutes as the catharsis of tears flowed.

"I feel so stupid," Karen cried.

"Not at all," Anna said, comforting her. "Would you like to get together today, maybe at lunch or even after work?"

"I'm supposed to go somewhere after lunch with my boss today, but thanks," Karen smiled. "Speaking of which, I need to be getting myself downstairs and letting you get your store open for the day."

"If you change your mind, Karen, I'll be at the food court at noon."

Karen thanked her again, and turned to go. It had been three years since Karen had cried about how she felt. As she took the escalator down to the first level, she wasn't sure she still wanted to take that trip today. She wasn't sure about a lot of things.

Howard parked in front of the courthouse and walked into the police station. Parking places were never a problem on a Saturday. Rusty met him in the lobby and introduced him to the officer that handled visitors. They signed the necessary logs and were given small plastic badges that clipped onto their shirt pockets. Rusty knew most of the men in the lobby by name.

"Arnie and Betty have already gone up," Rusty said.

"How is Arnie taking all this?"

"Pretty hard. It seems that Alex and his friends wanted to borrow a car last night to go to some amusement area in La Mesa. So they end up taking the bus, and as they are getting off, Alex sees this purse on a seat. He grabs it and runs from the bus stop with the other boys. They split up the money and have a great time and all is well, till they start home. Would you believe it, they get the same bus driver? Anyway, he holds Alex because he was the one he saw snatch the purse and he calls the police."

"The other boys?" Howard asked.

"Not taken in. Alex spent the night here on his own."

"Spent the night! When was Arnie called?"

"Last night sometime late. Arnie said that the night in jail would do him good."

Howard huffed in disagreement. They walked to the stairway that led to the second floor and the holding cells. Rusty knew his way around and greeted the guards he recognized. As they entered the visiting area, Howard saw the Johnsons standing near a table. Betty looked up and greeted the two men.

"Thank you for coming, Bro. Pennington," Betty said sincerely. "We just saw Alex. He had to go back to the holding cell for now, but we are going to be getting his bail worked out. We should be able to take him with us in about an hour."

Howard nodded and looked toward Arnie. He extended his hand to shake and Arnie hesitated, then accepted the courtesy.

"Morning, pastor," he mumbled.

"How can we be of help," the pastor asked, looking back toward Betty. It was obvious, she had called and she wanted him to be present.

"I'm not sure," she began. "I know he once was active in church and I thought maybe him seeing you while he was still in here would bring him to a greater sense of conviction. He hasn't really been listening to either of us very much lately."

Rusty stepped forward.

"Mrs. Johnson, I was Alexe's Sunday school teacher when I first got here a couple years ago. He seemed pretty levelheaded then. Do you think it would be OK if I spoke with him?"

Betty looked to her husband. He gave a nonchalant response and then approved. Rusty showed his special minister's badge to the guard at the door and was allowed in the cell area. Howard suddenly felt unneeded. Betty leaned towards her husband and whispered something to him. He looked disagreeable, but finally gave in.

"Pastor, would you mind if we talked some while Rusty is with Alex?" Arnie said with difficulty.

"Whatever you wish, Arnie," Howard responded. He wasn't that excited about talking with him either.

The two men stepped away from Mrs. Johnson, who took a seat at the visiting table. They walked towards one of the barred windows. Arnie took a deep breath and began.

"I guess you've figured that I wasn't really in favor of calling you," he began.

"I gathered," Howard confessed.

"Well, that's what I want to talk to you about," the big man began to sound softer. "You see, I have had a real problem and I don't know how to deal with it. On the one hand, it concerns Alex, and on the other hand it concerns you."

"Me?" Howard responded in surprise.

"Yes. You see, the problem I have with you is . . . well, I see too much of myself in you and it really bothers me."

Howard had no response. He just continued to let Arnie talk.

"When you first came, I thought you were cocky and full of yourself. No offense, mind you, but you were just out of seminary and had just gotten those initials after your name and, well you made a point that we all knew it. I didn't mind the Greek lessons in the sermons, but it was always, 'the scholars . . . this' and 'the scholars . . . that!' It made me feel like I couldn't study the Bible for myself. Then I realized that you were just good at what you knew - like I was - and that you wanted to pour yourself into what you did. Well, I know that feeling too."

Howard looked confused. He wasn't sure if he was being complimented or criticized. He let Arnie continue.

"Then I began to notice something in both of our families. It was about five years into your being here. Both Alex and Karen became teenagers and both of us started losing ground with them. We both poured ourselves into our jobs. I tried to push Alex into construction and he got so turned off, he never wanted to go to a work site again. I can still see the point when your daughter quit singing in the choir and started missing services. I wanted to come to you then for help with Alex, but when I saw you were having the same problems, I thought to myself, 'what could he possibly have to offer?' "

Howard dropped his eyes. He had no defense and worse - he knew there was more.

"I guess the hardest part for me was the coming of the building proposal. What should have brought our two worlds together, was actually the driving wedge between us. You were about to let a building come between you and your family and I wanted nothing to do with it. Not because I don't believe the church needs the building. You've heard me speak my mind about the design. The real problem is that I just hate the thought of you letting it be the final thing to finish driving Karen away from you. You see I felt like I had already lost Alex. This weekend should be pretty good indication of that. But if you were able to somehow straighten out your relationship with Karen, then maybe there would be hope for Alex and I."

Howard looked up to see Arnie's eyes redden.

"If your pastor can't work out his own family problems, what hope is there in seeking his counsel. Don't you see, every week I saw your situation worsen, I was seeing my own grow hopeless," Arnie concluded.

Howard put his arm around Arnie. He had no words of wisdom that seemed appropriate. Then he began to open his own heart to hear. As he heard, he shared.

"Arnie, everything you have said is true," he began. "Though I had no idea that you were experiencing similar struggles. I guess I don't know my church body as well as I should. I've been making a lot of mistakes lately, and I wish I could tell you that things aren't nearly as bad at home as you think they are, but to be quite honest, they may actually be worse. But something I have been learning just this week. God can change hearts. The key is . . . listening to Him in the middle of the situation instead of after the dust settles. We tend to look to God for damage control after the fact, when He wants to keep us from causing the damage in the first place. I have been one of the worst, when it comes to listening to God - for some of the very reasons you have just mentioned. But a couple nights ago, I remember hearing Him while I was angry with Karen. I actually found myself saying words that moments before I would never have imagined uttering because of my own state of mind."

Now Arnie looked confused.

"What I'm saying is that most of the time that I have had problems with Karen is when I was determined to handle the situation MY way! Well, sometimes, my way and God's way are diametrically opposite to each other. What I have been learning, is that, it is possible to yield your way to His at just that right moment when He gives you the words and the heart to deal correctly with your child."

Arnie seemed to understand. At least he was listening.

"Now to be honest, I'm the last man to be giving you this advice, because, just this morning I blew it again. But maybe, the fact that I'm a work in progress helps me to be able to share it with you. Does that make sense?"

Arnie nodded.

"Even now. God is using your words to speak to me about my priorities," Howard continued. "I feel that I needed as much of what you had to say, as maybe we both need what is coming out right now. I do know this. I certainly have never given this counsel before, and it is not some pat answer I learned in seminary."

Arnie chuckled.

"Now if Rusty is able to do what I believe he is capable of with Alex, I would dare say that both of you will have a shot at a new start. I know I certainly am going to work on a new start with Karen when she gets home today."

Howard meant every word. He extended his hand and this time Arnie took it firmly. They passed a look of mutual appreciation and Howard knew he had just taken two more steps forward.

"Listen, pastor," Arnie said heartily. "If you need any helpful advice on that building and not just 'a piece of my mind', let me know."

"I'll be calling you first thing Monday morning - trust me," Howard assured him.

Arnie walked back to his wife and they held each other.

After about ten more minutes, Rusty reentered the visiting room. He smiled at Bro. Howard and walked toward the Johnsons.

"Bro. Arnie," Rusty began cordially, "I have been asked to relay a special message to you from your son."

The couple looked on eagerly.

"Alex says he is more sorry than he could ever express. He knows he must pay for what he has done, and if you want him to stay in that cell, he knows he deserves it. BUT, if you are willing to not only accept his apology, but also see that he gets the necessary counseling, he would love to go home with you two today."

Peggy began to cry.

"I don't know what to say," Arnie stammered. "When he was out here with us, he wouldn't say two words."

"He was afraid of how you would respond," Rusty confided. "He says, he has been wanting to please you for years, but he feels you gave up on him when he couldn't drive a straight nail. He isn't really a bad boy. In fact, he just rededicated his life to the Lord in front of the others standing around. I think he's got a lot of intestinal fortitude."

"Thank you, Rusty," Arnie said, shaking his hand. "I'll go make sure they are arranging bail now. We'll get through this . . . as a family."

He looked back to Bro. Howard. They shared another exchange of hope. Then they headed for the stairway to the front desk.

Howard shook Rusty's hand as well and thanked him for coming. As he turned for the exit, Rusty stopped him.

"Oh we can't go yet," Rusty announced.

"Why not, we're through here, aren't we?" Howard asked puzzled.

"Not quite," Rusty smiled. "There's someone I want you to meet."

The two men walked back to the doors leading to the cells and presented their ministers' badges. The heavy doors were opened, and Howard entered a new world.

Chapter Twenty Four:

"The News"

Donna waited for the room to empty before approaching the missionary. She was slightly nervous and yet exhilarated. She had not slept much the night before. Marnie's devotion spoke directly to Donna's heart. She had wanted to talk to her then, but the conference leaders had been whisked away for a planning meeting. Donna went to her room instead to study the passages that the missionary had shared.

She was interested in talking to her about the call to missions. Marnie had shared her personal call, but alluded to characteristics that others on the field seemed to share. What Donna mostly wanted to know was, if someone felt called at an earlier time in their life and didn't act on it. Did God withdraw the call? She wasn't sure what she would do about the answer she may receive, but she had to know something. Donna was willing to forgo her next conference to able to talk to Marnie during the next session.

As she waited, she realized that she hadn't thought about Howard or the children since the conference began. She didn't even call home the night before to check on how things were going. She was beginning to wonder if she was taking too large a step away from her family. Donna paused to pray.

"Lord, You know how confused I have been these past days. I have felt things and thought thoughts that I have never entertained before. I don't want to leave my family, and yet, I feel trapped. I need to know exactly what Your will for my life is. I pray you can use this woman to speak Your wisdom to me. I will listen. Please just give me the strength to do what You want me to do. I give this all to you today. In Christ's name I pray, Amen."

Donna looked up and Marnie stood before her. They introduced themselves and Donna asked if it would be possible for them to take the next hour together to talk. Marnie was sensitive to what she saw in Donna's eyes and smiled. They found two chairs in the conference room and Donna began to pour her heart out. It was not easy, but Marnie was patient. Donna began to cry as she spoke of her family and their struggles. She had never been more vulnerable in her life, and yet, she had never been more transparent either. She opened her soul and God began to heal it and to fill it anew.

———

Karen arrived at the shop a few minutes after Sheila had opened the doors. Sheila was going over some invoices on her desk when Karen looked in and announced her arrival for work. Sheila glanced up and smiled. For the first time, Karen felt uncomfortable about that smile.

"Hope you're ready for a fun day," Sheila asked.

"Oh, yeah . . . sure," Karen responded faintly.

Sheila decided not to question Karen's lack of enthusiasm. She discounted it for being early on Saturday morning and Karen not fully awake. She handed Karen a small list of tasks for her to be working on during the morning. Floor traffic would pick up from 10:30 on. There were enough jobs to do to cover an hour and a half. Karen was glad for the busy work. She didn't feel like talking to Sheila just then.

Karen took the list and began putting away the clothes that had been left at the dressing rooms. As she rehung the dresses on their stands, she began to think about the picture in the Bible bookstore. She didn't look anything like the girl in the picture. She wore nice clothes - like the ones she was rehanging. Why did she feel such a kinship with her then.

"It's not the clothes. It's the girl."

Karen shook her head. 'Where did that come from', she thought. And yet the voice was right. Inside, Karen was just a lost little girl. She wanted to be older. She wanted her independence, but the truth was - she wasn't ready for it yet. She thought life could be easy. She thought success came with just wanting it. She wasn't ready to live on her own - especially with Sheila or her help.

"I'm still just a young girl," Karen said to herself.

She continued to fold clothes, but she now saw more than that small shop.

———

Rusty introduced Bro. Howard to one of the jailers, whose name was Antonio. His tawny complexion and jet black hair suggested a Latino heritage. Antonio walked with the two men back to the cell area. Howard saw Alex sitting in the corner with a Bible that one of the other guards had provided. He was about to speak to him when Rusty turned him in another direction.

"He's over here. . .in this cell," Rusty said. "He's the skinny one standing alone."

Howard turned and saw a group of men standing around the sides of the walls. He then noticed one man apart from the others. He was gaunt and looked completely out of place with the other men.

"Now normally, when we come up here on Saturdays I just preach to the whole group," Rusty explained. "But as you know, we aren't scheduled to be here till later this afternoon. While I was talking to Alex, I noticed a man watching us carefully. When I tried to speak to him, I discovered he knows no English. But he still looked interested in talking. I asked Antonio if he could translate for me."

"His name is Flaco," the officer stated. "He is an illegal who was picked up just yesterday. Because he had a gun, they brought him here. I don't know what the plans are for the man. He won't talk to me much. I try, but he sees the uniform and clams up. If you want, I can see if he would let you talk to him and I can translate."

Howard walked to the bars and looked at Flaco, who had heard his name mentioned by the officer.

"*Qué tal amigo?*" Howard asked with a fairly good accent. His years in Texas and his classes in Spanish started coming back to him.

Flaco's eyes brightened and he stepped towards the bars. Rusty looked at Antonio and they shrugged their shoulders. Antonio returned to his desk.

"You speak Spanish?" Flaco asked with his Honduran accent.

"A little," was the common response for most gringos, who didn't want to get in over their heads too soon.

"Is that young man with you?" Flaco asked pointing to Rusty.

"Yes he is, we came to see that boy over there," Howard replied.

"I have been watching that boy all night," Flaco said. "He is scared. Were you able to help him."

"I think so," Howard smiled. "He will be going home with his parents soon."

Flaco sighed.

"Where is home for you, my friend," Howard asked innocently.

"Far from here, *amigo*," Flaco replied.

"Deep in Mexico, I take it."

"Farther than Mexico. Farther than Guatemala. Farther than El Salvador," Flaco responded, almost boasting.

Howard tried to think of the Central America countries and their locations.

"Are you from Nicaragua," was his only guess.

"No, my friend. I am from Honduras."

"You are far from home," Howard agreed.

"I left there to come here. I came to find work. I came to find a better life," Flaco announced.

"Didn't work out that way, did it?" Howard noted.

"What are they going to do to me?" Flaco asked.

"I have no idea," Howard said honestly. "I don't know the procedures for illegals. And they say you had a gun."

"Yes, I had the power," Flaco said proudly. "Little good it did me here."

"Is that what you think? That a gun is power?"

"Do you not fear a gun, my friend?" Flaco asked.

"If you are asking, would I be nervous if someone pulled a gun on me to rob me, of course. If you are asking am I afraid of a gun taking my life from me . . . well, no," Howard said flatly.

"You are not afraid to die?" Flaco sounded incredulous.

"I am concerned, of course about leaving my family behind, but that could happen on the road. I have to deal with that every day. If you are asking me if I am personally afraid of leaving this earth in death, I would have to say, 'NO'!"

"How can you say that," Flaco questioned. "There is nothing worse than death."

"But, there is, my friend," Howard stated calmly. "It's dying twice!"

"What do you mean, 'dying twice'?" Flaco replied genuinely confused.

"Let me share something with you."

Howard turned to Rusty. He asked him to see if there were any Spanish Bibles around. After a couple minutes, Rusty returned with a small colored New Testament. He handed it to Howard, who looked at the cover. It had been brought by the Gideons. Howard smiled, then opened to the back of the book.

"This is part of the Bible," Howard began to explain. Flaco knew what a Bible was, though he had never seen one that little. "The Bible tells us what the God who made us wants us to know about Him. It is His Word to us. We can believe what it says, because He wrote it - not men."

Flaco had never heard it explained quite that way. His few times in Mass he had heard the book opened and read from without explanation of where it came from. He decided he would listen.

"In the last book of the Bible, God tells us about many things that will happen. Included in those things is what happens after we die. You see, it doesn't just end there. We will all stand before God to give an account of our lives. Then he will look in a book to see what should happen to us next."

Howard found the passage he was looking for and began to read from the Spanish New Testament.

" 'Then Death and Hades were thrown into the lake of fire. This is the second death. And those who were not found written in the Book of Life were thrown into the Lake of Fire.' That is Revelation 20:14, 15."

Flaco stared with a look of surprise. He had never heard those words before.

"So there is a second death?" he asked.

"Yes, it is described in the Bible in many ways. Sometimes it is referred to as fire, sometimes to a deep pit, and sometimes as just darkness. But it is always described as a place of eternal separation from God and torment."

"But I already don't feel close to God, what's the difference?" Flaco asked.

"You're right. Sin has a way of separating us from Him and we sense that. But eternal separation from God means that not only do we have nothing to do with Him, but He will have absolutely nothing to do with us. You see, even though you don't feel close to God here, He is still involved in your life. If He wasn't, you couldn't even exist. God still deals with you as one of His creations, but He wants to know you as one of His children."

"I thought we were all children of God?" Flaco replied.

"We are all part of God's creation, that is true. That is why He is still involved in our lives. But our relationship with Him has been affected by sin. We were created to know Him personally like a Father and His child. But sin keeps us from knowing Him in that way. That's why He sent His Son, Jesus Christ. His life and death made it possible for us to know God as our Father."

Flaco was beginning to look confused.

"You see, my friend," Howard continued slowly. "Just as there are two deaths, there are two births."

Howard began to turn the pages of the New Testament back to the Gospel of John. He located the third chapter and began to read the story of Nicodemus visiting Jesus one night. As he reached verse 7, he read slowly.

" 'Don't be amazed when I tell you, it is necessary that you be born again.' "

At this point, Flaco stopped him and countered.

"Yes, BUT . . . how can a man be born when he is already old?"

Howard looked up into Flaco's eyes. He couldn't believe the question he had just heard.

"Do you know, that is exactly the question that the man Jesus was talking to asked him?" Howard exclaimed.

Flaco's eyes widened with expectation.

"You must tell me. What did he say to him?"

Howard smiled. He held the small Bible where Flaco could see it. Together they read through the account. When Howard reached John 3:16, he read it with all the feeling of having discovered the verse for the first time.

" 'For God so loved the world, that he gave his one and only Son. That whoever would believe in Him would not die, but have eternal life.' "

Flaco looked up with a spark in his eyes.

"That means they will not die the second time, right?" he asked.

"That's exactly what it means. When we believe in God's Son, Jesus Christ, as our personal Lord and Savior, he writes our name down in the Book of Life, because at that point, he gives us a new life. That is when we are born again - with a new life. This life means we now are Children of God, not just creations. We can know Him as our Father and will do so for all eternity. He will never leave us or forsake us."

"I have never heard this before," Flaco said amazed. "Why have I never heard this before? Why did I have to come all this way to hear this news?"

"Because God loves you enough to bring you all this way," Howard replied wisely.

For the next few minutes, Rusty looked on as Howard explained how to receive the Lord Jesus through repentance and prayer.

"But what if I may have killed a man?" Flaco asked painfully.

"You aren't sure if you killed a man or not?" Howard replied.

"I shot and robbed him and left him in a ditch. I don't know if he died or not," Flaco explained.

"Then after you pray for God to forgive you, we will pray together for the man you shot. If he did not die, then we will be helping him," Carey offered.

Flaco did not understand how God could forgive a possible murderer. But he knew some things he would just have to accept on faith. The two men bowed their heads and prayed together with Howard leading and Flaco repeating.

When they finished, Flaco added, "Dear God, I pray for Felípe. Please let him live. Let him return home to his family. And God, I pray for the missionary that Moncho's family is looking for. Please be with him and protect him, too."

Howard closed the prayer and the two shook hands. Rusty stepped to the bars and Howard introduced him. The three men talked longer, with Howard doing the translating. He was amazed how much of the language he was able to recall.

This had been a good morning, Howard thought, in spite of how it had begun with Karen. As they made their way back to the car, Howard said a silent prayer for Karen. He would definitely begin to improve things when she got home that evening.

———

Capitán Mendoza recognized the scene. As he drove up to the curve, cars were pulled over and a large crowd was standing in the road. Traffic had to slow to a crawl for two reasons: to avoid hitting people and to get a glimpse of the accident. If it looked like someone may have been seriously hurt, they would pull over at the next convenient spot of the shoulder and walk back. Capitán Mendoza had to park quite a distance down the hill, across the road from a semi with a crumpled front fender. If that were the extent of the damage, he would not be too long.

As he walked up towards the large group, he could see another vehicle on its side against the hill. The red Toyota pick-up was a common vehicle in Honduras. But as Mendoza got closer, he passed the broken white camper shell that had detached when the truck turned on its side. A sick feeling came over him as he quickened his step pushing the onlookers aside. The crowd opened up and the Capitán swallowed hard. It was the missionary's truck.

"When did this happen?" He asked the young man beside him.

"About five minutes ago," he replied.

Mendoza ran to the driver's door, but he could barely see from that angle. The truck lay on the passenger side and the bodies were all positioned against that door. He pushed his way around past the front of the truck and looked in from the windshield. As he peered down into the front seat, he saw slight movement.

"Some of these men are still alive, someone help me!" he shouted.

Several joined him against the downed side of the truck and pushed it back over on its wheels. They forced open the passenger door and began to gently pull the bodies to the embankment. Mando was moaning and holding his arm. Luís was unconscious and Carey wasn't moving either. Mendoza laid them back easily and began to check for vital signs. A minute later he stood up shaking his head.

He pointed to two men nearby.

"You two help these men to the road, while I bring my truck up. Put the one holding his arm in my front seat and place the other gently in my back seat."

Mendoza then looked at the restful pose of the missionary. He choked back a tear and instructed the men.

"Then come back and place the body of that tall man in the back of my truck. I will take them to *Choluteca*."

"Do you know these men," one asked.

"Yes I do. They are good men. Please be gentle with them."

––––––

Karen looked at her watch. It was fifteen more minutes till lunchtime. She was starving, especially from not having had any breakfast before leaving the house. Sheila came out onto the floor from her office. Karen took a deep breath. Much had changed for her since she had arrived that morning.

"Amber should be here pretty soon. Have you thought about what you might like to do for lunch before we head out?" Sheila asked.

"Sheila, I hope you don't mind, but I think I may be changing my mind about our trip today," Karen said timidly.

"What are you talking about," Sheila sounded angry. "I'm taking some special time off just to carry you out to the mountains. You're not going to be some flaky high school girl who can't make up her mind now what she wants, are you?"

Karen was taken aback. She had never seen Sheila upset before.

"I'm not being flaky," Karen retorted. "I've just had some things come up that I would rather take care of today. I'm sorry if that upsets you."

"I'm not upset," Sheila responded without changing her tone. "I'm disappointed in you. I thought you wanted to be your own person and do things you'd never done before. I mean, that's what you told me."

"I am being my own person," Karen reacted in kind. "Changing your mind is part of being yourself, isn't it? I just think I need to do something else more important today. I thought you would understand."

"I think I understand just fine," Sheila replied cryptically.

Karen let the conversation pass for the moment before one of them said something unkind.

"Listen Sheila, I'm sorry I ruined your plans. Maybe we can do it another time. Believe me, I wouldn't be changing my mind if I didn't think it was important."

"Whatever," Sheila huffed. "If you need to go on now, that's fine. Here's your paycheck for this past week. I'll watch things till Amber gets here."

Sheila turned her back on Karen and began straightening the counter. Karen walked to the back to get her purse. She started to say good-bye, but could see that Sheila was hurt. She thought it best to just let her go. She walked through the doorway and heard the familiar electronic tone . . . for the last time.

———

"Would you like to join me for lunch" Marnie asked Donna.

Donna looked at her watch and gasped. They had been talking for almost two hours.

"Have we been talking that long?" she asked.

"Oh, I don't mind," smiled Marnie. "In fact, I would like to spend more time with this, but why don't we do it over a salad."

"That would be wonderful," exclaimed Donna.

The two women walked to the hotel restaurant and ordered lunch. Donna waited till the waiter brought them water. She took a deep drink and then continued with her questions.

"How do you know where God wants you to serve?"

"That answer is as different as there are missionaries. For some, it doesn't matter. They feel drawn to a task and tell God, 'it doesn't matter where you send me.' For others, it is as definite as the call. I have heard of people who have seen themselves in dreams in a certain country and know that there is where God wants them to serve. For others, it's a matter of following the 'open doors' till they reach the right place."

"What do you mean," Donna asked sipping her water.

"You may think you are being called to one area. You train for it, you study the language, you learn about it. But before you arrive, something happens. It may be VISA problems, or a sudden war, or any of a number of reasons and suddenly, you find yourself heading in another direction. When you get there. You discover that this was where God wanted you all along."

Donna listened intently. Each of her questions was responded to with humility and wisdom. She felt she was getting some of her answers.

———

Howard made it back home shortly after lunchtime. He called the house where Terry was staying and discovered they had gone go-cart riding and would be away most of the afternoon. He wasn't sure when Karen would be returning home, so he went to the kitchen and made himself a sandwich.

After eating, he went to his office and cleared his desk. He took his Bible and a notepad and made himself comfortable. Howard had at least five hours before him. He intended to do some serious soul searching, some Bible study and some qualitative prayer time. If necessary, he may have to do some rewriting for his Sunday message.

God was speaking, and Howard was listening. . . for a change.

———

Karen looked around the food court for Anna. She had just started to walk the perimeter a second time when she saw Anna waving from a table. Karen motioned that she was going to get some food and join her, then stepped into the line for pizza slices.

"Are you through for the day?" Anna asked, as she placed her tray beside her.

"Most definitely, and maybe for good," Karen remarked.

"What do you mean? Did she fire you?"

300

"No," Karen replied. "I'm just not sure that's where I want to work."

Karen decided to let it go at that.

"I have till 4:00, and then I'll take the bus home again," Anna said. "How are you getting home?"

"I can hang out till then," Karen replied. "My Mom is away on a retreat and my Dad isn't expecting me till later in the afternoon anyway. I can wait till you get off if you like."

Anna smiled.

"That would be great. Why don't you come by the store and let me show you some cool music. I also know a book I think you would like."

"I can't remember when I last listened to contemporary Christian music," Karen said. "I bet it has changed some."

"Personally, I prefer some of the older music. My Dad and I listened to Christian groups when we would go out to the field," Anna remembered.

"You and your Dad have a good relationship, don't you?" Karen said enviously.

"We do."

"It's funny, you are closer to your Dad and he is hundreds of miles away, then I am with mine, and he's right here."

Anna saw the longing in Karen's eyes. She thought for a moment and then shared, "Dad used to drive with his arm around me all the time when I was a little girl. I would sit between him and Mom in the front seat and he would just wrap his arm around my shoulders and I would feel so safe. I remember, one time we were taking a trip out to one of his churches and Mom wasn't with us. I climbed up in the seat, but wanted to look out the window. So we drove like that for awhile. Later, I realized how far I felt from him and said, 'Daddy, why don't you put your arm around me like you used to?' He looked across the seat and smiled with those big blue eyes and said, 'honey, I'm not the one that scooted away!' I got the point, and I slid back across the seat towards him. Sometimes, Karen, we don't think about what pulls us away from our fathers, but we let it, and we find ourselves looking out the window thinking about other things and then when we start to feel lonely, we blame him. When the truth is, we were the ones that moved."

Karen heard the message loud and clear. God was speaking to her through this new friend. She began to ask Anna more questions about how they spent time together and what Anna did when her father got "too busy" for her.

The lunch hour was not enough. Karen decided to spend the next three hours (as well as some of her money) reacquainting herself with materials for getting to know God and her father better.

When 4:00 arrived, the two girls made for the bus stop. They looked like two sisters. In many respects they were. Karen decided she would visit with Anna and call home from her house. She didn't want her father to worry any more about her.

———

Mando was in extreme pain from his broken arm. Luís drifted in and out of consciousness, as Capitán Mendoza drove swiftly, but carefully over the remainder of the mountains leading down to the south.

"How did this happen?" Mendoza finally asked, when he felt Mando could speak.

"It was all so fast," Mando strained to say. "We were rounding the curve . . . a truck was coming, and another was trying to pass."

"Why didn't he take the edge?" Mendoza wondered out loud.

"There were some girls walking on the side of the road. They were too close to the edge. Bro. Carey didn't want to hit any of them, so he broke while still on the road. I guess the truck knocked us on our side."

He winced with pain, but then looked directly into the Capitán's direction.

"But we didn't hit any of the girls!" he said proudly.

"I know, I know"

They traveled along in silence, for the longest time. Then Mando spoke again.

"You are taking me to the hospital for my arm?"

"Yes, and to get your friend some help also. He needs to see a doctor."

"Can you wait for me to get my arm set, before you go to Bro. Carey's home? I need to be there when you tell his wife."

Mendoza nodded. This would be one of the hardest things he had ever done. He had informed many widows of the death of their husbands, but never a man like this. As they traveled along the southern highway, Mendoza asked Mando how a North American could come to one of the poorest areas of his country, and work among the people for so many years, and even put his life in danger as he had this past week? Then, he added, to ultimately trade his life for that of others in his path. What causes a man to do something like that?

"Only one thing I know, and I am still learning," replied Mando.

"What is that?"

"His love for God."

Mendoza expected to hear about his great love for the people, or to show the love of God, but this answer was different.

"What do you mean?" Mendoza asked.

"He loved God more than his own life. He was willing to let God take him wherever He wanted. He was willing to serve God how ever He chose, and he was willing to let God use him, in whatever means necessary."

"So why did God let him die?"

Mando didn't have a quick answer. He let the question soak in his own mind for a few kilometers. Then he ventured a response.

"Capitán, do you remember the night Bro. Carey and I brought you the body of Moncho?"

"Yes, that's partly why I am asking these questions now," he replied.

"That night, we had no idea why God let Moncho die. He could have prevented the robbery without the loss of life - we know that. But today, on the way home, we were talking about that, and it occurred to us, looking back, that because of Moncho's death, two villages are responding in a mighty way to the good news of Jesus Christ."

"But is this good news worth an innocent man's life?" the Capitán asked honestly.

Mando thought for just a moment, then replied confidently.

"Yes sir. That's how it became the Good News in the first place. An innocent man died! His name was Jesus Christ. His death was not tragic - it was triumphant because of what God accomplished through it. I ache with all my being for losing Bro. Carey today, but I know that his death will not be tragic. If Moncho's death could be used for the glory of God, how much more the death of Bro. Carey Eldridge."

Chapter Twenty Five:

"The Breach"

Howard heard the front door slam. He glanced at his clock on his desk. It was 5:10pm. He called out from his study and Terry answered from the kitchen. He told him not to ruin his supper, there were some prepared dishes in the Tupperware that his mother had left them before leaving.

Howard suddenly realized that Donna would be home within the next two hours. He was just coming to grips with some of what he was gleaning in his quiet time and study, how could he begin to share those things with her? He felt an anxiety begin to build in his stomach. They were going to have to talk. . . and he dreaded it.

———

Donna walked Marnie to the lobby where the vans would soon be coming to pick them up and take them back to their home churches. Donna would have an hour ride back to the church and then the thirty-minute drive home. Marnie took Donna's hand into hers.

"I will be praying for both of you," Marnie told her. "Trust me, God knows what he is doing. Sometimes we don't see how, but trust me, he knows."

"I know one thing," Donna said with confidence. "We're going to have to talk, and the sooner the better, and you know what? I am really dreading it."

Marnie gave a sympathetic smile.

"You don't know Howard," Donna began to tear up. "This is the last thing he needs right now."

"Just trust God," Marnie repeated.

The two ladies embraced one last time. Donna knew that God had spoken to her through this woman.

———

Karen and Anna walked the last couple blocks from the bus stop to Anna's house. They let themselves in and Anna introduced Karen to her Aunt Helen.

"Nice to meet you Karen," Helen said politely. "Uncle Billy will be home by 6:00. Do hamburgers sound OK for supper tonight?"

"That's sounds great," Anna responded. "Can Karen stay?"

"Fine with me, I have plenty of meat. Why don't you let your folks know where you are and make sure it's OK."

The girls agreed and headed for the den to use the phone. Karen stopped her though, and signaled to put the phone down.

"Let me call him just a little later," Karen asked in a low voice. "I'm not sure I'm ready for that yet."

"If you think so," Anna replied hesitantly. "I'm sure he is wondering where you are right now, especially from what you said earlier."

"I know, but I just want to be ready."

Anna winked with understanding and they left for the girls' bedroom. Karen had a few more things she wanted to talk about. As best she could tell, she was getting straight on a lot of things about her relationship to God and to her father. God was speaking through Anna.

———

Susan Eldridge had given the boys a project in the backyard to occupy them. They had all expected their father to arrive sometime around lunch and it was already late afternoon. Susan didn't usually feel uneasy when Carey wasn't on time, but today she did.

When she heard the truck pull up in front of the gate, she waited for the three blasts of the horn. That was the signal for one of them to open the gate. It never came. Instead, she heard the engine shut off. She slowly walked out to the front to see who had arrived. As she approached the large metal gate, she could see through the opening that Carey used to unlock it from the outside. The truck was gray, not red. It wasn't Carey's truck. She opened the lock and saw Mando. His face was bandaged and his right arm was in a cast and a sling. She knew immediately that there had been an accident. Susan turned to see Capitán Mendoza step around from the driver's side and close his door. She quickly looked in the backseat, but there was no one else in the truck.

"Where is Carey, Mando?" Susan called out.

The two men passed a quick look, then Mando spoke.

"He's at the hospital, Susan," he began. He knew his first comment was misleading, but he wanted to break the news as gently as he could. "There was an accident on the mountain. We were hit by a truck and Bro. Carey's pick-up was knocked over."

Susan looked straight into Mando's eyes as he continued to step toward her and talk at the same time.

"Carey was trying to not hit some others who were walking on the side of the road, so he let the truck hit his side of the cab and knock us backward.

There was another man in the backseat. He is being operated on now for a head injury."

"And Carey?" Susan asked slowly.

"*Hermana* Susan . . ." Mando spoke, slowly forcing the words from his lips, ". . . Brother Carey was killed. His body is at the hospital so that it can be prepared for burial in the States. I knew you would not have wanted to bring him here."

Susan's legs buckled and Mando caught her. The Capitán rushed to help carry her back into the house. They assisted her to the kitchen where she took one of the chairs and cradled her head in her hands. The boys were too preoccupied to notice the distress of their mother. She began to cry.

Mendoza did not know how to comfort in this kind of loss. Most of the death he dealt with was among those who had been guilty for contributing to their own demise. He stood helpless to know how to give consolation.

"Senora Eldridge," he began nervously. "If I may say, I have only just met your husband these past two weeks. But I have seen him for many years driving up and down the road around this department. He has even given me rides before without knowing who I was. He was a kind man. But from what I have seen these past couple of weeks, he was more than that. He was a man of courage and conviction. I was on duty the night of his accident - I know how the death of Moncho so deeply hurt him and this was a man who tried to kill him. He had a love for the people . . . "

Mendoza paused and rethought his words.

"He had a love for MY people, that I have rarely seen. He gave his life to them. Today, he gave his life for them. I know this. His friend Mando tells me it is because of his love for God. I go to church, my wife and I attend the Mass and we say our prayers. But I do not know this depth of love that your husband had for his God. I know now is not the time, but when I can, may I come back and talk to you, with my wife about what you and your husband tell the people of these villages about God?"

Susan looked up at Capitán Mendoza through tear stained eyes. Her grief was profound. She still had much pain to endure just in telling her sons. She dreaded the call she would have to make to Billy that night. And yet, through all that pain, she was hearing words of praise for her husband that would ultimately bring glory to God. A verse of scripture came to her mind, 'Except a grain of wheat fall into the earth and die, it abideth alone. But if it die, it bringeth forth much fruit.' Was she looking at the first of much fruit to come through Carey's death? One thing was for sure. God was speaking to her through Capitán Mendoza. He was speaking words of comfort and Susan allowed the words to come.

Donna opened the front door to her home. She called out. Howard responded from the kitchen. She walked in and found him seated at the table with two plates of dinner nicely prepared. Once again, Terry had eaten in the den and was now involved in a video. It was as though they both had something serious to talk about . . . and they did.

Howard rose and helped her with her suitcases. He left them at the foot of the stairs and walked her back to the kitchen. She was overtaken by his manners and followed him completely without comment. He escorted her to her chair and pulled it out for her. She sat down daintily and watched him take his seat. He had an unusually calm and humble disposition about him.

"How was your retreat, dear?" He asked.

He hadn't used 'dear' all week.

"It was wonderful, thank you for asking. And this dinner is a wonderful surprise."

"I used your 'left-oversee' and added some salad," Howard replied simply. "Hope you like it."

They ate their meal together and chatted lightly. It was as if both were waiting for the right moment.

After the meal, Howard began to clear the table.

"Just leave it, honey," Donna said. "I'll get to it later, why don't we just sit and talk a little."

She was opening up the door, he thought. It was obvious they both wanted to deal with the problems they had been having lately. There would be no better time he thought. Howard took a deep breath. He wasn't sure how to begin. He wasn't sure exactly where this conversation was going to carry them. He knew she was ready for a change, but there was such a thing as too much change.

He was obviously leading up to something big, she thought. He had apologized before and tried to straighten things over, but he had never gone to this level of production to prepare her for it. She began to think of the things she had been dwelling on that day. This was not going to turn out like he thought it would. She hoped he was ready for it.

"Donna," he began, "I had an incredible day today."

"Me too," she said.

"We need to talk and I need you to listen till I get through before you say anything," he stated, more as a request than as a demand.

"I will do that," she agreed. "If you promise to then listen to everything I have to say without interrupting."

"It's a deal," he replied.

307

Howard than took the next twenty-five minutes to deliver what he had been rehearsing for the previous hour. Donna listened. It was not what she expected to hear.

———

Karen and Anna lost track of the time. The next thing they realized, Uncle Billy was calling them to wash their hands for supper. They bounced out of the bedroom and raced each other to the sink in the hall restroom.

At the table they began talking about schools. Karen was beginning to think that going to college may not be such a bad idea after all. Helen was just about to ask Karen if she had called her father when the phone rang.

Billy answered it in the hall. There was a long pause and then a whispered response. Helen watched him from the kitchen table and knew something was wrong. He turned back to look at Anna who now was sensing a problem. Billy motioned for her to come from the table. He handed her the phone and placed his arm around her. Karen looked on as her new friend received the hardest news of her life. It was the last thing anyone expected to hear.

———

Howard had been listening to Donna for nearly thirty minutes when the phone rang. It was hard for him to tear himself away. He held one finger up to indicate that he would be right back. As he stepped into the hall for the phone, he shook his head. This was not what he was expecting to hear from Donna.

"Pennington's," Howard announced into the receiver.

"Daddy," the voice cried.

"Karen? Is that you? Are you OK?"

Donna jumped up from the kitchen table and ran to his side.

"I'm OK, Daddy," she sniffled. "It's a long story and I want to tell you all of it, but right now, I am at a girls home and she has just lost her father. May I stay the night to be with her?"

"Who is the girl, honey?" Howard asked. "Where are you?"

"Her name is Anna, and she's living with her uncle. I can let you talk to him if you want. It's just that she is so hurt and, like . . . we just met today at the mall. Well, not for the first time, but we really got to know each other today and I came home with her. Well, she just got a phone call from her mom and her father was killed in an automobile accident today, and I would just like to stay with her if I can."

"Let me speak to the uncle," Howard said. He turned to Donna and whispered, "It's Karen, she's OK. She's at a girl's house who just lost her father and she wants to stay over."

Howard turned his attention back to the phone.

"Yes, this is Howard Pennington," he responded. "May I ask who this is?"

Howard's eyes widened. He listened without comment as Billy Eldridge related the details of the phone call.

"Billy, if you would give me directions to your house, I would like to come see you. That is, if you don't mind," Howard said with slow deliberation.

He took a pen and began to make notes.

"That is not far from here," Howard said. "We can be there in ten minutes. Is that OK?"

Donna looked up surprised.

"We?" she asked.

"I'll explain in the car," he said aside from the phone.

"What about Terry?" she asked.

"He can go with us. It's just up the road and they have a younger child he can meet. I know this family."

Howard quickly returned to the phone. It was Karen again.

"Daddy," Karen said in a low voice. "If you will go up to my bedroom, you will see a suitcase by my bed. Open it up and take out my sleeping things. The rest you can just throw back on the bed. And you can put the suitcase back up in the closet."

Howard expressed a little shock, and then relaxed his forehead. He never knew how close he came to losing his little girl. But then, after today, he would never take anything for granted.

———

Adam finished the dishes and wiped down the dining room table. Gertie sat in the den with her needlework. She felt good about the afternoon. The prayer time had lasted nearly an hour and a half with different ones taking turns. During the fellowship time, Gertie had shared some of the newsletters so that the class would have a better understanding for Carey and his family.

Gertie turned her attention to Karen and her family that evening. She found herself praying not just for the father, but the mother as well, since she knew that tension had to effect the whole household.

Adam brought two small bowls of vanilla ice cream into where she was sitting.

"Would you like some ice cream?" he offered.

"Sounds good," she replied setting her needlework aside.

"Well, do you think that about wraps up this prayer vigil you have been on?" Adam asked.

"I don't think so," Gertie replied. "I have been praying for Karen and her family off and on since the group left. I'll let you know in the morning."

Adam shook his head. Tomorrow was church. He needed his sleep to be able to teach. He wasn't opposed to her prayer schedule, he just hoped she didn't wake him when she got up. Little did either realize, that this was to be a critical night for prayer.

———

(Sunday)

The Coronado Baptist Church had not yet moved to two morning services, but plans were being made. That was one of the reasons for the building project. Parking was always a problem, especially following the Sunday School hour.

Howard sat in his office with Donna. She was rarely in this office, but this morning, he needed her support. This was not going to be an easy message to preach. Rusty tapped at the door.

"Did you want to see me?" Rusty asked.

"Yes, Rusty, come in for moment and close the door please."

In the sanctuary, the youth began to file in taking their usual seats. The instrumentalists began their prelude and after a few minutes the choir marched in majestically. The Sunday School director walked to the pulpit and began to give the morning report while a low level of conversations continued in the pews.

Normally, the pastor was seated in one of the large oaken chairs just in front of the choir on the piano side. He would share the platform with the Worship Leader, who directed the choir and led in the congregational singing. The hour came to begin and Bro. Howard was not in his chair. The organist and pianist completed their piece and a brief moment of silence filled the sanctuary. Immediately, the Worship Leader stood and stepped to the pulpit and began to recite from the book of Psalms. The passage naturally flowed into the first hymn. The congregation stood, took their hymnals and began to sing.

During the hymn, the pastor, his wife and Rusty entered from the doorway nearest the piano. Instead of taking his place at the platform, Howard sat with Donna on the front row. Rusty sat with them. The usual order of service was followed with rigid ritual. The only difference in the routine was that Rusty rose to give the welcome and announcements in place of the pastor. He then returned to his place on the front row. Bro.

Howard would be expected to preach following the special music after the offering was collected. But by the time the offering plates were being passed, it was evident that something different was going to take place that morning.

The soloist gave an inspirational interpretation of a familiar Christian song that was popular at that time and then took her seat. There was an awkward moment of silence again. Howard squeezed Donna's hand and walked up the steps of the platform to take his place behind the pulpit. He looked out over the crowd. He saw his son sitting with his friends to one side. He thought about how this was going to effect him. He then glanced to the other side of pews and saw Arnie. He was smiling. He sat with his wife and son. Howard smiled back.

He opened his Bible and began to read from 2 Peter 1:5-10:

> *" For this very reason, make every effort to add to your faith goodness; and to goodness, knowledge; [6] and to knowledge, self-control; and to self-control, perseverance; and to perseverance, godliness; [7] and to godliness, brotherly kindness; and to brotherly kindness, love. [8] For if you possess these qualities in increasing measure, they will keep you from being ineffective and unproductive in your knowledge of our Lord Jesus Christ. [9] But if anyone does not have them, he is nearsighted and blind, and has forgotten that he has been cleansed from his past sins.*
>
> *[10] Therefore, my brothers, be all the more eager to make your calling and election sure. For if you do these things, you will never fall, [11] and you will receive a rich welcome into the eternal kingdom of our Lord and Savior Jesus Christ.*

"My friends, this morning I am doing something I have never done before. I am setting aside the message I prepared earlier this week in order to share with you as a church family, something that God has been doing . . . not just in my life, but in the lives of several. How this has all come together is more than I will ever be able to understand. I ask that you be patient with me as I try to share these events."

Howard could tell that everyone was interested, and even the youth had quit passing notes.

"As long as I have been your pastor, I have put my entire self into this church. For nearly ten years I have served you all faithfully, visiting your sick, marrying your sons and daughters, burying your beloved family members, and doing the best I could to feed you as a flock. We have grown together in many ways. And yet, in all that time, I was blind to the needs of one of the church families - my own. I was blind to the fact that the man who builds his ministry at the sacrifice of his family will eventually lose both."

Howard looked over at Rusty and smiled.

"This was recently brought to my attention. I was blind to the needs of my wife whose own dreams and aspirations didn't fit into my agenda. I was blind to the needs of my own daughter, who, if you will notice, isn't even here this morning. Last night, I found her packed suitcase in her bedroom. She had planned to run away."

Arnie gasped.

"I'm glad to say, she didn't, but that will come later in the story. For now, suffice it to say, I was blind because I allowed the ministry to take the place of the character qualities I have just read to you.

This past week, I was introduced to another quality I had been lacking. It is the fear of the Lord. I wish I had the time to share all the insights that I have been gleaning over that one, but I have another message to bring you all this morning."

Howard took a breath and refocused.

"This past Wednesday, many of you will remember the Gideon speaker we had. I would not be honest if I didn't say, I was less than excited over the prospect of having another Gideon service. I even commented to one of the staff, that the only thing more boring to me than a Gideon speaker is a missionary presentation."

This brought a couple low chuckles from among the sympathetic.

"What I didn't know was that our Gideon speaker was the brother of a missionary. He and I talked before the service and he opened my eyes to some things that I didn't really understand about missions. Again, I wish I could develop those themes, and perhaps very soon I will. But again, suffice it to say, I was blind to the purpose of God concerning missions. I thought that a man who trained as much as those who go, would be wasting his education in an area where it would never be used. Worse, I thought he was wasting his life. I was blind. Then God began to go to work on me. Like I say, I will never know all the details of how He brought these things together, but I want to tell you what I can."

Howard grasped the sides of the pulpit for reinforcement. He had no notes for what followed.

"As I have stated, my daughter and I have been having serious problems. While I was busy building a building for the church, I was allowing my own house to crumble. Karen took a job about a week ago. We were in agreement, but had no idea that little by little, the lure of independence was being dangled before her. She packed her bag yesterday with the full intention of moving out of the house. But a young girl who also worked at the mall helped her to see the importance of family. More importantly, she helped her restore her relationship with the Lord. Like myself, she had become blind to the fact that her sins had been forgiven and she was not growing in the qualities we read. She rediscovered the love of her Lord and this morning she is with that other girl. I'll explain why she is not with us in just a moment."

"At the same time, Donna and I had been experiencing ongoing tension in the home. My dominance had kept her from ever sharing the cries of her heart."

Howard looked directly at Donna.

"I have asked her to forgive me, and she has. Sometimes the one lost sheep in the fold is the one closest to you. This weekend, Donna attended the ladies retreat. There she found someone who would listen to her. Ironically enough, it was a missionary. The very type of person I felt was wasting their ministry, was the very person that was able to minister to my own wife. Talk about humbling. But she did more than just listen to Donna. She helped her with an issue that has been part of her since before we met. Knowing me, I would have dismissed it and would not have been able to help at all."

"Then two very significant events took place yesterday. To adequately share them without burdening you with all the details, I need to put each in its context. The first had to deal with a trip to the county jail."

Arnie stiffened. He was not prepared for the pastor to air their problems along with his own.

"Some of you are aware of the jail ministry that Rusty conducts on Saturdays. Some of you have even accompanied him at times. I must confess, he has tried several times to get me to go. But yesterday was my first time. While there, we met a man that had been arrested as an illegal alien."

Arnie relaxed. Bro. Howard was not going to mention Alex. Alex had told him of their encounter with the Spanish prisoner after he and his wife had left.

"Now, I really wish I could tell you the whole story. It was incredible. But he had traveled all the way from Honduras, through three other countries, just to cross the border and to be arrested within two hours of entering the United States. Now that may sound tragic, if you are sympathetic to illegals, but God used his time in that jail to bring him to an encounter with Jesus Christ. I had the privilege of sharing the gospel, and you know - I honestly think that he had never heard the plan of salvation ever presented before. That was a real eye-opener for me. In all my years of preaching and sharing my faith, I don't know that I have ever met anyone who had never heard the gospel. That got my attention, but not near as much as one of the statements he made after praying. I'll never forget. He looked at me and asked, 'Why have I never heard this before? Why did I have to come all this way to hear this news?' "

"I have to tell you folks," Howard stepped out from behind the pulpit. "Those words stung my heart. I could not get them out of my mind for the rest of the day. I went home and got alone with my Bible and God and asked Him the same question."

Howard began to walk freely about the platform. This was not his usual form of address and it was obvious, he was not preaching.

"I have preached you sermon after sermon over the great commission. And yet, I have always seen it in the context of just where I was, and not where I wasn't. I missed two important words in those verses. One is at the beginning and the other is at the end."

Several began turning in their Bibles to Matthew 28:19, 20 to see which two words he was referring to.

"I don't believe in coincidence. A Gideon with a missionary brother, a missionary conference leader, my wife, and an illegal alien were challenging the way I thought about missions. You all know what little emphasis I have placed in the past on this subject. I'm here to say this morning, that that is going to change. The first word of the Great Commission is 'Go!' The last word is 'Amen' or 'so be it'."

Several "amens" were heard across the congregation.

"This church will no longer grow to serve itself, I pray. It will begin to see the world around it and then the world it can't see."

More "amens".

"I have been blind to missions. Please forgive me."

He stepped back to the pulpit and paused.

"The second event that occurred yesterday is much more difficult to share. Again, let me reiterate. I do not believe in mere coincidence. We serve a God of purpose and that purpose is good. We don't know why many things that transpire around us happen, nor do I believe we will ever fully understand. I feel there is a need to see how our decisions and God's sovereignty work together. I don't blame God for the evil things that happen around us anymore than I can blame the devil when I catch a cold. Some things are the result of choices. God works all things together for the good to those who love Him - that is the promise. 'We need to see where God is working and join Him', to quote a familiar writer."

"Yesterday I learned of a tragic death of a missionary on the field. I use the word tragic because he left a wife and three children. I say tragic because it was an automobile accident and that is the usual word we use to describe the sudden death of an individual. But maybe I should be careful how I use the word 'tragic'. Because 'tragic' implies something completely negative without a positive perspective. I wish I had known this man. His name was Carey Eldridge and he had been on the mission field for sixteen years. Two of his children were born on the field. He has labored diligently to start new churches in the area where he was placed. He was a good worker. He was more than a good worker, though, he was a good father. He took time for his family. I would dare say, his schedule was fuller than mine. He left a legacy of Christ that will carry on in the south of Honduras for years to come."

"You say, 'how could I know so much about a man I've never met?'"

Howard glanced back at the choir. They were hanging on every word.

"Because he is the brother of the Gideon who was with us last Wednesday."

A soft murmur swept across the congregation.

"What's more," Howard turned back to the front. "His daughter is here in San Diego attending high school and she is the girl my daughter met. Her name is Anna, and yesterday, she shared with Karen at the point of her greatest need. Last night, she received the phone call that her father had been killed and now Karen was with her, comforting her in her hour of greatest need. I don't believe in coincidence!"

Howard continued.

"While all this was going on, Donna and I were having a serious family conversation about the things we have been learning this week - each of us from our different sources. We had just about reached a point of a critical decision when the phone rang informing us of the death of Carey Eldridge. We left immediately to be with the family and to be reunited with Karen who was already with them."

"I have to admit, at first I felt a strong frustration at the thought of the loss. This was my argument just three days before. Missionaries take all their training, and then waste it on people who would never appreciate a third of it and then place themselves in danger doing it. Mr. Billy Eldridge, the gentleman who was with us Wednesday set aside his personal grief to share some insight. Much of it, he tried to tell me the other night, but one statement escaped me then. He repeated it for me last night. 'Carey didn't lose his life - he gave it. He gave it the moment he committed himself to the God that called him to the field. The martyr is not just the wild-eyed zealot who bears his chest to the sword and refuses to denounce Christ. True, we are seeing modern martyrs today who are accepting death rather than deny Jesus, but the blood of martyrs includes those who are taken from us as they are found faithful in their obedience to God's call upon their life, whether by a machete or an automobile accident.' Carey was found obedient in his death. What an inspiration to us."

315

"I said earlier that I need to be careful about using the word tragic. That infers that nothing good has come out of this. But good has come, and I believe will continue to come. Carey's death, though a deep wound to us and his family, is seen by God as a seed . . . a seed that has fallen into the earth to die, but in dying will bring about fruit. Like our scripture reading this morning, I believe that Carey has received a 'a rich welcome into the eternal kingdom of our Lord and Savior, Jesus Christ'. And that my friends is anything but tragic."

Howard stepped out from behind the pulpit again and looked down at his wife for strength. She smiled and nodded her head.

"That brings me to one other point from the last portion of the scripture we have read this morning."

He turned back to the pulpit to read from the Bible.

"... Therefore, my brothers, be all the more eager to make your calling and election sure."

Howard closed his Bible and stepped away from the pulpit.

"The message this morning is for me. I have been the one that was blind. I am the one who needed to examine himself before the Lord. Yesterday, I spent much of the afternoon doing just that. I came away with a startling discovery. I wasn't sure how I would even begin to approach Donna about it. And yet, God gave me peace and grace. He is also a God with a sense of humor. Because at the same time, Donna was discovering God's will for her life and was trying to decide how best to approach me. When we sat down at the table last night - it was undeniable. God had led us to the same discovery. But it was not until the phone call we received from the Eldridges with the news of Carey that I was 100% sure of what God was doing."

Howard took a breath.

"Let me put in this way. Carey's death has caused a gap. A soldier has fallen. There is a breach in the wall. God has called us - Donna and I both - to fill the breach. We are going to the mission field!"

There was shocked silence that covered the crowd. Then a lone voice was heard.

"AMEN!"

Howard looked out and saw Arnie standing to his feet.

"Dr. Pennington, God bless you!"

Others began to agree. Then a small wave of applause rose from the youth. It swept across the pews until it thundered. Rusty stood to his feet and took Donna's hand. He walked her up the platform steps and she stood beside her husband. The ovation rose to its feet. Tears began to rain as the sound of a mighty storm filled the sanctuary. Howard lifted his hand asking the applause to subside. He took Donna's hand in his own.

"I want you to know that this has been a calling that my wife has sensed most of her Christian life, even before she met me in Texas. She has set her dreams aside and that was part of the reason she was so miserable. God has brought us to the same page finally and we are now both ready to go"

"Karen wants to stay here and to attend college with her new friend, Anna. We will work out the arrangements. Terry doesn't know much about these plans yet, but I see him standing and applauding as well, and can only assume that he is in agreement."

"As for the church, I wish to stay on as long as it takes to process the appointment."

"AMEN!" came a unified voice of those standing.

"But I plan to ask Rusty to take more of the responsibility in preaching. I have heard this young man, and he has much to offer this congregation. He has been a tremendous inspiration to me, especially these past two weeks."

"As for the building project, I would like to ask Bro. Arnie Johnson to begin overseeing the plans and budgeting. I believe he has some ideas this church should listen to. I only wish I had listened to him sooner."

They exchanged nods.

"I would like to add one last thing. While we are all standing, I would like the accompanists to come and for Bro. Perry, our Worship Leader, to lead us in 'Wherever He leads I'll go.' "

The congregation opened their hymnals and began to sing. One by one, many came forward - some to pray with the Penningtons, some for the Eldridges. Some came to pray for themselves, while others came to pray for missions. The prayer service extended itself into the next hour. Carey's death was bearing fruit in the Coronado Baptist Church. It would not end there.

Epilogue:
(Monday Morning)

Startled! Gertie rose up suddenly. Adam was standing over her with the sun at his back shining through the curtain sheers. He had a tray with a plate of eggs and bacon in his hands. She focused her eyes and then stretched.

"How long have you been standing there?" she asked.

"Not long, I'm afraid I woke you when I hit the tray against your walker. I meant to kiss your cheek. Do you know it's 9:00am?"

"You're kidding?" Gertie replied. She sat up against the back of the bed so that he could place the tray over her lap. "I slept the whole night through! I never got up once."

"What does that mean?" Adam asked.

Gertie smiled tucking the napkin under her chin.

"That means, all is well." She said with a grin.

A week later, Gertie received a letter from Billy Eldridge. He was so impressed with her letter to Carey, he had kept her address. In the letter, he explained about the accident and the impact it was having both in Honduras and in Southern California. He told her of how he would be helping a "soon to be missionary family", by assisting Karen get settled in college with his niece, Carey's daughter. He shared the decision that Karen's father had made in church that past Sunday. He took the time to thank her again for her prayers. They had protected Carey as God had put all things in order. He added that she must not think of Carey's death as a defeat. But her prayers had been part of a greater victory. Gertie read the letter several times and then placed it in her Bible for safekeeping. She smiled and thanked God.

"All is well," she said.

ABOUT THE AUTHOR

Randy Pool, native of Tennessee, is the son of a career Navy officer, and lived on both coasts and Puerto Rico before becoming a teenager and returning to Tennessee. He received his B.A. from Union University (Jackson, TN) as a Religion/Greek composite major. He went on to earn his Master of Divinity from the Mid-America Baptist Theological Seminary of Memphis, TN.

Randy's labors in ministry have included children's work, youth work, prison work, the pastorate, international mission service and now local missions among the poor. His mission service includes a year in tropical Costa Rica, seven years in the south of Honduras, and one year in Nicaragua. Randy returned to Tennessee with his family where he now works with the Mississippi River Ministry of Tennessee and the Gibson Baptist Association.

He is a husband and father of three, Timothy, Tiffany and Christina. He has striven diligently to pass the legacy of the 70's and it's music on to his offspring with some degree of success. This has made long family car trips endurable. Writing is his favorite pastime. He has written a devotional with poetry entitled "*Poolside Reflections*". He has several articles printed in various mission publications.

It has been said that men are defined by what they do. If such were the case, then Randy Pool would be a missionary. But those who know him – know there is more. Randy enjoys telling stories and finds humor to be a means of equalizing most conversations. Even his wife, Cindy, is not sure how to define Randy after twenty-five years of marriage, but one thing is for certain. He is not just a missionary.

Printed in the United States
1219900004BA/49-147